History and
Computing II

Table of Contents

vi

IX. Regional Data Banks

Introduction

The idea that the discipline of history has much to gain from the widespread use of computers in teaching and research is nowadays uncontroversial, accepted by almost all but the most determined of technological reactionaries. Yet, despite the remarkably swift advance in awareness and practice of the last few years, the nature of historical computing and its potentialities remain imperfectly understood. Many teachers and scholars, seemingly mesmerised by the glories of word-processing, still conceive of the microcomputer as a sophisticated typewriter, whilst others continue to identify computers solely with quantification. This book, like its precursor, *History and Computing*, aims to demonstrate that computers have much more to offer the historian than mere secretarial or numerical assistance. Each of the chapters, in one way or another, suggests that historical computing is concerned with the very fundamentals of teaching and research. It is evident that new methods of enquiry, which utilise the power and flexibility of modern computer systems, are already adding significantly to historical knowledge and understanding.

History and Computing II is one of the fruits of the Second Annual Conference of the Association for History and Computing held at Westfield College, University of London, in March 1987. It is not a complete collection of the papers presented, but a selection chosen to illustrate the state of the art in historical computing: the variety of work currently being undertaken, the problems faced by teachers and researchers, and likely developments in the future. The papers have been placed in sections which reflect the main preoccupations of authors and the organisation of the Westfield conference. Several sections deal with applications, others with techniques, sources, teaching and general methodological issues. However, it must be admitted that the divisions are somewhat arbitrary, and many papers were candidates for inclusion in more than one section. Certain of the articles in the applications sections, for example, raise important methodological issues as well as dealing with the findings of particular research projects. A case in point is the essay by Schurer, Schofield and Oeppen reviewing recent advances in historical demography; another is Morgan and Moss's innovative approach to wealth-holding, which stresses the importance of the accumulation process rather than the value of holdings at the time of death.

The important point to note is that methodological innovation is an important feature of much computer-assisted historical research. This is not to assert that using computers directly encourages the development of new methods, but that best use can be made of the machines when historical problems are explicitly and formally defined. Indeed, the solution to a problem may have been specified well before the advent of low cost computing power. Many advances in demography fall into this category, and so too do others in historical psephology, as O'Gorman makes clear in his essay on electoral behaviour in England. The application of advanced quantitative methods in economic history likewise pre-dates the modern computer era. But, this said, there can be no doubting that the cause of formalism and explicit theorisation has been boosted by the forward march of information technology.

A second feature of historical computing, which is illustrated by many of the essays in this collection, is the adoption, modification and application of the techniques of information systems analysis and design. The section on databases, for example, contains a series of essays which demonstrate the relevance of data analysis and modelling to much historical research. The argument developed in the papers by Hartland and Harvey and by Dunk and Rahtz, for example, is that a true understanding of the nature of an historical source is likely to be critical to the success of a project. There is nothing original in this. What is original, however, is the approach to sources, and the application of methods of investigation first used in the development of business systems. The message that the nature and form of the data matters more than software or hardware specifics finds confirmation in many of the more empirical papers, notably those by Itzcovich on masters and apprentices in medieval Genoa and Doorn on central Greece in the early Ottoman period. The papers by Schulte and Carvahlo on artificial intelligence and expert systems again confirm that historians have much to gain from remaining alert to developments in those branches of computer science and information systems directly concerned with advanced techniques for data interrogation, manipulation and processing.

An acute concern with sources and their potential value is the third and perhaps most important feature of historical computing reflected in this volume. This is hardly surprising. Large storage capacities and rapid data processing are two of the blessings of modern computer systems, and scientifically trained social historians have for long appreciated the worth of software packages like SPSS-X. More recently, and more generally, the historical community has embraced database management systems, especially of the relational variety, as invaluable tools for research. Rapid searching and sorting, and the capacity to link records, are the most basic attractions. Historians of all periods and all interests are nowadays involved in the construction of large databases, often merging many sources, in an effort to shed fresh light on old issues or open up new avenues of enquiry. The papers of Doulton and Kitts, Nault and Desjardins, and Jaritz and Müller, each illustrate the thinking behind the database approach. Essentially it is a grass-roots technique of historical research. Once a worthwhile problem has been identified, sources are located, a data model is devised and implemented using appropriate software, and the available data is entered onto the system, and subsequently analysed using the facilities of the database management system and other software packages (statistical and cartographic, for example). In this research model, generalisation is the product of meticulous data collection and analysis. The role of theory and previous studies is to furnish interesting questions and hypotheses for detailed investigation.

The ease with which sources can nowadays be rendered machine readable has led to further developments in historical computing. The first is the growing acceptance of the notion that computer data files might be shared by many historians rather than limited in use to a single project. As a result there are now many projects devoted to establishing large scale data banks through the computerisation of existing collections of documents or through the deposition of files by researchers in a data archive. The section of the book on regional data banks gives some indication of the scale and importance of this work. A second and related development is the spread of computer-based project work in the teaching of history. The fact that data files can be freely circulated and that others can be created without difficulty has given history teachers the opportunity to integrate project work within existing courses. The possibilities for historical computing laboratories in which students analyse and classify data are discussed by Wild and by Trainor in their papers on history and information technology. Both authors raise issues which are sure to figure high on the educational agenda in the next few years.

Taken together, the papers in this book point to the emergence of new methods of historical teaching and research. In both spheres of activity the emphasis is on a more systematic and intensive approach to sources. Students should gain from a heightened awareness of historical materials, methods and reasoning. Researchers should benefit from the discipline of a more formal approach, not least in being able to trace more exactly the reasoning of other scholars. Moreover, historians working in higher education now have the opportunity to integrate research and teaching activities much more fully than in the past. In these respects, history might be thought of as becoming more like the natural and social sciences, and indeed there are those who already speak in terms of historical science.

It would be misleading, however, to represent history as proceeding down a path long since trodden by the social sciences. Historical computing is not the same thing as social scientific history, as Manfred Thaller makes clear in the first chapter of this volume. Thaller attaches great importance to the inherent complexities and distinctiveness of historical research, which stem ultimately from the need to explain interrelated phenomena over time and across space on the basis of incomplete and imperfect data. If historical computing is to thrive, Thaller believes, the subject must assert its own identity through the development of a more robust conceptual framework. For this to occur, computing historians must draw on the researches of computer scientists, and in turn their writings should be of sufficient generality to make a worthwhile contribution to information science.

There are many who do not accept the elevated vision of historical computing advanced by Thaller or the way forward proposed by him. Many computing historians take a more prosaic view of computers, computer science and historical research. However, few would dispute that recent developments in computing have stimulated ambitions and brought a fresh sense of purpose to many a flagging specialism. One of the brightest prospects is the initiation of comparative and thematic projects which involve collaboration between scholars in several countries. The Association of History and Computing — sponsors of this volume and the Westfield Conference on which it is based — has already done much to promote the cause of international cooperation. New members are always welcome!

Peter Denley
Stefan Fogelvik
Charles Harvey

Acknowledgments

This book was photoset on Oxford University Computing Service's Monotype Lasercomp phototypesetter. It was prepared using facilities generously provided by the Computer Unit, Westfield College. The editors wish to thank the staff of the Unit, and especially Mr Brian Place and Dr Felicity Rash, for their help with its production.

The Association for History and Computing

The Association for History and Computing is an international organisation which aims to promote and develop interest in the use of computers in all types of historical study at every level, in both teaching and research.

The Association was proposed at a large conference at Westfield College, University of London, in March 1986. At a second conference at Westfield, in March 1987 (of which this volume constitutes the proceedings), it was formally founded and its constitution approved. A central co-ordinating body, the Council, organises the Association's international activities, including an annual conference (in 1988 this was held in Cologne, in 1989 it will be in Bordeaux). Branches of the Association have been or are being formed for countries or groups of countries where a large membership exists, and these organise activities at a local level. Sub-groups dealing with specific aspects of computing (such as the standardisation and exchange of historical data) have also been formed. Within eighteen months of the Association's official foundation its membership grew to over 600, from 23 countries.

A vital part of the AHC's work is its publications policy. A newsletter, *Computing and History Today*, is issued free to members; in 1989 this will be replaced by a more professional magazine, *History and Computing*. Proceedings of conferences at international and branch level are published and are available to members at a discount on the published price. A series of Research Reports has been inaugurated, and the publication of introductory material is also planned.

The Association has a particular commitment to the dissemination of computing techniques among history teachers. Courses and summer schools are being organised at both international and branch level, and publications directed specifically at teachers are in hand.

Further details of the Association's activities, and membership application forms, are available from Dr Veronica Lawrence, Membership Secretary, Association for History and Computing, 3 Crown Terrace, Stadhampton, Oxon OX9 7TY. On general matters relating to the Association contact Dr Peter Denley, Secretary-General, Association for History and Computing, Department of History, Westfield College (University of London), London NW3 7ST.

List of Contributors

A. Balthasar *Forschungszentrum für Schweizerische Politik, University of Berne*
Heinrich Best *University of Cologne*
Neithard Bulst *Fakultät für Geschichtswissenschaft und Philosophie, University of Bielefeld*
Lou Burnard *Oxford University Computing Service*
Joaquim Carvalho *Department of History, University of Coimbra*
Bettina Callies *University of Regensburg*
Frank van Deijk *Department of Social and Economic History, State University, Leiden*
Peter Denley *Department of History, Westfield College (University of London)*
Bertrand Desjardins *Département de Démographie, University of Montréal*
Herman Diederiks *Department of Social and Economic History, State University, Leiden*
Peter K. Doorn *Department of History, University of Leiden*
David Doulton *University of Southampton*
Julie Dunk
Stefan Fogelvik *Stockholms Historiska Databas*
Edmund M. Green *History Department, Royal Holloway and Bedford New College, University of London*
Philip Hartland *Royal Holloway and Bedford New College, University of London*
Charles Harvey *History Department, Royal Holloway and Bedford New College, University of London*
Oscar Itzcovich *University of Genoa*
Gerhard Jaritz *Institut für mittelalterliche Realienkunde Österreichs of the Austrian Academy of Sciences, Krems*
Arno Kitts *Department of Social Statistics, University of Southampton*
Lothar Kolmer *University of Regensburg*
Ingo H. Kropač *Forschungsinstitut für Historische Grundwissenschaften, University of Graz*
Nicholas Morgan *University of Glasgow*
Michael Moss *University of Glasgow*
Albert Müller *Ludwig Boltzmann-Institut für Historische Sozialwissenschaft, Salzburg*
François Nault *Département de Démographie, University of Montréal*
Jim Oeppen *Cambridge Group for the History of Population and Social Structure*
Frank O'Gorman *University of Manchester*
Christian Pfister *University of Berne*
Sebastian Rahtz *Department of Electronics and Computer Science, University of Southampton*
Roger Schofield *Cambridge Group for the History of Population and Social Structure*
Hannes Schüle *University of Berne*
Theo J. Schulte *Cambridgeshire College of Arts and Technology*
Kevin Schurer *Cambridge Group for the History of Population and Social Structure*
Peter Taylor *Bristol Polytechnic*
Peter Teibenbacher *Institut für Wirtschafts- und Sozialgeschichte, University of Graz*
Manfred Thaller *Max-Planck-Institut für Geschichte, Göttingen*
Richard H. Trainor *University of Glasgow*
John Turner *History Department, Royal Holloway and Bedford New College, University of London*
Martyn Wild *The Advisory Unit, Microtechnology in Education, Hatfield*

I.

Methodology

The Need for a Theory of Historical Computing

The application of computers in history can be seen in two ways: as part of a distinct methodology, or as a purely technical collection of recipes for the performance of specific tasks. Today we probably need not emphasise that the second of these approaches requires no defence: there is, in text processing, simple statistics, data retrieval and many other fields an increasing number of tools, the application of which results in such immediate gains in efficiency that they are best left to themselves to explain why they should be used. This author is of the opinion, however, that there are many reasons why we should not stop here: that there are indeed reasons why we should strive towards a consistent formulation of the ways in which information as contained in historical source material — or describing historical phenomena — differs from the information cropping up in contemporary administrative processes, or, indeed, the academic study of contemporary phenomena as well.

In pleading why this would be so we will follow three different lines of argument. We need a theory of historical computing because:

1. We need it to structure our own academic discourse.
2. There simply *are* properties of history which make it different from other disciplines intellectually.
3. It is needed to defend our requirements against academic competitors for funds which are becoming constantly less ample — and, indeed, against the academic bureaucracies themselves.

1. Academic Discourse

Computing in history has in its early years had many similarities to a sectarian endeavour: the need to defend the small group of people engaging in it against an overwhelmingly sceptical majority led to a situation where at most conferences about the subject, almost everybody was so happy to meet other people with the same interest that there was not very much argument about the advantages of a specific approach.[1] We need not be ashamed of that: every new intellectual and/or academic movement has to run through this phase, where a kind of collective brainstorming is undertaken, everybody being welcome who is ready to accept very basic common concepts. Such is the case with other developments in history as well. Women's history is a material example; even more so oral history, to quote a methodological one.

Computing in history has a tradition longer than both of them: so it is very appropriate that the almost messianic utterances of the early years have in general given way to a much more sober evaluation of the subject by practitioners. Beyond being sober, the next step has to be the development of a common ground on which all those problems can be discussed, which are not as self-explanatory as might sometimes appear. To mention just a few points on which this author is in disagreement with some of the arguments presented at this year's Westfield conference: I would *disagree* with the assumption that quantitative studies are the most appropriate way to use a computer as a methodologically relevant tool in history; I would *disagree* with the assumption that the relational data model is the most appropriate one for the design of historical databases; I would, finally, *disagree* with the notion that present artificial intelligence techniques hold a promise, if they are taken over unchanged.

This is by no means to be understood as a blanket rejection of the proposals brought forward by colleagues. It is to be taken rather as call for discussion of the specificity of historical research with respect to avenues of enquiry. And the necessity for an academic subdiscipline which is coming of age to provide a framework for precisely this kind of discussion is the first reason why a theory of historical computing is needed. In order to explore what such a framework would have to provide for, we will mention some of the background to the disagreements noted above. Of course this author *himself* considers his arguments valid; he admits, that he does not see a methodological framework, however, in which to prove that conclusively.

Disagreement with the concept of quantitative studies being the primary use for computers in history does not imply that these methods should not be used at all: indeed, students of history trained in quantitative methods are usually better able to adapt to other techniques than colleagues without such a background. One could argue, however, that there is an inbuilt problem in the whole philosophy of quantitative methodology, as developed in the social sciences, which makes their application in history difficult beyond a certain point. One of the problems is that all present-day studies make, often implicitly and tacitly, the assumption that for many aspects of the problems they are dealing with, authoritative expert knowledge exists, which is readily available. Large parts of modern linguistics assume that if you want to know what a phrase in a given language really means, all you have to do is to go and ask a native speaker — which in itself makes their methods useless for the treatment of any language-related phenomenon before 1880. In the social sciences many studies assume that for important areas of inmation — such as for occupation for example — there are experts able to relate surface information (the occupation in a questionnaire) to the underlying reality (the social position). So they are trying to produce hypotheses about what is going on between observable phenomena, testing hypotheses about the interrelationship between established facts. Historians have to become experts of the systems they are exploring themselves; indeed that is, what history is all about. So a statistical treatment of phenomena of a past society deals with hypotheses about the way an assumed reality was projected into the surviving source material. The whole concept of falsification has to change, therefore, if applied to the past: indeed, one might argue, we cannot falsify any hypothesis to begin with, as we never can isolate it completely for testing. What we *can* do, however, is finding out about the consistency of a certain number of interrelated hypotheses.[2] A theoretical background for such an evaluation procedure would be one example of what a theory of historical computing should be about; and a prerequisite for the decision as to which quantitative methods are appropriate at which times. This should not discourage interdisciplinary discourse with the Social Sciences: rather it should make it more fruitful.

In disagreeing with the proposition that the relational data model[3] is the best tool for database work in history, I do not wish to imply that it is wrong to use database management systems which implement it for historical studies. While no one doubts, however, that such current systems as dBASE can make one's life very much easier, I would like to emphasise that structural restrictions of existing software are no substitute for methodological reasoning. So another example of the kind of discussion for which a background is needed, and which we will have to undertake as a discipline some day, is the following. Are there not properties of our data which simply do not fit into the clean rectangular tables of relational software? And what alternatives are there for the organisation of data?[4] This is not intended to belittle the gains to be had from current commercial software; but we should look also to provide the base upon which to build software tailored for historical use.

Nor does my disagreement with some notions relating to the applicability of artificial intelligence imply a denial that this is one of the most fascinating developments in the information sciences of today. There is a split in present-day computing, however. On the one hand, there is database technology,[5] doing wonders with the administration of extremely large, but inherently trivial, data structures like lists of spare parts or patients in hospitals. On the other hand we have artificial intelligence,[6] providing the background for the simulation of extremely complex reasoning on the computer, but with amounts of data, which, for the not-so-enthusiastic spectator, border upon the ridiculous. Historians may be singularly well positioned to help to find the means to bridge this gap, since their data, being considerably more plentiful than that used nowadays by artificial intelligence, and definitely beyond the complexity administered by current database technology, can provide problems of a kind for which both techniques, if successfully combined, might yield a solution. To help in defining the basis for such a combination would be a third example of the kind of discussion that should be undertaken within the framework provided by a future theory of historical computing. It is not suggested that historians should teach computer scientists, but they should approach them with problems of sufficient interest to justify interdisciplinary research, with profit to both sides, instead of looking to them as providers of black boxes to be mechanically applied.

2. Intellectual Requirements

Is there indeed something about historical data which makes it different from other data processed by computers?[7]

One of the most frequent uses made of computers in historical studies is the ordering of information, to find specific documents by some information retrieval technology. A typical example for such an application could be to ask a database management system for the processing of records within a suitable database dealing with persons

— *coming from Prussia,*
— *being fifty or younger and*
— *having a fortune of 100 or more units of a currency 'x'.*

Straightforward as such a request may seem to be at first glance, we (or a natural language shell, if we apply a very sophisticated software system) would have to rephrase it first, somewhat along the lines of:

Provide information about entries in the database, where
— *the field 'country of origin' contains the string 'Prussia',*
— *the field 'age' contains a number smaller than '50'.*
— *the field 'fortune' contains a number greater than '100' ('x').*

In principle, these statements are sufficiently formal for processing by a computer. The problem, however, is, that this is still not what we really want: if we stick to the letter, we would, for example, always have to enter a field 'country' of origin to make such a question feasible, even if our source contains the relevant information in some other form such as 'place' of origin. What we *want* to express with the first of our three conditions in our query is actually something like the following:

I'm interested in entities where the field 'place of origin' contains a string which can be looked up in a table of place names. If that is done, the 'places of origin' I'm interested in shall in that table be connected with a pair of geographical coordinates, which fulfil the following condition: in the same table the string 'Prussia' is assumed to be associated with a polygon coded in the form of geographical coordinates; the coordinates of the 'place of origin' we started from, have to be contained within the polygon describing Prussia.

Incidentally just the possibility of making a query system able to replace a single term of comparison (like 'Prussia') with a chain of alternative search terms (like place names being located within Prussia) more or less automatically, has been heralded in one session of the annual conference of the AHC in Westfield 1987 as a major advantage of the use of artificial intelligence techniques. This author, coming from a database background, would disagree with that, and would suggest that this kind of substitution rule is a tool which any decent DBMS has to provide. Be that as it may, with formulations like that we are very close to the limits of what present-day DBMS-oriented software makes possible.

For an historian it is immediately clear, however, that what we asked for can intellectually just be the starting-point. 'Prussia' was taken as an example, not because it is assumed to be a particularly popular country, but because it has a property *in extremis*, which all geographical terms in historical research have inherently to some degree: its meaning fluctuates over time. To decide, if a particular place is located 'in Prussia', we have to know of what period that question is being asked, for example in 1730, 1794, 1811, 1830 or 1868. More generally, what we actually mean by the query we are discussing would have to be augmented by something like:

Assume that 'Prussia' is actually described not by one polygon, but by a whole series of such. To decide which one has actually to be used, proceed as follows. Take the field 'date of record' and subtract from it the content of the field 'age': then compare the resulting date with the timeframe that shows to which period the various polygons representing Prussia are applicable, and choose the appropriate one.

In any in-depth treatment of the subject, we would have to go on much further from this. For the purpose of the present paper, it may suffice to introduce a first statement about the intellectual requirements put up for any software that is supposed to be truly historical in nature:

Thesis 1:
Any software system able to accommodate inherent properties of historical data has to be able to make all processes of deduction dependent on the temporal context within which the items of data upon which the deductive process is based occur.

Looking now at the second of our questions (*the field 'age' contains a number smaller than '50'*), we encounter a different problem. Our forefathers, while virtuous in many respects, never paid much interest to precision in questions that seemed superficial to them; it is a well-known fact that sources as late as the nineteenth century censuses contain information about seemingly hard facts like the age of a person, which are just an approximation. Indeed, one could reasonably argue that *all* information supplied in historical sources is inherently vague or *fuzzy*, to use the term employed in the relevant literature[8] of information science.

The way to a formalisation of this problem is unfortunately thornier than in the previous case, so here I sketch it out even more roughly. The solution requires that we arrive at some estimate of the imprecision inherent in the age information of our source. This could be gained if we collect information on such things as whether the source contains vague expressions ('Approximately fifty years of age', 'an octogenarian' etc.). How many expressions does it contain, and how vague are they? And when we bring together information from different sources, how great is the observed difference between the age of one and the same person as given in different sources? Out of items such as these, we should ultimately be able to arrive at a statistical estimate of the distribution of errors in the age-related items of a single source or collection of sources. Using this, we could reformulate our original condition somewhat along the lines of:

The field 'age' has to contain a value which is smaller than x, where x is defined as the threshold one obtains by adding to 50 the standard deviation of 'age'-related errors. When the database in question has come into existence over a longer stretch of time, take into account its inherent context sensitivity: that is, when computing the error distribution for age, weight the terms entered into the distribution proportional to their temporal distance from the value of 'age' with which the comparison is made.

While the practical implementation of this example may be one of the most complicated to be solved by specifically historical computing, we note, as a second hypothesis, what requirements software has to fulfil to be — on a theoretical level — appropriate for information derived from historical sources:

Thesis 2:
Any software system able to accommodate inherent properties of historical data has to provide means to take account of the inherently fuzzy character of the information contained within historical source material.

So context-sensitivity and fuzziness are two inherent properties of historical data. We keep that in mind when we continue to look at the third of our original conditions, that *the field 'fortune' contains a number that is larger than 100 currency units 'x'.*

The first refinement to our initial formulation has obviously to assume that 'x' is a term that is contained as a character string both in the database and in the query posed to the retrieval system. So we could start with the re-formulation:

I'm interested in persons, where the field 'fortune' contains a string, which, when converted to a numerical entity, yields a value that is greater than the one that results when the string '100 x' is undergoing the same conversion process.

Having been alerted to the fact that the interpretation of the terminology of a source is dependent on the moment in time at which that source has come into existence, we can immediately add:

Start this conversion process by computing out of the field 'date of record' the timeframe within which the currency has been quoted. If the 'fortune' given has been recorded at a time other than that at which the record as such was written, take this into account.

Now, 'x' obviously stands for a currency. The exchange values of currencies change over time; they change also, however, when one moves from one territory to another one, coins being struck under the same name at different places having quite different values. So we have to add:

Continue the conversion process by examining which spatial frame might be appropriate. To get at that, take into account where the source has been written; check also, however, whether the information given in the field 'fortune' might have been originally recorded somewhere else.

After that we come to:

Now use the timeframe and the spatial frame obtained to decide which of the varying exchange rates between the currency used in the source and the 'x' used in the query apply in our case. For this purpose consult an independent database, which contains exchange rates for variant currency denoting terms.

Bearing in mind that historical sources are inherently fuzzy, we add, finally:

When comparing the temporal and spatial frames derived from the source with the entries in the currency database, check whether these frames are close to a point where different ones would apply (i.e. whether the exchange rate changed shortly before or after our information was fixed in writing, or the place where it was recorded lies very close to a border between two territories with different coinage). If so, consider the original conditions to be already fulfilled if it is fulfilled within a wider margin, to take care of the discovered disambiguity.

It should be emphasised again and again that considerations like these are just the beginning. In the case of spatial terms, for example, one would have to consider *where* the term was written down in order to discover which area is covered by it; in the case of temporal information, one might have to consider *when* it was fixed in writing in order to understand what date is actually meant by the feast of a particular saint, used as a temporal reference point. Both observations imply that our context-sensitivity is something which has to be applied recursively,[9] that is, to itself. It will not always be as simple, as in our example, to discover which temporal and spatial frames apply: this information will very often be hidden in parts of the data to which a conventional data model does not necessarily provide any connection.

At the same time the question of the level at which such considerations should be implemented is open to argument. The author is in favour of solutions where some reference mechanism[10] is built into the data by the researcher collecting them — or even by the person developing the software. So we could discuss means which would guarantee that historical software 'knows', for each definition, that it is necessary to look for a 'place of origin' if a 'country of origin' is not within the data. On the other hand it is obviously important that these reference mechanisms have to remain under control of the user, that the user has to have the possibility to redefine some of the implicative mechanisms. And some historians are, indeed, afraid, that the user would lose control over the source material on which they are basing their reasoning, if that source material is administered by a database with a very enhanced reference mechanism which remains oblique.

How much data do we need so that the results we gain will actually be markedly different from the ones we get by conventional software, when compared to inference mechanisms like the ones discussed here? If we ever reach a stage where the large collections of printed editions are available as databases, we will obviously have to provide mechanisms in the direction to which I have pointed. Do we further our aims better if we start to develop the necessary tools now, testing them with smaller amounts of material — or should we, for the time being, concentrate mainly on the rough-and-ready provision of data, leaving the refinements for a later stage?

None of these questions can be answered off-hand; none of them can be answered by anybody from the information sciences, as all of them are completely, or at least have components which are inherently, historical. And my purpose here was not to *answer* such questions, but to show that they are there and that they constitute an intellectual and theoretical challenge for the historian discussing the application of computers to his or her field.

3. Institutional Requirements

Intellectual problems, and the tackling of them, are a delightful part of the academic historians experience; dealing with funding agencies is an equally integral, though far less exciting, part of the same. This second part of the historian's experience, has, at least during the last few years, been dominated by the so-called 'micro-revolution'. In most parts of Europe, historians encountered the strange phenomenon that bureaucrats of the local research administration, while very hard to convince to spend money on historical research as such, were much more easily persuaded to provide funds for the introduction of computing into historical research and/or teaching. Indeed, in a few European countries, historians, like other academic teachers of the humanities, have been asked to provide the inclusion of some data processing knowledge into the curricula they offer. Now when I argue that historians should explore possibilities to assure their access to these funding possibilities for the future, I do not consider that we are working towards a policy of a sell-out of history to some other discipline. It is a fact, however, that at many universities there exists already the necessity to provide some kind of teaching on the use of computers in history; it is a fact, furthermore, that in the near future the number of students who enter university with quite a bit of working knowledge of computing will increase. Today it is of course possible to teach, under the heading of *computer-literacy*, wordprocessing skills (and it is possible to improve ones funding position by that). But this teaching is going to become pointless as soon as the various projects to emphasise computing in secondary education become successful. So historians should try to avoid dependence on developments which are likely to become redundant in a relatively short time. It would be much wiser to move to a higher intellectual plane and show what a computer can do specifically for the historian.

I repeat, we should *not* advocate any sell-out of the historical disciplines, I am against exchanging 'a truly historical education' for the possibilities of acquiring funds. One should see realistically, however, that for every history student today who ends up with a job as historian, there are at least four who find themselves in professions where they are paid for having acquired the ability to argue according to some intellectual standard, to express themselves easily in writing, and for other abilities which somehow come as a windfall profit from the classical historical education. If we accept the view that the universities' role in teaching history consists also of training people for the society in a number of skills, which are very valuable intellectually, but not necessarily and inherently linked to the chronology of the Saxon kingdoms, we will have to think seriously about how far and in what ways a specific understanding of formal reasoning has to be introduced into our dealings with our past.

This quest for what is specific about computing in history should also be undertaken for the sake of another aspect of funding. Right now it is relatively easy to convince the administration of a university that it is a major methodological innovation if an historical department starts using standard programs on standard computers. Already now, however, there have been cases in Europe where historians applying for computers have had a rude awakening, when the funding bodies approached for some project told them that, while their projects would certainly hold great historical merit, from the data processing point of view they were not innovative at all, and therefore it would not be possible to provide any additional money for a project which would have to be paid out of the regular budget. Interdisciplinary cooperation with the information sciences, if inaugurated by a historical discipline from the basis of a secure knowledge about one's own need for innovative solutions, can in some cases produce very material rewards.

To conclude: I think that we need a theory of historical computing. Because computer usage is an established fact for many historical departments, and in order to exchange our knowledge about it, we need a firm conceptual and theoretical base. Because there *is* a difference between data in historical sources and those in the accounting books of a hospital. It has been said that history as an academic profession consists of interpreting the past in the light of the knowledge and the conceptions of the present. If we take this seriously, and notice that formal reasoning, as it accompanies the advance of computing, seems to be destined to become much more important in the general intellectual background of our society, it is indeed hard to see how we can avoid the problem of creating some conceptual framework, just to come to grips with these developments in our discipline's eternal confrontation with our heritage.

Notes

1. A comment of a participant of one of the earliest of these conferences: 'That is, though some of the projects described may have seemed confusing, superficial, inconsequential, or just plain long to a number of onlookers, even the most suspect of the undertakings explained could hardly have been called diabolical'. (Edmund A. Bowles (ed.), *Computers in Humanistic Research*, Englewood Cliffs, 1967, vii.)

2. See the more extensive treatment of this point in Manfred Thaller, 'Ungefähre Exaktheit. Theoretische Grundlagen und praktische Möglichkeiten einer Formulierung historischer Quellen als Produkte "unscharfer" Systeme', Helga Nagl-Docekal und Franz Wimmer (eds.), *Neue Ansätze in der Geschichtswissenschaft*, Vienna, 1984 (= Conceptus Studien 1), pp. 77–100.

3. Indeed the author suspects that there are a few historians who tend to think that the relational model is the only one around: a more sophisticated introduction can be found in Dionysios C. Tsichritzis and Frederick H. Lochovsky, *Data Models*, Englewood Cliffs, 1982.

4. As a lengthy example of this kind of problem constitutes the second section of this paper, none is provided at this point.

5. William Kent, *Data and Reality*, Amsterdam, etc., 1978, is a very good introduction for some of the less trivial properties of databasing.

6. Challenging reading for an historian, but a very good introduction into the less superficial links between traditional computer applications and AI techniques: J. F. Sowa, *Conceptual Structures: Information Processing in Mind and Machine*, Reading, Mass., 1984, pp. 310–18.

7. The following example is discussed in much greater detail — including aspects of a possible solution — in: Manfred Thaller, 'Warum brauchen die Geisteswissenschaften fachspezifische datentechnische Lösungen? Das Beispiel kontextsensitiver Datenbanken in der Geschichtswissenschaft', in Albert Müller und Manfred Thaller (eds.), *Computer in den Geisteswissenschaften*, Frankfurt/New York, 1989 (= Studien zur Historischen Sozialwissenschaft 7).

8. Good introductory reading: Lotfi A. Zadeh, 'The Concept of a Linguistic Variable and its Application to Approximate Reasoning', *Information Sciences*, 8 (1975), pp. 199–249, 301–57 and 9 (1975) pp. 43–80. B.R. Gaines, 'Foundations of Fuzzy Reasoning', *International Journal of Man-Machine Studies*, 8, 1976, pp. 623–68.

9. More precisely we would need tools to perform the varieties of lookup simultaneously. On recursion as an artefact, derived from the current hardware architecture, see Stoyan O. Kableshkov, *The Anthropocentric Approach to Computing*

and Reactive Machines, Chichester, etc., 1983, pp. 25–27.

10.   Here, indeed, AI techniques, which tend to blur the differences between data and rules, might be applied very profitably: see Richard Ennals, *Artificial Intelligence: Applications to Logical Reasoning and Historical Research*, Chichester, etc., 1986.

Prosopography and the Computer: Problems and Possibilities

Let me start with a brief comment[1] on a current problem which is much discussed at the moment in Germany: the census of May 1987 and the opposition to it of large numbers of the population and many experts. Newspapers have evaluated the total cost of this project at 100 million DM; about 600,000 people will be employed as enumerators in what is really a massive prosopographical research project. Both the government's interest in the census and the resistance to it are mainly due to the same set of circumstances. There are two main issues: first, the enormous possibilities offered by new computer techniques in handling this data and the consequent fear of abuse through the unification of the census data with fiscal, police or other data banks; second, the charge that the whole business will be an enormous waste of time and money, because the same data is already available elsewhere.

This debate is in my opinion very relevant to the subject of this paper. Undoubtedly the boom in the use of computers by historians is also stimulated by the possibilities offered by the computer for record linkage. One of the reasons for the recent growing interest in prosopography comes precisely from the specific needs of prosopographical studies in which the computer can be helpful. But the second issue, that of cost, should equally be kept in mind by any prosopographer, though in a slightly different way: it must be asked whether the use of the computer offers real advantages, or whether it may not result in in wasted time, effort and money.

In this paper I will discuss 1) the prosopographical approach to historical research, its special problems and possible solutions, and 2) the advantages and dangers of implementing computer-based solutions. I will do this mainly from the point of view of a medievalist, but my arguments apply to modern and contemporary history as well.

Prosopography is one of the oldest approaches of the historical sciences.[2] Yet the more systematic interest in prosopography is quite new. I do not need to stress the pioneer works of Namier[3] and Syme.[4] But these innovative efforts had relatively few immediate consequences. It was only with the publication in 1970–71 of important articles by Nicolet and Chastagnol[5] and Lawrence Stone[6] that a real increase in prosopographical research could be noted.

Where did this new interest in prosopography come from? Is Stone right in suggesting that 'In terms of psychological motivation, these obsessive collectors of biographical information belong to the same category of anal-erotic males as the collectors of butterflies, postage stamps, or cigarette cards; all are byproducts of the Protestant ethic'?[7] Or should we follow Ronald

Syme, who in his day thought that a pessimistic and materialistic view of humanity was the inspiration of the prosopographical approach?[8] Does this pessimistic view still fit better in our day than other historical approaches? I think that nowadays, whilst we cannot totally exclude a passion for collecting as a motivation for microscopic research, the truth lies more in the direction to which Syme alluded. Firstly, for reasons which I have no time to discuss here, there is a new orientation towards social history which found favour amongst German scholars only a few years ago. Secondly, and here I come back to my opening statement, when historians first cautiously approached the computer some fifteen years ago, prosopographical questions were soon found to be congenial topics for electronic data processing. So, for instance, German and international interdisciplinary conferences on electronic data processing in Rome (1975), in Paris (1978) or in Tübingen (1979) were also concerned with prosopographical approaches.[9]

But certainly the main impetus came from social history. 'Après beaucoup d'autres j'ai seulement éprouvé le désir et presque le besoin de m'intéresser à tous les hommes, et non pas seulement à ceux qui brillèrent par leur naissance, par leur état, par leur fonction, par leur richesse ou par leur intelligence'.[10] This conception of social history, formulated by Pierre Goubert, could not be realised without studying the people themselves together with their conditions of life, their families, occupations or professions, careers, earnings and so on, by means of prosopographical research. Furthermore, this prosopographical interest involved not only the protagonists of history but everybody including those at the margins, or, as Irène Marrou formulated it, 'l'histoire à travers ses fantassins'.[11]

Before we start to discuss the consequences of this argument for historical research, a definition of prosopography should be given. There have been many attempts to define prosopography, but what they nearly all have in common is a concern with the individual and his community. This aspect, the individual seen in relation to a given totality, is contained in the definition offered by Stone: 'Prosopography is the investigation of the common background characteristics of a group of actors in history by means of a collective study of their lives'.[12] The only thing perhaps which needs here to be defined more precisely is the notion of 'life'. Because in nearly all cases it is impossible for medievalists or even historians of more recent periods to get enough real personal data about an individual to enable the effective reconstruction of his life.

This is not something to be regretted, since prosopography should not be confused with biography. The prosopographer is interested in the research of life-cycles, which means he must look for pure demographic data on persons and their families, as well as data on professional careers, on education, income, wealth, and the like. Apart from purely personal data, the set of data assembled varies according to the subject under investigation. Thus only a well-defined selection of data should be of specific interest to the researcher.[13] We will consider later the question of bias in these selections and of the standardisation of data which is often required when evaluation is assisted by a computer program.

Another definition of prosopography has been offered recently by Karl Schmid: 'An essential object of prosopographical studies is the identification of individuals through their personal or family or similar relationships'.[14] This surely is misleading; the individual can only ever be an intermediate aim of prosopographical research, not the final one. But the dividing line between biography and prosopography is not the only difficulty we are concerned with here.[15] A matter of major importance, in my opinion, is the question of whether we should conceive of prosopography as a method or not. Stone was imprecise on this point in his article. He began with 'Prosopography . . . has developed into one of the most valuable and most familiar *techniques* of the research historian'. Later on he spoke of the relatively new invention of 'prosopography as a *historical method*'.[16] The same inconsistency can be found in many articles and books. I would like to emphasise that prosopography can not be characterised by the use of a specific method but by its interest in specific questions in the field of social history. To succeed, the prosopographer must therefore use the whole range of methods and techniques of history and social sciences, from paleography, sigillography or heraldry to statistics and last but not least to electronic data processing. It is according to the nature of the specific topic that the historian chooses his methods and approaches. So unless we refer to the combination of all these techniques and approaches as a new method, which is not justified in my view, prosopography cannot be defined as a new method.

The possibilities and limitations of prosopographical research have been discussed these past years in a series of four conferences devoted exclusively to the subject. The first of these was devoted to methodological questions in medieval history, and was held in Bielefeld, in December 1982.[17] Its aims were to discuss prosopographical approaches to different groups and strata of society, from bishops to peasants, from students to townspeople. Two conferences followed in Paris in October 1984. The first, organised by Françoise Autrand,[18] was concerned with research into the personnel of the early modern state (thirteenth to seventeenth centuries); the second, organised by Hélène Millet,[19] concentrated on the use of the computer for prosopographical research, covering ancient to contemporary history. The last of the four conferences took place at the École Française of Rome in December 1985.[20] Its general topic was 'La prosopographie. Problèmes et méthodes', and it covered again a wide range of research fields from the Romans to the exiles from fascist France. During these conferences more than a hundred papers were presented and discussed which dealt with a large variety of prosopographical interests covering topics as diverse as warships of the seventeenth and eighteenth centuries and Byzantine seals. In addition, I should mention the discussion going on in the review *Medieval Prosopography*, founded by George Beech, Bernard Bachrach and Joel Rosenthal and published in Kalamazoo,[21] and various special issues of other reviews.[22]

From a consideration of the research papers presented at these conferences and published in learned journals — and that includes many which are in the conceptual phase and many which may never reach completion — two points emerge more strongly than any others. First, prosopography has succeeded in overcoming the traditional barriers between institutional, legal, economic and social history. As examples I could mention the history of universities,[23] of the peasantry,[24] of representative institutions, of cathedral chapters[25]. In each of these cases the prosopographical approach has demonstrated its validity. Only a better understanding of the participants can lead us to a better appreciation of the functioning, success or failure of medieval or early modern institutions or of peasant or urban revolts. Here it is possible to work prosopographically not only on the leaders but also on the people acting in minor positions and sometimes, as in the case of the revolts, on quite ordinary participants. The enumeration of examples could easily be enlarged. Second, there are the dangers of prosopography, those outlined in my quotation from Stone. The collection of prosopographical data can easily degenerate into an end in itself. The damage is greater because in most cases the data collected remains inaccessible to others. The temptation to press ahead and collect data regardless of its value and purpose is greatly increased by the possibilities offered by the computer. Another problem lies in the handling of data which has been collected but which cannot easily be integrated into an historical narrative. On the other hand prosopographical studies in which results and interpretations are published without the database, i.e. the prosopographical catalogue, however they might increase the interest of the general reader, decrease the value of the work to other researchers.

Let me come now to my second main question. What can the computer offer the prosopographical researcher? Here again I must confine myself to some short guidelines which result from recent experience, and I must leave apart purely technical aspects. Of course computer techniques have made an enormous difference to prosopographical studies. Equally, there must be a minimum size of population to make computerisation worthwhile: for example, some hundred members of parliament or deputies to representative assemblies, Huguenot refugees, or many thousands of students, or even 400,000 dead monks and the people they pray for. This last project, a well as many others, is based on an enormous database. The number of new projects which have in view the creation of a database, for example on biographies of artists, on Domesday Book, on a whole urban society (Avignon in the fourteenth century) etc. is ever increasing.[26] And here the computer offers us an inestimable service. It allows us for example, in the case of the Münster project on necrologies, to identify groups, to date populations of monks, to check newly discovered necrologies, etc. Comparable results can be hoped from the Domesday Book database.[27] These two projects have one thing in common. Both databases contain all the data available. But a comparable procedure is excluded in most other cases.[28] In some cases such large databases might hinder the progress of historical prosopographical research. If the research and the prosopographical database is not done for a precise scientific purpose, the project is not very likely to succeed.

Another possible difficulty of very big database projects can lie in the fact that even if their intention is to facilitate access to the sources and make the data more available for all scholars, they might hinder further research in this field because there is no free choice any more: either you agree to work on this specific topic using the computer or you elect to study something else. A further danger lies in the computer's capacity to quantify. The techniques of record linkage, factor analysis and so forth must be carefully handled, or the results can be very misleading or incomprehensible.[29] It is up to the historian to decide whether computer-generated results are significant or not, whether they establish wrong correlations, whether they invert causes and effects, etc.

Two other problems which have been at the centre of recent discussion are far from being solved. The first is how to constitute a group. Many prosopographies are diachronic.[30] Others concern groups living together for a certain time. The members of a cathedral chapter from the thirteenth to the fifteenth century are a different group to the members of a specific nation at the council of Constance 1414–18. This of course has consequences for the research itself. The other problem concerns the choice of data model or schedule. What data items should be chosen, what should be left out? This choice is of course crucial for what can be done afterwards with the assembled data. If the schedule is too detailed nothing very significant will come out of it. The lacunae in every file will be too numerous. If on the other hand it is too restricted only banalities will result. A. Zysberg has very adequately formulated this danger: 'éviter le codage qui écrase comme un rouleau compresseur ce qu'il convenait de faire ressortir'.[31] The database — an artificial new source or meta-source — should not be mistaken for the reality or even as a reliable copy of it. It should be open to revisions and it should be kept in mind how it has been constructed. But once the construction of a database has reached a certain stage it can be very difficult to modify it to meet fresh research demands.

Let me conclude with two remarks. Prosopographical research has enabled the discovery of people who up to now, at least in medieval and early modern history, have lain somewhat outside the mainstream of historical interest, for example migrants, refugees, students, monks, peasants or even social outcasts. Many of the research programmes which are concerned with rather large populations depend on the computer and could not have been conceived and cannot be realised without the aid of sophisticated computer programs. This does not mean that a general revision of former research must take place, but we may perhaps achieve a better balance in our knowledge of different members of past societies. My final point is an appeal or rather a personal statement. Further progress which historians and prosopographers may make with the help of the computer will depend very much on efforts to unify computer-aided approaches to historical research, and the success or otherwise of such efforts.[32]

Notes

1.   This text is an only slightly altered draft of the text presented at the conference.

2.   Cf. N. Bulst, 'Zum Gegenstand und zur Methode von Prosopographie', in *Medieval Lives and the Historian. Studies in Medieval Prosopography*. Proceedings of the First International Interdisciplinary Conference on Medieval Prosopography, University of Bielefeld, 1982, Kalamazoo, 1986, p. 1.

3.   L. Namier, *The Structure of Politics at the Accession of George III*, London, 1925, 2 vols.

4.   R. Syme, *Roman Revolution*, Oxford, 1939.

5.   C. Nicolet, 'Prosopographie et histoire sociale: Rome et l'Italie à l'époque républicaine', *Annales E. S. C.*, 25, 1970, pp. 1209–28; A. Chastagnol, 'La prosopographie, méthode de recherche sur l'histoire du Bas-Empire', ibid., pp.

1229–35. Cf. also the more recent critical article by J. Maurin, 'La prosopographie romaine; pertes et profits', ibid., 37, 1982, p. 824–36.

6. L. Stone, 'Prosopography', *Daedalus*, 100, 1971, pp. 46–79.

7. Ibid., p. 49.

8. Syme, *Roman Revolution*, ed. Oxford, 1974, p. VIII.

9. *Informatique et histoire médiévale. Communications et débats de la Table Ronde CNRS (Rome, 20–22 Mai 1975)*, ed. by L. Fossier, A. Vauchez and C. Violante (Coll. de l'École française de Rome, 31), Rome, 1977, pp. 227–46 (with contributions of J. Glénisson, J.-P. Genet and F. Autrand on 'Prosopography and Social History'). *L'histoire médiévale et les ordinateurs — Medieval History and Computers. Rapports d'une Table ronde internationale, Paris, 1978*, ed. by K. F. Werner (Documentations et recherches, ed. by l'Institut Historique Allemand), München/New York, 1981, pp. 61–109 (with contributions of K. Schmid, J. Wollasch and F. Neiske). *19. Kolloquium über die Anwendung der EDV in den Geisteswissenschaften*, Tübingen, 1979, in *ALLC-Bulletin*, 9,3, 1981, p. 19–21 (with contribution of D. Geuenich).

10. P. Goubert, *Beauvais et le Beauvaisis de 1600 à 1730. Contribution à l'histoire de la France du XVIIe siècle*, Paris, 1960, p. VII.

11. Quoted by L. Fossier, in *Le Médiéviste et l'Ordinateur*, 10, 1983, p. 1.

12. Stone (as n. 6) p. 46.

13. Examples of different prospographical catalogues may be found in C. Bozzolo and H. Loyau, *La cour amoureuse dite de Charles VI*, t. 1, Paris, 1982, pp. 47 ff.; H. Millet, *Les chanoines du chapitre cathédral de Laôn 1272–1412* (Coll. de l'École française de Rome, 56), Rome, 1982, pp. 321 ff.; R. Descimon, 'Qui étaient les Seize. Étude sociale de deux cent vingt-cinq cadres laïcs de la ligue radicale parisienne (1585–1594)', *Paris et Île-de-France. Mémoires*, 34, 1983, pp. 101 ff.

14. K. Schmid, 'Prosopographische Forschungen zur Geschichte des Mittelalters', in *Aspekte der Historischen Forschung in Frankreich und Deutschland. Schwerpunkte und Methoden* (Veröffentlichungen des Max-Planck-Instituts für Geschichte 39), Göttingen, 1981, pp. 60 ff.; cf. M. Hillebrandt, 'The Cluniac Charters: Remarks on a Quantitative Approach for Prosopographical Studies', *Medieval Prosopography*, 3,1, 1982, p. 9.

15. This problem is discussed at length in Bulst (as n. 1) pp. 6 ff.

16. Stone (as n. 6) p. 46 and 49.

17. Bulst/Genet (as n. 1).

18. *Prosopographie et genèse de l'État moderne*, ed. by F. Autrand (Coll. de l'École Normale Supérieure de jeunes filles, 30), Paris, 1986.

19. *Informatique et prosopographie*, ed. by H. Millet, Paris, 1985.

20. *La prosopographie. Problèmes et méthodes* (Mélanges de l'École française de Rome, 99), Rome, 1988 (in press). This conference served also as a preparatory meeting of the 'Action thématique programmée' (A. T. P.) 'Prosopographie'.

21. Vol. 1 ff., Kalamazoo, 1980 ff.

22. Cf. especially *Le Médiéviste et l'ordinateur*, 10, 1983: La Prosopographie.

23. Cf. the excellent work of R. Schwinges, *Deutsche Universitätsbesucher im 14. und 15. Jahrhundert. Studien zur Sozialgeschichte des Alten Reiches*, Stuttgart, 1986, which could not have been done without the computer.

24. L. R. Poos, 'Peasant "Biographies" from Medieval England', in Bulst/Genet (as n. 1) p. 201–14 (with computer use).

25. Millet (as. n. 13) (with computer use).

26. For references see Bulst/Genet (as n. 1) and Millet (as n. 19).

27. A. Ayton and V. Davis, 'The Hull Domesday Project', in *History and Computing*, ed. by P. Denley and D. Hopkin, Manchester, 1987, pp. 21–28.

28. Another Domesday Book database in Santa Barbara will work with a selection of data, cf. R. Fleming, 'A Report on the Domesday Book Database Project', *Medieval Prosopography*, 7,2, 1986, pp. 55–61.

29.   For a convincing demonstration cf. H. Millet, 'Une expérience: essai de classification des chanoines de Laon, *Le Médiéviste et l'Ordinateur*, 7, 1982, pp. 14–17.

30.   Cf. Bulst/Genet (as n. 1), Introduction.

31.   Fossier (as n. 11) p. 2.

32.   See for example the enumeration of the different programs which the projects presented at the conference in Paris worked with (see n. 19) p. 354.

II.

Education

History and New Technology in Schools:
Problems, Possibilities and the Way Forward

This paper is about New Technology in schools — the problems and possibilities accompanying the use of this technology for both teachers and children, now and in the future.

It is pertinent to introduce one such teacher, a teacher that had a prolonged effect upon my own education. Miss Page taught 'her children' in a provincial primary school. A history lesson would invariably consist of Miss Page standing in front of her charges, holding aloft a rectangular 'flash card' with a phrase or word writ large. Scanning slowly a sea of sullen faces, each progressively sinking lower and lower into its shoulders the awesome silence would suddenly be broken by fierce and humbling tones: 'What does REVOLUTION mean, Wild?' (revolution being the word on the flashcard). After what seemed like hours but was in fact a matter of seconds, it was established that I would not be able to tell Miss Page what revolution meant. After some admonition that this was the third time I was unable to give the right answer I invariably had to sit out the rest of the day in a lower class, squatting upon smaller seats at miniature tables and alongside younger children.

Although history lessons might give way to English and then maths, the method by which each was taught varied little. Although as a nine-year old I did not fully appreciate the subtleties of Miss Page's pedagogical approach I know now that it had profound effect. But my reminiscences are much less important than what happened to Miss Page — and I shall continue her story towards the end of this paper.

1. The Context

To appreciate the problems and possibilities for the use of microcomputers in history education we need to consider the wider influences that have produced very mixed patterns of teaching and learning in all parts of the curriculum to date.

Programmed Learning   The notion of individualised learning relates closely to theories of behavioural psychology first given credence in the 1950s by Skinner.[1] This led to the design of individualised programme learning systems. The basic premise for such systems is that learning occurs when a specific response from a learner has been elicited in response to a particular stimulus in a particular situation. After initial research work had been carried out with pigeons, early findings were then applied to classroom situations. In effect, this meant providing children with a linear learning sequence, a degree of predictable interaction between teacher and learner and continual reinforcement of the learning.

The influence of theories of programmed learning has proved a pervasive if, as Maddison[2] would argue, vestigial ingredient in some of the thinking about computers and their applications in education. Whereby both Skinner's research and his philosophy have received popular and more general educational criticism,[3] his influence has permeated more deeply ideas about the use of computers in education. The reasons for this are probably largely historical. Programmed learning was in its heyday in the 1960s, a time when computers were beginning to be applied to learning, particularly in the USA. As with all innovations, the application of computers to education needed a methodology, a need that could be satisfied by behaviourist theories — 'instruction' rather than 'learning' and 'training' rather than 'education' became pivotal parts of the emerging methodology. It is not coincidence that CAI (Computer Aided Instruction) was and still is the dominant term used to describe the general application of computers in education in the USA; it is also no accident that the same term has been used extensively in Britain to describe computing (especially software) development. In 1977 the Director of the first major national research project felt compelled to write in his final report:

Many people equate computer assisted learning with programmed learning, and with the provision of cost-effective teaching through the reduction of labour costs (i.e. fewer teachers). This image of CAL (Computer Assisted Learning), largely inherited from North America, must be put to one side if the National Programme, and this final report, is to be understood. Computer assisted learning, and its twin, computer managed learning, as defined and developed by the Programme, are characterised by a versatility of applications, some of which have nothing to do with programmed learning at all.[4]

Despite this statement the subsequent development of educational computing since the 1970s has been marked indelibly with programmed learning techniques: one only has to turn to examples of software still being produced to see the lasting effects of Skinners' behaviourist influences. Interestingly, another mark of this period of educational computing was a fear that the computer would eventually replace the teacher — a fear generated out of ignorance and equated with notions about the 'intelligent computer', an idea popularised by the media at every turn.

Cognitive Approaches   Later in the 1970s the theories underlying cognitive psychology found expression in education, notably through the work of Piaget, Donaldson and others.[5] Educationalists began to focus upon the nature of the educational experience children received and to the context the child itself brought to that experience. With regard to the use of computers the influence of this school of educational thought became particularly powerful. In *Mindstorms — Children, Computers and Powerful Ideas* Papert gave the most persuasive account to date of such thinking.[6] He and others consistently spoke of the importance of creative problem solving, wholistic and experiential learning and, later on, peer-group inter-action.

Techniques said to facilitate this type of learning include games and simulations. Indeed, simulation activity has influenced both pedagogical theory and classroom practice since the late 1960s, especially with respect to the 'New Movements' in the humanities.[7] In general this school of thought promoted the idea that learning should be about awareness and understanding rather than simply about factual knowledge; that children should be involved in the processes of active enquiry rather than passive instruction. It has also been said that learning should concern itself with the affective as well as cognitive development of the learner. In the 1970s and 1980s these ideas were embodied in a number of curriculum development initiatives, such as the Schools Council History Project[8] and Nuffield Science. It is no coincidence that computer simulations and modelling activities are currently so much in vogue amongst both software and curriculum developers working in educational computing.

The Place of the Computer
The inter-connections described above between general educational developments and the evolution of educational computing should not surprise us. They are evident in all aspects of educational computing, from software designs to teaching strategies. So from the 1970s through to the present, and no doubt beyond, we can point to examples of educational computing practice developed in the full light of behaviourism, bearing either the tell-tale acronym CAI (Computer Aided Instruction) or often and less

Figure 1

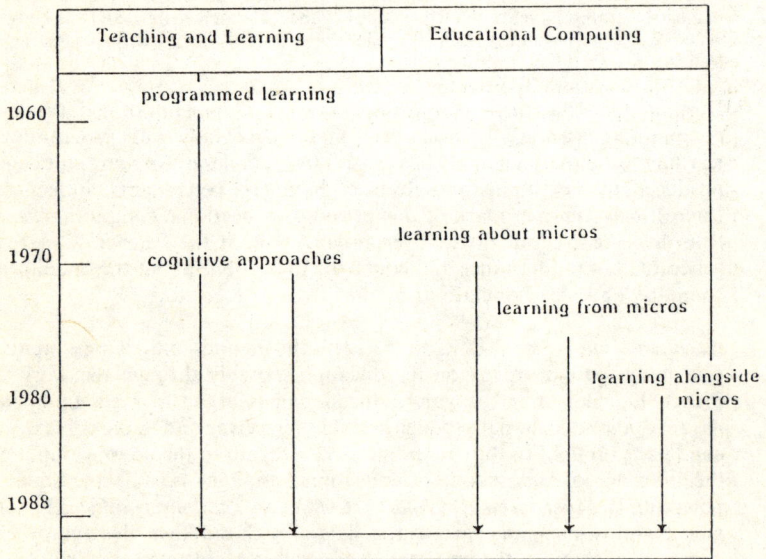

honestly, paying lip-service to the umbrella term CAL (Computer Aided Learning). Since the early 1980s, the idea of experiential and group learning processes has became increasingly influential; 'learning by doing' has become the implicit catch-phrase of many new software applications.

Amongst many of those who advocate the unique advantages of using micros in education the most recent 'buzz' might be about such things as 'peer group inter-action', 'transferable skills', 'content-free software environments', or 'microworlds' — but such phrases should not blind us to the mixed practice which permeates all educational computing, reflecting in part, teacher-centred, child-centred, programmed learning and experiential learning strategies.

2. The Practice and Potential of Computers in History Education

It is necessary from time to time to ask a fundamental question of ourselves and our work: Why use the computer in history education? It is possible to address this question in a variety of ways. It may, for example, be persuasively argued that computer technology is quite simply and unashamedly a major lifeline to a threatened profession. The Historical Association's (HA) submissions to the former Secretary of State for Education, took the view that 'History in the schools has diminished, is diminishing and ought to be increased'.[9] The position taken by the HA in the National Curriculum debate is only the latest manifestation of a long-festering concern to defend against encroachments of more 'relevant subjects' in both schools and institutions of higher education.[10]

There can be little doubt that the political and economic climate of the time places greater emphasis upon the importance of the market place and by doing so puts pressure upon the arts and humanities. Ministers exhort educational establishments to ensure that education should meet 'national needs' for 'vocationally-oriented . . . work of use to the creation of wealth in the country'.[11] Newly formed government sponsored organisations, such as the Manpower Services Commission (MSC) have responded in part by favouring an expansion of a 'more appropriate' technological input into education. Indeed, the national Technical and Vocational Education Initiative (TVEI) has sought to provide direct answers to the general clamour that the education of our children lacks relevance to the 'real world'. Schemes like TVEI are revolutionising schools' curricula, particularly in the arts and humanities.

The response of those who take it upon themselves to represent history education in these threatening times is predictable. Eager for both recognition and financial support, history educationalists are jostling with the best of them, seeking to establish the potential of history as a technically rich and vocationally relevant subject.[12] The current trend to slap the IT label on anything that moves only blinds us to the real educational opportunities of the new technology. To apply and develop new technology in history education can begin to focus critical attention on the learner, the learning process and the changing role of the teacher in that process. For example: *(i) Child Centred Learning*   Computers can provide the student with responsibility for his/her own learning. The computer can become the tool which shapes and structures students' activities;

(ii) New Activities   Those very activities open to the student will become less restricted and be potentially of better quality; activities will be possible that are not so without the use of the micro. This is particularly true in terms of software that provides for the use of sophisticated simulation and modelling programs;

(iii) Social Contexts   Used in social situations the computer may become the focus for discussion and communication amongst peer groups and between teacher and student(s);

(iv) Cognitive Modelling   In some circumstances the computer will involve the student in modelling his/her understanding, that is, representing ideas and knowledge within a flexible framework. This framework may be made of rules which determine the relationships within a knowledge base. Used in this way the computer may provide the environment for children to engage in reasoned and logical thinking, tracing and forming various types of association between discreet items of knowledge;

(v) Learning Processes   In some cases the computer reflects certain processes of learning where the student is actively encouraged towards reflexive thinking and techniques involving problem-solving or/and decision making. Some software will not only provide the context for students to answer questions but also to question answers.

(vi) Learning Environments   Computers may also provide the learning environment for students to progress when they would not have done so otherwise. For example, the computer can remove the psychological barriers in presenting written work where the fear of making mistakes is no longer a dominating one;

(vii) Pedagogy   The use of computers in certain situations may affect relationships within the classroom where the teacher is no longer seen as the font of all knowledge but is now the facilitator, providing support where it is appropriate and guidance when necessary. Teachers may well find themselves in a position to be able to address individual student requirements and to monitor and evaluate processes of learning.

However, this is largely concerned with what is possible; we also need to look specifically at examples of current practice.

The State of the Art: New Technology in History

There are a range of activities practised in history classrooms across the country, although the teachers and children involved are no doubt a small minority of potential participants (see Part III, below).

Information Handling

Information Handling (IH) is perhaps the most influential and potentially promising of computer related activities in history classrooms. The IH software allows information of a structured type (for example, a burial register or census return) to be represented in the computer and then investigated by questioning, sorting and general manipulation and the results then displayed (textually or graphically). Such activities have been said to facilitate learning experiences that are rich and perhaps not otherwise available.[13]

Figure 2 describes the involvement of children in one such learning experience. Starting with a series of related activities (in this case these ranged from cooking a meal from rations typically available to those living in war-time London to watching a TV drama based on a contemporary family) the children began to build up knowledge about the home front in the Second World War. Working together, the children and teacher then organised the collection of information from those who had lived during the war in the childrens' home area (viz. Luton, Bedfordshire). This was achieved through interviews conducted by the children. The information collected was entered into the computer in a structured format for later analysis. Not all the data

Figure 2

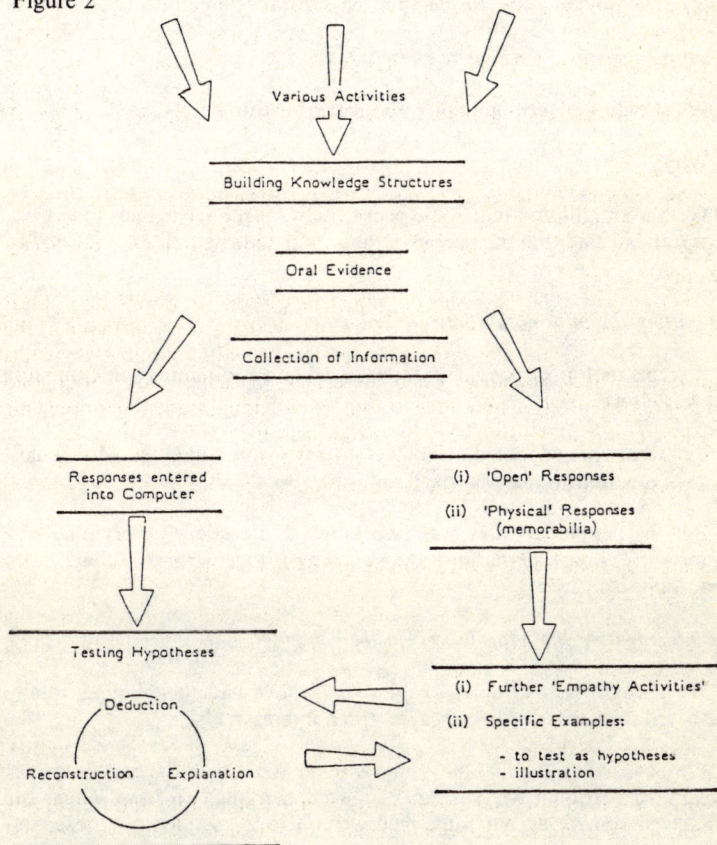

collected was to be represented on the computer — the more open ended questions and responses were used in other classroom activities, as was the range of memorabilia brought back (including, ration books, medals, photographs, etc.). The analysis of the data now on computer was used to answer specific hypotheses the children had formulated throughout the whole project as well as providing further material to support other classroom activities (including a re-enactment of the life-style of a contemporary family and a 'News at Ten' war-time news bulletin). As such, the processes embodied in using the computer and in the other activities were complementary.

As an information handling tool, the specific contribution made by the computer in this respect (i.e. allowing the questioning, display and general manipulation of information) is perhaps less important than the role the machine played as a catalyst for a whole series of powerful experiences with the children very much in control of their own learning. A number of the recorded dialogues between the children serve to highlight this:

When the questions were being chosen:

'We should include something about their eating habits'.

'Why?'

'Well, we might find that some people didn't just have rations to live on. My Grandad said that the people in the countryside had all sorts of food to eat'.

On putting the information into the computer:

'It seems that most people we interviewed had a job doing something for the war effort'.

'But what sort of jobs did they do — one woman filed nails for mules' shoes? How important was that?'

'But the people felt they were working for a cause — everything was important. People said that there was a feeling of togetherness — that's more important, isn't it?'

On interrogating the information via the computer:

'We thought that a lot of people would have had their houses totally destroyed. But most people escaped the bombing raids'.

'We expected to find that most men would have been in the armed services because of National Service. Lots of women seemed to have joined the WRAF or something but some men weren't in the services — those who delivered food or were too old. But everybody seemed to do something in the war effort'.

'And *everybody* had jobs — no-one was unemployed. People must have had money to buy food when they could'.

'Most people missed not having fruit or chocolate, especially bananas. Not many said they missed meat. Perhaps people found it easier to get meat if they lived in the country. The people we interviewed in our group mainly came from country areas'.

'The memories people had were mainly good. It was as if everybody joined together to get through. No-one talks about death in their memories only danger and how exciting it was . . . even though the evidence suggests just about everyone had friends and family dying in the war. Perhaps it's like one person said, "time heals bad memories"'.

The whole project saw children encountering fundamental historical concepts such as change and causation and using a series of skills, including: inferencing; hypothesising; synthetising; extrapolating; communicating.

Generally the role of the computer served to: focus the children's activities, providing a framework for investigative study; foster co-operation and communication between pupils; enable the children to think in a structured and possibly historical way; allow the children to think at appropriate conceptual levels and to advance their understanding of the nature of historical study.

No doubt this project or something like it, could have occurred without the use of the computer but how effective would it have been? Importantly, in this context, the computer provided for positive changes, not only in the way in which children managed their learning but also since the teacher was able to encounter and experiment with a different pedagogical approach.

With developments in technology, such as the Interactive Video Disc and Compact Disc Interactive (manipulating both analogue and digital data) and more powerful computers (witness the present adoption by schools of 32-bit micros, such as the Research Machines VX and Acorn Archimedes 410) the possibilities for the use of information handling software in history education can only expand.

Viewdata

With viewdata systems the educational possibilities are also interesting but less apparent than those described above.[14] Viewdata is a generic term used to describe different information systems all of which provide pages of text and graphics through the telephone system. Information is divided into screensful (or pages) and each page is linked to a number of others. This linking structure allows an 'information tree' to be searched hierarchically (although individual pages may also be accessed via a unique page number).

Using software to simulate the operation of an extensive viewdata system such as Prestel, it is possible both to construct and save information (as a viewdatabase) and search it without having to incur telephone charges. When used in this mode a viewdata program is open-ended — that is, it provides a structure within which the user is able to represent information and ideas of his/her own choice. It may be that the users are children 'doing' some history and it might follow that the viewdata software is used to create a historical adventure or to simulate a past event, such as the Norman Conquest. The multiple routeing structure of viewdata is particularly useful for representing and developing understanding of historical causation.

And of course, with most viewdata software it is possible to tap into mainframe-managed viewdata banks such as those offered through Prestel, The Times Network for Schools (TTNS) and the educationally exclusive National Educational Resource Information Service (NERIS). Currently material on these large viewdatabases that might appeal to history teachers/students is very limited. However, the HA, ever optimistic, is presently compiling a list of relevant pages available on Prestel and TTNS.

Computer Aided Learning (CAL)
CAL is very often equated with the use of the computer simulation. Certainly simulation and modelling programs, often described as 'games', are the most well-known software amongst history teachers.[15] Such software usually offers ready-made solutions to the teaching of specific topics such as the outbreak of the First World War or the events surrounding the Elizabethan Court patronage system of the 16th century. Whilst lists of such simulation software are long,[16] their contents are often of a dubious educational value. However, occasionally, some such software is supported by considered history education theory.

In this light we might consider the efforts of a long-standing and well-publicised software production venture. A number of simulations for use in history education have been developed by the Computers in the Curriculum Project (CIC); these are each marked with the stamp of the Schools History Project (a team involved with the design and production of the software) and, by association, the current history teaching orthodoxy.[17] This orthodoxy is not under consideration here, although it has been criticised elsewhere,[18] suffice to say that it represents the most successful curriculum development movement in history education to date. It is characterised by various features but is essentially based on the notion that history should be relevant to all children and that the study of history should reflect something of the subject's perspectives, logic and methodology.[19]

Consider an example CIC simulation package. Palestine 1947 is described as a 'counterfactual game'; it is based on a software approach that allows children to explore the effects of a range of policies that were available (in theory and practice) to the major political powers involved in this conflict. Thus, it principally aims to (i) extend students's understanding of the Arab-Israeli Conflict; (ii) to enable students to learn about the complexity of cause and effect.[20]

Despite impressive aims perhaps the most notable feature of the simulation in practice is its 'closed nature' (that is, it is limited to one historical situation and to a pre-determined number of outcomes). But perhaps this feature is its strength: the simulation seeks to meet clear objectives by limiting the amount and nature of interaction available to students.

Undoubtedly, this type of simulation owes as much to the gaming and simulation movement of the 1960s/1970s[21] as it does to the earlier days of CAL/CAI development. Its significance to the future development of history software lies less in its classroom aims, aspirations and the potential success it has in achieving these things than in the lessons that can be learnt from its closed design and thereby the limitations it places upon the user. The user should be able to interact with the simulation at every level and not be limited to making only first level decisions; the user should be able to add to the choices from which decisions are made; the user must be able to expose and influence the computer's reasoning at any point; the consequences of computer-generated decisions must appear real and not perpetually limited by the author's/designer's knowledge (which, in this type of software, is fixed and therefore always flawed). Why limit and entrust a student's learning to a single interpretation of events or possibilities encapsulated in the computer by the program's author? Indeed, why not allow the student to become the author?

Whilst it is arguable that there is a role for this type of software in the classroom it should be of some concern that the design of such programs is intended to restrict inter-activity between children and the computer and that such programs also serve to promote, in practice, a rigid model of learning. We need to exploit the power of this and the next generation of micros to build more flexible software items that are not limited either by the technology or, more fundamentally, by a narrow model of childrens' learning. At the very least we need software that puts teachers in charge of curriculum development and allows children responsibility for their own learning.

Knowledge Based Systems
Knowledge Based Systems (KBS) offer perhaps the most promising prospect for bridging what is happening now (in terms of pre-programmed software) and what will be possible in the near future in both history and other classrooms.

KBS can take various forms; the essential characteristics of those being considered here include the provision of a software 'shell' in which both children and teachers can represent knowledge in the form of text and conditional rules.[22] The use of rules determines the relationship between knowledge items. All knowledge is determined by the user, the knowledge-base being freely extensible. Importantly, all user-input is in the form of natural language.

In terms of their educational potential, KBS do offer new possibilities: (i) teachers with a tool to generate 'customised CAL' programs, typical of the 'closed' software commercially available; (ii) children with more control over the micro and greater levels of student-student-computer inter-activity. It is a measure of the educational significance of KBS that they can encourage teachers to use the software to meet their own and their childrens' needs, to regard the computer as entirely organic to classroom practice and to develop that practice in ways which enrich the childrens' learning experiences. A case study of the application of two KBS (i.e. (i) Linx; (ii) Adex Advisor) in the history classroom will illustrate this.[23]

Linx is a KBS shell which allows the creation of a model or simulation of a branching type, plotting nodes in a branching structure where each node might, for example, represent an historical event. At each or selected events choices can be presented; each choice having single or multiple consequences within the framework of the model or simulation. Other facilities offered by the system include the ability of the software to trace and reveal the progress of the user in the simulation at any point and to 'carry forward' the consequences of earlier decisions made by a user to effect the subsequent progress of the simulation or model. Moreover, information may be embedded within the simulation or model and recalled by a key-words search by a user (perhaps, for example, to provide more information to make a particular decision).

Adex Advisor is an expert system shell and allows a user to represent knowledge in the form of conditional rules and advice. The system seeks to provide advice to a user on the basis of a user-system dialogue of questions and answers. The on-board inference engine handles the knowledge (i.e. the rules); the inferencing made by the system in the provision of advice can be made explicit to the user by the use of an explanation facility.

The use of Linx and Adex Advisor can be complimentary. A history teacher recently made use of Linx to (i) produce a simulation based upon the Norman Invasion; and Adex Advisor to (ii) construct an advisory system for the choosing of an appropriate site for building a castle. When children came to the appropriate point in the simulation they were able to turn to the advisory system to explore the reasons for building the castle site(s) most suited to their needs. Indeed, at this first level of classroom interaction the students were simply engaged in following 'closed' exercises not very different to the type outlined elsewhere in this paper — other than that the teacher had engineered the software, so that the use of the computer was a wholly natural extension of other classroom work. The teacher intended that the children should use the software to encounter certain historical concepts and experiences; these related to exploring causation and to what Peel calls 'possibility involving' thinking.[24]

From being involved with a 'closed' situation the children were then exposed to the reasoning implicit in the teacher's construction of each of the knowledge bases. As such, children were put in a position to question and influence: (i) the fundamental premises on which the original simulation had rested; and (ii) the rules which underlay the advisory expert system on choosing Norman castle sites. In essence, the children were able to represent their own understanding of the events of the Norman Invasion as well as their understanding of what is a 'good site' for building a Norman castle. There is some evidence to suggest that the processes described here, (i.e. children exploring 'teacher-centred' knowledge and then representing and developing their own understanding), are progressive and a function of the software used. There is also a suggestion that this software encourages teachers to explore different models of pedagogic practice.[25]

3. The Real World

Part II has sought to introduce some of what is possible in history classrooms; it does not, however, consider how widespread effective use of the micro is in history education. For this we might turn to a series of surveys.

The BBC survey conducted in 1984 revealed that a mere 8 per cent of school history departments were making use of the micro.[26] The Womack survey in 1985 suggested that non-users had fallen to 47 per cent.[27] Again in 1985, a DES survey pointed out that only 23 per cent of history depts were using the micro.[28] The results of recent moves by the MESU to research and encapsulate good practice in the use of micros in history are equally not optimistic. But it is perhaps not too surprising to find that 'good practice' seems even more elusive than practice *per se*. Jackson came to similar conclusions after her survey of computing practice in Hertfordshire schools.[29] She revealed that when any form of practice could be identified it was, in a large number of cases, practice that reinforced limited learning experiences.

Kenneth Baker's opening address to the 1987 High Technology in Education Exhibition revealed a similar story. He announced that a DES survey had shown that in November 1985 there was an average of one micro to every 60 children in secondary schools. primary schools had an average of one micro to every 107 children. It is not surprising that only 20 per cent of secondary head teachers said that micros had made a significant contribution to teaching in their schools.[30] What is surprising is that Kenneth Baker announced these figures with pride and self-congratulation.

Despite the efforts of the Micro Electronics Program between 1979–86, despite DES and DTI moves on various occasions to provide the technology required, despite MSC funding of vast TVEI initiatives in almost all LEA's, we are still faced with a disappointing picture. A MESU priority is the establishment of a 'consolidation programme' — consolidating what good computer related practice exists in schools.[31] Perhaps we can talk of consolidating the use of computers but can we legitimately talk about the consolidation of good classroom practice when that practice is seemingly almost non-existent outside a number of 'demonstrator-projects'?

The obvious question remains: why is good practice in the use of micros difficult to identify in history education in our schools? To furnish an answer we might legitimately echo the concerns constantly expressed by other educationalists — about the need for good and powerful software; about the need for appropriate resourcing; about the need for extensive teacher INSET programmes. But the problem is rooted more deeply than this. The answer is to do with fundamental barriers to educational innovation and change — barriers that are political, educational and institutional.

Barriers to Educational Change
The barriers inhibiting increased use of the micro in schools and in school history teaching in particular, are manifold. They begin with the student, traditionally at the receiving end of education and a notoriously conservative force in the teaching-learning process. They include the teacher, who is inclined to take refuge in a particular subject area and protect his/her

specialist knowledge jealously. How many times have we come across a school Information Technology (IT) Co-ordinator (who used to be called the Computer Studies teacher) with a request to use the computer in a history lesson only to be told:

Yes, by all means use the computer room to look at the First World War. By the way, I picked up a marvellous programme listing from BeeBug magazine which lets you put your own questions on the computer — you must use it. Oh, you don't know how to operate the network; well, I've got this system, easy really, which lets you use level I software on the Econet level II; but then this printer I've configured for my own use — its not that easy to reset. And of course, you can't use the Master machines without loading sideways ROM images. Do you know how to do all that?

There is safety in knowledge and there is safety in making sure that no one else shares in that knowledge. And this is as true for the history teacher as it is for the IT Co-ordinator. Teaching staff continually reinforce artificial subject boundaries only to the detriment of the learner. Also, we must acknowledge that the history teacher may well have contracted 'technophobia' or 'novophobia' — the real fear that here is something new which is not within their expert knowledge.

From here we can look for barriers in the school as an institution where the timetable and the 35 minute lesson is the focus for all activity; where examinations are short and long term objectives; where the influence and power of the head teachers alone direct school policy and attitudes to change. We could go on to identify barriers in parents and their conservative aspirations for their off-spring; in the often negative resourcing policy of the LEA; in central government policy (for example, consider the potential conservative and narrowing effects of establishing a national curriculum), often caught between political expediency and educational awareness. And we might consider the inhibiting nature of social and economic influences upon education and in particular, the general tendency towards 'training' rather than education.

But these barriers and any strategies to overcome them must be the subject of another paper. It must suffice to suggest that there are successful models for moving forward, for effecting change and innovation, for establishing effective and long-term use of new technology in history education.

Conclusion

This paper has sought to explore some of the possibilities and problems that new technology represents in history education for both teachers and children. It has also made some tacit suggestions as to what the future may hold and how we might now move forward to make the best possible use of micros to develop and extend both teaching and learning experiences.

I should conclude with an up-date on the career of Miss Page, the primary school teacher responsible for my early education. Miss Page eventually came out of teaching and only then took to the use of the computer. She is in fact now working for a publisher, producing educational (including history) software thick and fast; software that generates short questions and answers and puts the child under competitive pressure to answer 'correctly' — indeed, not unlike the 'flashcards' she originally employed to teach history when I was in her charge. With an occasional burst of graphics and shrill noises to indicate either success or failure, Miss Page is designing software Bernard Barker has typified as the 'Dr Who approach to History'.[32] But perhaps the most disturbing factor is that her software sells like hot cakes!

Notes

1. B. F. Skinner, *The Technology of Teaching*, Appleton-Century-Crofts, 1968.

2. J. Maddison, *Education in the Microelectronics Era*, Open University Press, 1983, pp. 34–41.

3. N. Chomsky, 'A Review of B. F. Skinner's Verbal Behaviour', *Language*, 35,1, 1959, pp. 26–58.

4. R. Hooper, *National Development Programme in Computer Assisted Learning — Final Report*, Council for Educational Technology, 1977, 10 pp.

5. M. A. Bodin, *Piaget*, Fontana, 1979, which provides a readable account of Piaget's work from 1915 to 1978; M. Donaldson, *Children's Minds*, Fontana/Collins, 1978.

6. S. Papert, *Mindstorms: Children, Computers and Powerful Ideas*, Harvester, 1980.

7. D. Birt, and J. Nichol, *Games and Simulations in History*, Longman, 1975); M. Ballard, ed., *New Movements in the Study and Teaching of History*, Temple Smith, 1972.

8. Schools Council, *A New Look at History*, Holmes McDougall, 1976.

9. D. Read, 'History: Core Subject Within A Core Curriculum', *Teaching History*, 9, Autumn 1985.

10. D. Read and M. Roberts, 'Six of the Best — The National Curriculum', *The Times Educational Supplement*, 11/12/87. This article provides an introduction to the debate and the stance taken by the Historical Association, self-appointed saviour of history teaching in schools. It also mentions a number of other documents that are indicative of the same defensive mentality.

11. P. Beck, 'Going Up in History', *The Times Educational Supplement*, 21/2/86.

12. F. Blow and A. Dickinson, eds., *New History and New Technology*, Council for Educational Technology, 1986. This book is one of a number produced by different subject associations with the support of funds from the Micro Electronics Programme (MEP). The theme running through each of them is conspicuous, viz. 'IT is *especially* relevant to History/Geography/Home Economics/etc.'.

13. M. Wild, 'What's this got to do with History, Sir?', in *The Times Educational Supplement*, 13/6/86; idem, *Quest in History*, The Advisory Unit, 1986; idem, 'Information Handling, History and Learning. The Role of the Computer in the Historical Process', P. Denley and D. Hopkin, eds., *History and Computing*, Manchester University Press, 1987.

14. M. Wild, *Viewdata in History*, The Advisory Unit, 1986. This describes in detail the possibilities for the creative use of viewdata software in History.

15. A. Martin, 'Computers and Simulation in the Humanities: Modes of Description, *Computer Assisted Learning in Social Sciences and Humanities*, Conference Edition, ESRC, 1986, pp. 75 ff.

16. S. Bennett, ed., *Update of Computer Software for History*, MESU, 1988 (a list which does not attempt to distinguish between good and poor software); F. Blow, A. Dickinson and M. Wild, *New History and New Technology: Suggestions and Considerations*, Council for Educational Technology, 1986.

17.   e.g. F. Blow, ed., *Palestine 1947*, Longman, 1986; D. Watson, *Developing CAL: Computers in the Curriculum*, Harper and Row, 1987. This describes the CIC Project in detail; it also outlines the history software produced by the Project to date.

18.   S. Lang, 'The Sacred Cow History Project', *The Times Educational Supplement*, 4/4/1986.

19.   D. Schemilt, *Evaluation Study: Schools Council History 13–16 Project*, Holmes McDougall, 1980.

20.   Blow, *Palestine 1947*, cit., p. 7.

21.   J. Chorley and P. Haggart, *Models in Geography*, Methuen, 1967; R. Walford, *Games in Geography*, Longman, 1969; J. Nichol, *Simulation in History Teaching*, Historical Association, 1980; J. Nichol, 'Models, Microworlds and Minds', J. Nichol, J. Briggs and J. Dean, eds., *Prolog, Children and Students*, Kogan Page, 1988.

22.   J. Briggs, 'Why Teach Prolog? The Uses of Prolog in Education', Nichol et al., eds, *Prolog, Children and Students*, cit.; idem, *Education: A Starter Pack*, The Advisory Unit, 1988; J. Nichol, J. Briggs and J. Dean, *Authoring Programs and Toolkits, Logic Programming and Curriculum J. Development* (unpublished); J. Nichol, J. Briggs and J. Dean, *Linx*, PEG, Exeter, 1988.

23.   M. Wild, 'A Catalyst for Change : the Computer and the Use of Prolog in Teacher Education', PEG 1987 Conference Proceedings, 1988 (in print); idem, 'Teaching Perspectives', R. Lewis, ed., *Learning Through MicroWorlds*, ESRC, 1988.

24.   E. Peel, 'Some Problems in the Psychology of History Teaching', W. H. Burston and D. Thompson, eds., *Studies in the Nature and Teaching of History*, Routledge, 1967.

25.   Wild, 'A Catalyst . . . ', cit., and 'Teaching Perspectives', cit.

26.   *Microcomputers in Secondary Schools: a Survey of England, Wales and Northern Ireland Secondary Schools*, BBC, 1984.

27.   S. J. Womack, 'An Investigation of the Role of Computer Assisted Learning in the Teaching of History', M.Phil. thesis, University of Sheffield, 1985 (unpublished).

28.   *Results of the Survey of Microcomputers in Schools — Autumn 1985*, DES, 1986.

29.   A. Jackson, B. Fletcher and D. Messer, 'A Survey of Microcomputer Use and Provision in Primary Schools, *Journal of Computer Assisted Learning*, 2,1, pp. 45–55.

30.   DES survey (see note 28 above).

31.   *MicroElectronics Support Unit*, MESU, 1987; J. Foster, 'The Well-Kept Secret', *The Times Educational Supplement*, 16/10/87.

32.   B. Barker, 'Computer Update', *Teaching History*, 47, 1987, pp. 30–31. Figure 1.   *Learning About Computers* — a period when computers were first introduced into schools and when computer studies and computer science were both exclusive terms and exclusive subjects. *Learning From Computers* — a period when terms such as CAI and CAL were applied to describe applications of micros to various areas of the curriculum other than computer science. This period saw many schools getting micros for the first time as part of a national government initiative. *Learning Alongside Computers* — a period when generic software, such as word processors, information handling tools and knowledge based systems were seen to offer more powerful learning environments. Computers were re-assigned as a resource for curriculum development and as major teaching and learning tools.

History, Computing and Higher Education[1]

For many years academic enthusiasm for computer-based history teaching lagged behind information technology's rapid emergence as an important tool for historical research.[2] Historians tended to view computer-based teaching as an activity distinct from computerised research and intellectually inferior to it. Basing their assumptions on early generations of CAL in the natural sciences and modern languages, some historians feared that computer-based teaching meant rudimentary learning, administered through a drill-and-practice method. Others suspected that more adventurous use of the computer involved complex software and highly sophisticated 'number crunching'; both seemed remote from the nuances of historical sources and the mainstream of historical discussion. These academic anxieties reinforced worries that history departments could not obtain the equipment, materials and time necessary for such teaching.

Recently, however, academics have begun to realise that computer-based teaching, in history as in other 'arts' subjects, can be closely linked to research and challenging for instructors and students alike. The increasing storage capacity and cheapness of microcomputers, combined with the comparative simplicity of recent software, allow researchers to share their sources and modes of investigation with undergraduates, thereby enriching the curriculum while sharpening the research process. Students as well as academics can now take an active, step-by-step role in manipulating uncoded material rather than rely on complex programs to spew out results following laborious coding and multiple instructions. Thus it is becoming increasingly clear that computer-based teaching can be rigorous and open-ended rather than elementary and tedious.[3]

The educational utility of the computer is at least as great in history as in other subjects in the humanities and social sciences. Because history is a highly word-intensive discipline, its students and teachers can profit greatly from the computer's facilities for word processing, note-taking and bibliography. More central to the learning process is the computer's ability to unlock the frequently bulky and complex sources of history for students whose previous access came only through lecture summaries and photocopied examples. Sources as diverse in time, period and type as medieval monastic surveys, early modern pollbooks, nineteenth-century census schedules, business records and lists of twentieth-century political leaders are appropriate for student exploration through tailored teaching datasets constructed from larger research databases. Likewise, the increasing availability of simple but powerful textual software allows systematic searching of large historical documents for usage, style and context. Thus historians can use the computer in their teaching in a fashion complementary to their long-standing classroom use of printed primary sources. Similarly, student use of the computer is well suited to undergraduate dissertations and postgraduate theses which are both adventurous and thorough.[4]

In all these contexts, students can use the computer as a tool to enhance key traditional historical skills such as the critical assessment and the systematic handling of evidence. Thus information technology, when appropriate to the subject matter and sources, can be incorporated into traditional teaching formats, notably the small class or collective tutorial. Even in lectures the computer can provide vivid examples and illustrations of general points. Moreover, the increasing number of historians who use the computer in research can find in computer-based teaching an outlet for their expertise, which in turn will be enhanced as it is adapted to the testing demands of the classroom. Thus history is well placed to yield three key benefits of computer-based higher education: a deepened knowledge of subject matter, an enhancement of general skills of analysis and expression, and familiarity with information technology.

Especially in the United Kingdom and the United States but increasingly in Continental Europe as well,[5] significant numbers of historians are beginning to acknowledge the educational utility of the computer. In Britain the Government-funded Computers in Teaching Initiative (CTI)[6] established in 1984 has boosted an interest hitherto largely confined to courses dealing with quantitative methods in economic and social history.[7] Likewise, the Association for History and Computing (AHC) gave higher education a prominent role at its first conference in 1986. The programme featured two CTI Projects (Glasgow University's DISH — Design and Implementation of Software in History — Project and Edinburgh University's Computers in Education Project) and cognate developments at Teesside Polytechnic and at Durham and York Universities.[8] Further recognition of the growing importance of computer teaching in higher education came a year later when the Association's United Kingdom Branch coupled higher education with schools, where computer teaching was more deeply rooted,[9] in one of its major subgroups, Education.

Increasing enthusiasm for computer-based higher education heightens rather than diminishes the need for relevant discussion by historians. In addition to specifying their objectives, practitioners must begin to devise criteria for appropriate software, data, course materials and pedagogical methods. The relationship of such teaching both to traditional instruction and to research also demands attention. For example, how can computer-based teaching best be integrated into the curriculum? How much computer-based teaching should be offered, and how should it be assessed? Moreover, it is important that those active in the field share experiences concerning the hardware, financial, managerial and career implications of such teaching.

It was highly appropriate, therefore, that the AHC gave a 'Higher Education Seminar' a substantial place on the programme of its 1987 conference. The increasing interest in computer-based teaching resulted in a large attendance despite strong rival attractions. The seminar included papers from participants in four of the more prominent computer teaching projects in British higher education. Two presentations dealt with projects seeking to apply existing software to history courses. Dr Donald Spaeth of the University of Exeter gave a paper on 'First Steps in Computing for Arts Students: Project Pallas', a CTI enterprise based in an entire Arts Faculty but affording history a prominent role. Dr Virginia Davis of the University of Hull, one of the pioneering institutions in computer-based history teaching, outlined the aims and plans of a newly launched CTI Project in her paper, 'Historical Databases and Coursework'. The other two speakers' projects involved extensive software development as well as coursework applications. Dr Steve Jefferys of Manchester Polytechnic described his Viewbook program in 'Users and Winners: The problems and potential for historians of information retrieval'. Finally, Dr Frank Colson spoke from the perspective of an IBM-financed initiative in his paper, 'How not to Reinvent the Wheel: Early days on the HIDES Project'. Thus the speakers encompassed comparatively old and new initiatives and private as well as public funding in addition to contrasting approaches to software.

When Project Pallas began in 1984, Exeter's Arts Faculty had few computer users and no hardware devoted to them. Pallas constructed a facility with 27 BBC micros linked to a mainframe; open around the clock, it is staffed by two full-time teachers who also provide an advisory service to the Faculty's academics for research as well as teaching. According to Dr Spaeth, Pallas has three aims: to increase student awareness of computers in general and of their potential in arts subjects in particular; to encourage students to use the computer voluntarily for word processing and information retrieval; and to enable staff to introduce information processing into their courses.

To these ends, the Pallas team provides a general introductory course on information technology and supports computer-based modules in courses in particular departments. It was decided to keep the approach simple in order to combat fear among a student population largely unused to computers. During its first two years the project reached 1300 students. The impact on this group was greatest in terms of word processing, usually including composition on the screen; this activity defused anxiety and enhanced information processing skills. History and Archeology have been the two greatest users of the project; they soon required their students to produce word-processed essays. In addition, Archeology staged a special computer-based course on principles and methods. Yet, in general, subject-specific courses have been less successful than word processing. According to Spaeth, this contrast results from the greater complexity of the software needed for disciplinary applications, the undergraduates' ability to understand their subjects without databases, and the time required for individual instructors to devise computerised modules. Nevertheless, Pallas plans to launch a new course on arts computing methods that will provide two or three streams — on, say, databases, textual analysis and statistics — culminating in subject-based projects.[10]

At Hull computers have for some years played a part in history teaching at both the undergraduate and postgraduate levels, including work both on Domesday Book and on eighteenth-century elections.[11] As Dr Davis pointed out, the CTI grant has allowed the History Computing Unit to plan a significant expansion of teaching, which will now occur in a laboratory equipped with a network of 16 IBM-clones with colour monitors adapted to map displays. From 1987 all first-year history students at Hull will have to enroll in a historical computing course, including training in word processing, information retrieval and communications but emphasising exploration of a wide variety of historical databases. For example, students probing a dataset on medieval religious houses can discover the clustering of particular orders in specific areas. In addition to this foundation course, from the outset other first-year courses will make a modest use of databases, and in due course databases will find their way into second and third year courses as well.

Although the Hull project eschews further significant software development, opting instead to use a few existing packages, it has ambitious plans for developing databases ranging from English placenames to pollbooks. Some will be small-scale, suitable for use in a single essay or seminar; these datasets will promote experimentation by academics and students alike. Others, though surprisingly quickly typed into the computer, will be more permanent and larger in scale: some of these databases will be based on staff research and applicable to several courses. Colleagues will be encouraged to participate in database construction; otherwise they might resist computer-based teaching as an alien intrusion. Properly approached, they will sympathise, Davis implied, with the fundamental aims of the project: to encourage students to explore data more systematically and, by removing tedium, to encourage active historical curiosity.

These aims were echoed by Dr Colson, whose Historical Document Expert System (HIDES) project concentrates on enhancing student analysis of the documents used in final-year special subjects. The format of these courses had come under pressure from rationalisation, yet department members still hoped to realise a long-held goal of persuading students to read primary documents more carefully. The computer, by providing the means for undergraduates to test their understanding of the evidence, provided a way out of this dilemma. As at Hull and (to a lesser extent) at Exeter, the computer-based material will be integrated into existing courses, which have been suspended in the interim to give instructors time to adapt materials. Indeed the computer exercises were preparations for the usual special subject classes.

Yet, in contrast to those other two projects, HIDES intends to develop and adapt software rather than to use what is already available. Phase one of HIDES is adapting an existing concordance package to allow students to test the use of evidence in documents; phase two, using expert systems, will allow them to test inferences as well. Also, whereas Exeter and Hull emphasise databases, the focus of the HIDES project is textual analysis. Colson illustrated the technique by demonstrating how computer-assisted analysis of the words 'slavery' and 'labour' in a nineteenth-century travelogue can undermine the credibility of a source much used by historians of Brazil. These document-specific 'shells' will be research-led, as will the database work which is associated with the project.[12] In addition, HIDES is collaborating with a CTI project, based in Southampton's History and Education Departments, which is working on 'history information trees' for first-year students.

Manchester Polytechnic's Dr Jefferys decided to develop software because of extreme pressure on library resources. Lecturers were expected to transfer information to students more intensively, an unrealistic and inefficient strategy. Could innovative software provide a solution? If so, it must cope with limited computing resources, students suspicious both of information technology and of statistics, and staff lacking the time and inclination to revolutionise teaching methods.

Jefferys' solution, Viewbooks,[13] are disk-based books. They allow highly flexible retrieval of textual databases with minimum loss of storage space and interactive facilities. The books consist either of historical documents (with introductions and conclusions by historians) or of texts and tables. Designed in a dialogue with a 'friendly programmer',[14] Viewbooks provide a common 'front end' to fit the many types of machine in use. Input and output occur through word processing files, allowing students to concentrate on manipulating material rather than on copying it out into essays. Viewbooks allow a student dealing with a topic such as the New Poor Law to move very fast within a text. Now that approximately twenty-five such books have appeared or are about to do so, attention is turning to plans for a Viewbook author, a shell program into which teachers could insert texts. It is also hoped to produce packages which mix texts and graphics. Moreover, Jefferys would like to supply packages that will automatically generate indexing and cross referencing as text is inputted through a word processing file. Future advances in storage capacity and intelligent interfaces may enable users to move easily among many such texts.

The speakers in the higher education seminar differed to some extent on software strategy, extent of subject specialisation,[15] preferred teaching level, degree of student compulsion and commitment to databases. Nevertheless, the panelists implicitly agreed that computer-based instruction was worthwhile and practical. The utility of pursuing advances through projects within individual institutions also drew tacit support.

In contrast, the subsequent discussion reasserted some of the fundamental problems that historians engaged in computer-based higher education must resolve. One worry concerned whether such teaching made students better historians. Sometimes marks for computer-based projects were used as part of continuous assessment. Such testing and the results of conventional examinations produced fragments of positive evidence, but the need for systematic educational evaluation was evident.[16] Related to the question of educational results was an anxiety about educational motivation. How far did computer-based teaching represent an unholy alliance with the utilitarian, even philistine, environment in which higher education was operating? In this respect the panel had firm answers, insisting that the computer helped historians to improve their students' basic historical skills such as the ability to evaluate evidence, whatever information technology might do for graduate employment prospects and history departments' budgets.

The mention of cash inspired another member of the audience to question the cost-effectiveness of such projects at a time when history departments found it difficult even to afford traditional resources such as books. Panelists answered by emphasising the relatively low cost of generating software and datasets, which were resources of enduring value. The case for the defense drew reinforcement from Nigel Gardner, Head of the Computers in Teaching

Initiative Support Service, who argued that programmes like the CTI brought money to subjects such as history which otherwise would have gone elsewhere. Nevertheless, he cautioned, historians will bankrupt their departments and alienate funding bodies if they pretend that all aspects of history could profitably be computer-taught. Gardner's view that priorities must be established deepened earlier anxieties that 'evangelists' might alienate those historians not yet using the machine.

On the whole, however, the audience was more concerned to discover the means by which worthwhile work such as the featured projects could be spread throughout higher education. A key concern — methods of sharing software and datasets — elicited the news that a national coordinating organisation, NISS (National Information for Software and Services) was being launched, primarily for universities.[17] There was a consensus at the seminar that the AHC should commit itself to NISS and, more generally, to the sharing of resources. In terms of methods, a closing comment suggested that higher education could learn much from schools, whose pupils soon would be so computer literate that universities, polytechnics and colleges would have to implement computers in teaching effectively, or face the consequences!

Where does the 1987 higher education seminar leave the field? In addition to the questions on which the panelists differed and the problems raised by the audience, practitioners must confront issues such as the extent to which historians should teach their students about quantitative methods and the technical aspects of computing. The differing strategies which may be appropriate to advanced and introductory courses should also be explored. In addition, further consideration should be given to the heavy time commitments that computer-based history teaching demands of participating instructors. Moreover, there are significant problems of management, in particular the need to encourage effective cooperation both within and between departments.[18] Furthermore, those active in computer-based history teaching in the United Kingdom, who have little to fear from international comparisons, nonetheless could enhance their performance by much closer links with those involved in the field elsewhere.

Yet it would be perverse to conclude on a negative note. Many of the pedagogical and organisational difficulties discussed in the seminar are no more serious than those found throughout higher education. Also, the differences of view which emerged in the session emphasise the many legitimate ways in which the computer is being applied to history teaching. Overall, much has been achieved in a very few years. In addition to the work of the projects featured in the seminar, there have been further developments by the teaching initiatives represented at the 1986 conference.[19] Moreover, there is activity at a range of other institutions, notably Bristol Polytechnic, the College of St Paul and St Mary Cheltenham, Lancashire Polytechnic, the Polytechnic of North London, Royal Holloway and Bedford New College, the University College of Wales Aberystwyth, Westfield College and the Universities of Leeds, Leicester, Manchester, Newcastle, Oxford, St Andrews and York. Aside from the potentially crippling problem of finance, the major challenges that the field faces are growing pains rather than terminal illnesses: to involve many more institutions, to deepen the teaching programmes in currently active locations, to continue to insist on the quality as well as the quantity of computer-based teaching, and to ensure that the computer remains a historical tool rather than a marketing gimmick.

Notes

1. The chapter uses the term 'higher education' to refer to polytechnics and colleges as well as universities.

2. On the latter see, for example, B. Collins, 'The Computer as a Research Tool', *Journal of the Society of Archivists*, 7, 1982, and numerous illustrations in P. Denley and D. Hopkin, eds., *History and Computing* (hereafter referred to as *History and Computing*), Manchester, 1987, Parts I and II. For evidence of reluctance to use the computer in history teaching in American higher education, see R. C. Rohrs, 'Sources and Strategies for Computer-Aided Instruction', *Historical Methods*, 20, 1987.

3. For the general argument, see R. H. Trainor, 'The Role of the Computer in University Teaching: Potential and Problems', in S. Rahtz, ed., *Information Technology in the Humanities: Tools, techniques and applications*, Chichester, 1987.

4. Simulations and programmed learning are also available, but although these methods have used frequently in higher education in the United States (see: C. Lougee, 'The Would-Be Gentleman: A Historical Simulation of the France of Louis XIV', *Outlook*, 19, 1986; J. E. Sargent & S. P. Hueston, 'Simulating History: Programming the American Revolution', *History Microcomputer Review*, 3, 1987), in Britain they have been largely confined to the school sector.

5. For recent American developments see for example: M. P. Gutmann & K. H. Fliess, 'Reconstructing a Historical Community', *Proceedings of the 1986 Academic Information Systems University AEP Conference*, IBM Academic Information Systems, 1986; V. Burton et al., 'Historical Research Techniques: Teaching with Database Exercises on the Microcomputer', *Social Science History*, 11, 1987. On Continental Europe see: J. Ehmer, 'The Teaching of Computing for Historians in Austria', in *History and Computing*, and Trainor, 'The Promise and Pitfalls of International Historical Computing', *History and Computing Today*, 3, 1988.

6. See N. Gardner, 'Integrating Computers into the University Curriculum: The experience of the U. K. Computers in Teaching Initiative', *Computers and Education*, 12, 1988.

7. Leading practitioners in the field's pre-CTI phase, with enduring influence, included Professors Michael Anderson (Edinburgh University), Michael Drake (Open University) and Roderick Floud (Birkbeck College).

8. See the articles in *History and Computing* by: D. Mealand, N. J. Morgan, R. J. Morris & C. Anderson, D. Taylor, R. H. Trainor, P. Wardley, and R. B. Weir.

9. See: J. Nichol and J. Dean, 'Computers and children's historical thinking and understanding' in R. Ennals et al., eds., *Information Technology and Education: The changing school*, Chichester, 1986; articles in *History and Computing* by F. Blow and M. Wild; and the works cited in Trainor, 'An Experiment in Computer-based Teaching and Research', ibid., p. 301 n. 2; articles by B. Labbett, A. Martin, Blow, and Nichol et al. in W. A. Kent & R. Lewis, eds., *Computer Assisted Learning in the Humanities and Social Sciences*, Oxford, 1987.

10. For more extended discussions of Project Pallas see: J. Buckett, 'Project Pallas. . . ', *University Computing*, 7, 1985; M. Waddicor, 'Progress Report from Project Pallas', *CTISS File*, 1, 1986.

11. The latter was the work of Professor W. A. Speck (before his appointment in 1985 to the Chair of History at the University of Leeds) and Mr P. Adman (see Adman, 'Computers and history', in Rahtz, *Information Technology*, and idem, 'Micro-MIST',

in *History and Computing*). On the Domesday Project see J. J. N. Palmer, 'Domesday Book and the Computer', in P. Sawyer, ed., *Domesday Book: A Reassessment*, London, 1985; A. Ayton & V. Davis, 'The Hull Domesday Project', in *History and Computing*. Both these streams of work included software design as well as database development.

12.   See A. Kitts et al., 'Using the Database Management System SIR to Link Political Data from Viana de Castelo, Minho, Portugal, 1827–95', in *History and Computing*.

13.   Available from Information Education Ltd, Unit 33, Enterprise Centre, Bedford St., Stoke-on-Trent, ST1 4PZ.

14.   For a parallel method, see F. Candlin, 'Software to make the most of your Dataset', in J. M. McArthur, ed., *Databases in History Teaching*, Glasgow, 1986.

15.   For a discussion of general 'computing in the humanities' courses, see the special issue (No. 4) of *Computing in the Humanities*, 21, 1987.

16.   Gardner, 'Editorial: Less Rhetoric: More Evaluation', *CTISS File*, 3, 1987; K. Day, 'Comments. . . ', ibid., 4, 1987.

17.   NISS is paired with CHEST (Combined Higher Education Software Team); both are located at the South West Universities Regional Computer Centre (SWURCC) at the University of Bath.

18.   Trainor, 'Implementing Computer-Based Teaching and Research: the Need for a Collaborative Approach', *Computers and Education*, 12, 1988.

19.   For example, idem, 'History and Computers: The First Two Years of Glasgow's DISH Project', *Humanities Communication Newsletter*, 9, 1987; R. J. & T. Morris, 'Computers in Teaching: Economic and Social History at Edinburgh', *University Computing*, 9, 1987.

III.

Database Systems, Methods and Applications

Information Engineering and Historical Databases

1. Introduction

No subject in historical computing has aroused more interest in recent years than that of databases. Enthusiasm is running high for projects of all descriptions covering all historical periods. At one college of the University of London alone, the current project list includes topics as diverse as crusaders in the Latin east, Italian merchants of the fourteenth century, voting and occupations in eighteenth-century Westminster, London music halls, aspects of British direct investment overseas, newspapers and the musical scene in London, and shop-floor workers in the railway towns of England. The attractions of database-centred research are manifest. Efficient data storage, rapid searching, sorting and information retrieval are standard features of modern database systems, and major savings in time and effort can be made simply by upgrading existing systems based on cards and sets of notes. Database technology, moreover, by its very nature encourages the progressively-minded to think of new and exciting research possibilities. Not only might individual data-sets be computerised, but also associated data-sets might be gathered together for collective interrogation. The historian can thus connect disparate pieces of information to obtain a fuller and more accurate view of the subject under examination. Furthermore, once a substantial historical database has been constructed, it might be viewed as a facility available to a community of users, not just an individual researcher. Data sharing, as it is called, holds out the promise of more incisive research, and, in the longer term, considerable savings in time, effort and cash.

The current enthusiasm for databases is in many ways similar to that shown by data processing professionals in the later 1970s. At that time, senior computer staff were aware of how effectively sophisticated software packages — database management systems — could be used to create, manipulate and maintain databases, and there was already a small army of converts to the general 'philosophy' of database systems. This states that the operational data of large organisations should be held centrally, rather than controlled by individual departments. A database is defined as an integrated collection of files structured in accordance with natural data relationships; it is more than a large collection of data. Corporate databases are viewed as common resources for many departments and applications. This arrangement has a number of important advantages. Data redundancy or duplication is much reduced. Problems of maintaining data consistency and accuracy are minimised, as when data are entered, updated or deleted a single operation or action is automatically 'exploded' across all files. Another advantage is that programs and data are made independent of each other. Programmers are thus freed from the responsibility of determining how data are stored, and can develop applications more rapidly. Additionally, and perhaps most important of all, data can be shared and manipulated to serve fresh purposes: the database becomes a valuable corporate asset.[1]

The theoretical advantages of databases have not always been achieved in practice. Indeed, in the early 1980s complaints abounded that databases were costly to establish and maintain, that key database operations were painfully slow, that databases were inflexible and difficult to restructure, and that information retrieval was far from perfect. There were many reasons for such complaints, including inadequate hardware and software. However, the single most important cause of difficulty was that database designers paid too little attention to the details of the information required by client organisations, whilst failing to develop databases in a manner that would admit restructuring, rapid searching and sorting, and complex querying. All this was symptomatic of a wider problem: that large numbers of organisations lacked the expertise needed to migrate from data processing based on functional areas to modern systems which take a more data centred view of the world.[2]

A great effort has been made in recent years, by large firms, government agencies and consultancies, to come to grips with the common problems of designing advanced information systems. One important result has been the widespread adoption of structured methodologies for systems analysis and design. These methodologies take a data-oriented view of a system through analysis of its data structure (the form of the data), data flows (who uses the data) and processes (what is done with the data). The approach involves the division of projects into stages — for instance, strategy, analysis, design, construction and implementation.[3] At each stage, certain well-defined tasks are undertaken and the foundations laid for further work. The fundamental idea is to move from the general to the specific, progressively decomposing the work to produce a hierarchy of steps consisting of increasing levels of detail. The governing principle is that of divide-and-conquer. A good deal of effort is put into project documentation, management and the monitoring of progress.[4]

Experience has shown that substantial benefits stem from the adoption of structured systems analysis and design methods: better information systems result, with efficiently structured databases at their core. The database approach has returned to fashion, and there is general acceptance that database technology embraces design methods as well as the hardware and software components of a system. There are valuable lessons in this for the historian. One is that handsome dividends should result from a disciplined and systematic approach to database problems. It may not be necessary for lone researchers, handling small, unified data-sets, to trouble too much about the intricacies of database design; common sense and the support of a good database management system will probably suffice to ensure the success of the project. However, this is unlikely to be so if the projected database is large in scale and scope, involving complex data-relationships. If the intention is to develop a major resource, to meet the needs of a mixed community of users, nationally and internationally, then considerable thought must be given to project planning. Another and related point is that historians should not hesitate to make use of selected systems analysis and design techniques. These are sometimes referred to as information engineering tools,[5] and they are used to build data and other types of models, which, amongst other things, form the basis of correctly structured databases.

This chapter reviews some of the information engineering techniques commonly used in database work. No attempt is made to be comprehensive, nor is there any direct reference to particular methodologies. A staged approach is taken, but this is as much for expositional as prescriptive reasons. The data analysis and modelling process is not intended as an intellectual strait-jacket, and more or less effort may be required at each stage. The examples given are highly simplified owing to lack of space. Original material is included which is largely derived from practical experience.

2. Nature and Scope of Project

The logical way to begin a major project is to specify its aims and requirements. The project specification can then be used as a guide for associated staff and as a basis for funding applications. Several aspects of the project require preliminary investigation.

2·1 Community of Users

The nature and scope of a project are largely defined by the size and interests of the user community. There are a number of aspects to this. The first concerns whether the database is intended as a direct or indirect research facility. A direct facility is one which aids scholarship by yielding information of immediate relevance to a research topic; whereas an indirect facility simply guides the researcher toward the information sought. An example of the latter is the database currently under development by the Construction History Society. In this case, the database is seen as a means of helping historians locate documents relating to building firms, important construction projects and major figures in the industry. Data will be gathered on repositories, collections of documents, and records relating to individual firms. The community of users will be all those interested in the history of construction in modern Britain.

Most database projects are not of the archival type. Research databases provide the means, through systematic querying, to discover associations between data items that might otherwise pass unnoticed or be impossible to find, and selected data can be dumped for detailed analysis, statistical or otherwise. One important class of research project is that concerned with extracting data from a discrete collection of documents. Essentially, the aim is to computerise the source — port books, crew lists, business accounts or whatever — and the user community is by definition all those who recognise the potential value of the original material.

Not all research projects are source driven. Some take as their inspiration a topic, concept or theory. A case in point is the work on crusaders currently being undertaken by Prof. J. S. C. Riley-Smith. In attempting to understand the motivations of crusaders, Riley-Smith is examining such things as geographical location, family and feudal relationships, individual and community wealth and relevant prior activities. Data are also gathered on crusading activities and associations between individuals on crusades. The data are drawn from a rich variety of sources, including narrative accounts, hagiographical material, charters, epic poetry and wills. In such cases as this, the database system must be designed to accommodate likely data occurrences; it serves as a tool for guiding and organising the research. The user community consists of all researchers in the field. Prof. Riley-Smith's ultimate ambition is to construct a directory of crusaders, settlers in lands conquered by crusaders and members of military orders from 1095 to 1798.

A further important class of project, and the last to be mentioned here, may be thought of as a hybrid of the direct and indirect types distinguished above. The aim of projects of this type is to store a large volume of data that has no obvious structure and to provide a comprehensive index to it. The index serves as a database in its own right as well as a finding aid. The data core is a form of text base. An example is the register of musical data in London newspapers, 1660–1800. Newspaper advertisements, news articles and editorials are rich in details of performance, musicians, composers, musical venues, music publishing, and a host of other things. They are a prime source for research in many branches of history. Economic, business, social and cultural historians, with many specialist interests, are numbered amongst a large community of users.

2·2 Forms of Data

Most historical database projects are concerned, in one way or another, with the computerisation of sources. At an early stage, the researcher should investigate the character, consistency and quantity of data available. Data entry, staffing, hardware and software are all affected by data considerations. It is particularly important to identify the extent to which data are structured and the degree of consistency with which data are represented. Close scrutiny of original sources is a vital preliminary task.

Historical data-sets vary considerably in the degree of order imposed upon them, and this in turn reflects the original purpose of collecting and preserving the data. Administrative functions demand order, whether these functions are carried out by government agencies or privately. Lists and tables — of members, customers, voters, debtors, products and places, for example — are generated by organisations of all sorts, from churches to the inland revenue. Documents like poll books, cost accounts and registers of births, deaths and marriages are all the product of systematic administrative effort, and the resulting data may be described as explicitly structured. This means that the data are generally presented as a matrix of rows and columns; an easily identified collection of records with a fixed number of well-defined fields and a high frequency of entry in most fields (few null values). Each field contains either a single unambiguously defined item of data or, where the item is not completely decomposed (for instance, date of birth decomposes to day, month and year), its constituent parts are strongly related.

A second category of historical data may be described as implicitly structured. Implicitly structured data do not appear in list or tabular form, and the underlying structure of the data in a collection of documents or objects is only revealed through detailed examination of the source. Newspapers might at first sight appear as little more than a miscellany of textual and graphical material. However, an underlying structure is revealed through the successive decomposition of the text into progressively lower levels of information. Figure 1 shows a partial decomposition of the text within a newspaper.

Figure 1   *Newspaper Content Analysis*

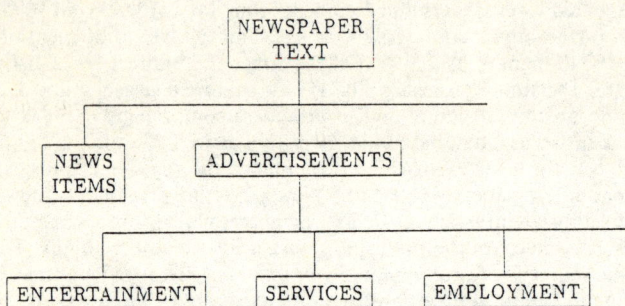

The process can be taken further with certain types of information. Examination of entertainment advertisements, for instance, reveals a number of regularly repeating data items, such as venue name, venue location, name of act and names of performers. A sufficient degree of order exists to classify the data as implicitly structured. The frequency of a particular data item is likely to be much lower than in the case of explicitly structured data (many null values), and the researcher must cope with the problem that data are often immersed in other textual or graphical material designed to catch the eye or convey a more subtle message. Depending on how the user community is defined, this type of material might itself form part of the database. A fascinating example of how to cope with complex, implicitly structured data is provided by Julie Dunk and Sebastian Rahtz in 'Strategies for Gravestone Recording'.[6]

2·3 Volume of Data

In order to estimate the time and resources needed to build a large historical database, it is first necessary to know the extent of the available data and the proposed method of data entry. Matters are usually complicated by the tendency for the amount of data to vary between years covered by the project. Some form of estimation procedure is usually required. A case in point is the project mentioned above concerned with musical items (advertisements, reports, editorials and the like) in London newspapers. Stage one of the project covers the period 1660–1745 when the number of newspapers, frequency of publication and number of musical items per edition were all on the increase.

An estimate of the total number of characters relating to music in a given period (year n to year m) is given by the following:

$$N = \sum_{i=n}^{m} \bar{\rho}_i \cdot P_i \qquad (1)$$

where $\bar{\rho}_i$ is the average number of characters per musical item and P_i is the total number of items in each year i through the period. Estimates for both $\bar{\rho}_i$ and P_i have been made following examination of the newspapers for selected years. A representative subset of all newspapers has been used to determine the average number of characters per item. Estimates have also been made of the number of items concerned with music in each of the sample years. These are presented in Figure 2.

Figure 2   *Estimate of Number of Musical Items in London Newspapers, 1660–1745*

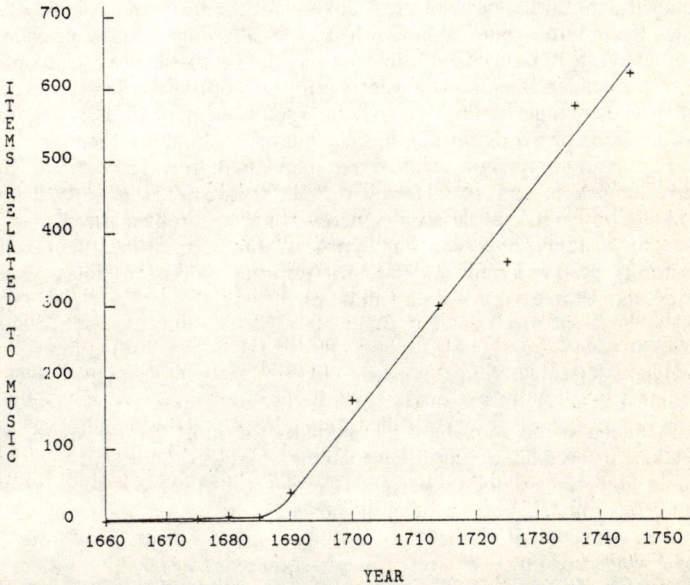

A continuous function P_{mn} (year) has been obtained by fitting a curve to the sample data. If we assume that the variation in the average number of characters per item is small over the period, such that $\bar{\rho}_i$ may be regarded as a constant $\bar{\rho}_o$, the estimate for N can be obtained from:

$$N = \bar{\rho}_o \cdot \int_{year_n}^{year_m} P_{mn}(year) d\,year \qquad (2)$$

For the entire period, 1660–1745, the total number of characters in London newspapers spent on musical matters is estimated to be nine million (18,000 items with an average number of characters per item of 500).

2·4 Project Specification

A project specification will normally include three main elements: a statement of aims and objectives; a plan of work; an analysis of resource requirements and costs. The statement of aims and objectives should specify the type of the project, the extent of the database, the means by which the database will be accessed, and the size and diversity of the user community. Enough should be said to make evident the value of the work to be undertaken. The plan of work should list the phases through which the project will pass, and the tasks to be carried out during each phase. Two possibilities are open to the researcher. One is to undertake a pilot project with a view to finding out more about what is really entailed and what resources would be needed for an all out effort; the other is to prepare a detailed plan on the basis of prior analysis of the form and volume of the data. If the latter route is chosen it is especially important to provide an estimated rate of data entry. It may or may not be possible to use an optical character reader. If manual data entry is the only option available, as is often the case, there must be a trial to arrive at a sound estimate (usually expressed as characters or words per minute). Details of this kind can then be used in preparing an analysis of resource requirements (hardware, software, staff, travel monies etc) and costs. Hardware and software needs are not difficult to evaluate; research and data entry needs are more problematic. Keying in data, for instance, may be a simple process, but account must be taken of operator speed, training and fatigue.[7] Important decisions must also be made about the extent of data validation.

3. Data Analysis

Data analysis and modelling are perhaps the most critical stages of a database project. Some authorities treat the two stages singly, and refer to the whole process as database design.[8] The general purpose is to produce a conceptual model that can be implemented using a database management system. Conceptual models are software independent. They must be developed according to correct principles, otherwise the resulting system will not function efficiently in terms of either data entry, storage and update or speed and quality of information retrieval. A conceptual model does not describe the way in which data are physically stored. It is a logical view taken by the database designer, and it should be capable of supporting many external views of the database. An external view is a partial view of a logical data model taken by an individual user or application. In supporting many such views, the needs of different specialists within a user community can be accommodated.[9]

There are two main approaches to data analysis and modelling: entity-relationship diagramming (ERD) and relational data analysis (RDA). ERD proceeds top-down, whereas RDA is a bottom-up approach. Top-down methods begin by taking a wide view of the subject under consideration, and progressively add fresh levels of detail. Bottom-up methods begin with a close examination of the raw data and progress towards a general design. Either method can be applied in most cases, but certain types of project lend themselves more readily to one method rather than the other.

3·1 Entities, Attributes and Relationships

Data analysis is founded on the notion that real world situations can be described in terms of entities, attributes and relationships.[10] An entity is simply something in which we are interested and about which we store data. Workmen, managers, contracts, suppliers, customers, equipment and workshops, for example, are entities which form part of a railway workshops database. Entities are described by attributes. A workman, for instance, may be described by works number, name, trade, wage rate and previous employer. Relationships exist between entities. There are three types of direct relationship. (i) One-to-one (1:1) is where one entity 'A' can be associated with one entity 'B' and vice versa — monogamy, for example.

Figure 3·1

```
┌──────────┐              ┌──────┐
│ HUSBAND  ├──────────────┤ WIFE │
└──────────┘              └──────┘
```

(ii) One-to-many (1:m) is where one entity 'A' can be associated with many entities 'B' — polygyny, for example. The many end of the relationship is indicated by a crow's foot at the end of the relationship line.

Figure 3·2

```
┌──────────┐              ┌──────┐
│ HUSBAND  ├─────────────<│ WIFE │
└──────────┘              └──────┘
```

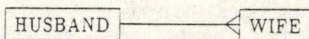

(iii) Many-to-many (n:m) is where one entity 'A' can be associated with many entities 'B' and vice versa — universal promiscuity, for example.

Figure 3·3

```
┌──────────┐              ┌──────┐
│ HUSBAND ├>─────────────<│ WIFE │
└──────────┘              └──────┘
```

Data analysis, following the top-down approach, begins with the selection of a set of primary entities. This process varies according to the type of project in hand. If a project is source driven, entities are chosen that best reflect the actual form of the data. If, however, the project is topic or concept driven or of the archival type, then the entities selected are those about which it is intended to gather data. A considerable degree of forethought is required in these circumstances, and there is much to be gained from first undertaking a pilot study. In either case, definitions of entities should be unambiguous. The process of definition is especially valuable in helping expose the underlying nature of implicitly structured data. Once entities have been defined it is a fairly easy matter to group the attributes associated with each. A further advantage is gained when projects involve researchers from different specialisms: the effort taken to define entities produces a higher degree of common understanding and fewer conflicts of interest.

Entity definitions may conveniently be represented in an entity description table such as that reproduced in Figure 4. This is part of a table drawn up for a project concerned with London music halls, 1865–90. The raw data is implicitly structured and contained in advertisements in the trade newspaper The Era. Other data are gathered from sources of a similar nature.

Figure 4   *Entity Description List: London Music Hall Database*

ENTITY NAME	DESCRIPTION / DEFINITION
Venue	Name and address of music hall given in an advertisement.
Act	The name of an individual, individuals or collective title given to a perform or performers named in a hall advertisement, and forming a recognisably distinct (in the context of the advertisement) unit of entertainment.
Performer	Individual performer named in the advertisement and forming all or part of an act.
Performance	The ancillary details given in an advertisement (ticket prices, times of performance, etc.) associated with the entertainment.

Once a set of entities has been selected, the researcher must explore the nature of relationships between entities. The first step is to determine whether a relationship is direct or indirect. A simple example of a direct relationship is that between the entity *child* and the *school* attended by the child. An indirect relationship exists between two entities where they require a third entity to support the relationship; *parent*, for example, is only related to *school* through *child*. An entity relationship table may be used to record the nature (direct or indirect) of relationships between entities. In Figure 5, which relates to the music hall entities described above, the entities form the rows and columns of a diagonalised table. At the point of intersection of a row and column, the nature of the relationship is recorded. Direct relationships are marked with a X, indirect relationships with an O, and if the relationship is neither indirect nor direct the relevant cell is left empty.

Figure 5　　　　*Entity-Relationship Table: London Music Hall Database*

	V E N U E	A C T	P E R F O R M E R	P E R F O R M A N C E
VENUE				
ACT	X			
PERFORMER	O	X		
PERFORMANCE	X	O		

All that remains to complete the data analysis is to determine the degree of the direct relationships that have been established. These are most clearly shown in diagrams such as those presented in Figure 3 where entities are presented as labelled rectangles and relationships as lines drawn between them. The music hall example is taken to its conclusion in Figure 6. It can be seen that one relationship is of the one-to-many type: a single venue may host many performances. The other relationships are many-to-many. Many acts may appear at a venue, whilst a venue may stage many acts. Likewise, an act may use many performers, whilst a single performer may participate in many acts.

Figure 6　　　　*Entity-Relationship Pairings: London Music Hall Database*

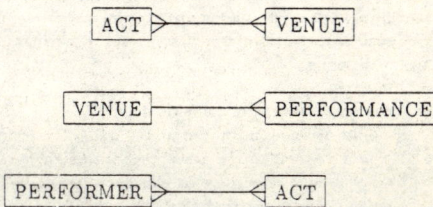

3·2 Data Item Lists
Relational data analysis begins with a detailed examination of the available data. The researcher studies relevant document types and extracts from each in turn a list of attribute names (known also as data item types or simply data items). This is a straightforward process when dealing with explicitly structured data as the attribute names are often given as the column headings

of a document. When dealing with implicitly structured data the researcher must identify all the data items that occur regularly in a particular type of document. Suitably descriptive attribute names must then be thought up.

A good example of a class of documents that contain explicitly structured data are the Crew Lists and Agreements held by the Public Record Office (classes BT98 and BT99). These documents contain details of ships, voyages, individual seamen and seafaring occupations. They are a prime source for maritime historians. The data item list presented in Figure 7 is derived from the standard document used in the Port of Liverpool. It is not a complete list as data are also to be found on ship captains and their remuneration, and for ease of exposition it is assumed that we are only dealing with the post-1854 period when an official number (unique identifier) was allotted to all newly registered ships. It should be evident from the example that an important purpose of the listing process is to produce a tight definition of each of the data items selected.

Figure 7   *Data Item List: Merchant Seamen Database*

DATA ITEM LIST	
Attribute Name	Definition & Explanation
Ship_Name	Name of ship.
Ship_Number	Number of ship in register; uniquely identifies ship following 1854 Act.
Ship_Burden	Notional figure of tonnage according to formula.
Date_Reg	Date on which the ship was registered.
Delivery_Date	Date agreement delivered to the Comptroller of the Port.
Departure	Port of departure.
Destination	Port of destination.
Duration	Maximum duration of agreement with the ship's master.
Entry_Place	Port at which a mariner joined the ship.
Entry_Date	Date on which a mariner joined the ship.
Name	Name of mariner (Forename & Surname in full).
Stated_Age	Age given by mariner at date of joining the ship.
Date_Birth	Full date of birth: day, month, year.
Place_Birth	Town County or Country of birth of the mariner (Country only if foreign).
Occupation	Job title.
Wage	Amount of wages per calendar month.
Advance	Amount of wages advanced at the date of entry.
Signature	Mariner's assent to the agreement with signature or mark.
Witness	Name (in full) of witness to mariner's signature .
Last_Ship	Name of ship in which mariner last served.
Reg_Ticket	Register ticket possessed by every mariner (foreigners were not eligible for a ticket).

4. Data Modelling

Data modelling builds upon the work done in the analysis phase of a project to produce a conceptual data model. Entity-relationship diagramming takes as input the entities and relationships defined during analysis. Relational data analysis, which is often referred to as normalisation, applies a set of rules to develop a data model from a data item list.

4·1 Entity-Relationship Diagramming

An initial diagram may be drawn simply by combining the binary relationships identified during the analysis phase. The music hall example used in section 3·1 is extended in this way in Figure 8.

Figure 8   *Initial Entity-Relationship Diagram: London Music Hall*

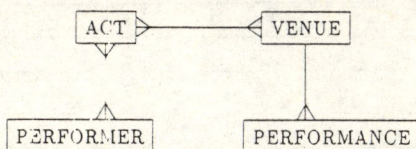

There may be problems, however, with data models of this sort. The most important stem from the existence of many-to-many relationships. In order to sustain these, identical attributes must be attached to each entity. Data redundancy is the consequence, which in turn might damage the integrity of the database. The solution to the problem is to decouple the offending entities through the insertion of a link entity. The result is shown in Figure 9.

Figure 9   *Entity-Relationship Diagram with Link Entities: London Music Hall Database*

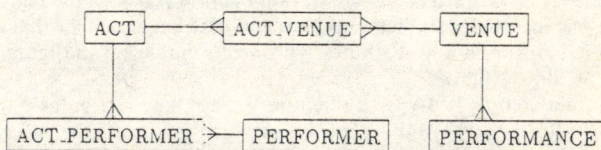

The process of refining an ERD may be taken further to eliminate other sorts of redundancy. These matters need not detain us here, and the reader is referred to a good textbook on the subject.[11]

Once an ERD is in an acceptable form, attributes are associated with entities, beginning in each case with the attribute or attributes that uniquely identify an entity occurrence (a record). Record identifiers are known as primary keys. The data content of a link entity is decided by placing in it attributes common to the two entities which it was introduced to separate. Attributes can be displayed on an ERD; more commonly they are recorded on a form for use when implementing the database. An example entity description form is provided in Figure 10.

Figure 10   *Entity Description Form for the Entity Act_Venue: London*
                   Music Hall Database

ENTITY DESCRIPTION FORM				
PROJECT: London Music Hall				
DATE: 06 / 12 / 87				PAGE 1 OF 1
ENTITY NAME: Act_Venue				
ENTITY DESCRIPTION: Details of the appearance of an act at a venue				
DATA ITEM	KEY	FORMAT	LENGTH	COMMENT
name_act	y	char	80	source 'ERA'
date_performance	y	date	dd-mmm-yyyy	ditto
venue_name	y	char	80	ditto
venue_location	n	char	80	ditto

4·2 Relational Data Analysis

RDA is a step-by-step procedure which breaks down a data item list into smaller groups of related attributes called relations or tables.[12] These relations are structured so that they may be *joined* and information retrieved in response to even the most complex queries.

The first step in RDA is the selection of a key from a data item list, or unnormalised relation as this is often called. The key should be composed of one or more data items that collectively uniquely identify the values of some or all of the remaining attributes. If there is more than one possible key, the researcher should choose that composed of the least number of attributes, and preferably a standard code like the number of a vessel on the register of shipping. When a choice still remains, the candidate key should be that which identifies the most non-key attributes. The most suitable key in Figure 7, for example, is Ship_Number.

The second step in RDA is to separate the non-key attributes into two groups. The first consists of those attributes which can be uniquely identified by the key. An example is Ship_Burden, for which, given the registration number of a ship, there can only be one possible value. The second group consists of attributes which can have several values for any given value of the key. These are generally referred to as repeating groups. In the shipping example, for instance, there will be many names of seamen for every Ship_Number. The original key is added to the second group of attributes as well as the first, and a new key selected which includes it. The second group is now subjected to the same procedure for dealing with repeating groups, and this continues until all attributes are in groups with keys that uniquely identify them. The resulting data structure is said to be in First Normal Form (FNF), as illustrated in Figure 11.

Figure 11   *Relational Data Analysis: Merchant Seamen Database*

FNF	SNF	TNF
Ship_Number	Ship_Number	Ship_Number
Ship_Name	Ship_Name	Ship_Name
Ship_Burden	Ship_Burden	Ship_Burden
Date_Reg	Date_Reg	Date_Reg
Ship_Number	Ship_Number	Ship_Number
Delivery_Date	Delivery_Date	Delivery_Date
Departure	Departure	Departure
Destination	Destination	Destination
Duration	Duration	Duration
Ship_Number	Name	Name
Name	Date_Birth	Date_Birth
Date_Birth	Place_Birth	Place_Birth
Delivery_Date		
Place_Birth	Ship_Number	Name
Stated_Age	Name	Date_Birth
Occupation	Date_Birth	Delivery_Date
Entry_Place	Delivery_Date	*Ship_Number
Entry_Date	Stated_Age	Stated_Age
Wage	Occupation	*Occupation
Advance	Entry_Place	Entry_Place
Signature	Entry_Date	Entry_Date
Witness	Wage	Signature
Last_Ship	Advance	Witness
Reg_Ticket	Signature	Last_Ship
	Witness	Reg_Ticket
	Last_Ship	
	Reg_Ticket	Ship_Number
		Delivery_Date
		Occupation
		Wage
		Advance

N.B. Primary keys are underlined. Foreign keys (an attribute which forms part or all of a key in another table) are marked with an asterirk in TNF column only.

The next step in RDA involves the elimination of partial dependency. According to relational theory, all non-key attributes should depend on the whole key and not just part of it. Composite keys are studied to ensure that this is the case. An example of partial dependency is to be found in the third of the FNF relations in Figure 11. In this case, a mariner's place of birth (Birth_Place) depends on his name (Name) and date of birth (Date_Birth) but not on the date on which his contract of employment was delivered to the Comptroller of the Port (Delivery_Date) or on the registration number of the ship (Ship_Number). Partially dependent attributes are removed from the original relation and placed in a new relation. The key of the new relation is formed from the elements of the original key on which the non-key attributes actually depend. Once partial dependency has been eliminated the data structure is in Second Normal Form (SNF).

The final stage in normalisation involves the removal of indirect dependencies. Two examples are provided by the fourth relation in the SNF column of Figure 11. In this case, Name, Date_Birth and Delivery_Date determine Ship_No, so this is no longer needed as part of the key to the relation. The key is then formed by Name, Date_Birth and Delivery_Date, but the wages paid to seamen can be seen not to depend directly upon it. In fact, Wage depends on the the the mariner's occupation and the particular agreement he signed. It is on Ship_Number, Delivery_Date and Occupation that Wage depends, and these attributes are used to form the key of a new relation. Removal of indirect dependency places the data structure in Third Normal Form (TNF).

In TNF all non-key data items depend on the whole key and nothing but the key. A final step may be taken: that of merging any relations which have exactly the same key. This produces a data model known as Optimised Third Normal Form (OTNF). In the example used in this chapter, the relations shown in the TNF column of Figure 11 have no identical keys and thus are already in OTNF.

4·3 Comparison of ERD and RDA

ERD and RDA are alternative ways of producing a conceptual data model, and, as one might expect, there is much discussion as to the relative merits of each technique. The advocates of ERD point out that the approach is very positive in obliging project sponsors to think exactingly about the requirements of a database system. This is true, and the method undoubtedly scores heavily when it comes to scoping and detailing projects that are not data driven. Moreover, ERD can be applied very neatly in source-based projects where little difficulty exists in identifying the main entities, attributes and relationships. This is not always so, however. In cases where the structure of the data is obscure or difficult to disentangle, it is better to apply RDA. One major advantage of RDA is that it obliges the researcher to study the sources very closely before moving to a higher level of abstraction. Another is that the method merely requires the application of few simple rules. Providing that the rules are applied correctly, the same data model will always emerge from the same data item list. No such assurances can be given with ERD, where much depends on the initial choice of entities and the skill and judgement of the individual modelling the data. Essentially, RDA is a simpler and more natural technique than ERD; it makes few conceptual demands and produces consistent results.

5. Implementation

The conceptual model developed during analysis and design forms the basis of an operational database system. The system is implemented using the facilities of a database management system (DBMS). Implementation may take place in a single operation; alternatively, a prototype may be developed, tested and refined before a final version of the system is released. An operational system must cater for the needs of the user community whilst protecting the data from corruption.

5·1 Database Management Systems

Database management systems are software packages used to create, maintain and access databases. They offer the facilities needed to implement a database system. Conceptual models are independent of any particular DBMS. They are generalised models: vital but intermediate products in the process of database development. The data models actually supported by DBMSs are specific to each, and any given conceptual model must be *mapped* to a DBMS-specific data model.

DBMS are classified according to the type of data model supported by the system. There are many types, but the most popular are the hierarchical, network and relational models and corresponding DBMS. The hierarchical model recognises that a relationship between two entities is often like that between superior and inferior. An inferior entity may have only one superior but it may itself have many inferiors. Arrangements in the armed forces conform to this pattern; the Supreme Commander stands above all, the lowest ranks stand over nobody. The model can be represented as a series of one-to-many relationships between entities. The network model is more flexible than the hierarchical model. It is defined in terms of a set of nodes (records) and links between the nodes. Many-to-many relationships are supported. In the relational model, all data are organised into simple two-way tables known as relations. The tables are manipulated by the DBMS in storing, amending and retrieving the data. All operations that can be performed on tables can be mathematically defined.[13]

It is not within the scope of this chapter to evaluate the various types of DBMS available. Each model has its devotees. Relational database management systems (RDBMS) are currently the most popular type, due largely to the neatness and simplicity of the underlying concepts. It is not possible in the space available to discuss the specifics of mapping from a conceptual model to each of the DBMS-specific models outlined above. The following section refers solely to RDBMS.

5·2 Database Design and Prototyping

A major advantage of leading RDBMS is the provision of facilities for the rapid development of operational database systems. All fully-fledged DBMS have at their core a data dictionary for recording data about database systems (such data are often called metadata). Definitions of relations, attributes and other items are held in the data dictionary and are used in creating a prototype database. This facility, and others, make it possible to move straightway from conceptual modelling to the implementation phase of a project.

The details of mapping from a conceptual model to a tangible design are DBMS-specific. With the ORACLE RDBMS, for instance, the database designer is offered a set of guidelines. The following are examples:

(1) Each entity identified during ERD or RDA becomes a table in the database.

(2) Each attribute in the primary key is specified as NOT NULL.

(3) Each attribute in the primary key is indexed.

By following such guidelines it is quite easy to take the conceptual model embodied in entity description forms and create the tables of a prototype database. The data in Figure 10, for example, are used as follows in constructing a table of an ORACLE database:

```
CREATE TABLE act_venue
(name_act CHAR (80) NOT NULL,
date_perf DATE NOT NULL,
venue_name CHAR (80),
venue_loc CHAR (80));
```

ORACLE stores table and attribute definitions in its data dictionary and these are called by its applications generator to build default data entry/query screens. Little difficulty is experienced in moving from conceptual model to prototype database system.

Prototypes are used to test the underlying logic of a conceptual model. Test data, selected to include the extraordinary as well as the ordinary, are entered into the system. The database is then systematically queried and its performance assessed. Trials of this kind, which vary considerably in length and sophistication, provide the feedback needed to correct, improve or modify the database design. The technique is essentially one of refinement through a cycle of test-observation-modification-test. It might be thought that countless iterations could result, but experience shows that a refined system usually emerges after very few cycles. Rapid implementation is made possible by the existence of a sound conceptual model. An equal measure of success is not likely to accompany database development on a purely trial-and-error basis.

5·3 An Operational Database System

The testing and validation of a database is followed by all-out data entry and release to the user community. A database may be made available through a single release or a number of staged releases: the more onerous the task of data entry, the more appropriate the staged approach. But whatever policy is adopted, clear guidelines must first be established concerning the management of the database. A database is a resource shared by a community of users, and, like any shared resource, it must be managed to prevent degeneration. The guidelines needed to regulate a database should be established well before a project is completed, after consulting with potential users. A number of important questions should be addressed. Who is to have direct access to the database and what privileges should each class of person be given (like query, insert, update, delete, restructure)? By what method is the database to be accessed and queried? Is the database to be made available at one or many sites? How can the data be made accessible whilst protecting the database as a whole from unauthorised copying? Who is to assume responsibility for maintaining and running the resource? What provision should be made for recovery from disaster? What scale of charges, if any, should prevail? If reasonable answers to questions such as these are not found, a database, however well constructed, may still fail to meet the needs of its community of users.

From the standpoint of the user community, a major factor determining the value of a database is the ease and efficiency with which it can be queried. RDBMS typically offer two methods of retrieving information. The easiest of these is query-by-example (QBE). QBE allows the user to enter a set of search conditions through a data entry screen or similar. The information retrieved is that which satisfies the specified conditions. QBE is useful for the simpler sorts of query, but not all queries can be satisfied in this way. More complex queries are usually made by means of the query language supported by a DBMS. The standard query language for RDBMS is SQL (Structured Query Language), discussed by Lou Burnard in 'Relational Theory, SQL and Historical Practices'.[14] Languages like SQL are marketed as end-user tools, but whilst it is possible to learn very quickly enough about them to form orthodox queries, casual users might have difficulty interrogating a database as fully as desired. This problem can be overcome to some extent by writing macros to cover the most common queries. A macro encapsulates a query so that it might be activated by a simple command.

In addition to querying, DBMS provide facilities for the production of reports incorporating information retrieved from the database. Reports list data in the order specified by the user, giving sub-totals, totals, summary statistics and headings as required. The standard of report generators differs between DBMS; some are menu-driven, others require knowledge of a software-specific command language. Most DBMS provide facilities for the export of data from a database. The results of a query may be dumped to a flat ASCII file, and thence may be imported into other software packages (statistical, cartographic etc) for more complete analysis. The same facilities mean that entire databases may be transferred to different sites and run under different DBMS.

In the life of a project, the odds are that major difficulties will be met at some point along the way, either through technological or human failure. The more advanced DBMS are designed to offer a fair degree of protection against error. Transactions, for example, are logged automatically so that a database can be restored to its previous state in the event of a major system failure. Other procedures involve those responsible for a database in making back-up copies and other routine tasks. Dull such activities may be, but they are vital none-the-less. The data of an operational database system must be kept secure against corruption and unauthorised access. The facilities offered by a DBMS allow the database manager to restrict access at various levels (file, record, data item) and in many different ways. The quality and range of security offered by DBMSs is a major factor distinguishing between them.[15]

6. Conclusion

The number of database projects undertaken by historians is set to grow quite dramatically in the immediate future. Scholars with all kinds of specialist interest are aware of the tremendous potential of database-centred research, both in terms of their own needs and those of a wider academic community. Some even believe that database technology lies at the heart of a revolution in historical research methods. Whether this proposition can be sustained is not at issue here. What is of relevance is that database projects will surely absorb an increasing volume of resources, human and financial. If these resources are to be used well, and not squandered on the production of poorly specified, inaccessible and ill-structured databases, then due attention must be paid to project planning, management and information engineering techniques. The historian should be allied to database technology in the fullest sense, recognising that it is the data that really matter, not the specifics of a favoured software system.

Notes

The authors would like to thank Dr M. Goodland, Dr F. G. Kingston, Prof. J. S. C. Riley-Smith and Mr P. Taylor for their ideas and assistance in preparing this chapter for publication. They are not responsible for any errors or omissions that may remain. A debt must also be acknowledged to humanities researchers at Royal Holloway & Bedford New College and elsewhere whom the authors are assisting with database projects. These are: Dr R. McGuinness and Mr P. Baines (Register of Musical Data in London Newspapers), Dr J. S. Bratton (London Music Halls), Ms H. Bradley (Italian Merchants), Dr D. Drummond (Railway Engineering Workers), Ms K. Davidson (Construction History), Mr E. Green (Westminster Politics), Dr J. Press (Merchant Seamen) and Ms C. Harbor (Latin Liturgical Manuscripts).

1.   J. Bradley, *Introduction to Database Management in Business*, Holt, Rinehart & Winston, 1987.
2.   J. Lillywhite, 'Data in Humanities Computing', *Humanities Communication Newsletter*, no. 9, 1987.
3.   J. A. Senn, *Analysis and Design of Information Systems*, McGraw-Hill, 1985.
4.   I. T. Hawryszkiewycz, *Introduction to Systems Analysis and Design*, Prentice Hall, 1988.
5.   J. Martin, *Information Engineering* (vols 1 & 2), Savant Research Studies, 1986.
6.   J. Dunk and S. Rahtz, 'Strategies for Gravestone Recording', *History and Computing II*, P. Denley, S. Fogelvik and C. Harvey (eds.), Manchester University Press, 1988.
7.   D. Yeates, *Systems Project Management*, Pitman, 1986.
8.   L. Burnard, 'Principles of Database Design', *Information Technology for the Humanities*, S. Rahtz (ed.), Ellis Horwood, 1987.
9.   C. J. Date, *An Introduction to Database Systems*, 2 vols., Addison-Wesley, 1985.
10.   E. Oxborrow, *Databases and Database Systems*, Chartwell-Bratt, 1986.
11.   D. R. Howe, *Data Analysis for Data Base Design*, Edward Arnold, 1983.
12.   Martin, *Information Engineering*, cit.
13.   C. J. Date, *Database: A Primer*, Addison-Wesley, 1983.
14.   L. Burnard, 'Relational Theory, SQL and Historical Practice', *History and Computing II*, P. Denley, S. Fogelvik and C.Harvey (eds.), Manchester University Press, 1988.
15.   H. F. Korth and A. Silberschaftz, *Database System Concepts*, McGraw-Hill, 1986.

Relational Theory, SQL and Historical Practice

1. What is a relational database?

For £99 in the UK you can now buy a software system called TAS which describes itself as a fully relational database system. Further inspection however reveals that this phrase is being used in a somewhat specialised sense: to quote from the manual that accompanies the software:

TAS-Plus is a 'Relational Database' in the modern sense of the word. By that we mean that in today's microcomputer terminology, the term 'Relational Database' is accepted as describing a powerful DBMS capable of handling multiple files (as opposed to a file manager which handles only one file at a time). In older mainframe and mini-computer terminology, the term 'Relational Database' was used to describe a DBMS that met a specific set of criteria as described by Dr Codd (one of the first proposers of relational theory for databases). . .[1]

It is in this latter, 'older' (also sometimes disparagingly described as 'academic') sense that I use the word 'relational' throughout this paper. Informally, we might say that a 'file management' system is concerned with the manipulation of 'files' (whatever they might contain, and however many), and is hence much concerned with the mechanical quiddities of a particular computer system, while a 'relational database management' system is concerned only with the manipulation of 'relational data'. In the rest of this paper, I have attempted to describe that 'specific set of criteria as described by Dr Codd'[2] in as accesssible a way as possible, without I hope too grossly over-simplifying it. Fortunately several excellent texts are now available which describe the concepts with more precision and in more detail.[3]

Relational database management systems are so called because all of the data they manage is held (conceptually at least) in the form of *relations* (a technical term; for the moment, read 'tables'). All of the management carried out by such systems is also describable solely in terms of relational operations. Because the mathematical properties of relations and the operations possible on them can be formally derived from well understood (by mathematicians at least) set-theoretic notions, it is fair to say that true relational database have a sound theoretical basis, conspicuously missing from most other areas of contemporary computing practice.[4]

From this basic principle follow a host of other desirable characteristics which do not in themselves necessarily characterise a system as relational. The first of these is *non-procedurality*: which simply means that you tell the computer what you want, and it works out how to do it for itself. There is no notion within the relational model of how a particular operation is to be carried out by a given machine. (After all, the notion of 'multiplication' on such a machine requires no additional specification of whether it is to be performed for example by repeated additions or by some other means). Instead, relational operations are described solely in terms of their input (one or more tables), the constraints on the operation itself (i.e. properties or rules concerning the input tables) and the desired output (a new table). This arguably leaves designers of relational software free to make ghastly errors, but also frees users from the necessity of correcting them. It is possible to concentrate on the inherent logical structure of a problem without being concerned about quite unrelated methodological issues. Operations can thus be expressed in terms independent of a given machine or programming environment.

A second distinctive (though not definitive) characteristic of relational database systems is called *data independence*. In the same way as the user of a relational system is not required to know (and hence cannot be responsible for any decision concerning) exactly how relational operations are to be performed, so neither need he or she be concerned with how, where (or even whether) the tables being operated upon are actually stored or maintained. Note, incidentally, that 'the tables being operated upon' hold both data and meta-data; that is data about the data itself. The methods used to define a new table or change an old one are exactly the same as the methods used to change the data held in the tables.

As with non-procedurality, this separation of message from medium has important implications for the development of database systems which are *distributed*; that is, where programs running on different machines in different places appear to function as a single integrated system. It also means that different styles of operation can be efficiently delegated to the machinery best suited to handle them. For example, a sophisticated and 'friendly' front-end system running on a personal work-station can determine what database operations are required, and then instruct a powerful but perhaps not particularly friendly mainframe system to perform them. Such interfaces offer the best of both micro and mainframe worlds, yet are easy to provide because both machines can use the same relational language to describe the database operations required.

A third and perhaps less significant characteristic of the relational database approach is its current wide *acceptance* within the data processing industry. Historians more than others are aware of the dangers of jumping on band wagons; on the other hand they should also be keenly aware of the perils of marginalisation. While fashions in the computing industry change as rapidly as the hardware itself, there is a highly conservative solid centre to it (necessarily so in view of the amounts of money at stake), and it is only in the last few years, after nearly a decade of debate (an eon in computing terms) that the relational database model has become commercially respectable. It is central to the development of the next generation of IBM personal computers, and it is widely available on other manufacturers' systems. It is, perhaps most significantly, undergoing the arcane process by which custom is ratified into ISO standard. Unlike some other current computing fads, it is therefore unlikely to disappear.

Of course, this does not necessarily mean that a relational database system is the best tool for the historian's task, but only that it is the one which is most likely to come to hand. Certainly for some aspects of historical research (notably those primarily concerned with the processing of original documentary sources) it has serious limitations, which are described further below and elsewhere in this volume. However, there are many situations in which its limitations may be positive virtues. Before discussing these wider issues, however, a brief summary of the model itself may be helpful.

2. The relational model

In the relational model, as stated above, all information is represented by *tables* and all operations are carried out on and produce tables (including such operations as table definition or modification).

Tables consist of a set of *columns* each comprising zero or more *rows* of data. Each row contains the same set of defined columns. Each column of each row contains either exactly one *value* or (if permissible) nothing at all (it is said to be *null*). Each value is drawn from a known set of possibilities, called the *domain* of the column. A domain may be very small (YES or NO or MAYBE), or very large (any positive integer) or indeterminate (any meaningful English surname). It may also be determined by the contents of a column of some other table.

Figure 1   *Taxpayer Table*

FamilyName	GivenName	Title	TaxPaid	PageNo
Smith	John	Capt	1024	12
Smith	Henry		256	12
Wilcox	Henrietta	Ms	2301	15
Adams		Mrs	10	10
Smith	John		256	50

Figure 1 shows such a table, called Taxpayer, each row of which corresponds with the appearance of some name in a taxation record of some kind. Separate columns of the table hold FamilyName, GivenName, Title, TaxPaid, PageNo etc. for each occurrence of a taxpayer's name. Note that each column contains only a single value: this simple example will not cater for people with more than two non-FamilyNames. Note also that the combination of FamilyName, GivenName and PageNo is different in every row. The domain of the 'Name' fields is obviously indeterminate; that of Title is less clearly so: in some circumstances we might require that valid entries here come from a domain containing (Mr, Mrs, Ms, Miss, Dr, etc), though not in others.

The PageNo specifies the page of the source on which this name appears, and must therefore be a number greater than 1 and less than the number of pages in the source. The rules determining what is a valid entry in the TaxPaid column will be more complex than this; for the moment we will assume that the value must be supplied as a whole number of pence. These two columns and the FamilyName column cannot be null because we are entering information which must appear in the source somewhere (PageNo), and (for these purposes) a taxation record must specify both an amount and a payer. This obviously does not apply to the Title or GivenName columns.

Clearly such a table can be processed either row-wise or column- wise. Correspondingly, there are only two fundamental relational operations that can be performed on a single table, the technical names of which are *select* and *project*. The SELECT operation extracts complete rows from the table according to some criterion which can be tested against each row in isolation (for example, 'all rows in which the FamilyName is SMITH'). The PROJECT operation returns the contents of a given column. Assuming that the values in a particular column are different in each row, a projection of that column will also identify its current domain (for example, 'all different titles currently in use').

Figure 2   *Business Table*

```
Name           Type        Proprietor
-------------------------------------------
Baker          ABC         Smith
Butcher        ABD         Adams
Baker          ABC         Podsnap
Chandler       ABE         Wilcox
Butcher        ABD         Smith
```

As the third fundamental relational operation, the *join*, involves the use of more than one table, let us now assume that we have a second table, shown in figure 2, in which we hold information about businesses, such as the business name and type and also the family name of its proprietor. This column will be drawn from the same domain (valid family names) as the FamilyName column in our existing Taxpayer table. It will thus probably be meaningful to combine rows from the two tables where the values for this column are the same.[5] The JOIN operation merges together rows from two tables where the values of a specified column in each table are found to match. Such a join on the FamilyName and Propietor columns in our example will produce the table shown in figure 3. (Strictly speaking, both Proprietor and FamilyName columns should appear in the result, but as they are identical, I have suppressed one.)

Figure 3   *TaxPaying Businesses*

FamilyName	GivenName	Title	TaxPaid	PageNo	Name	Type
Smith	John	Capt	1024	12	Baker	ABC
Smith	John	Capt	1024	12	Butcher	ABD
Adams		Mrs	10	10	Butcher	ABC
Wilcox	Henrietta	Ms	2301	15	Chandler	ABE
Smith	John		897	50	Baker	ABC
Smith	John		897	50	Butcher	ABD

It should be apparent how the SELECT and PROJECT operations can now be used on this result table to answer such questions as 'Which of the people referred to on pages 10 to 12 of my source had family business connexions?' (Select on PageNo); 'What types of business were run by the Smith family?' (Select on FamilyName and Project on Type); 'How heavily taxed were chandlers?' (Select on Type and Project on TaxPaid).

The table in figure 3 has no rows for FamilyNames which appear in only one of the tables, and more than one row for FamilyNames which appear more than once in either of the tables. This is because there are no constraints on the relationship between peoples and businesses represented by this join: people in the Taxpayer table may or may not also be in business; owners of businesses may or may not also appear in the Taxpayer table. However, when we start to use the relational model to represent more complex relationships such laxity may be less appropriate.

It is of course quite probable that the 'Smith' who has a butchery is a different individual from the baker, in which case more than simply the family name would be needed to identify him in the Business table, as in the Taxpayer table. In this table however, the only way of distinguishing John Smith the elder (who is referred to on page 10 of our source) from John Smith the younger (who appears on page 50), is by specifying all three columns. Should there be two references to a 'John Smith' on the same page, even this expedient will fail. It would in any case be very tiresome to have to specify three pieces of information every time we wish to combine information from a variety of sources (business lists, baptism records, marriage records, address lists, etc). The simplest solution will be to define a single code number for each distinct individual we can identify in our source material. In both Taxpayer and Business tables we might add an Id column, which will have the value 42 for each row that we believe refers to Captain John Smith, and the value 98 for each reference to his son. In the same way, if we determine that Smith the baker is indeed John Smith the younger, we will specify a value of 98 for the Id column in the business table. In either case, where we have no idea to whom a given name refers, this Id column will of course be null.

We now resolve to create a third table Person, in which will be held all the facts we can glean about an individual using inspection of the available sources and our own skill and judgment. In this table, there will be a single row for each person so identified containing his or her unique Id, and perhaps a variety of other unchanging data such as dates of birth or death, principal occupation, social origins etc. Because the Id will be different in each row of the Person table, it is all that need be specified in a row in some other table which we wish to associate with a particular individual. This in turn implies that we must take care not to use in such another table an Id which does not appear in a row of the Person table — or we shall be unable to determine the intended individual. This requirement, known in the jargon as *referential integrity*, is one of two principles, an understanding of which is fundamental to the effective design of relational database systems.

The second such principle I have already introduced informally by requiring that values in each column of a table be indivisible: this is one aspect of the principle known in the jargon as *normalisation*. Pursuing our nominal linkage example, let us now suppose that we will record occupations as given in a variety of sources in a fourth table. The columns of such a table might include a name and classification for the occupation, a reference to the source, the name of the person concerned as given in that source, and (once we have determined it) the identifying number of the person concerned. Because of the requirement that the values in each column be indivisible, there must be one row for each distinct occupation of each distinct name found in a source. The two entries 'John Smith :butcher and baker' and 'John Smith: candlestick maker' will thus create three rows in the table. If we can determine the correct Id to associate with each Smith, we will have a more reliable method of determining how often the occupations of 'butcher' and 'baker' were shared by the same individual than simple collocation of these terms in a source.

A second aspect of normalisation has to do with what is called *functional dependency*. In simple terms, one column is said to be *functionally dependent* on another if in every case the value of the first column is entirely determined by the value of the second. A case in point might be the occupation codes in our example: everywhere that 'baker' appears, the code 'ABC' will also appear. The OccCode column is said to be functionally dependent on the OccName column. To normalise the data, we create another table, called Codebook, with two columns: one containing each different value in OccName and the other its corresponding OccCode, obtained by projecting the values in our existing table. We could then remove the OccCode column from the Occupation table entirely, thus (if there are several thousand rows in the latter) saving much space. To count the number of references with a particular OccCode, we need only join the Codebook and Occupation tables on the OccName column. Referential integrity will require that values do not appear in OccName for which there is no corresponding OccCode in the Codebook. More significantly, when we wish to revise our coding procedure, we need change only the Codebook table; to experiment with a different recoding we need add only a different codebook. In either case, our original data can be re-interpreted with no alteration.

3. Using the relational model

Space precludes anything more than the barest summary of the facilities available in software systems based upon the relational model and its de facto standard language, SQL.[6] This language emerged in the 1970s from IBM based research into the sorts of enquiry language appropriate to non-technical personnel, or 'end-users' as they are unflatteringly known. It is a simple English-like non-procedural language, which can be used interactively (i.e. typed straight at a computer) or embedded in a program written in some more conventional programming language such as Fortran or Cobol. Many large systems[7] also provide their own high-level programming languages of which SQL is an integral part.

It should be stressed that SQL itself has no facilities for bulk loading of data, formatting, report generation, statistical analysis, screen definition etc. because these are all to do with internal or external representations peculiar to a particular machine. Such facilities are however provided in one form or another with all existing implementations based on it.

SQL provides facilities for data definition, modification and enquiry. For example, to create the table in figure 1 one would use the CREATE command:

Create table Taxpayer (Familyname c24, Givenname c16, Title c6, TaxPaid integer, PageNo integer);

To add date into the table one can use the INSERT command

Insert into Taxpayer Values ('Smith','John','',1024,12);

to modify existing rows in the table one can use the UPDATE command

```
/* Recode TaxPaid as number of whole pounds */
Update Taxpayer set TaxPaid = TaxPaid / 240 + 1;
```

and to remove existing rows one can use the DELETE command

Delete from Taxpayer where Familyname = 'Smith';

The most complex part of SQL is the SELECT command, which is used to extract data from one or more tables. In full, this has the form

```
SELECT columns
FROM tables
WHERE conditions
ORDER BY columns
GROUP BY columns HAVING condition
INTO table
```

though all but the first two parts above may be ommitted. As this syntax perhaps indicates, the Select command is very simple for easy uses but quite hair-raising for complex ones. A further complication is that it is possible for example to nest (with some restrictions) one SELECT statement within another. A SELECT statement can also appear instead of the VALUES part of an INSERT to move data from one table to another.

Taking its major parts in turn, the FROM clause is used primarily to specify which columns are to be recovered and from which tables

```
Select familyname,pageno
from Taxpayer
```

It additionally specifies any functions to be calculated

```
Select avg(taxpaid)
from Taxpayer
```

The WHERE clause specifies which rows are to be recovered

```
select familyname from Taxpayer
where pageno > 10
```

A reasonably wide range of comparisons is possible, using standard arithmetic operators (< > =) and some simple string comparisons. For example:-

taxpaid < 2400
pageno between 10 and 20
givenname in ('Tom', 'Dick', 'Harry')
familyname like '%son'

In addition, the WHERE clause is used to specify how tables are to be joined

select Taxpayer.familyname,business.type
from Taxpayer, business
where Taxpayer.familyname = business.familyname

The ORDER BY clause is used to specify the order in which rows are to be
presented

select distinct familyname from Taxpayer
order by familyname

The GROUP BY clause is used to group together rows with duplicate values
in specified columns. The effect of such grouping is to reduce each set of
duplicate values to a single row. Arithmetic functions (total, count, average)
can also be performed on such groups. As a final refinement, a HAVING
clause may be added to restrict which of the groups so defined are to be
displayed.

4. Criticisms of SQL

Despite its wide spread (and spreading) acceptance, neither SQL nor the
relational model are to be regarded as panaceas. Some of the grounds on
which SQL has been criticised[6] may seem of little immediate relevance to
historians (its lack of orthogonality for example), while others on inspection
turn out to be illusory[8]. One significant class of criticisms has to do with
aspects of the relational model which are not in fact supported directly by
SQL implementations — most notably mechanisms to support the domain
concept as I have defined it above. Another, perhaps more immediately
evident, is the relatively restricted range of fundamental datatypes which
SQL can support — effectively numbers, modern dates, currencies and
character strings, often only of a fixed length. With the exception of the null
concept, SQL has no facilities particularly suitable for handling partial,
inconsistent or incomplete data.

   Some of these problems are being addressed, for example by proposed
extensions to the language to support new datatypes, together with
associated operations on them. There is of course no suggestion that the basic
relational operations should be changed; just that — for example — an 'ON-
TOP-OF' operator might be useful in the WHERE part of a SELECT
command dealing with a database of physical objects. One can easily imagine
new SQL objects (and associated operators and even storage mechanisms)
for such things as money values represented in LSD, dates in the Muslim
calendar, text strings conforming to a given structure or pattern and so forth.

   To criticise SQL for failing to support fuzzy or incomplete data seems
however to me to be a misconception. Inherently complex data requires

inherently complex solutions. Perhaps the greatest virtue of the relational model is precisely that it is a *model*: a powerful way of expressing ideas about entities and the relationships between them. Source material alone is not enough: if source critics agree on anything it is only in the inevitability of interpretation in the analysis of historical records. This is not just a matter of tolerating variant spellings or different methods of representing time or values, not just a matter of knowing what 'ditto' or 'the above named' mean, nor of being able to recognise the hierarchic structure of a list. It is also a matter of knowing what entities corresponded with the source in the real world, what social or historical acts or events we are extrapolating from these records. To represent such information structures a tool at once more flexible and more restrictive than a simple recording of document structure is necessary: I propose that SQL is the 'least worst' such tool currently available.

Notes

1. In fairness, it should be stated that TAS is, of its kind, excellent value for money. Its name is short for 'The Accounting Solution' — which it probably is.
2. The reference is to E. F. Codd, a researcher at IBM who first applied the relational model to database design. E. F. Codd, 'A Relational Model of Data for Large Shared Data Banks', *CACM* 13·6, June 1970, pp. 377–87.
3. See, for example, C. J. Date, *A Database Primer*, Addison-Wesley, 1984; Frank Lusardi, *The Database Expert's Guide to SQL*, MacGraw Hill, 1987.
4. David Maier, *The Theory of Relational Databases*, Pitman, 1983.
5. This is of course an unrealistically simplified account of the problems of nominal record linkage!
6. C. J. Date, *A Guide to the SQL Standard*, Addison-Wesley, 1987, provides a detailed and occasionally critical description.
7. Among such systems currently available may be mentioned Informix, Ingres, Oracle and DB2.
8. A good summary of common misconceptions about SQL is given in chapter 6 of C. J. Date, *Relational Database: Selected Writings*, Addison-Wesley, 1986.

Strategies for Gravestone Recording

1. Introduction

In recent years there has been a growing interest in the recording of graveyards and cemeteries for archaeological and historical purposes,[1] as a result of which a number of computer programs have been written, and database packages used, to record and analyse the information. However, such programs and packages have tended to be solely concerned with producing immediate answers to relatively simple prosopographical questions (for example, graphs showing number of deaths per decade, average age of death etc.),[2] and have not explicitly addressed the limitations imposed by the recorded data, or taken into account the needs of long-term research. This paper aims to show what we consider to be an ideal structure of database systems for the storage and manipulation of cemetery data, and how we arrived at this ideal. Examples quoted will, unless otherwise stated, be from the Protestant Cemetery in Rome, which was recorded on computer between 1984 and 1986, although the methodology can be applied to any graveyard or cemetery. The cemetery has been the last resting place of non-Catholic foreigners in Rome since the mid-eighteenth century, and contains some 2,600 stones commemorating over 4,000 people from over forty countries. The recording is part of a multi-national project under the auspices of the Unione Internazionale degli Istituti di Archeologia, Storia e Storia dell'Arte in Rome, organised by the Swedish Institute.

The cemetery was not recorded using the scheme we are about to outline;[3] while in some ways this paper is an attempt to shut the stable door after the horse has bolted, it does have the merit that all the peculiar possibilities we discuss have actually been encountered in the field, and caused problems — maybe this is the only practical way of devising a database structure, to do it wrongly and discover the pitfalls as one goes along. We would accept that while the Protestant Cemetery is not at all typical of what one would encounter in an English churchyard, nothing that we have met is specific to Italy or Protestants, and we suggest that gravestone recording which hopes to add to a long-term research archive must assume a situation at least as complicated as ours.

2. Establishing a 'Universe of Discourse' and a Conceptual Schema

According to the principles of database design, as recently expounded by Lou Burnard,[4] the first step in producing an ideal database system (in this case for the storage and manipulation of cemetery data) is establishing a 'Universe of

Discourse', or defining the limits of our recording and our enquiry. This immediately forces us to think about the world of the cemetery, the elements it consists of, and how they relate to each other. All the elements must be considered whether one intends recording them or not, as they will affect the overall conceptual model of a cemetery which one is aiming to produce.

First, then, we have to decide what the cemetery consists of. At first sight this seems relatively simple; we all know that cemeteries consist of memorials which commemorate people (Figure 1).

Figure 1   *A simple model of a cemetery*

However, on closer observation we notice that the memorials have inscriptions, and decorations which consist of motifs, and that the people they commemorate have probably entered the cemetery through burial, and that there may be plant life on the grave, and that the cemetery may have an archive of the burials. As we can see, then, there is more to a cemetery than just stones and people (Figure 2).

Figure 2   *A more complex view of a cemetery*

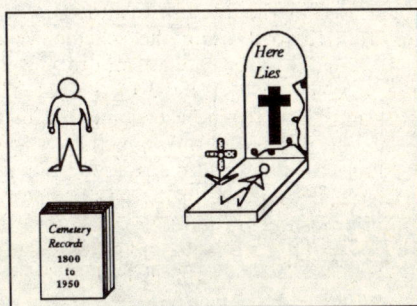

Although we can now establish a list of 'cemeterial' elements (Figure 3), we still have to decide how they relate to each other, and how to express these relationships in a clear manner. The way in which we can do this is by producing a conceptual schema diagram, where the types of relationships between elements are represented by different symbols, the meaning of which should become clear as we explain how we arrived at our conceptual schema.

Figure 3   *The elements of a cemetery*

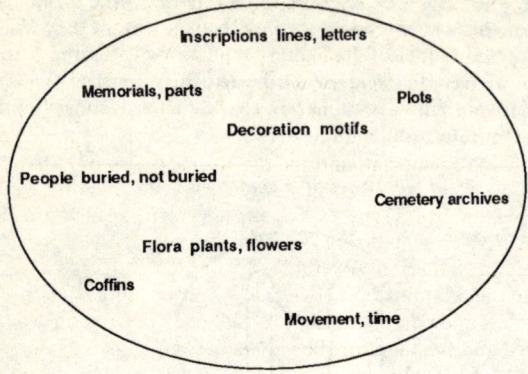

Starting with the most obvious element, *memorials*, we knew that they could be divided into *parts*, for example headstone, footstone, kerb etc. We also decided that, for recording purposes, it would be necessary to define which part of the memorial had, for example, an inscription on it, and that therefore all memorials had to consist of at least one part. This relationship is expressed in Figure 4 section a.

Figure 4   *A conceptual schema for cemetery records*

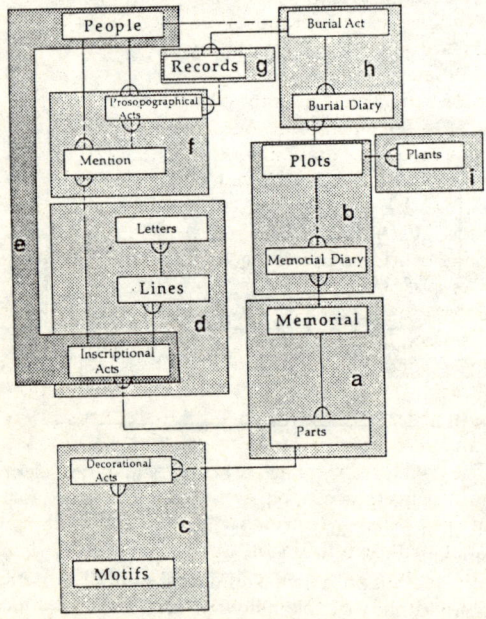

We also decided that for ease of recording it would be better to actually plan burial plots rather than the memorials themselves, as experience in the Protestant Cemetery has shown that memorials may move frequently, making updating of the cemetery plan difficult. This decision however necessitated defining what we meant by a plot. We decided that a plot is an area of action within the cemetery, which may be the subject of a burial or the erection of a memorial, or both, in the past, present or future; we must allow for not only the simple plot with a headstone, but also the plaque on the wall acting simply as a memorial, and the plot of ground purchased by a future 'client' but not yet in use. Basically it is a grid reference by which we can produce a meaningful plan of the cemetery without having to alter it drastically every time a memorial is moved. The actual recording of the extent of a plot may be somewhat arbitrary.

Expressing the relationship between plots and memorials is not as simple as for memorials and parts because, as has already been observed, memorials may be moved and can therefore be related to more than one plot. Also, plots may contain more than one memorial, as, for example, in a family plot. In order to take this into account we introduced the concept of a memorial diary, which represents every action memorials go through, including its initial erection. We can now show the relationship between memorials and plots (Figure 4 section b). This states that memorials may be subjected to one or many actions that each entry in the memorial diary has to be related to a memorial, and also to a plot, and that each plot may be related to many memorial actions, although it does not have to be related to any. Thus, at any given point in time a plot may have none, one, or many memorials on it, and one memorial may be moved from one plot to another through time.

Let us next consider decoration. Some memorials are highly decorated, whilst others are plain. Decoration can be of many sorts, for example traditional Christian symbols, classical scenes, or portraits of the deceased, and one memorial may have a combination of these, and they may appear on different parts of the memorial. We also recognised that decoration of memorials may take place gradually through time, so we decided to call each definable piece of decoration a decorational act to allow for this (Figure 4 section c). As we have just noted, decorations can be categorised into a number of forms, each form being what we have decided to call a motif. This can be anything from a complete scene to a cross. Each decorational act has to consist of a motif of some sort. One motif can appear in many decorational acts. Each decorational act has to be related to a part of a memorial, and any one part of a memorial may contain several decorational acts, although it does not have to contain any.

Parts of memorials may also have inscriptions on them. As with decorations, in order to allow for the addition of inscriptions through time, we decided to call each separate inscription an inscriptional act (Figure 4 section d). These have to be related to parts of memorials, and each part may have no, one or many inscriptional acts on it. Each inscriptional act has to be composed of lines, which in turn is composed of letters. Each inscriptional act may or may not mention one or more people; for example, an inscription may say 'here lieth Joe Bloggs,' or 'here lieth Jane Bloggs, wife of Joe', or it may just be a biblical quotation. The relationship between inscriptional acts and people is complicated by the fact that in order for us to know about a person who is in some way related to the cemetery, they do not necessarily have to be mentioned in an inscription: it is possible that they may be mentioned in a cemetery Archive. The relationship between people and inscriptions therefore appears (Figure 4 section e), which means that each inscriptional act may or may not mention one or more people.

Another problem with people is that they do not have to be buried in the cemetery in order to achieve a mention in an inscription or for us to be interested in them. For example, monumental masons may sign their work, or dead peoples' relations may appear in inscriptions even though they are not buried there. Relationships and other facts about people, i.e. prosopography, may be either directly stated in inscriptions, or may be implicit — for example, a memorial may state the date of birth and death of a person, in which case that persons age is implicitly stated in so much as we can work it out. So, each mention may state or imply none or one or many prosopographical facts (Figure 4 section f), and each prosopographical fact relates to a person. Prosopographical facts must relate to people, and people must have a prosopographical fact related to them, even if it is only their name. However, prosopographical facts do not have to appear in mentions, as they may appear in the cemetery records (Figure 4 section g).

We now have to consider how actual burials fit into this scheme (Figure 4 section h). Like memorials, burials may be subjected to movement through time, hence the necessity for a burial diary to cater for this. Obviously each burial act has to be related to a person, but a person does not have to be related to a burial act, although one person may be related to many burial movements through time. Burial acts and movements have to be related to a plot, and one plot may be subjected to many burials through time. Burials may be recorded in the cemetery records, and the records have to state burial acts.

The final category is the flora of the cemetery (Figure 4 section i). By this we mean the deliberate planting of flora on graves rather than trees or plants which are planted to enhance the landscaping of the cemetery. This establishes the fact that recorded plants have to relate to plots, but a plot may have none, one or many plants on it. This particular element of the record may seem odd to an English audience, who are used to broad green areas and yew trees, but one must remember that the climate and culture in Italy make individual plants in pots more common. We may also mention two documented cases of conscious planting; firstly, there are the flowers around the grave of Keats, which were planted to mimic lines from one of his poems, and secondly, there is a small tree in a newer area of the cemetery which has an associated plaque recording its dedication in memory of a Danish artist.

We have, then, a conceptual schema of a cemetery, which points us to the things we may wish to record and shows us that we should state whether information is explicit or implicit. The actual methodology of recording these entries need not concern us here. What we must now do is establish the most efficient system of databases for storage and manipulation of the data generated by such recording.

3. Implementing a Database

The analysis we have described of a cemetery record is, of course, idealised. It could, however, be implemented straightforwardly in a conventional relational or network database, and appropriate access strategies worked out. The primary needs in a working database fall into two parts, firstly those concerned with the extraction of information related to people, and secondly those which are concerned with memorial stones in abstract and their contents. We will need to take into account the following:

—Accessing the data by the names of the people buried or commemorated is an obvious route to take (but see below for problems).

—The cemetery records provide an important means of access for prosopographical information, based on dates of entry.

—Access by means of either a plot number or a grid reference is essential, as this will control whether things can be re-identified on the ground. It will be clear that there cannot be a single numbering system to categorise the gravestones, and that separate catalogue numbers will have to be allocated to a plot and to a memorial. The Protestant Cemetery has many examples of migrating gravestones, despite the apparently timeless stability of a graveyard, and complete plots undergo a thorough re-use.

—We need some way of quickly identifying information about a particular gravestone. For one major part of analysis, this will be the primary concern.

—For study of the inscriptions, we would like to access the texts word by word. This will be further discussed below.

—For art-historical purposes, getting at the stones by a particular design will be important, and we should therefore support access to the structure by motif.

With the exception of the words of the inscriptions, conventional indices will provide what is needed, and relational joins will provide the output we need for any purpose, such as input to a statistical program, as well as answering interactive queries.

3·1. Specific Problems
There are a number of detailed problems to do with the recording systems which must be solved once we have devised a global scheme. We shall examine two obvious, and one not-so-obvious, difficulties.

The first is to do with the prosopographical records. There are three conventional problems in such databases:

1. The fact that a European name has no universally accepted, life-long, form. It is quite possible to be born Mary Smith, and die Wendy Bloggs, with any number of names in between. No one name is 'right'.

2. The difficulty of establishing family or other links — is Mrs Trewhella *here* the wife of Mr Trewhella *there*?

3. The cultural and political dimension in recording an apparently innocuous field such as nationality. Do we record the name of the country in which the town of birth is now situated? This could make Anglo-Indian children come out as Pakistani. Or do we take the nationality at time of death? This would make the English woman who marries a White Russian in Rome become Italian. Do we record the nineteenth-century citizen of an obscure North European state, now in the USSR, as a Ruritanian or do we call him Russian?

There are no simple answers to these problems, and it is the *temporal* dimension of prosopograhical records that our concept of *prosopographical acts* is designed to cater for.

The second problem relates to iconography; do we describe the decoration on each stone in free text, and treat each one as unique? Or do we decide that there are a number of known possibilities (such as 'Classical mourning tableau', 'representation of the deceased', 'figure of Christ'), and categorise accordingly, with sub-groups ('with or without ivy leaves')? Or we do adopt a system of multiple keywords, recording the presence and absence of a known range of motifs? The latter was the system adopted for the Protestant Cemetery, on the grounds that this most accurately represented the needs of research — for instance, the Cemetery was under Papal authority until 1870, and the Pope forbade the use of the cross on Protestant gravestones. It is therefore of interest to locate easily the presence or absence of a cross on any particular tomb. This type of query is catered for by some degree of hierarchy in the coding list. Although each motif is given a number, and records are made using that number, there is an additional group number assigned to each motif for queries at a higher level (e.g. all Christian symbols are in the same group).

A third problem relates to the texts of the inscriptions; there is the simple problem of transcriptions of alphabets, particularly acute in the Protestant Cemetery, where conventional Greek, Russian and Latin alphabets mingle with various Slavonic, Japanese, Chinese, Arabic and other scripts. Even within the Latin family, there are problems of accentuation and other marks which must be encoded using the ASCII character set. To what extent should we record the style of the lettering, or is this best left to a photograph? Any one inscription can demonstrate a whole variety of different letters, and a detailed study of the inscriptions in the oldest part of the cemetery suggests that it may be possible to identify different masons' styles or at least stylistic periods in the cemetery. An allied question arises when we come to investigate the language used in funerary inscriptions; if we suspect that the same sentiments are used at a particular period, regardless of nationality, we must either translate all the texts into a common language, either real (Latin?

Table 1   *Iconographical Motifs*

Code	Group	Motif	Code	Group	Motif
1	7	altar	94		skull and cross bones
2	6	anchor	95	8	soul
4	1	angel	96	3	sphinx
5	7	arch	97		star
8	6	arrows	98		star of David
9	2	palette and brushes	99	2	statue, of deceased
12	0	bird in bush	100	1	statue, male (not deceased)
14	6	book	101	1	statue, female (not deceased)
16	7	column, broken	102		sun
19	4	bust	104		swastika
20	3	butterfly	105	5	thistle
21	6	caduceus	106	6	torch
22		celtic rope work	107	5	tree
23	6	chalice	108		triangle
24	8	chi rho	109		urn
25	2	children's toys	111		wings
26	1	Christ	112	5	wreath
28	5	clover	113	8	cross
29	2	coat of arms	114		star and + symbols (birth and death)
30	7	column	115		alpha and omega
31	6	compass	116	8	IHS
33	6	crown	117	5	olive
34	6	dagger	118	6	lamp
35	6	disc	120	5	acanthus
36	3	dog	121	5	lotus
37	3	dolphin	122	5	vines
38	7	door	123	8	cross, Greek
39	3	dove	124	8	cross, Orthodox
41	3	evangelical animals	125	5	wreath, victors
43	1	figure	126		statuary, broken
44	3	fish	127		meander
45	5	floral, unknown	128	5	pine
47		fravashi	129	5	garlands
49	3	griffin	130	5	wheat
53	6	hourglass with wings	131	5	poppy
54	8	icon	132	5	flower, falling
55	6	jug	133	5	ivy
56	3	lamb	134	5	oak
57	5	lily	135	5	laurel
58	6	lyre	136	7	capital
59	8	cross, Maltese	137	6	boat
60	5	maple	138		trefoil
61	6	mask	139		heart
62	2	mason's tools	140		quatrefoil
63	2	medal	142	8	cross, Celtic
64	2	military accoutrements	143	6	sword
66		mosaic	145	6	medical staff
68	2	music	146		leaf stop
69	2	musical instrument	147	6	vase
70	6	oar	149	3	toad
71		"tictactoe board"	150	3	lizard
72	3	owl	151	3	dragonfly
74	5	palm	152	3	insect, unknown
75	3	peacock	153	3	ox skull
76	3	phoenix	154	5	shamrock
77	2	photograph	155	6	rope
79	2	portrait	156	5	tree of life
80		praying hands	157	3	eagle
80		praying hands	159	6	cushion
82		putto	160		Romulus & Remus
82		putto	162	8	cross with dots in corners
84		sarcophagus	163		clouds
85	5	rose	164	5	cross, St Georges
86		rosette	165	5	holly
87		scroll	166	3	mouse
88	3	serpent	167	7	sculptor's tools
89	6	shells	168	3	sparrow
91	6	sickle	999		Extra - see notes
92		skull			

English?) or imaginary, or we must impose a concept of a range of known 'sentiments', parallel to the motifs in decoration, and somehow generate sentimental records from the actual texts.

Conclusions

We have purposely not given any illustrations of gravestones, printed any plans of graveyards or attempted to give any *results* of our work in the Protestant Cemetery, which is published elsewhere.[5] Our sole purpose has been to demonstrate the complexity inherent in recording a cemetery, to show what sort of theoretical structure we think it is necessary to adopt, and to share some of the problems encountered in a real application.

Notes

1.   J. Jones, *How to Record Gravestones*, Council for British Archaeology, 2nd edition, 1979.
2.   H. Mytum, 'Recording and Analysing Graveyard Data using the BBC Micro: a First Report', *Archaeological Computing Newsletter*, 8, 1986, pp. 3–4.
3.   S. Rahtz, 'Funerary Epitaphs and Iconography: An Analysis of the Protestant Cemetery, Rome', Master's thesis, Institute of Archaeology, University of London, 1981.
4.   L. Burnard, 'Principles of Database Design', *Information Technology for the Humanities*, Chichester, 1987.
5.   S. Rahtz, 'The Protestant Cemetery, Rome: a Study Undertaken under the Auspices of the Unione Internazionale degli Istituti di Archeologia Storia e Storia dell'Arte in Roma', *Opuscula Romana*, 16, 1987; P. Vian and A.I. Menniti (eds.), *The Protestant Cemetery, Rome: Parte Antica*, Unione Internazionale degli Istituti di Archeologia, Storia e Storia dell'Arte, Rome, forthcoming, 1988.

The Storing and Processing of Historical Data

1. Introduction

Developments in computer technology have permitted historians to embark upon research projects that would hardly have been possible manually. Recently, the advent of database management systems has provided more sophisticated tools with which to conduct such research. As a result, the historian need be less concerned with the writing of file-handling programs, and may therefore concentrate on other issues. In particular, the storage, indexing, and retrieval facilities of database management systems can be extremely useful in the storage of historical data; and it is with the application of these facilities that this paper is primarily concerned.

Historical data are available in many forms. This paper is concerned with any data that can be subdivided into components which occur repeatedly in the documents under consideration. Data such as these frequently arise in documents which were created for specific administrative purposes, and which thus have clearly defined structures; examples include: vital registration, local censuses, tax registers, etc.. When storing such data on a computer for later use in historical research, certain desirable characteristics of the storage system are particularly important: the data must be efficiently stored, efficiently accessed, readily manipulated, and accurate.

To develop these desirable characteristics it is possible to use some form of database management system which possesses certain features: the ability to store records with different formats containing data items of different types; the facility whereby new records can be constructed from one or more existing records; and the availability of other statistical, sorting and reporting functions on these records. Alternatively, it must be possible to export records to other packages for subsequent analysis. Finally, it is often necessary to link together different records pertaining to the same individual (record linkage), and so it must be possible to store and retrieve such links in the same way as the original data.

2. Example Data

While the software and techniques described in this paper can be applied in the processing of many types of historical data, for illustrative purposes, one particular example is described in detail. The data are taken from the Viana do Castelo database housed at the University of Southampton. The Port-City of Viana do Castelo is situated on the northern bank of the mouth of the river Lima which runs westwards through Minho — the northernmost province of Portugal. Histories of the demography of Viana and its hinterland can be found in the works of Reis and Kitts.[1]

The Viana database currently consists of approximately 60,000 records from four different types of document compiled in the nineteenth and early-twentieth centuries. In this section, these four documents are described briefly; a more detailed description can be found in the thesis of Kitts.[2]

2·1 Muster-Rolls
Muster-Rolls have been drawn up in Portugal since the mid-seventeenth century; the database contains those compiled for Viana between 1826 and 1833. They provide details of all males, and any female who might have affected a male's liability for recruitment.

2·2 Electoral Registers
Electoral registers have been drawn up in Portugal since 1834; the database contains most of those compiled for Viana between 1834 and 1931. They provide details of those individuals who were enfranchised; broadly speaking, these were Viana's wealthier males.

2·3 Passport Books
Passport books have been kept in Portugal since 1835; the database contains those compiled in Viana between 1835 and 1896. They contain the particulars of all passports issued, giving details of the passport holder and any accompanying persons.

2·4 Cemetery Lists
Cemetery lists have been kept in Viana since 1855, when the City's public cemetery opened permanently. The database contains those compiled between 1855 and 1922. They provide details of all people buried in the cemetery.

3. The Database Management System

The database management system chosen for the Viana database is SIR (Scientific Information Retrieval). The version currently in use is 2·1·3; it is available on a wide range of machines, from PC compatibles to mainframes. Machines used for the Viana database include IBM PC-AT and PS/2 microcomputers (donated by the IBM Institute), for data entry, and an IBM 3090–150VF mainframe for housing the whole database.

In SIR, data are stored hierarchically at three different levels known as Case, Record and Variable. These levels are used in the Viana database as follows. The case is the main identifier for an entity — all the information concerning one individual on a document. Variables are used to hold the attributes of that entity — the information recorded for that individual. Records are used to group the variables in order to increase storage efficiency.

4. Database Construction

As outlined in section 1, there are several desirable characteristics that need to be taken into account in the construction of a large historical database. First, the database must be efficient in its use of storage space. Second, access to any particular set of data must be efficient. Third, it must be possible to code and standardise the data for the purposes of record linkage and analysis. Finally, the data must be retrievable in the form in which it appeared in the original document, with spelling variations, intact. In this section, the development of these desirable characteristics is discussed.

4·1 Efficient Storage
There are two main areas in which space is often wasted in database systems. First, where a particular variable is only available in some cases, the storage of that variable — often as a missing value — for all cases is inefficient. Second, where variables often share the same value, it is sometimes possible to construct a code for that variable which requires far less storage space than the variable itself; this is particularly common in the computer-handling of historical manuscript sources which contain many textual variables. Considering the former problem, any variables which only occur for the minority of cases (e.g. birthplace) are stored in separate records which only exist when required.

With regard to the latter problem, textual variables which occur frequently with the same value are coded as numbers, and lookup tables are used to convert between the text and its code and vice versa. This process is used for names, occupations, addresses, and places, but not for text such as observations.

4·2 Efficient Access
All the data are indexed on the most likely key for access where this is practicable taking storage considerations into account. The main key in a SIR database is the case identifier; this is constructed according the type of case identified.

There are two different types of case in the database. First, there are those containing all the information concerning one individual on a document (see section 3); their case identifiers comprise 8-digit numbers, constructed from details of the document such as its type and the year in which it was compiled; this also allows cases to be processed in groups (see Appendix 1 for further details). Second, there are those containing the lookup tables described in the previous section; their case identifiers comprise 2-digit numbers which correspond to the record number containing the lookup table.

The lookup tables are stored in separate cases. Thus, while all the records for a particular case are stored physically close together, making retrieval of all the records of one case efficient, not all the information is stored close to the case. If frequent access is required via a non-key field, then a lookup table is used to index that field; an example of this usage is for access by name.

4·3 Standardisation of the Data

It is often necessary to standardise data so that variables which are not actually identical can be considered as such; this is especially so with textual data such as names of people and places. For example, unstandardised orthography often resulted in several versions of names, and (more peculiar to the Viana data) words were often abbreviated in an inconsistent fashion. The standardisation of such variables is accomplished using the same lookup tables as those described in section 4·1 for data coding. The lookup table which converts code into text is modified to include an extra field which contains the code of the text which is the standard form for that particular variable.

4·4 Retention of Original Data

By applying the techniques described in this section, all the data are stored as originally recorded on the document concerned; this enables the original document to be reconstructed exactly. This characteristic is important for practical as well as theoretical reasons; for example, should subsequent research show that the assumptions under which data are standardised were incorrect, corrections are quite straightforward.

5. Treatment of Names

The storage of names is always a problem and this is especially so with Portuguese names, which are not formed according to the relatively predictable patterns found in other societies; Portuguese names comprise one or more first names followed by one or more second names, any of which might be passed on to the next generation. Names are not always completely given; sometimes one or more first and second names are omitted. Further, names are often inconsistently abbreviated so that there is sometimes ambiguity over the name to which a particular abbreviation refers. Thus, apart from the spelling variations common to many historical manuscript source, Portuguese names present some interesting difficulties of their own.

To alleviate these problems as far as possible the names are split up into component names which are stored as codes, along with an indication of the position of the component within the full name. The process of name storage and standardisation is as follows.

During original data entry, into the micro version of SIR, names are split into their component parts. These components are used to build validation tables so that when a name not already known to the database is entered, the researcher can seek confirmation before continuing. However, this does not of course overcome all possible errors of data entry, as a name might be mistaken for another valid name. The data are checked again after entry by producing sorted listings of names, and examining these lists for possible errors. During this examination phase it is also possible to see which sets of names ought to be standardised to a single common version. The technique discussed in section 4·3 is then used to store names in a standardised form.

There are actually two tables of name standardisations. The first is for the first name, which is usually sex specific. The second is for all other names.

Where different component name endings might refer to the same name, they are replaced by a hyphen. Further, where confusion between certain pairs of component names is common, they are standardised to a version representing them both. As the individual parts of names are stored along with their position in the name, it is possible to reconstruct the full original or standardised version of the name from the codes of the original component names.

In the name standardisation table there is also a field which contains the frequency with which component names are standardised to that particular code. This information can be used to locate records efficiently, even where only some components of a name are available. In this respect, another facility developed in order to locate particular individuals is an index of all standardised name codes and the records that contain them, along with a note of the position in which it occurs.

In summary the steps in finding persons with a particular set of component names are: a) read in the complete name, b) split it into its component parts, c) look up the codes for these parts, d) look up the standard code for each part, noting both the code and its frequency, e) choose the one with the lowest frequency, f) use the index to find records which contain this name (note: if the complete name is being supplied the position information can be used to reduce the number of entries that need checking), g) look up the name codes for this record, h) check to see if all the given names occur in the given order, i) note the record found.

Once individuals are linked (see section 6), it is possible to use the link record to determine whether a record for this particular person has already been found in the search, thus only reporting the first record for distinct individuals, and using the links to find other records for the same person if this is desired.

6. Record Linkage

Since several records for the same person over several years are often stored in the database it is obviously useful to be able to access these records quickly. This is achieved by using link records which are held in a table in a separate case. The fields of this record are TID (this ID) FID (first ID) LID (link ID) and PID (prior ID). Therefore, using the IDs for any particular record, it is possible to access the first occurrence, next or prior occurrences of that person directly.

The problems of record linkage are discussed in general, and with respect to the Viana data in particular, in the thesis of Kitts.[3] The strategy adopted in the record linkage of the example data is a time consuming process largely due to the nature of Portuguese names. It is broadly tackled as follows: a) use a special name code of 1 for component names that are to be standardised out of the name (e.g. de, da, do), b) build a string of the standardised code for each record, c) send this to the report utility, along with the ID and the year (sorting by name code string, then year, then ID, presents the links in a time-sequence rather than a document-type sequence), d) set the break action on the code string, and generate the link records from the ID, e) read in the link records and produce the prior links by following the link IDs.

While this links together records with the same standardised name, the linkage process does not terminate here. There are the cases where one or more names may have been dropped, and there are the cases where one or more individuals shared the same set of component names. Considering the first problem, a check is made on all names with 3 or more components to see if there is another name containing those components; these can then be linked together to form larger possible sets of links. Turning to the second problem, while incorrect linkage is clearly identified in cases where a chain contains more than one cemetery record, sometimes it is far less obvious. These chains have to be separated using other data such as age, marital status, and occupation, in order to provide chains of individuals; however, details of this, and the development of probabilistic record linkage, lie beyond the scope of this paper.

7. Summary

The facilities of modern database systems provide the historian with sophisticated tools with which to conduct research. In their application to the storage of historical data, certain desirable characteristics are particularly important: the data must be efficiently stored, efficiently accessed, readily manipulated, and accurate.

The development of these desirable characteristics is illustrated in this paper using example data from the Viana do Castelo database, stored in a SIR database at the University of Southampton.

Notes

1.   Arno Kitts, 'An Analysis of the Components of Migration: Viana do Castelo, Minho, 1826–1931', unpublished Ph.D. thesis, University of Southampton; Elizabeth de Azevedo Reis, 'The Spatial Demography of Portugal in the Late Nineteenth Century: Evidence from the 1864 and 1878 Censuses', unpublished Ph.D. thesis, University of Southampton, 1987.
2.   Op. cit.
3.   Op. cit.

APPENDIX Construction of Case Identifiers

Muster-Rolls — DRRHHHFI, where

> $D\ (=1)$ is the Document type
> RR is a code for the Road.
> HHH is the House number in the Road.
> and FI identifies the Family and Individual within the House.

Electoral Registers, Passport Books, and Cemetery Lists — DYYYPIII, where

> D is the document type:
>> 2 Electoral Register
>> 3 Passport Book
>> 4 Cemetery List
> YYY is the year less its thousands digit
> P is the parish
>> 0 unspecified
>> 1 Santa Maria Maior
>> 2 Monserrate
> III is the position of the individual in the document.

For example, to retrieve the standardised name of the 282nd individual recorded on the 1856 electoral register of Santa Maria Maior, the Case 2-856-1-282 is located, and then the name Record it points to. From this Record the name code Variables are extracted, and used to retrieve the individually standardised component names from the name lookup table Record; these are then concatenated to form the full standardised name — Manuel Felix Mancio da Costa Barros, the mayor of Viana.

The coding is such that records can be processed in groups; for example, to examine passports issued in the period 1864–1877, the NIDs 3–864–0-000 through 3–878–0-000 are processed. Also, if data are sorted by NID, they are automatically sorted first within a document, then by parish, next in time, and finally by type of document.

IV.

Artificial Intelligence and Expert Systems

Artificial Intelligence Techniques for Historians: Expert Systems, Knowledge Representation and High-Level Programming

'Many of Gutenberg's contemporaries must have wondered what use — never mind what long-term implications — casting the alphabet in lead could possibly have. What we have here (with Expert Systems) is equally simple and equally important. It is easy to appreciate what the technique offers: an opportunity to solve problems that we could not tackle before using computers. But to assess its impact and significance requires the hindsight of history'.[1]

Artificial Intelligence (AI) is, of course, about much more than simply the creation of Expert Systems; even though this may appear to be the topic of most immediate relevance to historians. Accordingly, this paper addresses not only the specific matter of Expert Systems (Intelligent Knowledge Based Systems) but considers some of the wider issues raised by AI research; particularly knowledge representation in history, and programming for humanities students.

It would be useful at the outset to define our terms. Artificial Intelligence has been described by a leading commentator as 'the study of how to build and program machines (computers) that can do the sort of things which human minds can do.'[2] More specifically, practioners have seen the actual techniques involved as consisting of methods for searching 'problem' spaces, planning sequences of actions to solve problems, methods of reasoning and deduction, and techniques for representing knowledge.[3] Writing a conventional computer program to perform complicated statistical calculations would not be seen as an artificial intelligence activity, while writing a program to test an hypothesis would. Furthermore, while there are those who argue that AI programs can be implemented in any programming language, two so-called 'AI languages' have become the focus of much attention within humanties computing: LISP (and its list-processing variants such as POP-11) and PROLOG. These 'high-level' languages are able to handle something much closer to natural language than is normally associated with computers.

Expert Systems are computing programs capable of representing and reasoning about some knowledge-rich domain, with a view to solving problems and giving advice. Expert Systems have been likened to an 'assistant' which does much of the tedious appraisal of alternatives in the search for solutions, and rules out some of the less promising ones; but leaves the final decisions to the user.[4] Off-the-shelf systems are to be found almost exclusively in areas where there is a marked commercial interest. For those who cannot adapt such systems to their purposes and who do not wish to get involved in 'high-level programming' (that is using a language such as PROLOG or LISP) to construct their own Expert System, the task can be facilitated by the use of a software package referred to as a 'shell'. The idea behind these shells is that the 'domain dependent knowledge' is stripped from out of a standard expert system. This leaves behind a shell which consists of the system's reasoning component (inference engine) and its knowledge representation formalism. The user enters his or her own information in strict accordance with this formalism and this 'knowledge base' (facts, definitions, heuristics) is normally accessed by way of a 'production system'. In other words, by applying a series of antecedent-consequent ('IF-THEN') rules.

IF   the plaintiff did receive an eye injury
          and there was just one eye that was injured
          and the treatment for the eye did require surgery
          and the recovery from the injury was almost complete
          and visual acuity was slightly reduced by the injury
          and the condition is fixed

THEN   increase the injury trauma factor by $10,000.[5]

The above is one of the various rules which constitute ROSIE's pool of knowledge about legal heuristics for product liability. WHY, you may ask, have I chosen this example? WHERE's the 'history'? Both questions are, in fact, linked. I could have chosen virtually any package from DENDRAL (Mass Spectrograms) to HEADMED (pharmacological treatment in psychiatry). Recently, various other packages which deal with entitlement to Social Security benefit or financial analysis have been developed.[6] Clearly, such things are not the stuff which comes immediately to mind when one considers the content and function of history at its highest levels; a topic which will be discussed in due course.

This is not to say, however, that Expert Systems have nothing to offer the historian. If an historical research subject depends at its initial level on the manipulation of a great deal of data in a structered/patterned form that would be amenable to an Expert Systems approach, then the addition to the historian's tool-bag of a package or expert system development shell might be in order. A great number of shells are now available for a range of microcomputers, including ESP Advisor, Xi/Xiplus, Savoir, and APES.[7] Most provide an 'easy', natural-language format for entering 'knowledge', and can thus be used by non-programmers. In order to emulate mainframe performance, microcomputers based on 16/32 bit architecture with at least 1/2 M Byte of on-board memory (10 M Byte hard-disk) are required, but such powerful machines are now becoming the norm rather than the exception for all serious practitioners.

Expert Systems may thus be appropriate in very specialised, limited domains in which there is high-quality knowledge about the problem area. In such 'closed worlds' problem solving will have an enumerable set of states, well-understood start- and end-states, and a finite set of rules of legal actions which will move one through the problem space. Some of the building blocks of history may well be such 'closed world problems' in which there are a set of identifiable regularities or constraints which an implemented AI procedure can deal with.

However, larger, real world problems that are the ultimate concern of the historian are, given the intrinsic nature of the real world, never of this type. In most cases 'explanations' in expert systems are, to paraphrase Boden, merely recapitulations of the previous firing of rules which have strictly defined both the problem and answers beforehand![8] Pace the highly commendable efforts of Richard Ennals et al, I have yet to see an Expert System (whether using 'off-the-peg' shells or 'bespoke' high-level programming) that does justice to the complexities of history as an intellectual discipline.[9] Thus, while arguments can be advanced for treating Clausewitz on warfare, Mahon on seapower, Machiavelli on princely politics, or even Friederich and Brzezinski on totalitarianism, as potential Expert Systems (you may add others of your own choice), I remain unconvinced that work of this nature would be of any profound benefit.

This may not seem to be a matter for concern if historians confine themselves to the modest aim of using Expert Systems as mere 'assistants'. However, despite claims to the contrary, it seems unlikely that researchers will be able simply to borrow wholesale the standard packages of other groups; be these diagnostic software from the medics or accounting systems for financial records.[10] Moreover, even though we are promised great advances, the shells which are presently availabe tend to confine users to the kind of problems which correspond to the original problem from which the shell was derived by abstraction. To cope with such restraints the use of a high-level programming language is recommended for those who wish to implement their own AI applications.[11]

Fundamental issues emerge; for the debate not only enters into the the controversial area of 'programming for the humanities', but raises the whole question of the nature and form of 'historical knowledge' and 'problem solving' in history. The process of constructing an expert system from basic principles is usually referred to as 'knowledge engineering', and it can be argued that one of the primary motivations for undertaking any knowlege engineering exercise should be to gain insights into a discipline by attempting to codify and thereby render explicit the knowledge that an expert in that particular field possesses. Indeed, this activity might well be more intellectually rewarding and profitable than the elusive 'working' end-product. It may thus be a healthy exercise for historians to sit down and think about the form and structure of 'historical knowledge' and the way in which it can be utilised; rather than 'merely' engaging in the activity of being an historian.[12] In this regard some of the basic approaches adopted by Artificial Intelligence research seem apposite to debates on methodology in history. 'Forward-chaining' (working from a current situation towards a conclusion) seems very akin to Elton's view that in the 'practice of history' the evidence must be allowed to suggest the answers. On the other hand, 'backward-chaining' (working towards the known facts from an hypothesis) mirrors Carr's approach in which the question of 'what is history' cannot avoid approaching facts without theories and assumptions.[13] Given the heated debate, at least in German historical writing, on the methodological difficulties of 'history from below', the link is not that tenuous or escoteric.[14] Furthermore, the 'frame-problem' (how to keep track of changes occuring in the world and the consequences of an event) involves much that is of relevance for historians.[15]

This is not, it must be stressed, to assert that 'historical knowledge' can be easily formalised, if at all. AI research may assume that 'all our knowledge outside the field of mathematics is based on demonstrative logic, which consists of hypotheses'[16], but, as advocates of Foucault will concur, knowledge is, in the first instance, socially conditioned and culturally determined. The very description of the world is a subjective activity.[17] Moreover, history warns against the dangers of 'closed world assumptions' so favoured by current Expert Systems. Account must surely be taken of what we do not know; just as much as what we do know. Problem solving in the real world is also very much 'context determined' and as Arrow's theorem demonstrates, many problems are simply NOT solvable. Conflicts of interest, for example, which are surely the bread and butter of history, are often such that no rational solution is possible. To complicate matters, complex systems though causal may be highly unpredictable. Historians have already encountered Leibnitz's 'characteristica universalis', and would thus surely not be surprised to be told by AI researchers that 'there seems to be no universal theory of problem solving or knowledge representation which underlies everything else'.[18] All in all, knowledge is, to paraphrase one writer, a mysterious kind of entity, about which we know remarkably little. While there may be some point in applying tools as though we were dealing with a substantive material like wood or stone, knowledge engineering is still an art, and not a science.[19]

It should be apparent by now that historians who intend to consider the sophisticated use of AI techniques will no doubt find themselves involved with high-level programming. Clearly this goes against quite legitimate assertions that such activity is outside the purview of the historian.[20]

The view has emerged, of late, that programming is a beneficial intellectual activity for all; including, one presumes, historians. Advocates of this line range from those who see programming, in say LOGO, as akin to playing with sand in the Piagetian mode of learning, to those who boast that computer languages such as PROLOG offer an analytical training comparable to that previously provided by Latin.[21] Given that recent literature remains far from decided as to the merits of such claims, it seems appropriate to confine discussion to the use of high-level programming as an historical tool.[22]

Within the overall field of AI, two languages are most favoured: LISP (a so called procedural language) and PROLOG (a so called declarative language). It is the latter language which has gained an enthusiastic following amongst some historians on the grounds that the inherent character of PROLOG suits the needs of history and, perhaps of equal importance, it is seen as very accessible.[23] As its name implies, PROLOG (PROgramming in LOGic) is based on a form of logic known as the Horn clause subset of full first order logic; that is predicate logic and not classical Greek logic. Unlike a procedural language which specifies carefully and explicitly the steps that the computer must take to create a result, PROLOG requires that the user give a correct definition of the problem and its components. The definition is made up of facts and rules, with each fact or rule a logical sentence that makes an assertion about the problem. In other words, PROLOG allows for the creation of very flexible databases; with the historian concerned initially with the nature of the information, rather than with the mode of solution of a problem. Sophisticated facilities such as 'recursion' (the ability to use a rule which redefines itself) can be then employed as a powerful tool with which to infer say kinship relationships from demographic databases.[24] For example, a database of four facts, a rule for ancestor and a rule for descendant might be written as follows:

```
parent(william, charles).
parent(charles, elizabeth).
parent(elizabeth, george-v).
parent(george-v, george-vi).
ancestor(Old,Young) :-parent(Old,Young).
ancestor(Old,Young) :-parent(Mid,Young), ancestor(Old,Mid).
descendant(Y,O) :-parent(O,Y).
descendant(Y,O) :-descendant(Y,M),parent(O,M).
(or descendant(Y,O) :-ancestor(O,Y).).[25]
```

However, despite some claims to the contrary, PROLOG is still a programming language (like LISP) and not a 'knowledge representation language'. It should also be stressed that PROLOG does not 'know' the meaning of the terms contained in its database of propositions; merely whether or not they are present.Moreover, as practioners have stressed, the idea that PROLOG is somehow easy to program is a little misleading, and based upon an impression of the ease with which database entries and database queries can be constructed. In order to use the full facilities of the language you are into 'real programming'.[26] Indeed, at an advanced level (using modules) it is necessary to consider the procedural aspects of PROLOG (i.e. the order in which the program will do its various sub-tasks).[27]

More seriously, potential users of PROLOG should realise that as with Expert Systems (which are, afterall, often implemented in the language) fundamental matters of historical knowledge are again at issue. PROLOG operates on the principle of 'negation by failure to prove'and is thus only designed for a particular kind of problem; a 'self-contained' world of knowledge. In other words, PROLOG users must treat the knowledge representation as a closed system, where ALL the relevant information can be assumed to be present. The problem and possible answers tend to be strictly defined beforehand. Moreover, PROLOG relationships describe this closed logical system in static terms, and take no account of change. Clearly, the real world with which historians concern themselves is not like this. To be fair, AI researchers are all too well aware of this, as the interest in 'nonmonotonic' reasoning demonstrates. Reasoning, that is, in which new information is not only new but possibly inconsistent with some of the items already present in the database.[28] However, such mechanisms are not yet 'state of the art' and, therefore, without wishing to restrict research into the use of PROLOG as an historical technique, there does seem to be a need to voice caution in order to place the rather extravagent claims of its proponents in some context. To paraphrase one critic; 'much of what we would regard as common sense, involving purpose, cause and effect, process and creativity, could only be represented in PROLOG, if at all, after deep research and with deeper opacity. Isolated formal logic/reasoning is effective only with stark simplifications. It would be sad if historians believed that arguments which they could not express in PROLOG were somehow inadequate'.[29] Try, for instance, creating a system to which one could pose the question; 'Is the Third Reich best understood by a "structuralist" rather than an "intentionalist" approach?'.

Few serious studies of Expert Systems, let alone the recent wave of artificial intelligence writing, contain any references to 'history'; other than to the 'history of AI'. This might be attributed to the underdeveloped 'state of the art' of artificial intelligence, but at the heart of the matter is the nature of history; not the nature of AI. That said, historians should not ignore artificial intelligence or the techniques it offers. Afterall, AI promises to turn the computer into the quintessential artifact of the age because it holds out the promise of totally capturing the intellectual skills unique, until now, to people.[30] Given the present state of AI, however, its immediate usefulness depends on the type of historian we are dealing with. To employ Emmanuel Le Roy Ladurie's metaphor, AI techniques are probably more suited to the needs of 'truffle hunters' than those of 'parachutists'. The former, those supremely professional practioners — who are addicted to their archival source material, and precise and exacting in their methods — will no doubt be attracted by the promise of historical tools that will allow them to find out yet more about highly specialised domains. Parachutists, on the other hand, who range audaciously across time and survey a far broader panorama of the historical landscape may find that AI cannot, as yet, cope with the wide generalisations and deep underlying causes of which they are so fond.[31]

Notes

1. Peter S. Sells, *Expert Systems — A Practical Introduction*, Macmillan, 1985, p. 95.
2. Margaret A. Boden, *Artificial Intelligence and Natural Man*, (second edition), MIT Press, 1987, p. 478.
3. Mike Burton & Nigel Shadbolt, *POP-11 Programming for Artificial Intelligence*, Addison-Wesley, 1987, p. 2.
4. Peter Jackson, *Introduction to Expert Systems*, Addison-Wesley, 1986, p. 221.
5. F. Hayes-Roth, 'Rule-Based Systems', *Communications of the ACM*, 28/9, 1985, pp. 921–932. See also, Patrick Henry Winston, *Artificial Intelligence* (second edition), Addison-Wesley, 1984, pp. 166ff.
6. Michel Godron, *An Introduction to Expert Systems*, McGraw-Hill, 1986, pp. 68ff. Paul E. Lehner, 'Expert Systems for Microcomputers', *Expert Systems*, 2/4, October 1985, pp. 198–297.
7. 'AI for the Office', *Which Computer*, August 1986, p. 66.
8. Boden, *AI and Natural Man*, pp. 492ff. See also Michael Bell, 'Why Expert Systems Fail', *Journal of Operational Research Society*, 7, 1985, pp. 613–619.

9.   Richard Ennals, *Artificial Intelligence: Applications to Logical Reasoning and Historical Research*, Ellis Horwood, 1985, pp. 120ff. Jon Nichol et al., 'Logic Programming and Historical Research', Peter Denley & Deian Hopkin (eds.), *History and Computing*, Manchester University Press, 1987, pp. 198–205. The HIDES project (Historical Document Expert System) developed at the University of Southampton may be the exception which proves the rule.

10.   Karen Gould, 'History Makes a Date with Data', *THES Supplement*, 23 July 1987.

11.   Burton & Shadbolt, *POP-11*, p. 181. The Digital Equipment Corporation market a package (PILOT) which includes not only a variety of shells, but also LISP and PROLOG for those who wish to write their own AI applications.

12.   G Lee et al., 'AI, History and Knowledge Representation', *Computers and the Humanities*, September 1982, pp. 25ff.

13.   Eugene Charniak & Drew McDermott, *Artificial Intelligence*, Addison-Wesley, 1985, pp. 345ff. P J Rogers, *The New History; Theory into Practice*, Historical Association, 1978, pp. 14–16.

14.   Klaus Hildebrand, *Das Dritte Reich*, Oldenbourg, 1987, pp. 188ff.

15.   John Haugeland, *Artificial Intelligence: the Very Idea*, MIT Press, 1985.

16.   Michel Gondron, *An Introduction to Expert Systems*, McGraw-Hill, 1986, p. 52.

17.   Lewis Wolpert, 'The Tree of Knowledge', *Guardian*, 24 December, 1986

18.   Philip J. Davis & Reuben Hersh, *Descartes' Dream: the World According to Mathematics*, Harvester, 1986, pp. 13ff. Burton & Shadbolt, *POP-11*, p. 4.

19.   Jackson, *Expert Systems*, p. 204.

20.   Peter Adman, 'Computers and History', Sebastian Rahtz (ed), *Information Technology in the Humanities: Tools, Techniques and Applications*, Ellis Horwood, 1987, p. 103.

21.   Masoud Yazdani (ed), *New Horizons in Educational Computing*, Ellis-Horwood, 1984.

22.   Wendy Hall, 'The Art of Programming', in Rahtz, *Information Technology in the Humanities*, pp. 80–91.

23.   It has been suggested (Boden) that arguments in favour of one programming language rather than another may merely reflect a 'social phenonomenon'. For those interested in trying a procedural language, a Mac version of POP-11 (AlphaPOP) is available from Cognitive Applications Ltd., Brighton, BN1 2LR. (0273) 821600.

24.   See for example Joaquim Carvahlo, 'Expert Systems and Community Reconstruction Studies', in Peter Denley, Stefan Fogelvik and Charles Harvey (eds.), *History and Computing II*, Manchester University Press, 1988.

25.   Adapted from Jean B. Rogers, *A Prolog Primer*, Addison-Wesley, 1986, Section 6.

26.   Jackson, *Expert Systems*, pp. 184–5.

27.   Rogers, *Prolog*, pp. 163ff.

28.   Boden, *AI and Natural Man*, p. 494.

29.   John Self, *Computers in Education: a Critical Evaluation of Educational Software*, Harvester, 1985, pp. 105–6. See also; M Yazdani & A Narayanan (eds), *Artificial Intelligence: Human Effects*, Ellis-Horwood, 1984, pp. 143–156.

30.   J Rothfeder, *Minds over Matter; a New Look at Artificial Intelligence*, Harvester, 1985, p. 69.

31.   David Cannadine, Review of Lawrence Stone's 'The Past and Present Revisited' (Routledge, 1987), *Guardian*, 6 November, 1987.

Expert Systems and Community Reconstruction Studies

Community reconstruction studies: the computational needs

The main characteristic of community reconstruction studies, from the data processing point of view, is that the information dealt with consists mainly of references to persons, gathered in different sources, that must be linked together in order to obtain life stories or partial life stories of individuals in the community, which are then subject to quantitative and/or non-quantitative analysis. Normally, family reconstruction from parish registers plays a central part in the community reconstruction efforts, but a wide variety of sources can be incorporated.

The nominative nature of the information and the fact that several different sources are being used pose difficult problems of database design. Normally the database consists of a number of files, each with a certain type of record. In most cases there is a file for each type of source material (baptisms, marriages, deaths, wills, etc.) and records in the files correspond to individual documents. Persons appear in these records by their name and some additional information that varies from one type of source to the other. This database organisation raises two very important problems: nominal linkage of records and intensive exploration of the linked database.

Nominal record linkage is a classic problem in historical computing, and considerable literature exists on the subject.[1] The purpose of record linking is to produce some sort of index of the database that gives for each person in the files all the records in which that person occurs. Due to homonomy and name variations in the sources record linking is a very complex operation. When it is done by hand the historian examines all the information available using residence, profession, filiation and other variables to decide if two records correspond or not to the same person. Consistency tests are also made to detect erroneous linking and false duplication of records. Reproducing this by a computer program is not easy. It is an accepted fact that there is no straightforward algorithm able to deal with the complexities of record linking.

But the software difficulties of the historian do not end with record linking. As far as nominative reconstruction studies are concerned, demands on the linked database can be very complex and involve manipulation of relationships between records of all the files. For instance, if a database constructed from parish registers is used for illegitimacy studies, it is important that the computer should be able to allow the researcher to explore the network of kinship ties linking together bastard bearers. In general the historian recognises in a nominal database the existence of links among individuals, like geographical proximity, kinship ties or social affinity that are hard to express using conventional databases. The growing importance in social research of network analysis, even if implemented by informal methods, will increase the need for software that explores the complex ways in which real world data is interconnected.

The expert system approach

The sophistication of the historian's demands on a database system must be matched by software solutions that are necessarily complex. It is not always realised by historians and by the computer staff of institutions where historians work that most of the problems posed by nominative databases require state of the art software techniques. One software design architecture that could be very useful in the context described above is expert systems technology.

An expert system has been defined as '. . . a computer system that encapsulates specialist knowledge about a particular domain of expertise and is capable of making intelligent decisions within that domain'.[2] This type of computer program was developed for areas where the human expert's method of operation was hard to translate in a standard, algorithmic way (medical diagnosis, for instance). The idea of using artificial intelligence techniques to deal with the difficult problems of record linkage is an accepted fact, even if the expression 'artificial intelligence' is not always used.[3] However expert system technology has advantages over alternative techniques whenever a general solution is intended and not just a partial one. The characteristics of expert systems that are of interest to the designer of historical software systems are:

—   The capacity to work with uncertain information and uncertain rules of reasoning.
—   The rule-based architecture that allows the behaviour of the system to be modified by the addition, deletion or modification of rules.

The importance of the capacity to work with uncertainties is clear: historical information is sometimes uncertain in the sense that the historian might not be able to say that some information is true or not, but still be able to say that it is 'likely to be true' or 'unlikely to be true'. On the other hand, rules that apply to historical data can also be expressed in terms of likelihood, and not in the standard true or false boolean approach. Expert systems have the capacity to deal with this type of knowledge because it was found to be an important part of expert reasoning in general. Several formalisms are used, like Bayesean statistics or fuzzy sets theory, to express and manipulate uncertain information and uncertain rules.

The rule-based approach, on the other hand, allows for easier construction of a complex system and for generality. Rule-based programs are programs that incorporate knowledge about a domain by allowing the system designer, with the help of the domain expert, to express that knowledge as rules, instead of algorithmic steps. The system separates the 'facts', or information about a specific problem, from the 'rules' which are knowledge of a higher level about the problem domain. For example: 'a person named John Smith died in 1756' and 'on the 5th of October 1675 Mary, wife of Robert Smith, gave birth to John' are facts; 'people don't live usually more than 90 years' is a rule. This means that knowledge is treated by the system as a special kind of data that regulates the way the program deals with the 'facts' of the real world. The system in itself consists of a general mechanism (called the inferencing engine) that uses the rules to manipulate the facts. Rules can be added, deleted, or modified until the behaviour of the system over some test data is considered satisfactory. In this particular application the 'rules' represent the historian's knowledge about persons, communities, etc, and the 'facts' consist of the data transcribed from the sources. This process is simpler and closer to the way historians work than the traditional method of designing and debugging a traditional computer program. The rule approach, on the other hand, provides generality because it is easy to shift from a community (or region, or country) to another because all that is needed is to change the rules as required. The program in itself remains the same.

To conclude, expert systems have two main advantages: they provide a sophisticated formalism for representing the way historians deal with data, which is unavailable or hard to implement, in other system architectures; and secondly, dividing the rules from the data, they allow for gradual fine-tuning of the system, easy transportation to other situations, and also for the latter incorporation of sources other than original ones.

The structure of the system and the place of PROLOG

Current expert systems technology is still rather recent and development tools are not widely available, especially in institutions where historians work. Producing an expert system for community reconstruction studies would require a very specialised programming staff. A further complication of historical applications is that the system to be constructed must have the capacity of dealing with very large amounts of data, or, in other words, it has to have sophisticated database capabilities. Only very recently has the artificial intelligence community begun to face problems that require expert systems techniques applied to very large databases.[4]

These difficulties should not prevent some preliminary work being done. Even if the trend seems to be that artificial intelligence tools are becoming more and more available, it is always necessary to know to what extent the specific requirements of the historian fit into the commercially produced technology. The question is both technical and formal. The technical problems will arise from the capacity of building a system that is efficient in dealing quickly with large amounts of data and rules, in as much as this depends on aspects like computer speed, storage capacity and specialised development tools. The formal problems are related to the possibility to translate the historical data and the historians' ways of working with it into the framework of expert system's formalisms. While the technical aspects are mostly outside the historians' control, the formal aspects are not. In face of the current difficulties of obtaining appropriate and transportable software it is worthwile investigating the possibilities of this formalism even if a fully developed and self contained system is still far away.

With these considerations as background a small scale project was begun. The aim of this project is to test the capacity of the expert system approach to deal with the information processing problems posed by a community reconstruction study.

The project concentrates on the basic modules that actually require artificial intelligence techniques and relies on a traditional database to manage the information and to provide data entry and report generation environments. PROLOG was chosen as a development language for these modules, and conversion programmes were written to convert data from database format to PROLOG and vice-versa.

In this context the user works with the database for data input, error checking, report generation, etc., and exports data to the PROLOG programmes for complex analysis using artificial intelligence techniques. The results can be read back into the database. Such a hybrid system is usually more difficult to use than a complete program. But it is much easier to develop, and so a new technology can be tested with a fraction of the cost of building a full-featured system. Experience has proven that a relational database can be used in conjunction with PROLOG with little formal interfacing problems, due to basic isomorphisms in data representation. If a working and convincing prototype is built in this way it would be less difficult to make it evolve to a full system.

The PROLOG modules will cover record linking, life-story reconstruction, genealogical analysis and network reconstruction. They provide the basic inferencing mechanisms and rules that will accept for each new application the necessary case dependent rules and data. This implies a general formalism for data representation and for rule formulation in which specific data and knowledge are translated.

Data representation, rule hierarchy and the inference engine

The built-in inference engine of PROLOG is far too simple and primitive to cope with the mechanics of record linking. A more complex control structure has to be built on top of PROLOG and a hierarchy of rules is used to encapsulate several levels of knowledge.

The internal data representation obeys a simple formalism based on semantic networks where objects are classified in types and are described by a sequence of properties. Relations between two objects are labelled by type and value. Dependency exists between classes of objects: 'persons' is a class of objects that includes various other type of objects (brides, grooms, infants, witnesses, etc). For example: a bride in a marriage document is described as an object of type 'person' with certain values for the attributes that a person can have (name, age, place of residence), and the relations between her and the rest of the persons involved in the act have a type (kinship) and values (daughter, wife).

The atomic character of the representation is necessary to achieve generality but it is not necessary actually to input the data in this way. Data is converted from a database, as explained above, and stored in PROLOG in a format close to the original records. A first level of rules, called 'normalisation rules', tells PROLOG where the various types of objects in the records are, where (in what fields) their attributes are, and what types of relationships between the objects described can be inferred. The 'normalisation rules' provide the link between the variable database format that is used to collect and check the data and the formalism used by the inferencing mechanisms and the higher level rules. This first level of rules, although very simple to formulate, gives depth to the data in the sense that by classifying the items of information in the database records by object types they allow the system to use rules in an intelligent way. Higher rules can be formulated to encapsulate generic knowledge about persons, about certain classes of person or even, if necessary, about specific individuals. This has proved an extremely powerful mechanism in allowing concise expression of knowledge.

Once the normalisation of the data is done in this way record linking is the next step since all the other modules require a linked database. The inferencing engine of the record linking module regulates the classical 'generate and test' operation. The rules necessary for this step are of two types. The first type is used in the 'generation' phase and must produce 'candidates' for linking. These rules express knowledge of the type: 'to find the baptism of a bride in a marriage record search in the years between the year of marriage minus 12 and the year of marriage minus 60'. Rules are formulated according to the number of sources and the available information. Every time a rule like this succeeds a possible link is generated and stored eventually with an associated probability factor. The inferencing engine takes a reference to a person and applies these rules to generate all the candidates, and then applies the rules again to the candidates generated until no more persons are generated. The end of the generation procedure is a linking graph where the nodes are the candidates and the edges the possible links. Then the second type of linking rules is used. These take the graph and check for inconsistencies (for instance the existence of two baptisms) or produce further alterations in the strength of possible links, including deleting them, according to the graph configuration or consideration of other variables. The purpose of this second type of rules is to return a complete graph, that is to say, one where every candidate is linked to every other one with no inconsistencies, or to break the original graph into completed subgraphs (which is the frequent case where the first step collected candidates that really corresponded to more than one person). The result of linking, if completed successfully, is stored in the database as a special kind of facts that are used by all the other modules.

The rest of the modules are much more straightforward manipulations of the results of linking. They allow for manipulation of the linked database for the most common classes of queries. But here again the power of a declarative language like PROLOG and the level of abstraction provided by the data representation scheme prove to be very powerful mechanisms. The network reconstruction module, for instance, is nothing more than an application of graph searching techniques to the linked database. A special set of rules, called 'network reconstruction rules', express knowledge of the type 'if a person is godfather of a child infer a relationship of type "solidarity link" and value "spiritual kin" between that person and the father of the child baptised'. Other rules can cover economic relations, neighbourhood, or whatever can be inferred from the sources present. Using these rules and the linking information, the system can produce the networks in a form compatible with network analysis programmes or statistical packages (as network matrices, for instance).

Conclusion

The computational needs of community reconstruction studies require sophisticated software systems in order to solve the nominal record linking problem and explore, in a interesting manner, the linked database. Expert system technology has the required characteristics to provide such a system even if in the current state of the art problems of inefficiency might be important. Research centres involved in this type of historical research using computers should seriously consider this type of technique, as the converging paths of expert systems technology and database technology are likely to produce significant performance improvements in the near future. The ideal user environment would be an expert system front end to a database, with the overall characteristics of the one briefly described here, but with the interface between the two transparent to the user. Until this ideal becomes possible there is much that can be done with more rudimentary methods in order to have a closer understanding of how can the historian's knowledge and data be efficiently formalised in an expert systems framework.

Notes

The research described in this paper was partially done while on a grant from the Portuguese Instituto Nacional de Investigacao Cientifica (INIC). I am greatly indebted to Prof. Ernesto Costa of the Department of Electronics of the University of Coimbra for years of guidance in artificial intelligence techniques and literature.
1.   For a recent survey see G. Bouchard, R. Roy and B. Casgrain, *Reconstitution automatique des familles. Le système SOREP*, Centre Universitaire de Recherches sur les Populations, Chicoutimi, Canada, 1985, 2 vols.
2.   Richard Forsyth, *Expert Systems, Principles and Case Studies*, 1984.
3.   See Mark Skolnick, 'The resolution of ambiguities in record linkage', in E. A. Wrigley, ed., *Identifying People in The Past*, 1973; Gian Pierro Zarri, 'Constructing and Utilizing Large Fact Databases Using Artificial Intelligence Techniques', in Kerschberg, ed., *Expert Database Systems*. Proceedings from the First International Workshop, 1986, and Caroline Bourlet and Jean-Luc Minel, 'A Declarative System for Setting up a Prosopographical Database' in P. R. Denley and D. R. Hopkin, eds., *History and Computing*, Manchester, 1987.
4.   See Kerschberg, ed., *Expert Database Systems*. Proceedings from the First International Workshop, 1986.

V.

Quantitative Analysis

Computing the Unmeasurable: Estimating Missing Values in Legislative Roll-Call Analysis

1. The search for lost evidence: common ground for quantitative history and epigraphy

Introductory courses into ancient history familiarised many of us with epigraphy, the art of reconstructing fragmented texts by connecting single words or even letters to a complete wording. The basic message of this early experience was simple, although a bit contradictory: the vestiges of history are incomplete but reconstructable if we utilise knowledge of past societies. In every culture, subculture, organisation, or social group accepted norms and rules reduce the logically possible variation of expression and behaviour to a set of recurrent alternatives. The more rigorous were such norms and the better our knowledge of them, the more reliable are inferences from the known to the unknown likely to be. To return to my initial example: it is routine in epigraphy to reconstruct the *cursus honorum* of a Roman praetor if only small fragments of his epitaph are left, whereas it would be less promising to try the same with a piece of poetry or free prose on the basis of such spare evidence.

2. Legislative roll-calls: a case particuarly affected by missing values

I was struck by the analogy to epigraphy when my own studies confronted me with the methodological problem of missing values in quantitative analyses of historical data. This problem is frequently met, less frequently reported and scarcely ever systematically handled in quantitative historical social research.[1] It turned out to be an unescapable challenge in my research into legislative roll-calls.

These data are typically used for spatial analyses of policy dimensions in parliaments. For this purpose series of roll-calls are needed to identify the main policy dimensions in a legislature and to allocate the positions taken by representatives on these policy dimensions. A variety of scaling techniques are used for this purpose — from Guttman-scaling and its probabilistic variants to multidimensional scaling and factor analysis.[2] But summary measures such as scale-scores or factor-scores are particularly affected by missing values. The absence of only one parliamentary actor for a single vote will put this problem on the researcher's agenda. Factor analysis requires a positive-semidefinite coefficients matrix as entry-data; such a matrix is not necessarily obtained if the variance and covariance are calculated from different numbers of cases. For Guttman-scaling, in spite of some forty years of experience, an acceptable method of processing missing data has yet to be found and agreed upon.[3] On the other hand most studies into legislative behaviour are severely affected by missing values. The data I collected or reanalysed support this statement: in the Frankfurt National Assembly an average of about 48 per cent of votes per representative were missing, in the Paris National Assembly of 1848/49 this portion attained 27 per cent, and in the British House of Commons during the 1840s a tremendous 66 per cent.[4] Therefore, before I could make a systematic use of this data, it was inevitable that I should apply and eventually develop an appropriate routine for handling missing values; 'appropriate' meant according to my introductory statement that such a routine had to be isomorphic for the basic patterns of roll-call behaviour.

3. The empirical content of nonvoting: avoidance or nonavailability?

This required a rigorous definition of the causes of 'missing values'. If one accepts 'yes' and 'no' as truly valid reactions in a roll-call — an interpretation which is not uncontestable but followed here for reasons of simplicity — by far the most important reason for the occurence of missing values in legislative roll-call data was the absence of representatives. Decisive for the evaluation and treatment of absences is, whether they appear at random, whether they are correlated with some background chracteristics of the representatives, or whether they have to be interpreted as abstentions — i. e. an intended avoidance of a political decision. In this context it is helpful that the reasons why a representative did not vote were sometimes recorded in the sources. In the Frankfurt and Paris national assemblies of 1848/49 we could distinguish five types of 'missing values'. I expected each of them to be connected in a specific way with demographic background variables and political positions of the representatives.

1. The representative was not a member of parliament when a vote was taken. The number of absences due to non-membership may be correlated with those characteristics of a representative which have an influence on his 'availability' for the mandate, as for example his profession and place of residence.[5] But even for this type of a 'missing value' strategic nonvoting cannot be excluded. An example would be the members' previous resignation from parliament because he wants to demonstrate opposition against former decisions or to avoid impending conflicts of loyalty.

2. The representative was absent with excuse at the moment of the vote. This is assumed to have happened if the representative could not for a longer period participate in parliamentary decision making because of illness, professional or personal duties.

3. The representative was absent without excuse. Absences caused by competing duties of committee membership, the coordination of the decision making process, and other constraints in the personal time budget of the representative fit this category. Additionally the avoidance of voting in precarious situations or about controversial subjects are assumed to fall in this category. The classification of individual cases depends on the relevance

of the latter motive: whether unexcused absences should be treated as missing values or as a behavioural option in the strategy of voting.

4. The representative was present but did not vote. The last premise is certainly true for abstention, which can be included in the variants of missing values only under a very limited definition of the concept. In many studies abstentions are being treated as valid values, somewhere placed between 'yes' and 'no'. Empirically they pose only a minor problem, because abstentions were stigmatised by public opinion or even excluded in the standing orders of some parliaments. In the Frankfurt National Assembly, where abstentions were formally permitted, only in 0·2 per cent of all valid votes did representatives make use of this option.

5. The representative may have been present but his vote was not recorded. Cases were observed where the staff of the assemblies failed to record the vote of a representative who is known to have voted. In this case we have missing values in the strictest sense of the phrase. Fortunately this type of missing value is rarely found in legislative voting data.

The typology of missing values developed here can also be read as set of hypotheses about the determinants of parliamentary participation. Non-random absences would reveal indicators for a study of the cohesiveness of parliamentary leadership groups and the fulfilment of intra-legislative norms. We followed this strategy of research in an analysis of intra-parliamentary participation in the Frankfurt and Paris constituent assemblies of 1848/49. Three participation indices were constructed and used as dependent variables in multiple classification analyses.[6] The first participation index was the number of votes taken when a representative was enrolled in parliament. This is a simple indicator of the continuity of parliamentary membership. Two further indices were constructed: these were the proportions of excused and unexcused absences relative to all votes that took place during the membership of a representative.

The results of our study can be summarised briefly. In the Frankfurt National Assembly we found strong correlations between regional origin, profession, committee-membership and the continuity of membership in parliament. The results show that keeping a mandate was dependent on the degree to which the representative became socialised into his parliamentary role and participated in pre-existing networks of the political opposition movement. Another important factor was his loyalty towards the Frankfurt assembly and its attempt of state-building by constitution-making. In the French constituent assembly unexcused absences were strongly influenced by the location of the residences and the constituencies of the representatives: those members of the French 'classe politique' who lived in Paris and held mandates in a provincial *departement* were significantly more frequently absent than those who resided in their provincial constituencies. This difference could be explained by the necessity for the metropolitan élites to maintain their provincial power-basis and to keep in contact with the local dignitaries. Before local and national elections and during the presidential campaign of November 1848 the number of unexcused absences rose dramatically.[7]

While I do not want to go into further details of these substantial results two findings should be kept in mind. Firstly in both assemblies missing values were not distributed randomly among representatives and votes. Secondly, we found no indication that absences can be interpreted as abstentions. Both findings are of importance if one has to decide what method of handling missing values should be applied.

4. Trying to cure an evil by creating a bigger one: pairwise and listwise deletion of missing values

Pairwise and listwise deletion of missing values are standard options in statistical computer packages. Both methods follow a strategy of ignorance, and both require a random distribution of missing values. Pairwise deletion of missing values uses only cases with complete data on each pair of variables correlated regardless of whether the cases have missing values for other variables. Listwise deletion of missing values removes all cases where at least one item alone is missing from the data set. Typically the methods used in legislative roll-call analysis are variants of these options designed to minimise the negative effects of both standard methods of handling missing values. However, a systematic description or even a compulsory codification of these techniques is not found in the literature, although roll-call data is particularly affected by the problem of missing values. The introductory text-books on methods of legislative roll-call analysis deal with this problem only in a marginal and unsystematic way.[8]

Pairwise deletion of missing values is seldom used in its pure form because methods of transforming roll-call data into scales — like Guttman techniques and factor analysis — are not compatible with this method. Sometimes Riker's 'Coefficient of Significance' is used as a variant of pairwise deletion.[9] Riker's criterion for the selection of votes is their 'importance', which is conceptualised (1) as the number of members present and voting on a specific subject, and (2) as the degree to which the outcome of the issue is contested, expressed in the proportion of the 'yes' and 'no' votes. The application of Riker's Coefficient of Significance reduces the problem of missing values (without — of course — eliminating it) by excluding votes with many missing values from the analysis. It is doubtful, however, if this procedure is an adequate approach to the problem. For example decreasing participation-rates at the end of the day or during meals may have occured even if decisions on important subjects were to be taken. The exclusion of votes according to the rate of participation becomes extremely problematic if certain groups of representatives are absent during a series of roll-calls. Our analysis of participation rates have shown that exactly this happens in real world situations. Hence selection of votes according to the criterion of completeness may cause distortions in the analysis of policy dimensions which are identified by voting analyses and systematic biases in the population under study. Formal methods of selecting votes like Riker's Coefficient of Significance, however, should be preferred to approaches which exclude votes without giving any reasonable criterion of selection or decide on the basis of purely intuitive evaluation.[10]

The method of listwise deletion of missing values is not used in its pure form for voting analysis because the consequences would be disastrous. If only those representatives who voted on every possible occasion at the two constituent assemblies were included in the analysis, the number of valid cases would be reduced to four in each parliament. Strictly applied, listwise deletion of missing values is unsuitable for the majority of representative bodies. As an alternative it is sometimes proposed to include only those representatives whose number of missing values is below a free determined minimal value. Following this proposition, however, two already familiar problems appear: first, it is difficult to find an objective criterion for the proportion of missing values which would determine inclusion; second, it is reasonable to assume that participation varies non-randomly among different categories of representatives. Hence, the selection of cases according to their completeness may also cause systematic biases.

In her study of the House of Commons in 1861 Valerie Cromwell tried to avoid such distortions by creating subgroups of representatives with different participation rates.[11] She organised all cases according to the rate of missing values hierarchically and then formed ten overlapping subgroups of 100 representatives each. Subsequently multidimensional scaling was used to identify political positions of the representatives. These analyses were made separately for every subgroup.

I have my doubts, however, as to whether it is advisable to divide a parliament into artificial units which are not derived from its political structure and which are biased to an unknown degree. The interpretation of results will turn out to be difficult because different results among the subgroups may be caused by varying participation rates or by the different composition of subpopulations.[12] It is interesting to note that even after adopting this sampling strategy, Cromwell only published results for the 100 representatives with the lowest rate of missing values.

5. How a dead conservative turns into a posthumous liberal: replacing missing values by a neutral value

Estimation procedures offer alternatives to listwise or pairwise deletion of missing data. The advantages of an 'imputation' of missing values are obvious: (1) More extensive use of the data set can be made if cases or variables are not discarded because some information is missing. (2) Scaling procedures which demand a complete data matrix can be applied if estimated values for missing evidence are specified.

While the statistical literature and computer packages offer a number of estimation methods, only the standard options are considered here. The quality of the different estimation methods will be evaluated by the factor scores of the main factor found in a factor analysis of a sample of 98 roll-calls in the Frankfurt National Assembly. The main factor proved to be closely related to the left-right dimension of voting cleavages. We were able to use the variable party-membership as an external criterion to evaluate the quality of the estimation because parliamentary parties in the Frankfurt National Assembly were organised on a left-right spectrum too.

Graph 1   *The Distribution of Representatives on the Right-Left Scale*

After Replacement of Missing Values by the Mean

```
                              H
                              H
                              H
                              H                    EACH "H"
                              HH                  REPRESENTS
                              HH                      16
                             HHH  HH               COUNT(S)
                         HHH HHHHHHHHH
                         HHHHHHHHHHHHH
                   HHHHHHHHHHHHHHHHHHHHHHH
            L----------------------------U
```

```
              EACH "-" ABOVE =        .1500
                           L=      -2.4000
                           U=       1.9500

                                 MAXIMUM        1.2724280
                                 MINIMUM       -1.8530500
                                 RANGE          3.1254780
                                 VARIANCE        .3916139
NUMBER OF DISTINCT VALUES .       759   ST.DEV.         .6257906
NUMBER OF VALUES COUNTED. .       814   (Q3-Q1)/2       .4121415
NUMBER OF VALUES NOT COUNTED        0   MX.ST.SC.      2.03
                                        MN.ST.SC.     -2.96

LOCATION ESTIMATES
                  MEAN          .0000000    ST.ERROR
                  MEDIAN       0.0000000    .0219339
                  MODE         0.0000000    .0048902
```

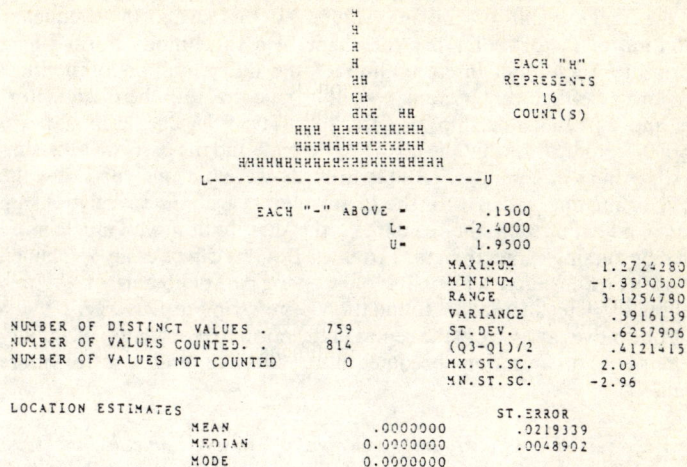

After Estimation of Missing Values by Stepwise Regression

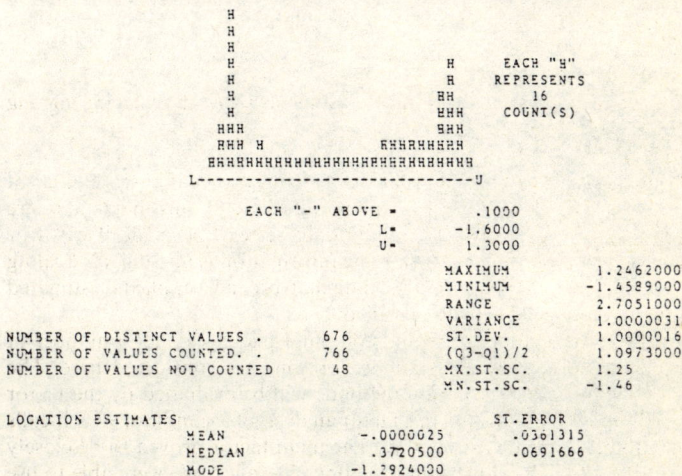

```
                   H
                   H
                   H
                   H                    H      EACH "H"
                   H                    H     REPRESENTS
                   H                   HH         16
                   H                  HHH      COUNT(S)
                 HHH                  HHH
                 HHH H             HHHHHHHH
             HHHHHHHHHHHHHHHHHHHHHHHHHHHHHHH
            L----------------------------U
```

```
              EACH "-" ABOVE =        .1000
                           L=      -1.6000
                           U=       1.3000

                                 MAXIMUM        1.2462000
                                 MINIMUM       -1.4589000
                                 RANGE          2.7051000
                                 VARIANCE       1.0000031
NUMBER OF DISTINCT VALUES .       676   ST.DEV.        1.0000016
NUMBER OF VALUES COUNTED. .       766   (Q3-Q1)/2      1.0973000
NUMBER OF VALUES NOT COUNTED       48   MX.ST.SC.      1.25
                                        MN.ST.SC.     -1.46

LOCATION ESTIMATES
                  MEAN        -.0000025    ST.ERROR
                  MEDIAN       .3720500    .0361315
                  MODE       -1.2924000    .0691666
```

The replacement of a missing value by the mean of the variable or another 'neutral' value may be considered the most conservative estimation method.[13] This judgement seems to be supported by the empirical evidence: after the replacement of missing values by the mean, the frequency distribution of factor-scores has the shape of a three-modal form which conforms to traditional interpretation of the differentiation of political camps into a 'left', a 'center', and a 'right'. The correlation between factor-scores and party-membership is acceptable: The ETA-coefficient takes a value of 0·77, indicating that the factor-score-scale and the party membership have something in common. Doubts arise, however, if one correlates the number of missing values with the factor-scores: a nonlinear relationship appears, indicating that the 'center' of the distribution was much more affected by missing values than the extremes. But this can be easily 'explained away' with an allusion to lack of discipline on the part of liberals, or — if one insists on a stricter theoretical foundation — referring to Duverger's thesis that as one moves away from the centre of the normative structure of a polity the units of organisation become more effective and control more centralised.[14]

Table 1   *The Effect of a Replacement of Missing Values by the Mean on the Localisation of Representatives on the Right-Left Scale*

Fraktion "Donnersberg" (Extreme Left)

Name	Number of Absences	Factor Score after a Replacement of Missing Values by the Mean	Factor Score after a Replacement of Missing Values by Estimated Values
A. Thieme	94	.11	-1.29
A. Ruge	91	.14	-1.28
F. J. Richter	80	.33	-1.27
M. Werner	50	-.44	-1.27
E.F.F. Schmidt	40	-.29	-1.20
N. Titus	29	-.72	-1.20
E.W. Zimmermann	18	-.59	-1.35
A. Boczek	10	-.74	-1.27

Fraktion "Café Milani" (Extreme Right)

Name	Number of Absences	Factor Score after a Replacement of Missing Values by the Mean	Factor Score after a Replacement of Missing Values by Estimated Values
H.A.E. v. Auerswald	93	-.02	.99
C.L.v. Bruck	91	-.07	1.11
E. Roß	86	-.03	1.07
F. Egger	57	.24	1.01
M.v. Schwerin	50	.65	1.09
E.H.v. Flottwell	42	.66	1.14
J.J.I. v. Döllinger	28	.77	1.13
W.C.F. Grävell	17	.71	1.02
W. Schultze	10	.96	1.10

But further doubts arise if one compares the factor-scores of representatives of antagonistic political parties. The results of Table 1 show that representatives of the left or of the right who voted only irregularly tend to be placed near the centre of the distribution, while their colleagues who were seldom absent at votes, were placed near the extreme left or the extreme right according to their party affiliations. The paradoxical effect of using this technique is particularly striking in the case of a hard line reactionary, von Auerswald, whose violent death during an insurrection in September 1848 removed him from parliament. In this example the use of 'neutral' value in the roll-call analysis turns an arch conservative into posthumous liberal. On the other hand Arnold Ruge, coauthor with Karl Marx, pronounced leftist, and very negligent parliamentarian approaches von Auerswald's position on the right-left continuum from the other side of the political spectrum. Clearly these 'findings' are sheer nonsense and the artifact of an estimating procedure which assumes implicitly and erroneously that absences can be interpreted as abstentions. This assumption should be rejected as our analysis of non-voting patterns demonstrates. The case of von Auerswald is a particularly macabre example of the transformation of involuntary non-voting into a 'moderate' political stance. Standard software packages and introductions into data analysis do not provide suffecent warnings against the possible distortions caused by unsuitable missing values techniques. Fatal consequences will very probably occur although seemingly plausible and statistically valid results are obtained at an aggregate level.

6. Intuitive regression: constructing contrived items

The misleading assumption of the neutrality of absences should not be made if we estimate each single value separately on the basis of the votes cast by each representative. This is a reconstructive imputation instead of an 'estimate in the lump' procedure. In the first category falls the method of 'contrived items' William O. Aydelotte applied in his study into voting behaviour in the British House of Commons 1841–1847. His data can be considered as a striking example for the problem of missing values in roll-call analysis: at 90 per cent of the 1,029 votes during this period less than 300 representatives of the maximum 658 members of the House of Commons were present.[15]

In a first step Aydelotte calculated a correlation matrix of all 186 votes he used in his study. He then formed pairs of roll-calls if they met a minimal criterion of similarity of Yule's Q = 0·65. Subgroups of items which met this criterion of similarity were then further combined to cumulative scales. To construct contrived items the roll-calls forming a scale were ordered according to their 'difficulty', i.e. the proportion of negative votes. Those roll-calls were considered to form a contrived item that had approximately the same difficulty. In a last step it was checked as to whether a representative voted predominantly with 'yes' or 'no' at votes which formed a contrived item. In the first case a positive, in the second case a negative value was attributed to the contrived item as a whole. The missing values were omitted in this final operation. The method used by Aydelotte has the advantage of significantly reducing the rate of missing values. The probability that valid values exist for none of the roll-calls which form a contrived item decreases dependent on the number of votes which were used for the construction of these summary measures.

Nevertheless missing values appear sometimes even if representatives participated frequently in roll-calls. This is the case if they were absent at all votes forming a contrived item or if the number of their valid 'yes' or 'no' votes in a contrived item was identical. On the other side a score may be attributed to a 'contrived item' even if the empirical evidence is very small, in extreme cases if the representative took part only in one of the votes forming the contrived item. Another serious objection is the enormous work this method requires. Aydelotte had to make 51·000 visual comparisons to form the contrived items. Twenty-four different scales had to be constructed manually. Furthermore, the criteria for the inclusion of votes in the scales and contrived items vary according to substantive and technical considerations. Changing selection criteria make it difficult, however, to interpret results even if the criteria are precisely documented. Last but not least, the contrived item technique is not neutral to results. Originally it was devised to improve the reproducibility of scales by eliminating idiosyncratic responses or random measurement error. Although it may be desirable to improve the quality of scales it is not satisfying that the reproducibility or scalability of a set of items is influenced to an unknown degree by the missing value technique applied.

7. Estimating missing values by stepwise multiple regression in BMDP

These reservations about Aydelotte's 'intuitive regression' motivated us to apply a more formal method of estimating missing values, combining the advantages of a casewise replacement of missing values with stricter criteria for selecting estimators and calculating estimates. Because SPSS (Statistical Package for the Social Sciences) is extremely uncomfortable for this purpose, we made use of the subprogram PAM of BMDP (Biomedical Computer Programs), which was designed to fulfil three primary functions:

— to describe the pattern of missing values — including a test of randomness;
— to estimate the covariance and correlation matrices;
— to replace missing values by estimated values.[16]

PAM has different options for estimating invalid values.[17] First using means (an option we have already rejected as unsuitable for our purpose), further, using regression on the variable most highly correlated with a missing variable (SINGLE), regression on a highly correlated set of variables (STEP), or regression on all available variables (REGRESSION). The application of any regression technique requires at least one estimator-variable being highly correlated with the variable having a missing value. The estimation will improve according to the number of equivalent indicators available. This favourable situation is typically given in legislative roll-call analyses. When all the correlations are very low it is usually difficult to improve on the MEAN-option.[18]

The choice of a regression technique is dependent on the multi-collinearity in the data. SINGLE may be appropriate if each variable is highly correlated with another variable and economy is essential. Simple Regression is appropriate when the number of cases is large and there are many large correlations. But too many predictor variables may be used, eventually entailing overfitting. A stepwise procedure is appropriate when the correlation matrix contains clusters of moderate or high correlations. This is the normal situation in legislative roll-call analyses and applied also to our data. It should be considered, however, that STEP requires substantially more computation time than the other methods.

In a stepwise regression the variable that has the highest correlation with the variable having a missing value is chosen first for the regression equitation. The variable chosen next is the one with the highest partial correlation with the dependent variable conditional on the variables already chosen, until all variables with acceptable values are used or a F-to-enter criterion is not satisfied. The linear equation system is solved by pivoting. Pivoting has the advantage that the determinant, the inverse of a matrix and a solution of the equations systems are found at the same time.

To find the best predictors for the regression matrix must be computed. BMDP offers two options for this purpose: COMPLETE and ALLVALUE. COMPLETE uses only those cases in the calculation which have valid values in all variables. This method is eqivalent to a listwise deletion of missing values, an option that we have already rejected as unsuitable in the present case. ALLVALUE uses all valid cases of each variable and a correlation matrix is calculated in every case. For this purpose a Kroneckers Delta is included in the formulas used to compute mean, variance and covariance. The Kroneckers Delta takes the value one if a valid value occurs, otherwise it is zero. With this method estimates of variance and covariance are obtained from considerably more information than with pairwise deletion. To obtain a positive-semi-definite correlation matrix a smoothing-procedure is performed and only the positive eigenvalues and corresponding eigenvectors are used.[19] Obviously the coefficient matrices transformed in this way do not have the same rank as they did previously but all relevant substantial dimensions in the data with an eigenvalue greater than one are preserved and the matrices are now positive semi-definite. The co-variance or the correlation matrix can now be taken as starting points for multivariate analyses and for the estimation of missing values by stepwise multiple regression.

The resulting estimates have metric properties and can be interpreted as the predicted probability of a 'yes' or 'no' vote, conditional upon the other voting behaviour of the representative. By a successive dichotomisation, the estimates can be transformed into the same codes as the valid values. Of course the ambiguities left after the estimation procedure are neglected and omitted by such a transformation.

One problem in the use of ordinary least square (OLS)-techniques in a regression model with binary variables should be mentioned here: the predicted values of the dependent variable need not lie in an interval that is

Table 2   *The Association between Party Affiliation and Left-Right-Scale Scores*

	Party	N	GUTTMAN-SCALE-SCORES x̄	s	FACTOR-SCORES x̄	s	q3 – q1
EXTREME LEFT	Donnersberg	62	0.2	0.4	1.25	0.13	0.03
	Deutscher Hof	54	0.7	1.8	1.25	0.15	0.03
LEFT	Nürnberger Hof	11	2.8	7.4	1.09	0.61	0.10
LEFT CENTER	Westendhall	55	3.6	5.2	1.11	0.48	0.12
	Württemberger Hof	48	7.1	5.3	0.98	0.48	0.32
RIGHT CENTER	Augsburger Hof	54	20.9	5.6	-0.33	0.56	0.74
	Landsberg	45	21.0	5.3	-0.33	0.52	0.75
	Casino	138	23.7	4.5	-0.80	0.47	0.26
EXTREME RIGHT	Pariser Hof	31	22.0	4.0	-0.89	0.34	0.92
	Café Milani	44	24.1	2.0	-1.07	0.13	0.12
	No Party	234	16.3	9.3	-0.24	0.88	1.70
	Total	771	14.7	10.6	0.00	1.00	2.20
	ETA (Representatives without Party-Affiliation Excluded)		0.81			0.81	
	ETA (Representatives without Party-Affiliation Included)		0.92			0.92	

LEFT-RIGHT-SCALE

compatible with the interpretation that they are estimated probabilities,[20] i.e. 'probabilities' greater than one and lesser than zero may occur. This undesired property of an estimate may be prevented by a logit or a probit transformation. But practically the reservations against an application of an

OLS*technique are not prohibitive if two heuristic criteria are fulfilled: The number of cases should be greater than 30 and the marginals of the variables should not be extremely shaped.[21] Both criteria are easily fulfilled in most roll-call analyses.

Another aspect is the quality of the estimates after dichotomisation. To test the validity of the estimation we correlated the 'right-left scale', obtained after missing values had been replaced by stepwise multiple regression, with the criterion variable 'party membership'. The ETA-coefficient of 0·92 was clearly higher than the value obtained after a replacement of missing values by the mean. The scale scores for the representatives are now correctly placed on the political continuum according to their party membership. Similarly good results were obtained in a study of voting behaviour in the Paris Assemblée Nationale Constituante.

Stepwise regression is at least equivalent to the method of contrived items suggested by Aydelotte: his main scale correlates highly with a right-left index constructed analogously in our study of legislative voting behaviour in the Frankfurt National Assembly (r = 0·95).[22]

8. Imputation by stepwise regression: the best method of handling missing values in legislative roll-call analysis

This discussion of the different methods for handling missing values should have made it clear that pairwise and listwise deletion and the common variants of these methods used in legislative roll-calls analysis will probably cause distortions and biases. Missing values are not distributed randomly among votes and subgroups of representatives. It is just as misleading to assume that absences in roll-calls can be explained generally by social predispositions as 'availability' or by political motives. It could be demonstrated that absences should not be interpreted as abstentions. Estimation methods for missing values which are based on this premise produce paradoxical results if scale scores are derived from voting-data. Political orientations of representatives and the rates of their participation are different dimensions of legislative behaviour. Accordingly it is not advisable to replace missing values by the mean or another neutral value.

The most suitable methods are those which reconstruct each missing value from existing information and rely on the high multicollinearity of voting data. The validity of estimates by the method of contrived items, such as that suggested by Aydelotte, and the method of stepwise multiple regression are of equivalent quality. However, given the necessary amount of work and the criterion of replicability, regression analysis is superior.[23] One should keep in mind, however, that the reconstruction of missing values from existent information may also cause distortions of the data, even if the consequences are not as serious as those caused by other methods: a complete parliament is simulated which never existed in historical reality. Insofar, however, as the choice of the best method to treat missing values is always a choice between evils, it is advisable to adopt a set of explicit criteria which can be used to assess the implications of such wickedness and to follow a strategy of imputation that is isomorphic for the basic patterns of roll-call behaviour.

Notes

1.   See H. Best and R. Kuznia, 'Die Behandlung fehlender Werte bei der seriellen Analyse namentlicher Abstimmungen, oder: Wege zur Therapie des horror vacui', *Historical Social Research*, 26, 1983, pp. 49–82.

2.   D. MacRae, *Issues and Parties in Legislative Voting. Methods of Statistical Analysis*, New York, 1970.

3.   J. P. McIver and E. G. Carmines, *Unidimensional Scaling*, London and Beverly Hills, 1981, pp. 64–65.

4.   See H. Best, *Struktur und Handeln parlamentarischer Führungsgruppen in Deutschland und Frankreich 1848/49*, unpublished 'Habilitationsschrift', Cologne, Wirtschafts- und Sozialwissenschaftliche Fakultät, 1986, p. 424; W. Aydelotte, *British House of Commons*, The Regional Social Science Archive of Iowa, Codebook 19, Iowa City, 1970, p. 6.

5.   The concept of 'availability' is a cornerstone of Max Weber's theory of political professionalisation. M. Weber, 'Wahlrecht und Demokratie in Deutschland', in *Gesammelte politische Schriften*, 3rd edition, Tübingen, 1971, pp. 272–74.

6.   Best, pp. 304–31.

7.   Ibid., p. 337.

8.   See L. F. Anderson et al., *Legislative Roll-Call Analysis*, Evanston, 1966; McRae.

9.   W. H. Riker, 'A Method for Determining the Significance of Roll Calls in Voting Bodies', in *Legislative Behavior*, eds. I. C. Wahlke and H. Eulau, New York, 1959, pp. 378–92.

10.   Cf. G. Hosking and A. King, 'Radicals and Whigs in the British Liberal Party, 1906–1914', in W. O. Aydelotte, *The History of Parliametary Behavior*, Princeton, N. J., 1977, p. 148.

11.   V. Cromwell, 'Mapping the Political World of 1861: a Multidimensional Analysis of House of Commons' Division Lists', in *Legislative Studies Quarterly* 7,2, 1982, pp. 285–87.

12.   Best and Kuznia, p. 59.

13.   Ibid., p. 64.

14.   M. Duverger, *Les parties politiques*, 10th edition, Paris, 1981, pp. 57–62.

15.   Aydelotte, *House of Commons*, p. 6.

16.   W. J. Dixon and M. B. Brown, *BMDP–77. Biomedical Computer Programs. P–Series*, Berkeley, California, 1981, pp. 217–34.

17.   J. W. Frane et. al., *Missing Data and BMDP. Some Pragmative Approaches*. BMDP Technical Report, 45, 2nd edition, Berkeley, Cal., 1979, pp. 27–33.

18.   A full description of the estimation procedure is given in Best and Kuznia, pp. 69–80.

19.   Frane, p. 33.

20.   D. P. Dagan et al., 'On Regression Models with Observation Specific Dummy Variables', in *Historical Methods*, 19,1, 1986, pp. 5–9.

21.   L. A. Goodman, 'A Modified Multiple Regression Approach to the Analysis of Dichotomous Variables', *ASR*, 37, 1972, pp. 28–46.

22.   Best and Kuznia, p. 79.

23.   The superiority of multiple regression as imputing method was recently confirmed by simulation techniques. Cf. R. Schnell, 'Zur Effizienz einiger Missing-Data-Techniken — Ergebnisse einer Computer-Simulation', in *ZUMA-Nachrichten*, 17, 1985, pp. 50–74.

At the Frontiers of Measurement: Non-Parametric Measures of Efficiency

Introduction

Economists and historians often wish to measure efficiency, usually for purposes of comparison. Traditionally, the simple measure of labour productivity, i.e. output per unit of labour employed, has been used, usually with the understanding, whether explicit or implied, that other factors of production affect labour productivity, that labour itself may not be homogenous, and that the data themselves may not be very reliable. Various measures are considered below which overcome these problems to some extent. The Farrell technique is shown to be very attractive as its properties overcome the first two problems fairly well, although it is more sensitive to the third problem than averaging techniques.

The concept of efficiency basically entails either the maximisation of a particular variable subject to constraints, at least one of which defines the maximum value of another functionally related variable, or the minimisation of a variable subject to constraints, at least one of which defines the minimum value of another functionally related variable. The problem used here as an example is the measurement of the relative efficiency of a set of firms, each of which use different quantities of capital and labour inputs. Figures 1 to 5 all represent the combinations of capital and labour that are used by the individual firms to produce one unit of output, and so points along the horizontal axis are found by dividing labour by output, and on the vertical axis by dividing capital by output. However, instead of the individual firm, some of the literature uses the concept of decision making unit (DMU) which emphasises the wide applicability of the technique. In addition the technique has been used to measure the 'efficiency' (i.e. value for money) of products.

Overall productive efficiency is derived from at least three sources: scale efficiency, allocative efficiency and technical efficiency. Constant returns to scale are assumed here for simplicity. Allocative efficiency is achieved when factors of production are used in such proportions that the ratio of their relative prices are the same as the ratio of their marginal physical products. This is illustrated in Figure 1 at point v where the budget line BB′ is tangential to the isoquant II′. Technical efficiency is illustrated in Figure 1 by any point on the isoquant II′. Thus point v is both technically and allocatively efficient, while all other points on II′ are only technically efficient. Any point beyond II′, such as X and Y are technically inefficient. It is technical efficiency which is considered here and which is measured by the traditional measure of output per unit of labour.

Figure 1   *Technical and Allocative Efficiency*

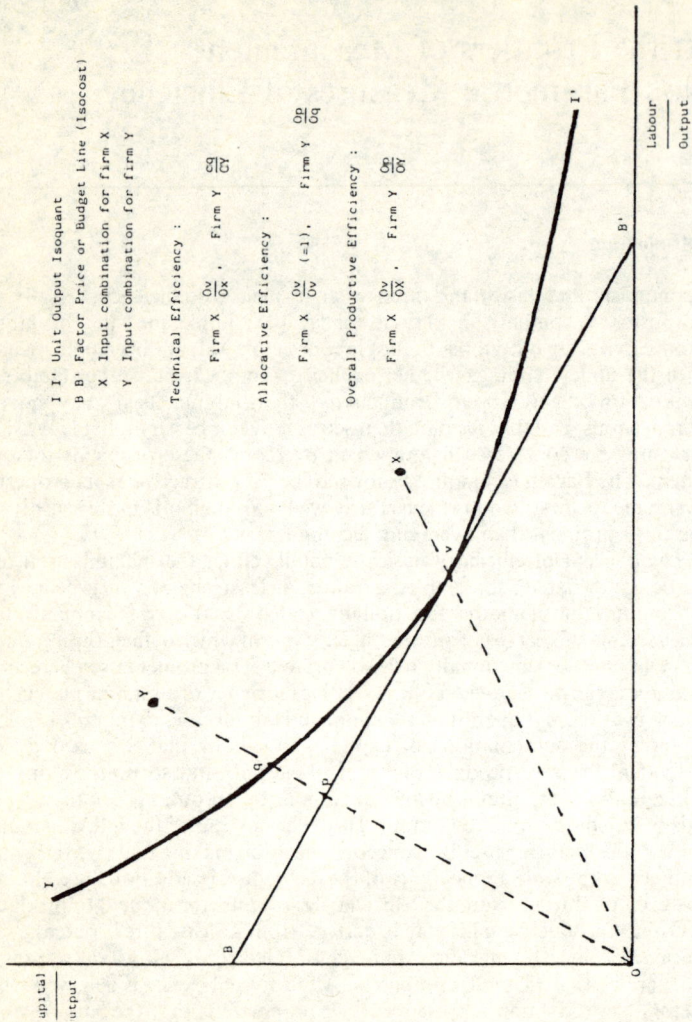

Various Measures of Efficiency

In Figure 2 measures of efficiency are illustrated which only consider the labour input and thus are unidimensional measures. The mean average amount of labour per unit of output is Ļ, and so firms using less than this amount are more efficient than the average, and vice-versa. An absolute measure of efficiency would be the distance from L (e.g. L — L), and a relative

Figure 2 *Unidimensional Measures of Efficiency*

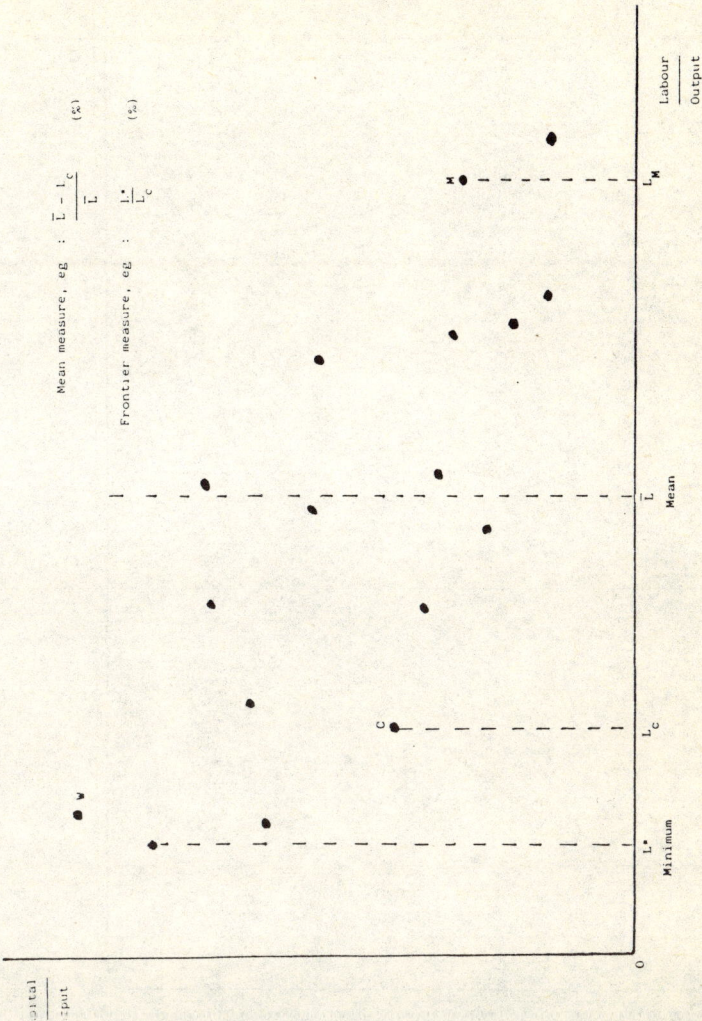

measure would be this divided by L. The minimum amount of labour per unit of output is L*, and a similar absolute measure (i.e. L* — L) and a relative measure can be derived. The former measures are therefore relative to the average performance, while the latter are relative to best perfomance.

The mean measure is extended into a multidimensional measure in the form of the regression line in Figure 3. It can be seen that the relative efficiency of points in Figure 2 is often very different from the relative

Figure 3   *Linear Regression Measures*

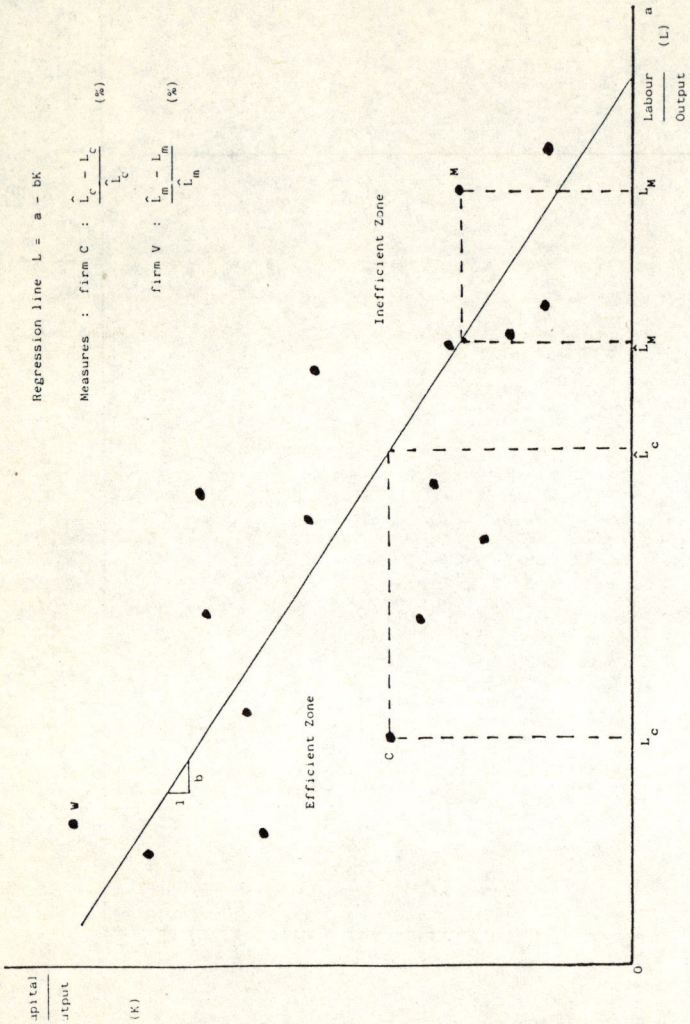

efficiency of those same points calculated using the simple mean. This implies that when another variable or variables are included in this type of measure, the efficiency score of each point will be affected in a somewhat unpredictable way. For example, point W changes from being very efficient to being very inefficient, and even the most efficient firm could become the most inefficient by the addition of an extra dimension.

Figure 4 *The Farrell Frontier Measure*

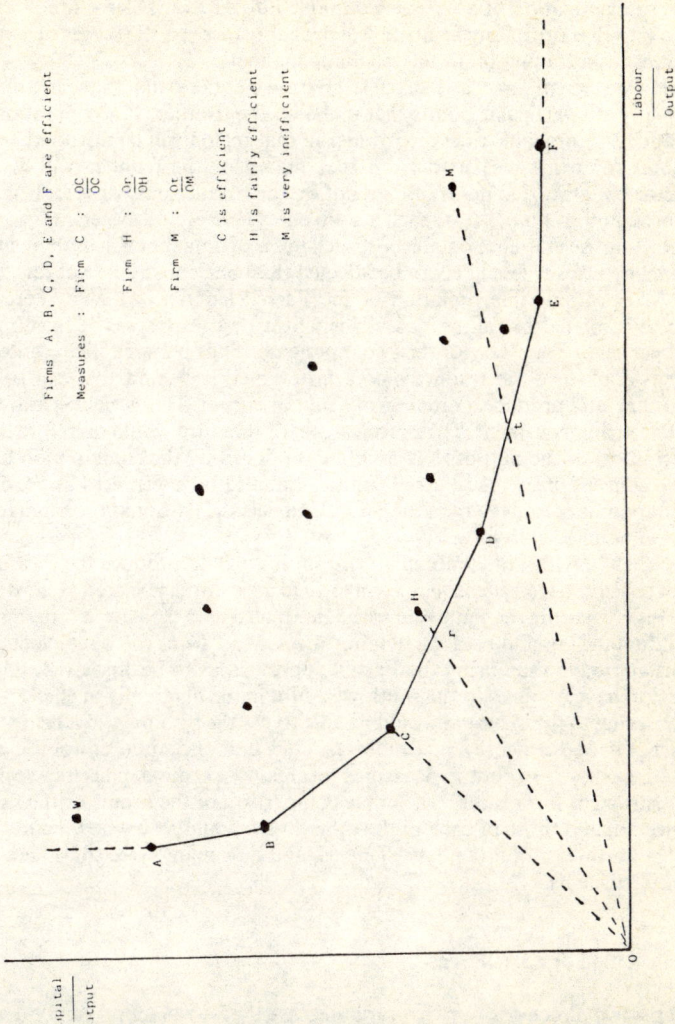

Firms A, B, C, D, E and F are efficient

Measures : Firm C : $\frac{OC}{O\bar{C}}$

Firm H : $\frac{O\bar{H}}{OH}$

Firm M : $\frac{O\bar{M}}{OM}$

C is efficient

H is fairly efficient

M is very inefficient

In Figure 4 the Farrell frontier is obtained by drawing straight lines between undominated points to form a convex frontier which encloses all the points not on the frontier itself. It can now be seen that the most efficient firm in Figure 2 (L*) which had the lowest labour input is on the frontier. Point L* in Figure 2 may thus be considered the one dimensional frontier. In turn this implies that any firm that is on a lower dimensioned frontier will also be on a higher dimensioned one. For a fuller treatment of this see Nunamaker[1] who also illustrates the property that an extra dimension, i.e. an extra variable, or the disaggregation of an existing variable into sub-variables, cannot reduce the Farrell score of any firm and will probably increase the scores of some of the firms, although in an unsystematic manner.

However, a major drawback of the Farrell frontier is that the scores may be sensitive to particular points that make up the frontier. If any point on the frontier is unreliable then the frontier in that region will be distorted and so scores for firms measured from that region of the frontier will also be distorted. Distorted items of data not on the frontier only distort their own scores, and so do not pose such a problem. There are no systematic ways of detecting the existence or effects of such items of data, but a frontier made up of many firms is less likely to be affected than one constructed of few firms.

An economic interpretation of the Farrell frontier is that it represents linear combinations of the most efficient firms, e.g. 40 per cent of one firm and 60 per cent of another for the two input case. Thus between them those two firms could use the resources of a firm which is behind that part of the frontier, and produce more than one unit of output. This is what is known as a Pareto improvement. The Farrell score for that firm would therefore be the reciprocal of the output that could be produced by the combination of the two efficient firms. The Farrell frontier can also be interpreted as the linear programming equivalent of the smooth Neoclassical isoquant so often found in economics textbooks.

Where the idea of combining firms in this way to produce the measure is not considered to be reasonable, an ordinal measure can be used as illustrated in Figure 5 using the same example data. It also uses the Pareto criterion but without the possibility of 'combining' firms. More firms will be efficient using this approach than using the Farrell approach, as to be efficient requires a firm to have no firms to the south-west of it in the diagram. An efficient firm according to this measure would be able to use the resources of a firm north-east of it, and either produce more than one unit of output, or not use up all the resources, or both. Measures of relative ordinal efficiency can be constructed. For example, a simple comparison of the inputs of the firm in question and those of each of the other firms would reveal how many firms were north-east of it (i.e. less efficient), and how many were south-west (i.e. more efficient).

Calculation of Farrell Scores

In the two dimension (i.e. two variable) case the Farrell scores can be derived by accurate graph plotting and measurement of the relevant distances. However, this is impossible in the much more common cases in which the number of dimensions is much higher. In such cases linear programming can be used to compute the scores. To do this, a linear programming problem is set up and solved for each firm. The firm's actual output divided by the linear programming optimum output, i.e. the theoretical output that a combination of other firms could produce using that firm's resources, yields the Farrell score for that firm. Firms with a score of 1 are thus efficient and so are on the frontier. Although the amount of computational effort is very considerable,

Figure 5 *Ordinal Measures*

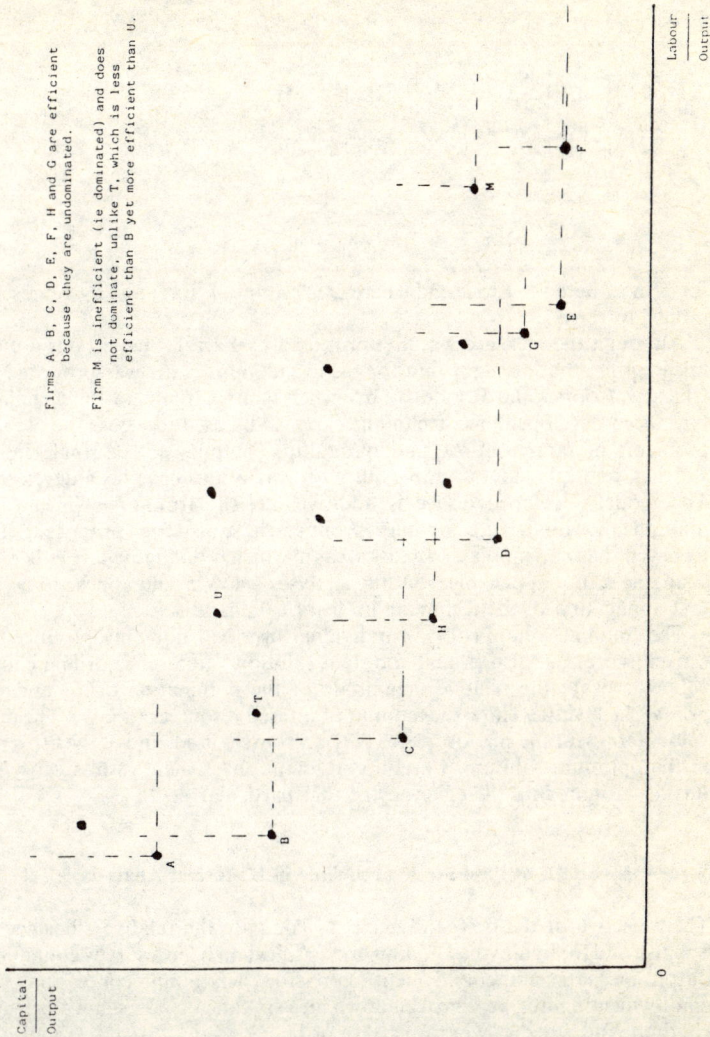

Firms A, B, C, D, E, F, H and G are efficient because they are undominated.

Firm M is inefficient (ie dominated) and does not dominate, unlike T, which is less efficient than B yet more efficient than U.

this is no real problem today with widely available computing power. A micromputer can formulate and solve the problem for each firm in succession and be left to produce the scores in its own time. A program to do this, written in a very general version of Basic, has been developed by the author.[2]

A formal statement of the linear programming problem for k firms using n resources is:

$$\text{Max } z_j = Q_1 x_1 + Q_2 x_2 \cdots Q_k x_k$$

subject to:

$$a_{11} x_1 + a_{12} x_2 + \ldots + a_{1k} x_k \leqslant a_{1j}$$

$$a_{21} x_1 + a_{22} x_2 + \ldots + a_{2k} x_k \leqslant a_{2j}$$

$$\vdots \qquad \vdots \qquad \qquad \vdots \qquad \vdots$$

$$a_{n1} x_1 + a_{n2} x_2 + \ldots + a_{nk} x_k \leqslant a_{nj}$$

for firm j where j = 1 to k and where Q is output of firm j and a_{ij} represents input i for firm j.

Although the measure was first proposed by Farrell,[3] he did not use the linear programming algorithm for his calculations. This was proposed by Charnes, Cooper and Rhodes,[4] since when many variants of the technique have been developed. The technique can also be used to assess the parallel problems of minimisation, and of multiple outputs and a single input. Further, multiple input multiple output formulations have been developed. The model developed above is additive, i.e. the frontier is linear, but multiplicative models, i.e. log-linear frontiers, have also been proposed.[5] The technique has been applied in many areas in which profit figures are either not available or not applicable,[6] but the analyses below would appear to be the first application of the technique in historical analysis.

The optimal solution for an individual firm will not only produce the Farrell score, but also primal and dual solution values. The primal choice values indicate the relative magnitude of the dominating firms, and the primal slack values show the amount of unused resources (if any). The dual values represent the shadow prices of the resources used, and of the firms not in the optimum solution. Careful consideration of these results can yield further insights into the efficiency of that particular firm.

Two Applications of the Farrell Technique in Historical Analysis

The objective of the first study[7] was to compare the relative efficiency of Spanish and foreign-owned mining firms using data from a survey containing output measures and employment figures for each mining concession. The employment figures were broken down into six categories: men, women and children, and whether working above or below ground. As the labour was therefore far from homogenous, the problems of the simple measures outlined above were likely to be severe. The employment figures were aggregated after being weighted by their relative wage rates for some analyses, but the statistical problem of multicollinearity meant that regression analysis was unable to provide sensible results from the disaggregated employment data. The Farrell approach therefore offered an opportunity for making use of this detailed data. Figure 6 shows the frequencies of Farrell scores for mining firms broken down by country, of

Figure 6   *Lead Mining: Comparative Technical (Farrell) Efficiency*

N = 241

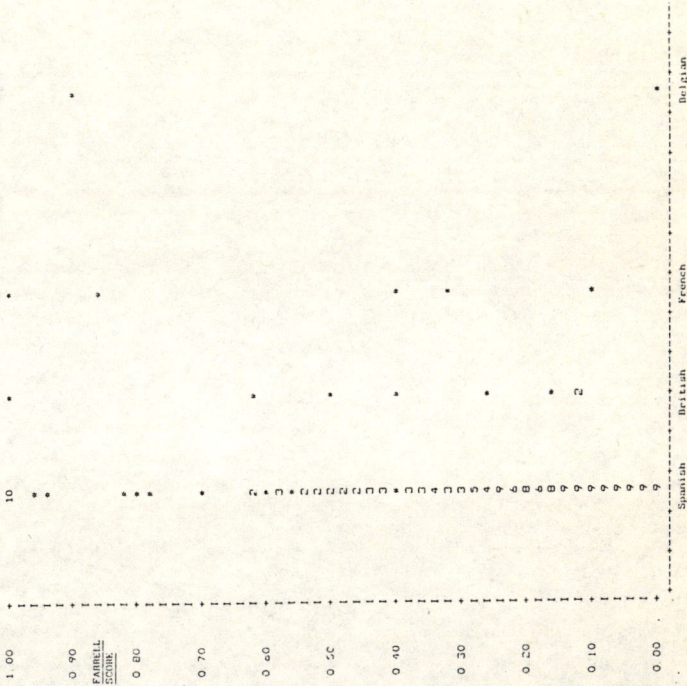

which ten Spanish, one British and one French firm were efficient, (i.e. on the frontier), while a very large number had efficiency scores of less than twenty per cent. If the columns are aggregated horizontally, it can be seen that there is a gap between about 0·64 and 0·76, with the exception of only one firm. The gap could either be the result of rogue data, or represent a true dichotomy between efficient and inefficient firms. In this particular case the rogue data explanation would have been hard to sustain. The study which used traditional, regression and Farrell measures, found no strong evidence to support the view that Spanish managements were significantly less efficient than their foreign counterparts in the three mining industries examined.

In the second study[8] which emanated from a debate on British economic growth,[9] the Farrell approach was not only an alternative method of analysis with certain technical advantages, but produced two-dimensional textbook isoquant diagrams, as in Figures 1 and 4. The diagram for 1856 with the Farrell scores for the sectors behind the frontier is shown in Figure 7. The preliminary results of the work indicate that manufacturing, although more efficient in the use of capital and labour than agriculture, was far from being

Figure 7   *Farrell Frontier for Major British Industrial Sectors, 1856*

Source of data: Matthews et al.[10]

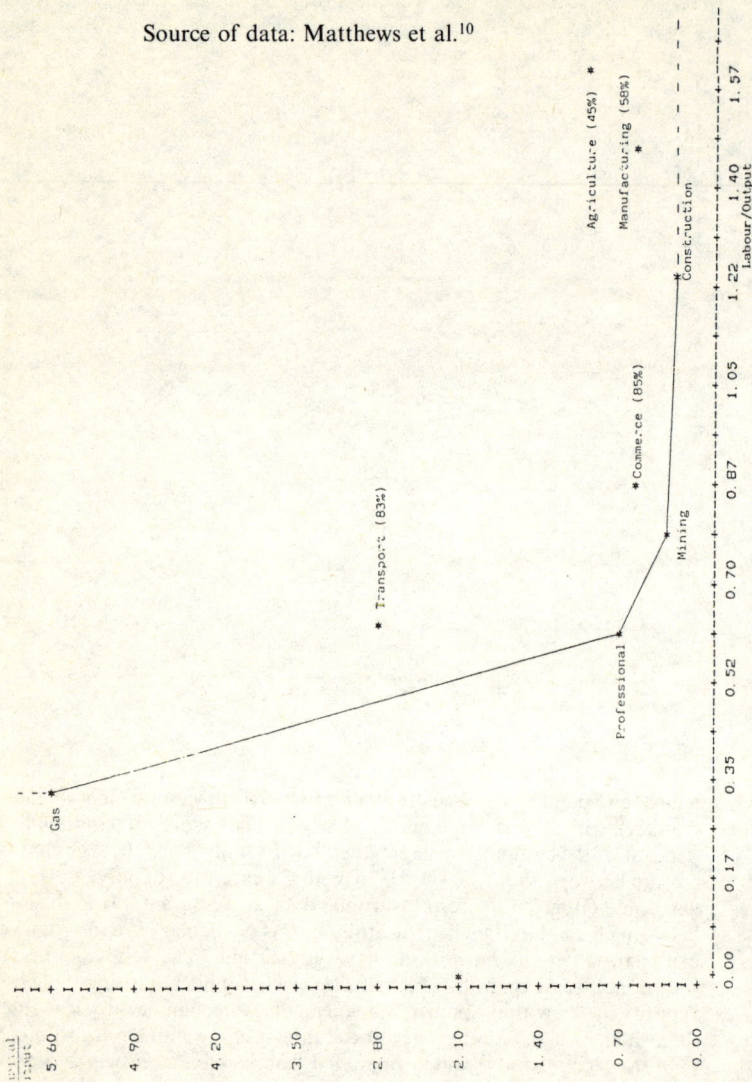

an efficient sector. In addition, there appears to have been a long-run rise (convergence) of efficiency for all sectors at least until 1964, although the 1973 analysis indicates a fall for several sectors. Further conceptual and analytical work has to be undertaken before any conclusions can be reached with confidence.

Concluding Remarks

The relative strengths and weaknesses of the various measures discussed above suggest that no single measure should be used in the evaluation of relative technical efficiency. However, non-parametric measures such as the Farrell approach, provide the historian with a new set of tools which complement existing statistical methods. Reliable conclusions are thus most likely to emerge when a combination of the measures provide consistent results.

Notes

1.   T. R. Nunamaker, 'Using data envelopment analysis to measure the efficiency of non-profit organisations: a critical evaluation, Managerial and Decision', *Economics* 6, 1985, pp. 50–58.

2.   P. Taylor, *A general computer program for Farrell frontier analysis, Occasional Research Paper in Economics*, Bristol Polytechnic, 1987.

3.   M. J. Farrell, 'The measurement of productive efficiency', *Journal of the Royal Statistical Society*, Series A 120 Part III, 1957, 253–90.

4.   A. Charnes, W. W. Cooper and E. Rhodes, 'Measuring the efficiency of decision-making units', *European Journal of Operational Research*, 2:6, pp. 429–44.

5.   For a full explanation see: R. Fare, S. Grosskopf and C. A. Lovell, *The Measurement of Efficiency in Production*, Kluwer Nijhoff, 1985; F. R. Forsund, C. A. K. Lovell and P. Schmidt, 'A survey of frontier production functions and of their relationship to efficiency measurement', *Journal of Econometrics* 13, 1980, pp. 5–25; S. Missiakoulis, *The current state of data envelopment analysis*, unpublished manuscript, University of Kent, 1984.

6.   For example see the following and those listed in Fare et al (Note 5): A. Bessent and W. Bessent, 'Determining the comparative efficiency of schools through data envelopment analysis', *Educational Administration Quarterly*, 16, 1980, pp. 57–75; H. T. Burley, 'Productive efficiency in US manufacturing: a linear programming approach', *Review of Economics and Statistics*, 62, 1980, pp. 619–22; A. Charnes and W. W. Cooper, 'Auditing and accounting for program efficiency and management efficiency in non-profit entities', *Accounting Organisations and Society*, 5, 1980, pp. 87–107; A. Charnes and W. W. Cooper, 'Management science relations for evaluation and management accountability', *Journal of Enterprise Management*, 2, 1980, pp. 143–62; F. R. Forsund and L. Hjalmarsson, 'Frontier production functions and technical progress: a study of general milk processing in Swedish dairy plants', *Econometrica*, 49, 4, 1979, pp. 883–900; B. P. Keating, 'Prescriptions for efficiency in non-profit firms', *Applied Economics*, 11, 1979, pp. 321–32; A. Y. Lewin, R. C. Morey and T. J. Cook, 'Evaluating the administrative efficiency of courts', *Omega*, 10, 1982, pp. 401–11; T. R. Nunamaker, 'Measuring routine nursing service efficiency: a comparison of cost per patient day and data envelopment analysis models', *Health Services Research*, 18, 1983, pp. 183–205; J. F. Pickering, 'Efficiency in a departmental store group', *Omega*, 11, 1983, pp. 231–37.

7.   C. Harvey and P. Taylor, 'The measurement and comparison of corporate productivity: foreign and domestic firms in Spanish mining in the late nineteenth century', *Histoire et Mesure*, 3:1, 1988, pp. 19–51.

8.   P. Taylor, *The relative efficiency of the major sectors of the British economy 1856–1973*, unpublished manuscript, 1987.

9.   N. Gemmell and P. Wardley, *The contribution of services to British Economic growth 1856–1914*, unpublished manuscript, University of Durham, 1986.

10.   R. C. O. Matthews, C. H. Feinstein and J. Odling-Smee, *British Economic Growth, 1956–1973*, Oxford, 1982.

VI.

Demography, Migration and Social Structure

Theory and Methodology: an Example from Historical Demography

In the mid-sixteenth-century the population of England numbered some three million. Three hundred years later the figure had risen to some sixteen and a half million persons. Yet the growth over this period was far from uniform or even. From the 1550s through to the late sixteenth century growth rates measured around one per cent per annum. The rate of growth slowed down from the 1580s, and between the 1650s and the 1680s the population was in decline. There followed a period of very low spasmodic growth, such that size of the population in the 1650s (5·2 millions) was not surpassed until the 1720s and 30s. From this date consistent population growth rates were resumed, initially on a modest scale, averaging around 0·5–0·8 per cent per annum, until the late eighteenth century when population growth rates witnessed a sharp upturn, reaching a peak of over 1·5 per cent per annum in the 1820s, reducing slightly to some 1·25 per cent per annum until the last quarter of the nineteenth century.[1]

Ever since the days of Malthus researchers have speculated on the relationship and interplay between population and economic growth. Writing in the 1790s, at the very point when the country was experiencing high population growth rates, the Revd. Malthus centred much of his attention on the potential conflict between people and resouces, mouths to be fed and food supply, a problem which two hundred years later is still so evident with regard to the developing nations. Living in a world where the effects and benefits of a more scientific approach to farming were still to be realised, Malthus believed that the production of food supplies would be subject to diminishing marginal returns, that output would grow only on an 'arithmetical' scale. However population, he suggested, was not subject to any such restriction. Since population growth was compound by nature it would grow instead on a 'geometric' scale. Consequently, Malthus argued that the two forces were in direct conflict, as the gap between the arithmetic and geometric rates inevitably increased food would become scarce, pushing up food prices and lowering the standard of living, perhaps to such a degree that starvation may occur.[2] Thus Malthus envisaged a demographic system in which uncontrolled population growth would lead to increased levels of mortality via lower living standards, which over the short-term would stem the rate of population growth. Such a system in which population growth and the supply of food are balanced by a 'positive check' of increased mortality is illustrated by the outer loop of the network of feedbacks depicted in Figure 1.

Figure 1

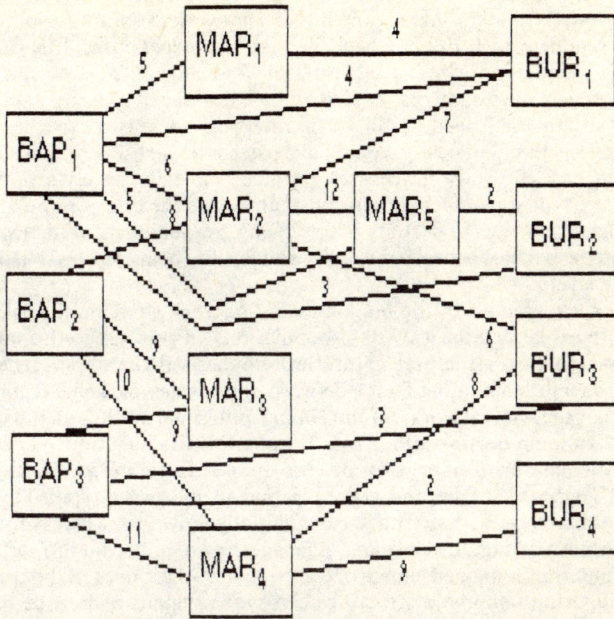

However, as this diagram suggests, Malthus also argued for the existence of a secondary demographic system operating in direct contrast to the 'positive check', as indicated by the inner loop of the diagram. As a response to falling levels of real income and standards of living Malthus postulated that young single adults might modify their behaviour and postpone marriage, and in so doing reduce fertility and the level of population growth, minimising as far as possible the potential of the 'positive check'. Controlling levels of population growth through the operation of a flexible system of nuptiality, Malthus appropriately titled this regulatory model the 'preventive check'.

Despite its simplicity the Malthusian model of population growth has served as a conceptual framework for much subsequent research into demographic patterns, both past and present.[3] The notion of a demographic system driven and controlled by the level of mortality is an essential feature of much traditional writing in historical demography, which in explaining increased levels of population growth lays emphasis on the effects of decreases in mortality over increases in fertility.[4] The primacy of mortality is also central to the stylised Demographic Transition Model, originally devised shortly after the Second World War yet still much used today, particularly to explain population trends in developing countries and the idealised transition from a 'traditional' to a 'modern' economy.[5] Stage One of the Model is characterised by a society experiencing high uncontrolled levels of mortality and fertility, with population size fluctuating spasmodically due to short-term differences between these two factors. From the 'traditional' demographic regime the society witnesses a transition to a 'modern' regime (Stage Four) which likewise also experiences little or no growth in population size as a result of low mortality rates due to improvements in environmental factors and medical facilities being paralled with low, strictly controlled, fertility rates. Between these two extremes the Model suggests that the society would have passed through a period of rapid population growth (Stage Two) as a result of mortality levels dropping sharply but fertility levels remaining constant, before the rate of population growth slackened due to fertility levels being gradually reduced, (Stage Three) and the balance between mortality and fertility being reached again at a new low level.

However, irrespective of the predominance of work stressing the role of mortality in explaining the growth of populations, in contrast to this much recent research of a structural nature has emphasised the importance of nuptiality as a differentiating factor between various demographic regimes. In particular, the seminal work of John Hajnal, published in 1965, identified a 'fault line' running north-south across Europe from Leningrad to Trieste, dividing the continent into two on the basis of traditional marriage patterns.[6] To the east of this line, argued Hajnal, marriage was typified by an early age at marriage with marriage being initially universal, whereas to the west of the line marriage took place at older ages and a significant proportion of the population remained unmarried throughout their lives. Subsequent works comparing household structures across the regions of Europe have combined to illustrate the potential effects of marriage upon patterns of family formation and household composition, pointing to nuptiality as a major causation factor in influencing household type.[7]

It was the basic conflict between the notion of the demographic system of the Malthusian 'positive check' controlled by mortality and that of the 'preventive check' centred on nuptiality that provided much of the intellectual framework for the research project carried out by the Cambridge Group for the History of Population and Social Structure and cumulated in the publication of *The Population History of England*.[8] In order to carry out this reconstruction it was essential that a long-term series of vital demographic events (births, deaths and marriages) be compiled for a wide geographical coverage. In the absence of other information this meant that the basic data source had to be ecclesiastical parish registers. In this respect it is fortunate that legal provision for the keeping of parish registers in England was made as early as 1538, however, since in the early years of the project such registers were still invariably maintained in the chest of the parish church, it soon became clear that the collection of an adequate data base was beyond the resources of the Cambridge Group. It was for this reason that local historians were called upon to help by filling in specially designed forms recording the aggregate monthly totals of the register events. The response was beyond all expectations and by the mid-1970s information relating to over 500 parishes had been received: it is in recognition of this mammoth undertaking that *The Population History* is dedicated to the local population historians of England.

In order to produce the required demographic rates the monthly totals of baptisms, burials and marriages abstracted from the parish registers had to be converted into measures of fertility, mortality and nuptiality. To achieve this a technique called 'back-projection' was developed to calculate artificial quinquennial censuses for the period 1541–1871 by combining the totals of vital events with the structure of a 'known' census population, in this case that of 1871. The application of this exercise is sketched out in volume one of *History and Computing* and detailed in the various appendices to *The Population History*.[9] Consequently it is not appropriate to discuss this operation within the confines of this short essay. However, since *The Population History* was published there have been three major developments which have caused the algorithm to be re-written and re-named 'generalised inverse projection', emphasising the link with Lee's 'inverse projection' which pioneered this approach.[10] The new version is more understandable and efficient and has been successfully applied to individual parishes, cities and regions as well as countries. Running it on the English data confirms the published results and suggests that back-projection can now be regarded as a clumsy implementation of the three basic elements: a system of demographic accounts, net-migration and mortality models and a method of finding the parameters that control them.

The first development came when a number of authors published articles on a 'new synthesis' of the demography of non-stable population systems open to migration. In particular, the work of Arthur and Vaupel has suggested that it is possible to calculate the structure of a population at a point on a population surface defined by age and time from the population at any other point, given the births, migration and mortality in the intervening years.[11] Consequently, the demographic accounting of back-projection, as defined by the crucial equation used in *The Population History*[12] now has an established pedigree. The 'new synthesis' also afforded another insight. In the original version back-projection moved backwards in time from the terminal census (1871) at time T and created preceding censuses to time 0, consistent with the observed totals of births and deaths, by selecting appropriate age-specific patterns of mortality and net-migration from 'families' of such schedules. At each five-year interval the processes of migration and mortality were reversed to move the population backwards, with the oldest age-group created as 'births'. The estimation of this age-group was critical to the operation of the projection yet was based partly on the same age-group in the terminal census, probably the least accurately measured in any period. The 'new synthesis' defines the information necessary to estimate one value in an open population system from any other and shows that it could have been estimated from a group in any later census that is thought to be most accurate.

Using Arthur and Vaupel's terminology, the estimation process can now be given a more 'formal' description than originally appeared in *The Population History*. As shown in Figure 2, the objective is to estimate the rectangular population or Lexis suface defined by time and age. The time dimension runs from 0 to the terminal census T 5-year periods later and the age dimension from birth in K 5-year age-groups to a maximum age. The bottom or 'youngest' edge of the surface is defined by the T 5-year birth totals

Figure 2   *Population or Lexis Surface*

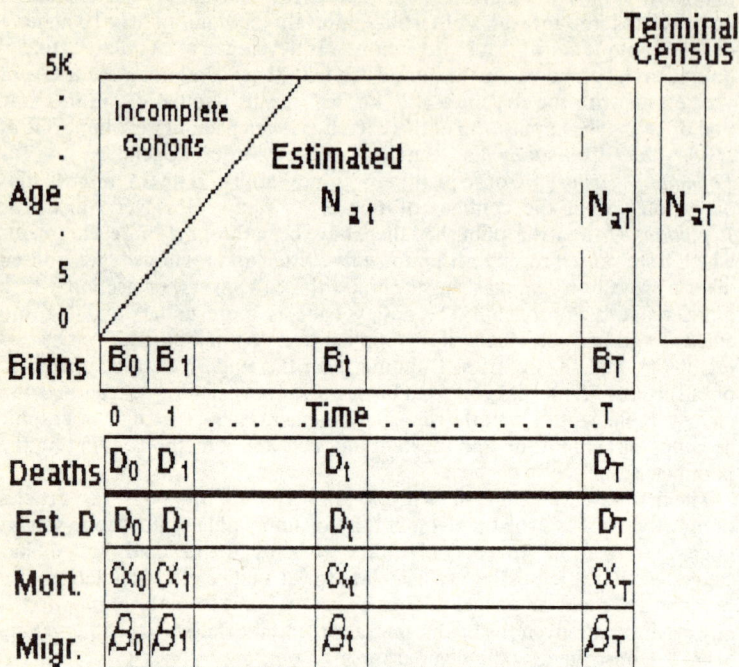

Terminal Census

| Age | Incomplete Cohorts / Estimated N_{at} | | N_{aT} | N_{aT} |

5K
·
·
·
Age
·
5
0

Births	B_0	B_1		B_t		B_T

0   1 . . . . . .Time . . . . .T

Deaths	D_0	D_1	D_t	D_T
Est. D.	D_0	D_1	D_t	D_T
Mort.	α_0	α_1	α_t	α_T
Migr.	β_0	β_1	β_t	β_T

and the 'oldest' edge is zero as no-one survives beyond 5K years by assumption. In Figure 2 the right hand edge of the Lexis surface is defined by the terminal census at T, but the left hand edge is undefined and is one side of a triangle containing the truncated cohorts who were born before the data start. In his initial workings, Lee, the originator of this approach to population estimation, resolved the problem of these cohorts by specifying a plausible initial census. Of the many alternatives, it is assumed here that they arose from a stable, open population process with a growth rate derived from the birth series, but the size of these groups is free to vary. To derive the population surface from the birth cohorts requires estimates of the age-specific mortality and net-migration rates. These are assumed to come from families of schedules where single parameters, alpha and beta respectively, define the level of each process. Thus there are T alphas and T betas to be estimated, one each for every 5-year period.

The second change concerns the method of estimating the levels of migration and mortality used in this calculation. In back-projection an *ad hoc* procedure was employed that moved backwards in time and made several such 'passes' through the data before the solution stabilised and the estimates matched the known totals of births and deaths. This backwards approach is necessary to maintain stability if the search procedure makes sequential and conditional decisions about the levels of mortality and migration at each period. In contrast, the search procedures in numerical algorithms libraries are 'omniscient' in the sense that they do not operate sequentially with regard to a time-scale and can make and assess changes at any point in the process they are required to search over, without losing stability. To understand the use of such an optimisation algorithm, suppose that two entirely arbitrary series of mortality and net-migration parameters are chosen and the demographic accounting system is used to reconstruct the population surface. Except by chance, the estimated census at T will not equal the observed one, the derived death totals will not match the registered figures and the net-migration rate will show random fluctuation. From the births and 2T parameters the mis-matches or errors can be calculated for T death totals and K age-groups in the final census. Normally, a non-linear optimisation routine would be called to minimise some function of the errors by varying the alphas and betas until the estimates 'matched' the data as closely as possible. However, with more parameters than targets (2T being generally larger than T + K), there can be no unique solution. This is known as an 'ill-posed inversion problem' and has been encountered in other disciplines using similar mathematical techniques.[13] One approach is to impose some other desired property on the system, or 'regularise' it, sufficient to guarantee a unique solution, although at present not enough is known about the dynamics of non-stable, open population systems to be able to prove what is 'sufficient'. Random fluctuations of the net-migration rate can be regarded as an undesirable feature. In the abscence of a model that linked migration to the economy, and following the spirit of Lee's original research,[14] the objective function could be augmented to 'penalise' departures from zero migration. In other words, the optimisation or search algorithm would be 'asked' to find the population surface that best fits the data with as little net-migration as possible, which within the constraints of the population model appears to define a unique solution. An alternative, which reflects the 'back-projection' algorithm, would be to make the net-migration rate as smooth as possible over time and, of course, near-zero migration could be one of the possible outcomes.

The formal expression of an objective function and the measurement of errors between data targets and estimates leads to the third major change. It is now possible to include additional pieces of demographic information in the objective function, to give them different weights and to assess the consistency of all the data with respect to the model. For example, a census in addition to that of the 'known' terminal census may give a total for the adult population which can be used as a target. The usage of such additional target information is given in the contribution to this volume by Andreas Balthasar in his detailed account of the application of inverse projection techniques to the study of the demography of Berne between 1720 and 1920. Consequently, there is little to be gained in duplicating a description of applied usage in this discusssion.

Although 'back-projection', or in its new form, 'generalised inverse projection', provided much needed information on the changing rates of mortality, fertility and nuptiality in England between 1541 and 1871, to fully test the operation of a nuptiality driven demographic system along the lines of the Malthusian 'preventive check', more detailed information was required on the mechanisms of the observed marriage and fertility patterns. In particular, it was desirable to calculate measures of age at marriage and age-specific fertility, both unobtainable from projection methodology. To ascertain these and other age-specific demographic indices a secondary methodological technique had to be implemented, that of family reconstitution. The method of family reconstitution was first perfected by the French demographer Louis Henry and involves the linking of individuals recorded in the parish registers in order to establish the ages at which marriage, death and the birth of children took place.[15] The major drawback to the technique is that the identification and reconstruction of family records when carried out by hand is very time-consuming. Thus it has long been a clear objective to automate as much of the process as possible.

Family reconstruction comprises two stages: the linking together and construction of family records; second, the subjection of these family records to demographic analysis. The computer has long been called in aid to help lighten the burden of calculation involved in this second stage. For example, the Cambridge Group began writing a comprehensive suite of demographic analysis programs for reconstituted families in the late 1960s, and other scholars have also developed similar sets of programs.[16] Using the computer to link parish register entries, however, as in the first stage of family reconstitution, has proved to be a far more difficult task. The problems are both conceptual and practical. Many were outlined and discussed at a conference held more than fifteen years ago, and the fruits of that exchange of views were published in 1973.[17] Since then several scholars have tried to tackle the problems raised by an automatic linking of register entries, and at least two major projects in French Canada have reported excellent results.[18]

Automatic record linking faces two main classes of problem. First, variations in spelling need to be overcome so that records referring to the same person can be linked. There is now a large literature on this subject; most of it concerned with phonetically-based representations of names, but an attractive alternative has been suggested which takes account of matches between individual letters within names.[19] In our experience, although algorithms can handle the vast majority of cases, variations in spelling in the past were so arbitrary that it is impossible to devise a set of standardisation rules that can achieve a 100 per cent success rate. Consequently, while the computer can provide an invaluable aid in making the standardisation of spelling both less burdensome and more systematic, it is essential that the historian checks the output carefully and takes final responsibility for the results.

The second class of problem relates to the linking together of records that refer to the same individual. While it is a trivial matter to sort files so that all records bearing the same name are brought together, it is quite another matter to determine whether or not they refer to the same individual. Indeed, in some circumstances it may be patently clear that this cannot be so, as when a burial entry is more than a hundred years after a baptism entry. On other occasions there may be several possible links that could be made, but which compete with each other leaving some uncertainty about which of the records refer to the same individual. For example, there may be two baptism entries and only one marriage entry bearing the same name. Which of the children being baptised was the one that got married? Put more generally, a simple comparison of records may reveal problems of multiplicities and incompatibilities, which must be resolved before records can be linked to form individual life histories. Yet in attempting to do this, we encounter a deeper problem in that we do not know how many individuals were alive at the same time bearing the same name who were being referred to in the records. Thus the essential task of the first stage of automatic family reconstitution is the identification of sets of linked records that refer to the life histories of an unknown number of individuals.

Since we do not know how many individuals were involved, we have to begin by making all possible links. It is only when we have done this that we can discover the existence of impossible or multiple links that can alert us to the presence of several individuals of the same name. In maximising the number of possible links, there is clearly no point in matching every record with each other record regardless of name, sex and age, since the number of potential links would be far too great, and many links would be wholly improbable. Providing spelling variations can be standardised, surnames usually provide the most stable and discriminating personal characteristic by which the set of records can be subdivided without fear of missing possible links to other records.[20] Within the surname set, the number of possible links can be further reduced by requiring links to accord with a number of logical, biological, or historical constraints. For example, first names must correspond;[21] baptism dates must precede burial dates, and by not more than a hundred years; and baptism entries must not be linked to records of women over age 50.

On the other hand, in the course of linking we may discover the existence of events which are implied by the occurrence of other events but are not recorded in the register. For example, children may die before they can be baptised and so lack a baptism entry, or baptism records for one or more children may imply the presence of a married couple in the parish for whom there was no entry in the marriage register. Consequently, we need to create dummy register entries for these implied events and include them in the linking process. We also need to take account of the fact that in England in the past women changed their surname upon marriage, and test whether baptism and burial entries for women that are linked to a common marriage can also be linked directly.

In many cases, once we have made all possible and sensible links, so as to gain the maximum amount of information about the possible individual life-courses that may be underlying the registered events, we may well find that the resulting sets of links fall out easily and unambiguously into individual life histories. However, there are bound to be occasions when incompatibilities between possible links, or multiple links between records, indicate the presence of more than one individual with the same name. For example, a baptism entry may be linked to a marriage entry, and the marriage entry to a burial entry, but the burial entry is too late in time to be linked to the baptism entry. In this case there are clearly two life-courses involved, but to which does the marriage entry belong? In practice, the frequency with which ambiguous clusters of links occur in any historical record-linking exercise will depend on the size of the pool of names that were used to discriminate between individuals in the past, and on the amount of additional information in the records. Where register entries mention personal characteristics, such as age, occupation or residence, or record the names of relatives, it will often be easy to discriminate between different individuals bearing the same name. Unfortunately, in England the pool of surnames most commonly used was not very wide in the past, and the parish registers contained little additional information. Consequently, the clusters of possible links can sometimes become very large, with a high proportion of multiple or incompatible links making their decomposition into individual life histories a far from straightforward matter.

Like many other scholars, in choosing between competing links we have taken account of the degree of confidence we have that the two records in each linked pair in fact refer to the same individual, and we have measured our confidence level in terms of the amount of agreement or disagreement over personal characteristics given in the records concerned. Thus each pair of linked records is scored depending on the presence or absence of congruent, or discordant, information on age, occupation, residence, relatives' names and so on, depending on the degree of information available from one parish register, plus any additional source that may have been used to supplement the linking process. The numerical scores to be assigned for matches, or mismatches, for any item of information can be determined in a simple probabilistic manner, taking account of the relative frequency of different personal states, or can be determined by the historian to take account of knowledge of the specific historical context.

For example, in a simple case, where two baptism entries are competing to be linked to a marriage, we could resolve the issue by preferring the link with the higher confidence score and deleting the competing link. But larger clusters of multiple and competing links pose a more challenging problem. Consider the network of links outlined in Figure 3, which shows the confidence scores for each possible link, and indicates impossible links by the absence of a line joining the records concerned. Evidently, as the different scores indicate, we have more confidence in some links than others, but how can we tell how many individual life-courses are being confused here? And how can we disentangle the network into the most probable set of individual life histories?

The usual response that scholars have made to this problem is to abandon any attempt to use the computer, referring problematic cases of this kind back to the historian for the exercise of personal judgment.[22] In our view, if the historian's judgment has any claim to intellectual respectability, the principles on which it is based must be capable of being specified in algorithmic form and so be executable automatically by the computer without further human intervention. Moreover, an automatic resolution of indeterminate networks of linked records would have the additional advantage of avoiding the unconscious biases and inconsistencies that can easily creep in when judgments are made for a long series of individual cases over an extended period of time. So while other scholars have concluded that a computer resolution of all possible combinations of links would not be worth the extra programming effort, for us the specification of a set of rules

Figure 3   *The Positive and Preventive Checks*

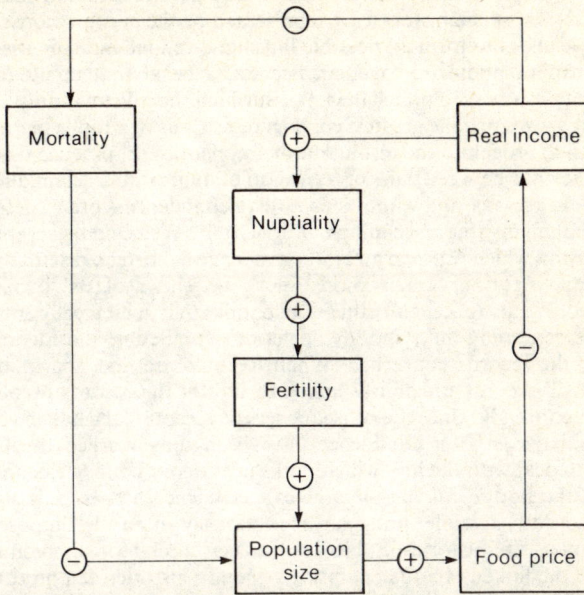

that would enable a full resolution of competing links to be made was the essence of the intellectual exercise that we set ourselves.

How, therefore, should one set about resolving a complex network of competing links, like the one illustrated in Figure 3, into an unproblematic set of individual life histories? So far, two basic approaches have been proposed. Skolnick has suggested that an appropriate strategy would be to search for the combination of links with the lowest aggregate total confidence score that would need to be deleted to resolve the network.[23] We have not adopted this approach, not least because it suffers from the disadvantage that there can be a very large number of possible combinations of links that could be deleted, for which the aggregate confidence scores need to be totalled and compared. Instead, we have proceeded sequentially. We begin by accepting the link in which we have the greatest confidence, and implement all the logical consequences for other links in the network. For example, any competing or incompatible links are deleted, and any links that are logically entailed by the acceptance of the strongest link are also confirmed, even though they may have low confidence scores in their own right.[24] In practice, however, there are often several links that attain the same confidence score. In such circumstances, we prefer links in which the records concerned have the fewest competing links, on the grounds that the more potential links a record has, the less confident we are that the link we are considering is the most probable one for the record concerned.[25] If there are several links with the same confidence score and multiplicity of competing links, then a choice of preferred link is made at random.

In summary, our approach to automatic record linking is based on two main principles. First, an agnosticism about the number and identity of individuals whose life histories are represented by the events recorded in the registers leads us to form all possible links, and to take note of cases where records cannot be linked together. Second, a belief that in situations of uncertainty it is best to prefer the links in which the information content of the records gives one the greatest confidence leads us to adopt a hierarchical, sequential approach to the resolution of ambiguities. In practice this means sorting the links between pairs of records of all types into a descending order of confidence scores, and within each level of confidence score by descending order of ambiguity (i.e. ascending multiplicity).[26] We begin by accepting the linked pair in which we have greatest confidence as correct, deleting all links that compete for, or are incompatible with, either of the two records concerned. We also accept all other weaker links that are logically entailed by the current winning link, and also delete all competing and incompatible links for the records concerned. When links are deleted, the multiplicity scores of all records previously linked to any of the records involved are revised accordingly. Once the consequences of accepting the link in which we currently have greatest confidence have been fully worked through, we proceed to deal with the link which ranks next in our confidence, and so on down to the bottom of the hierarchical confidence list. By this stage the clusters of all possible links have necessarily been decomposed into unambiguous life histories. Subject to further checks for impossible birth intervals, the linked records comprising the life histories can be combined into 'family reconstitution' histories in the usual way, with suitable cross-references between records of successive marriages, and between the marriages of parents and children. The family reconstitution records can then be submitted directly to other programs for the purposes of demographic analysis.

Combining the methods of aggregative analysis and family reconstitution, and applying appropriate techniques has proved fruitful in the reconstruction of the demographic history of England. Only through the creation of this demographic database and supplementing it with information on prices, wages and the standard of living could the link between population and economy be more fully understood. In particular, in relation to the strong case traditionally made for a pre-industrial demographic system governed by a Malthusian 'positive check', little evidence can be found to support such a view. Despite the fact that prior to 1640 mortality rates did correlate over the short-term to fluctuations in food prices, the strength of the relationship weakened considerably over the following century and disappeared entirely thereafter. Moreover, when viewed in a long-term perspective mortality levels show little response to secular trends in the standard of living, pointing to an absence of the 'positive check'. In contrast the presence of a 'preventive check' is far more evident. Fertility rates controlled through nuptiality respond in both the short and long term to changes in the standard of living, changes occurring in both the intensity of marriage and the age at which couples married. The response to economic conditions was sluggish, often lagged by thirty years, yet it was enough to forestall, to prevent, the calling into operation of a positive check on the population.

It is inappropriate to present a summary of findings within the confines of this short essay. Interested readers must turn elsewhere for such a discussion.[27] Instead the purpose of this essay has been to illustrate how appropriate methodologies have been developed and applied to a theoretical problem. In the exercise described here both sides of the coin, theory and method, were as important as each other. With a project such as this which involves the establishment of a large body of machine-readable data it is easy to be led by methodology and become entrenched in the data, not being able to see the wood for the trees. This is not to decry all exercises in historical positivism. On the contrary, in some cases the development of theory relies heavily on the observation of the trends and correlations that lie within a body of data. However, just as people can be fooled by coins bearing the same face on both sides, historians must not find themselves to be the producers of one-sided coinage.

Notes

1. E. A. Wrigley and R. S. Schofield, *The Population History of England, 1541–1871: a Reconstruction*, London, 1981, pp. 528–29.

2. T. R. Malthus, *An Essay on the Principle of Population*, London, 1798, (first edition).

3. See, for example, the collection of essays in D. Coleman and R. Schofield, eds., *The State of Population Theory: Forward from Malthus*, Oxford, 1986.

4. See, for example, G. T. Griffith. *Population Problems in the Age of Malthus*, Cambridge, 1926, T. McKeown, 'Fertility, Mortality and Causes of Death: an Examination of Issues Related to the Modern Rise of Population', *Population Studies*, 32, 1978, pp. 235–42.

5. K. Davies, 'The World Demographic Transition', *Annals of the American Academy of Political and Social Science*, 215, 1945, pp. 1–11. See also, R. I. Woods, *Theoretical Population Geography*, London, 1982, pp. 158–84.

6. J. Hajnal, 'European Marriage Patterns in Perspective', in D. V. Glass and D. E. C. Eversley, eds., *Population in History: Essays in Historical Demography*, London, 1965, pp. 101–43.

7. See the collection of essays in P. Laslett and R. Wall, eds., *Household and Family in Past Time*, Cambridge, 1972, and R. Wall, J. Robin and P. Laslett, (eds), *Family Forms in Historic Europe*, Cambridge, 1983.

8. *The Population History of England, 1541–1871*, esp. chapter 11.

9. K. Schurer, 'Historical Demography, Social Structure and the Computer', in P. Denley and D. Hopkin, eds., *History and Computing*, Manchester, 1987, pp. 33–45.

10. R. D. Lee, 'Estimating Series of Vital Rates and Age Structures from Baptisms and Burials: a New Technique with Applications to Pre-industrial England', *Population Studies*, 28, 1974, pp. 495–512.

11. W. B. Arthur, J. W. Vaupel, 'Some General Relationships in Population Dynamics', *Population Index*, 50 (2), 1984, pp. 214–26.

12. *The Population History of England*, p. 728.

13. F. O'Sullivan, 'A Statistical Perspective on Ill-Posed Inverse Problems', *Statistical Science*, 1(4), 1986, pp. 502–27. D. M. Titterington, 'General Structure of Regularization Procedures in Image Reconstuction', *Astronomy and Astrophysics*, 144, 1985, pp. 381–87.

14.   R. D. Lee, op. cit., pp. 495–512.

15.   M. Fleury and L. Henry, *Nouveau manuel de depouillement et d'exploitation de 'état civil ancien*, 3rd edition, 1985, Paris. For the application of the technique to English sources see E. A. Wrigley, 'Family Reconstitution' in E. A. Wrigley et al., *An Introduction to English Historical Demography*, London, 1966, pp. 96–159.

16.   See, for example, M. Hainsworth and J-P. Bardet, *Logiciel C. A. S. O. A. R: calculs et analyses sur ordinateur appliqués aux réconstitutions*, Paris, 1981; and R. Leboutte, G. Alter and M. Gutmann, 'Analysis of Reconstituted Families: a Package of SAS Programs', *Historical Methods*, 20, 1987, pp. 20–34.

17.   E. A. Wrigley, ed. , *Identifying People in the Past*, London, 1973.

18.   P. Beauchamp, H. Charbonneau, B. Desjardins, and J. Légaré, 'La réconstitution automatique des familles: un fait acquis', *Population*, numéro special, 1977, pp. 375–99; and G. Bouchard, 'The Processing of Ambiguous Links in Computerized Family Reconstitution', *Historical Methods*, 19, 1986, pp. 9–19.

19.   The two approaches are compared and evaluated in D. De Brou and M. Olsen, 'The Guth Algorithm and the Nominal Record Linkage of Multi-ethnic Populations', *Historical Methods*, 19, 1986, pp. 20–24.

20.   See E. A. Wrigley and R. S. Schofield, 'Nominal Record Linkage and the Logic of Family Reconstitution', in E. A. Wrigley (ed.), *Identifying People in the Past*, pp. 64–102.

21.   It is not the case that christian names have to match identically. Links can be made within groups of names with the same root, for example, John and Jonathan or Edward and Edmund.

22.   See, for example, Bouchard, 'The Processing of Ambiguous Links'.

23.   Mark Skolnick, 'The Resolution of Ambiguities in Record Linkage', in E. A. Wrigley (ed.), *Identifying People in the Past*, ch. 5.

24.   For example, suppose a baptism-marriage link is confirmed with the strongest current confidence score, and the marriage record in question has already been linked to a burial record with an even higher confidence score. In this case, if the burial record can also be linked to the baptism record; this link must be accepted as referring to the same individual that was concerned in the marriage entry, even though the burial record might also be linked to another competing baptism with a higher confidence score.

25.   For example, a baptism record may be linked with equal confidence to two marriage records, but while the first marriage record can only be linked to this baptism, the second marriage record can also be linked to a second baptism record, though with less confidence. In this case we prefer the link between the baptism and the first marriage, because that marriage can only be linked to a single baptism record, while baptism link for the second marriage is more ambiguous.

26.   Note that unlike some other scholars we do not allow the order in which particular types of links (e. g. marriage-child baptism) are made to influence the outcome. Only the confidence scores enable one link to prevail over another. Of course, if a particular type of register entry systematically contains more information than others it is likely to be more than proportionately represented amongst the links with the highest confidence scores.

27.   See in particular *The Population History of England*, chapters 10 and 11.

14 *François Nault and Bertrand Desjardins*
with the collaboration of Serge Poulard and Pierre Rosa

Computers and Historical Demography: the Reconstitution of the Early Québec Population[1]

Along with many other sciences, demography has experienced a tremendous evolution since the last World War. In particular, the importance of continuous and longitudinal observation has been recognised. One important development was the devising in France of 'family reconstitution', based on parish registers, to study what was called 'natural fertility'. The method set up very precise rules for procedures from the transcription of data onto forms to the analysis of results.[2] Blessed with instant success, it paved the way for the development of a new discipline, historical demography. Since then, a great number of parish monographies have been done, shedding new light on the life of past populations.

In this tradition, a major research program was initiated some twenty years ago at the Université de Montréal. Aiming at reconstituting a population reaching several hundred thousands, the project relied on computers from the outset. Recent developments have focused on structuring the data for consultation and analysis. After presenting the project, we discuss this latest contribution to our global methodology, which we feel constitutes an important advance in the field.

The Programme de recherche en démographie historique (P.R.D.H.)

The Canadian province of Québec presents a unique set of favourable circumstances for studies in historical demography:

1. It has very good catholic parish registers well kept and well preserved since the beginning of the colony in 1608. Missionaries crossed the Atlantic with the first pioneers and started right away to record vital events.

2. Immigration to Québec was relatively small, compared, for instance, to what the British colonies of America experienced. Consequently, the population did not grow to incommensurable numbers too quickly but, instead, expanded mostly from its own natural reproduction.

3. Emigration, although periodically involving large numbers, was in the final count relatively unimportant.

In this context, the Programme de Recherche en Démographie Historique was formed at the Université de Montréal to undertake the reconstitution and the study of the Québec population from the arrival of the first settlers up to the end of the French domination (around 1765) and eventually up to 1851, the year which marks the beginning of the statistical era in Canada with the first national census.[3] The aim has been to identify all the individuals who settled in Québec over the period studied and to sketch their biographies: dates and places of birth, marriage(s), death and family ties. This basic demographic data is completed by the individual's characteristics as found in the documents: sex, occupation, residence, origin and literacy (ability to sign).

The project is scientifically appealing for many reasons. Firstly, it is fundamental for Québec history. Secondly, it represents a unique occasion to follow the complete development of a human population. Thirdly, for historical demography itself, covering a large territory allows the study not only of the 'persistent' population, as is necessarily the case in a parish monograph, but also of the 'transient' families who moved from parish to parish.

Such a project could not be achieved without the help of computers. Despite a relatively slow population growth, the reconstitution of the population of Québec from 1608 to 1765 involves nevertheless around 300,000 certificates from some 110 parishes and relating to 180,000 individuals. Very long operations were undertaken:

1. microfilming all the certificates from every parish in the province of Québec

2. putting virtually all the content of the certificates on magnetic medium

3. automatically linking for each individual the events that concern him directly or through his children and spouse(s).

Computerising data is always a painstaking operation, especially when it originates from sources such as old documents, which add deciphering to the list of problems. The advent of microcomputers improved both performance and quality for the P.R.D.H., eliminating the need to transcribe the information on forms and bringing about the computerisation of longhand information instead of just codes.[4] Although intended for only a fairly small number of specialists, the data extracted by the P.R.D.H. generated a lot of interest in genealogical circles. Consequently, the P.R.D.H. has undertaken the publication of a 'Répertoire' where all the certificates appear in chronological order for each parish and where all individuals mentioned are indexed.[5]

Automatic data linking requires a lot of effort to succeed in having the computer deal with imprecise name identification and missing or inaccurate data which create ambiguities. A first approach to the problem was to have the computer identify all potential links and choose the most likely solution on the basis of name frequencies and demographic criteria.[6] Often incorrect at the individual level, the set of decisions yields results that are statistically valid. With the quality of data that we have, our approach evolved toward letting the computer handle only the trivial cases, by far the most numerous, and to resolve residues by hand.

Having traced through time and space what pertains to each individual in the documents, it remains to synthesise and to structure the information for analysis. In fact, the way this is done has direct implications on the results of the analysis. We will discuss briefly here three ways to manage a reconstituted population: family sheets, a computerised population register made of interrelated individual and marriage files, and a new idea about an evolving computerised population register.

Structuring and managing a reconstituted population

Family sheets

The family sheet has two parts: an upper part with information on the marriage and on each of the two spouses and a lower part containing the information about children. In the view of its designers, who had in mind the study of natural fertility, and in the absence of computers, the family sheet constituted a satisfactory medium to manage a reconstituted population. Scores of researchers have transcribed onto it the results of their manual family reconstitution and used it for their analysis.

From a data management point of view, though, the family sheet shows one poor feature: redundancy. Since an individual may appear on several different sheets, first on his parent's and then on each of his own marriages, the same information is repeated. Furthermore, it is not even interrelated, which somewhat limits analysis. Indeed, the rule has been to use each family sheet as a distinct unit for analysis, losing the benefit of the links established between each individual and his parents and between one's first marriage and remarriages in the reconstitution process. Because of the way the information is stored, the study of the fertility of women, taking into account their whole reproductive life or the study of the influence of parents on their children's behaviour, are out of the domain of analysis. Kin relations beyond the nuclear family and ascending or descending genealogies, in theory quite accessible after linking, cannot be established.

The computerised population register

A major breakthrough was achieved with the idea of storing the individual and marriage data separately, instead of together at the level of the nuclear family.[7] Specifically, the trick is to define two distinct but interrelated files: the individual file, which contains, for each person identified in reconstitution, name, sex, dates and places of birth and death, and the marriage file, which contains for each marriage, date and place of celebration, and other variables defined at the given moment. The files are interrelated through an efficient representation of the parent-children and the husband-wife-marriage links existing between the units of the files. Beyond eliminating redundancies, since each individual appears only once in this structure, the system considerably enhances analysis possibilities by putting in the hands of the researcher an efficient access to data across marriages and generations, instead of a simple sequential representation of family sheets.

Demography, Migration and Social Structure

Figure 1

```
LABBE, PIERRE (42690)                    SSP; C    PRECEDENT CONJOINT    BESNARD, CATHERINE (7397)              FICHE 60170
AR-EM * PERE LABE, FRANCOIS (42588)                FICHE 59977                                                  CATEGORIE MFI
1665 1 MERE FORET, MARIE (42689)

MEUSNIER, MARGUERITE (32704)                                                        CAT.: FAMILLE PIONNIERE
       PERE MEUSNIER, MATHURIN (47178)
       MERE FAFART, FRANCOISE (26363)
       FICHE 66863

         MARIAGE            UNION/OBSERVATION                              VEUVAGE                              REMARIAGE
      DATE   * L   *        FIN      * AGENO AGEFE DUREE  S *   DATE     AGE  DUREE   DATE      L     NOUVEAU CONJOINT:FICHE 45053
   10-04-674  1  381  04-01-709  1  067  049  034   F   5 04-01-709  1  049  17M   13 06-710  1  387  DEBLOIS, JEAN (16728)  0

                                                 MARIAGE                              DECES
         NAISSANCE                               MARIAGE
      DATE   * L   *   IR EM AGE AGE N  RES O  PROFESSION P  S C I      DATE    * INTERVALLE    L    EM  AGE  D  AGE  D  PROF I
                              O D C  N          S P M  P M                                          O D C
  EPOUX  31-12-641  3  842  2  2 V C 032             842                     04-01-709  1  01/1709  46  387  1  M  067  064  0
  EPOUSE 04-08-659  1  451  1  1 C C 014             381                     17-06-733  1  710/    2  387  1 V V 073  080  0

                                              ENFANTS
              NAISSANCE            MARIAGE            DECES
  NUMERO R  S I   DATE  * L  *    DATE            DATE OU        L  EM  AGE  D   PRENOMS: USUEL; B, M/S SI DIFFERENT
                                  (FICHE)         INTERVALLE     O D C                   CONJOINT
  42861  1  F 24-03-675  1  383  1              03-05-691  1  452  C C 016  016   MARGUERITE
  42862  2  M 08-10-676  1  383  1              07-11-676  1  383  C C 303  293   JACQUES
  42863  3  F 13-12-677  1  383  1              19-12-677  1  383  C C 063  153   MARIE
   673   4  F 16-07-679  1  387  103-11-694  1  387  015  1 19/       4              039*  ANNE
                                   (891)                                                  ALLAIRE, FRANCOIS (614)
  42864  5  M 10-09-681  1  387  1              14-08-688  1  387  C C 006  006  0 FRANCOIS
  42865  6  X 22-10-683  2  387  1              22-10-683  1  387  C C 003  NVR   0 ****
  18523  7  F 15-03-685  1  387  123-02-699  1  387  013  014 1728/     4              043*  MARIE
                                   (249459)                                              DUCHARME/ST-PIERRE, PIERRE (18530)
  42756  8  M 10-05-687  1  387  125-11-709  1  383  022  022 1727/     4              040*  JACQUES
                                   (600001)                                              DEBLOIS, FRANCOISE (16807)
  74034  9  M 28-03-689  1  387  1              07-04-689  1  387  C C 103          PIERRE
  16728 10  F 28-12-690  1  387  128-04-710  1  387  019  1 19-02-728  1  387  M M 037  027   MADELEINE, M=MARIE MADELEINE
                                   (22540)                                               DEBLOIS, JEAN BAPTISTE (16722)
  42066 11  M 01-07-692  3  000  16-06-715  1  387  022  110-08-720  1  387  C C 028  032  0 PIERRE
                                   (60006)                                               GUERINET, REINE (32985)
  42808 12  M 19-04-699  1  387  101-10-724  1  387  024  1728/     4              029*  JEAN
                                   (60040)                                               LEPAGE, MARIE (42809)
  42367 13  F 17-02-701  1  387  126-04-718  1  387  017  1728/     4              027*  GENEVIEVE
                                   (80607)                                               HARTINEAU, PIERRE (55856)
```

Confirmation of the adequacy of this new type of representation is given by the production of the family sheet itself (see illustration). To produce it, the computer successively accessed: 1) the filial and matrimonial ties to identify the spouses, their parents, their preceding and next spouses and their children; 2) the individual file to get all these people's names and characteristics; 3) the marriage file to find the information on the marriage itself; it then printed all this information in the appropriate format, adding the result of age and duration calculations.[8]

With the data structured in this way, the P.R.D.H. Québec population register presently includes data from 100,000 baptisms, marriages and burials up to the year 1729, covering some 65,000 individuals and 12,000 marriages. It was used to prepare a book on the first wave of immigrants, those who, having settled with families in the first decades of the colony, can truly be considered the founders of the French-Canadian population.[9] One of the chapters, thanks to the possibilities offered by the register, consists in an analysis of each immigrant's descendance, to see how date of marriage and differential nuptiality, fertility and mortality patterns interact to give more or less importance to some categories of people in the development of the population of Québec.

Evolving the computerised population register
But this kind of structure is not as yet enough to realise the full potential of the data base. Our experience leads us to think that the quality of the sources is so good that it is possible to present a near perfect picture of the population. We also think that the population register must not be strictly confined to demographic studies; an interdisciplinary approach, combining, for instance, social attributes and population genetics, is certainly preferable for a fuller understanding of population dynamics. The use of the population register for studies in genetics, where wrong genealogical ties can alter considerably the results, or in social history, where microanalysis is often important, requires a very precise reconstitution of the population.

In order to reach these more ambitious goals, an evolving and expanding population register is needed. Family sheets and present computerised population registers share a common limit: they are fixed entities. Once the family reconstitution process is completed, it is set aside and the analysis is done. But in the case of Québec, as analysis is performed and as researchers add data from other sources, the register is enriched and updating becomes a necessary function. Thus enhanced, the population register is perfectible, that is to say that it really can tend to a more complete picture of the population, in as much as it can incorporate data from sources other than parish registers.

Such a device is very complex, because it must ensure that the data are always consistent, first at the level of individual biographies and secondly at the level of entire genealogies. Adding new data can invalidate a set of linkage decisions that previously seemed consistent or it can help clarify the biographies of several related individuals, thus improving the population reconstitution. It is a little like throwing a pebble in a quiet pond, and it is the quality of the updating facility that ultimately determines the value of the results. Work at this last stage of our methodology is currently nearing conclusion.

Conclusion

Family reconstitution, based on parish register data, has been the core of the development of historical demography. The data available for Québec permits the development of a more ambitious approach, extending beyond the limits of classical parish register analyses. Covering a whole territory is a point of major importance, but the use of an efficiently designed computerised population register is also vital since it opens the door to analysis of a much greater scope than traditionally is done with family sheets.

We are now looking for a new kind of population register; an evolving population register. The ultimate result will be a register that can be used by all those interested, in whatever aspect, in population history.

Notes

1.　The preparation of this text was made possible by the financial support of the Social Sciences and Humanities Research Council of Canada, the FCAR funds of the province of Québec and the Université de Montréal.

2.　M. Fleury and L. Henry, *Des registres paroissiaux à l'histoire de la population. Manuel de dépouillement et d'exploitation de l'état civil ancien*, Paris, 1956. Editions de l'INED, 84p.; E. Gautier and L. Henry, *La population de Crulai, paroisse normande, Etude historique*, Paris, 1958. Editions de l'INED, 269p.

3.　J. Légaré, 'A Population Register for Canada under the French Regime: Context, Scope, Content, and Application', *Canadian Studies in Population*. (Forthcoming).

4.　B. Desjardins, 'Introduction des micro-ordinateurs dans l'élaboration des données au Programme de recherche en démographie historique,' *Cahiers québécois de démographie*, vol. 8 no 3, 1979, pp. 39–57.

5.　Programme de recherche en démographie historique. *Répertoire des actes de baptême, mariage, sépulture et des recensements du Québec ancien*. Edited by Hubert Charbonneau and Jacques Légaré. Montréal, Les Presses de l'Université de Montréal. XVIIth Century series: vol. 1 to 7, 1980, xxvi — 4116p. 1700–29 series: vol. 8 to 17, 1981 and 1982, xvi — 5928p. 1730–49 series: vol. 18 to 30, 1983 to 1985, xvi — 8177p. 1750–65 series: vol. 31 to 35, 1986, xv — 3611p.; vol. 36 to 45.

6.　B. Desjardins, P. Beauchamp and J. Légaré, 'Automatic Family Reconstitution: the French Canadian Seventeenth-Century Experience', *The Journal of Family History*, vol. 2, no. 2, 1977, pp. 56–76.

7.　M. H. Skolnick, L. L. Bean, S. M. Dintelman and G. P. Mineau, 'A Computerized Family History Data Base System', *Sociological and Social Research*, vol. 63, no. 3, 1979, pp. 506–523.

8.　B. Desjardins, 'Quelques éléments de l'expérience informatique du Programme de recherche en démographie historique', in *Informatique et prosopographie*, Paris, 1985. Edition du CNRS, pp. 159–77.

9.　H. Charbonneau, B. Desjardins, A. Guillemette, Y. Landry, J. Legare and F. Nault, *Naissance d'une population. Les Français établis au Canada au XVIIième siècle*. Paris and Montréal, 1987. Institut national d'études démographiques and Les Presses de l'Université de Montréal, 232p.

The Move into the Town: Urban Migration and Generalised Inverse Projection. The Example of Berne, 1720—1920

Historical demographers investigating large regions, where migration is marginal, know that Generalised Inverse Projection (GIP) is a very powerful method of analysing demographic trends. This has convincingly been demonstrated by Wrigley and Schofield in *The Population History of England 1541 — 1871*.[1] Since GIP delivers a set of consistent estimates of the size and the age structure of the population under investigation, at regular points in time the path of fertility and mortality can be studied in great detail. Yet while the relevance of the method on a national level has already been displayed, there has been little discussion of its applicability in urban demographic history, where migration is a variable of major influence.[2] Unfortunately, the main handicap of GIP is that it treats migration as a residual. The authors of *The Population History of England* state: 'Missing deaths, in short, appear as emigrants', and we can add that missing births appear as immigrants.[3]

However, detailed knowledge in urban demographic history is desirable, not only from a economic point of view. Contemporary urban problems might better be understood, not least by planning authorities, if a longer view were taken. A brief comparison of the crude measurement which can be calculated from the Swiss censuses shows an obvious correspondence between long-term economic cycles and the growth of the towns.[4] A further comparison of the migration flows between towns and the surrounding areas might point to different migration patterns.

A major problem for the urban demographer is that basic information on the size and the age structure of the urban population at regular points in time is often lacking. GIP can deliver this data. However, to run the GIP program some fundamental knowledge about the demography of the place under investigation is necessary. Some of the problems connected with the collection of the input data necessary for the program are considered in this paper. We concentrate on the special problems involved in working on an urban area, using data for the city of Berne. Berne has been the Swiss capital since 1848, in which year it had about 25,000 inhabitants. By way of conclusion we make some comments on the use of GIP in the analysis of urban demography, especially of urban migration.

GIP requires aggregate numbers of births and deaths, and data on the age structure of the population at the end of the period under study. In addition, age-schedules of mortality and migration which give the relative probability of dying or migration at different ages are necessary. The actual levels are estimated by the projection.[5] All this data should correspond as far as possible with historical reality. The program begins by calculating initial values for several demographic measurements including the size and the age structure of the population, and mortality and migration over the whole period of time.[6] The actual projection compares the number of deaths, the population size and the age structure implied by the starting values with the numbers actually recorded in the historical data. In an optimisation procedure the levels of mortality and migration are varied until the differences between the estimated and the registered values reach a minimum. At the same time the program tries to match estimated and registered numbers of two other variables, namely the sizes of the age groups in the final census and — if available — observed population sizes. For the stabilisation of the model it is also necessary to smooth the net migration rates over the first periods.[7] So, GIP requires aggregate numbers of births and deaths per interval (in this study we use quinquennial intervals), a life-table, a net-migration schedule, the age structure of the population at the end of the period being studied and, if available, some information on the population size in the course of the observed period of time.

What information do we have on the size and the structure of the Berne population between 1720 and 1920? Since the official incorporation of the suburban community of Bümpliz into the community of Berne took place in 1919, the published age distribution in the census of 1920 already includes Bümpliz. For a subsequent separation we had to assume parallel age structures in the town and the suburban community.[8] No special difficulties were caused by the Federal censuses of 1850 to 1910 and the Cantonal censuses of 1818, 1831, 1837, 1846 and 1856. We can consider all of them as reliable enough for our purpose.[9] Only the Helvetic census of 1798 is problematic, since its results are generally considered as too low.[10] It was not, therefore, included as a target in the projection. The first census in Berne was organised in 1764.[11]

The second group of data used for GIP are aggregate numbers of births and deaths. In the case of Berne this data is available with no serious gaps. However, there remain at least four major problems, if we want to use the registers of baptisms and burials for GIP:[12]

1.   The difference between birth and baptism in protestant Berne was relatively large. Of the 160 baptisms conducted between 1750 and 1780 (which give information on the date of birth as well as the date of baptism), 33 (21 per cent) children were baptised during the first four days of their life, 100 (64 per cent) between the 5th and the 8th day and 23 (15 per cent) between the 9th and the 14th day. The remaining four children were baptised more than a fortnight after birth.[13] Between 1841 and 1870 baptisms took place even later, on average about a month after birth.[14] Since babies dying before baptism generally were not registered and private baptisms were not allowed in protestant regions, a serious underestimation of births resulted.[15] A correction factor of 10 per cent has thus been applied to the baptism figures to estimate births. The correction factor was calculated on the basis of a study of

separate registration of deaths before baptism covering 15 per cent of the parishes in the canton of Berne.

2.   A second problem is caused by the fact that some of the rich citizens temporarily lived in the country; some because of their official function, some because they prefered to live on their estates.[16] However, if they did not want their children to lose their full political rights, they had to baptise them in the cathedral. All of them are therefore mentioned in the birth registers but their death registration is much less reliable. In addition, the practice of some families of handing over children to nurses in the country again reduces the completeness of the registers.[17] The tendency is to underrecord numbers of deaths. This becomes obvious in a comparison of the percentage of children who died in the first week of their lives in different places: Vienna 18 per cent, Lucerne 10 per cent, Berne 6 per cent.[18] To convert burials into deaths, information on the number of deaths before baptism was used.

3.   The registration of the population in a town, even of one in the size of Berne, caused serious problems for the authorities. In Berne, separate birth, marriage and death registers were kept for members of the aristocracy and for ordinary citizens. In a third register, births, marriages and deaths of the immigrant Huguenots were listed. Unfortunately, some of them are also mentioned in the ordinary register.[19] In 1704 a register of foundlings and illegitimate children was started.[20] Different registers offer the best conditions for missing registration and double counting. In addition not all the baptisms and burials are noted in the registers. Generally the priest wrote the personal data on a card. Every now and then he copied the data into the registers. If he had lost cards the entries were missing. There was an additional risk of underregistration when a new priest took over a parish.[21]

4.   In general, people living for just a limited period of time in the observed place are also included in the GIP procedure. However, a special problem is caused by hospital patients, because here the risk of birth or death clearly differs from the average. It is therefore important to know more about the extent of such events (birth and death) in these institutions. Graph 1 shows the number of births and deaths in Berne, relative to the number of events registered in the hospitals.[22] This graph must be considered with great caution, since the data stems from a contemporary table. It was not possible to check it on the basis of the original sources (the proportion of births before 1870 is much higher than the expected level).

In the series of births and deaths in the hospital people who came into the town just for medical care are included. Only about 21 per cent of the patients were resident in the town in 1871. From 631 patients in the maternity hospital (Entbindungsanstalt) about two thirds came from the countryside.[23] The situation was similar for deaths, where 81 per cent came from out of town. Unfortunately, we do not know if and to what extent birth and death of non-resident people were included in the registers of baptisms and burials. Only after 1876 is more data available. In 1876/77 and 1899/1900 11 to 13 per cent of the parents of new born babies were not resident in Berne, in 1917/18 about 23 per cent. The proportion was even higher among the deaths: 21 per cent in 1876/77, 24 per cent in 1899/1900 and 27 per cent in 1917/18. Based on these figures and the numbers of events in the hospital we had to correct the numbers of births and deaths between 1830 and 1920.

Graph 1   *Age Structure of Migrants. A Comparison of Distributions*

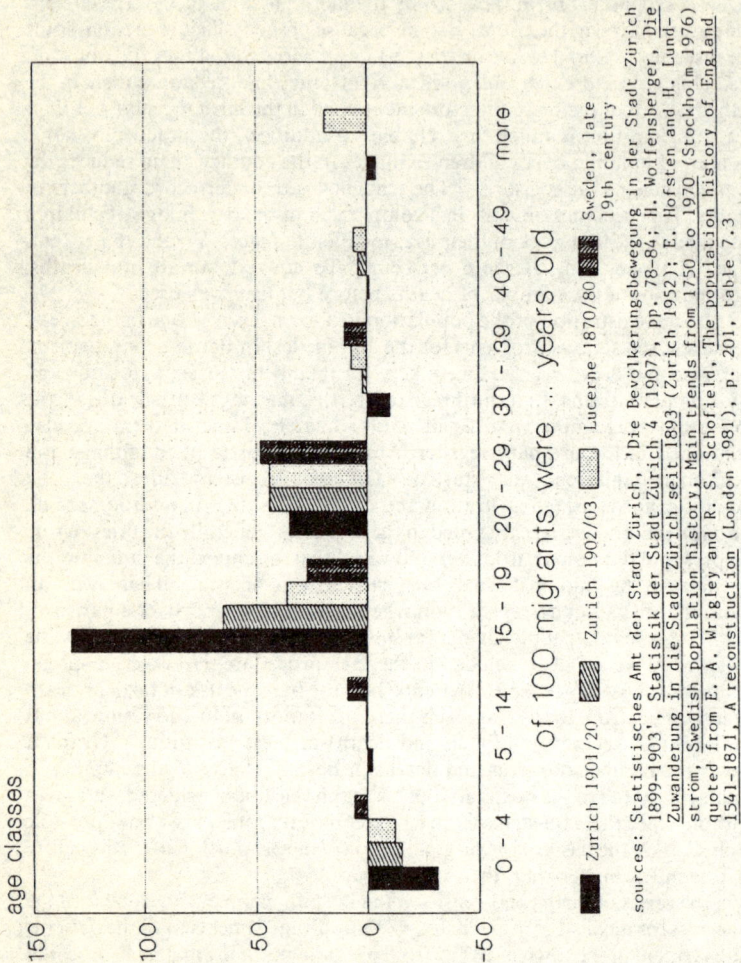

sources: Statistisches Amt der Stadt Zürich, 'Die Bevölkerungsbewegung in der Stadt Zürich 1899-1903', Statistik der Stadt Zürich 4 (1907), pp. 78-84; H. Wolfensberger, Die Zuwanderung in die Stadt Zürich seit 1893 (Zürich 1952); E. Hofsten and H. Lundström, Swedish population history, Main trends from 1750 to 1970 (Stockholm 1976) quoted from E. A. Wrigley and R. S. Schofield, The population history of England 1541-1871, A reconstruction (London 1981), p. 201, table 7.3

The large number of births in the hospital convinces us of the importance of the hospital in the urban demography of Berne. This observation is in opposition to the results of a study, dealing with the case of Lucerne. There 'mad and incurable persons and women in childbed' were excluded from the hospital.[24] In the 1890s only 3 out of 100 births in Lucerne happened in the hospital and non-resident people are included.[25] Although the reliablility of the Berne data may be questioned, it seems to be realistic to assume that about 30 per cent of births took place in the hospital. More than three quarters of mothers came from out of town.

Life-tables and a net-migration schedule form the third group of information on which GIP is based. In this study we use the Swiss life table of 1876/80. Although it still reflects the high infant and child mortality of the nineteenth century, it is based on a large amount of statistical evidence. But it is clear that it does not take into account local and urban characteristics.[26] Since migration is of special importance for the urban demography, the net-migration schedule will now be discussed in some detail. What we need are figures about the relative probability of migration at different ages. Unfortunately not much material could be found regarding this. The cohort net-migration schedule which Hofsten and Lundström have calculated from Swedish data and which had been used in the *The Population History of England* is based on national emigrants.[27] We have to assume, though, that an urban schedule is considerable different form a national one. Supposing the necessary source material is available, the 'life-table survival-rate method' can offer one way of finding a local migration schedule on a period basis.[28] This method is based on the comparison of the size of an age cohort between two censuses. Serious problems can occur in small age groups when the life-table is not entirely appropriate to the data. This effect can explain the overestimation of old people in the schedule of Lucerne 1870/1880 displayed in graph 2. A much better distribution can be calculated if we know the age at death in a period between two censuses. This sort of data is available for the city of Berne since the 1840s, but it has not yet been analysed.[29] Therefore we had to use statistical evidence on the age of the migrants in Zurich from about 1900.[30] For Berne similar data is only available after 1931.[31]

Graph 2   *Births and Deaths in the Hospitals of the City of Berne*

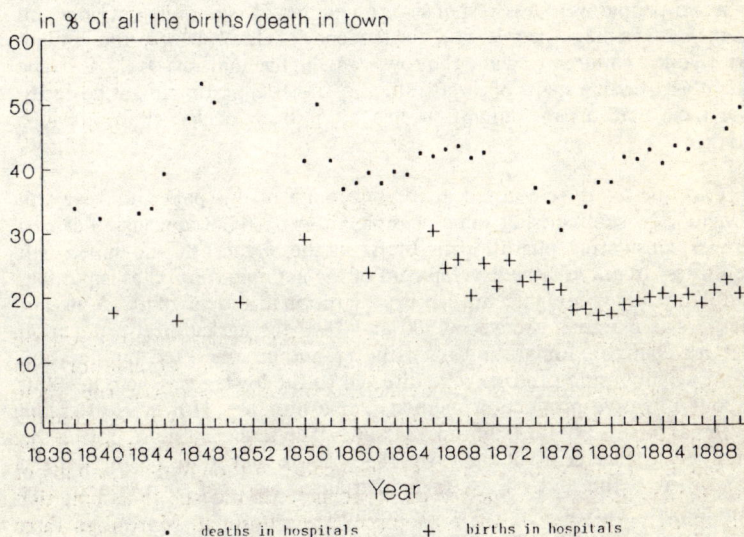

in % of all the births/death in town

· deaths in hospitals   + births in hospitals

In graph 2 all the age schedules of net-migration have two characteristics. On the one hand most of the migrants are between 15 to 29 years old. This has been observed many times before.[32] A more surprising finding is the concentration of the 15 to 19 year-olds, in contrast to 20 to 24 year-olds. The reason for this becomes clear when we look at the volume of migration, i. e. the sum of immigrants and emigrants together. 20 to 24 year-olds contribute most to immigration, but their large share among the emigrants reduces their proportion among the 'net migrants'.

A second characteristic of the net migration schedules in graph 2 relates to young children under four. Even if the majority of the migrants were immigrants, members of this group were more often leaving town than coming in. E. Wolfensberger, who wrote a thesis in 1952 on the immigration to Zurich, does not have a very convincing explanation for this:

Of major influence might be the fact that mothers came from the country into Zurich to give birth to their child and that they went back to their place of residence after a few days or weeks. In this case the child was considered as emigrant. However, it is surprising that the largest proportion of emigrants was not among the 0 to 1 year-olds, but among the 1 to 2 year-olds. This loss of migrants can only be understood if the relatively high proportion of illegitimates is taken into account, and if we assume that only after a year or so a place for these children could be found.[33]

More important, in my opinion, was the emigration of families with young children.

What can we conclude from these remarks on the net migration schedule? First, even if there was more immigration among the whole population, a negative balance among young children is possible. Secondly, there are reasons to believe that the proportion of the 15 to 19 year-olds in net migration was higher than that of every other age-group. Thirdly, old and married people were less responsive to changes in economic development than younger, single people. Still, the tendency of elderly people and families with young children to leave the town was higher than the average.[34] The slightly surprising shape of the age stucture of net migration might be due to the fact, that urban emigration has often been neglected in previous studies.[35]

Two questions were posed at the beginning of this paper, and we will conclude by summarising some possible answers. What conclusion can be drawn considering migration in Berne in the eighteenth and nineteenth centuries? In graph 3 the development of the net migration rates is plotted. Until the end of the eighteenth century migration in and out of the Canton of Berne was marginal. Between 1800 and 1840 the agricultural production pattern changed. Emigration from the mountain zones and immigration from neighbouring cantons were directed to the lowlands, where new but labour intensive production methods came into use. However, after the outbreak of the potato-blight in 1845 and 1846 and even more during the mild subsistence crisis of the early 1850s, more and more people left the canton of Berne and moved to industrialised parts of Switzerland, like Aargau and Zurich, or to overseas countries.[36]

The growth of the town population in the eighteenth and the first half of

Graph 3   *Net-migration Rates. Estimated and Observed Values, 1727–1917*

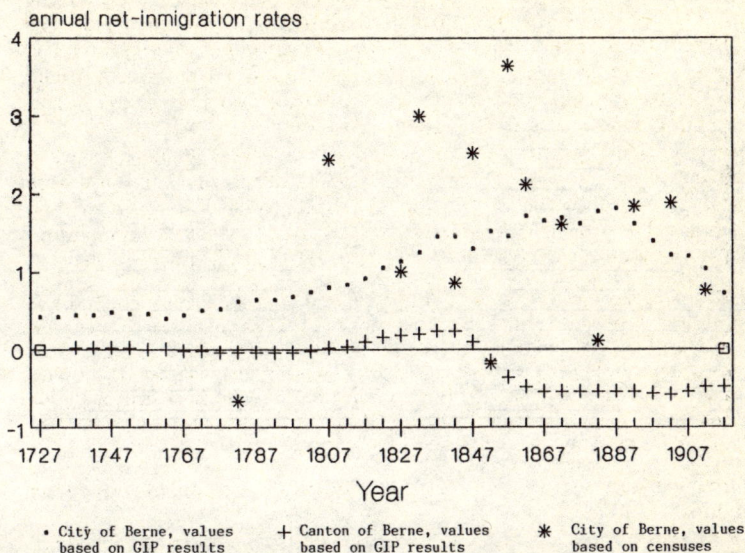

annual net-inmigration rates

- City of Berne, values based on GIP results
- Canton of Berne, values based on GIP results
- City of Berne, values based on censuses

the nineteenth century was slow but continuous. The two periods of low increase between 1850 and 1860 and between 1880 and 1890 were followed by times of rapid growth. The peak was around 1900. Towards the end of the nineteenth century more and more migrants were attracted by jobs in the town. Between 1901 and 1920 Berne had a higher surplus than most other Swiss towns, including Basel, Zurich and Geneva.[37] The percentage of foreigners is given in the censuses: 1850, 5·6 per cent, 1880, 7·8 per cent, 1900, 8·4 per cent and 1910, 10·6 per cent.[38] The city of Berne was declared as Swiss capital in 1848 and became a city of civil servants.[39]

What were the results of the large immigration on the age structure of the population of Berne? The estimated age pyramids in graph 4 show the bulk of young people between 15 and 29 in the town from the 1750s onwards. Since GIP at its present stage does not allow to distinguish between women and men, all our results are given for both sexes combined.[40] In comparison with the observed data the results of the estimation are encouraging, especially considering the uncertainties we had in constructing series of births and deaths, a life-table and a net migration schedule.

The second question asked at the beginning of this paper deals with the use of GIP in the analysis of urban demography, especially of urban migration. At first sight the benefit in the case of Berne appeared to be small. The first census was taken as early as 1764, so defendable migration values can be calculated from then on. But having the data at regular intervals is a clear advantage. GIP has other strengths as well. First, it forces us to think

Graph 4   *Observed and Estimated Age Structure of the Population of the City of Berne*

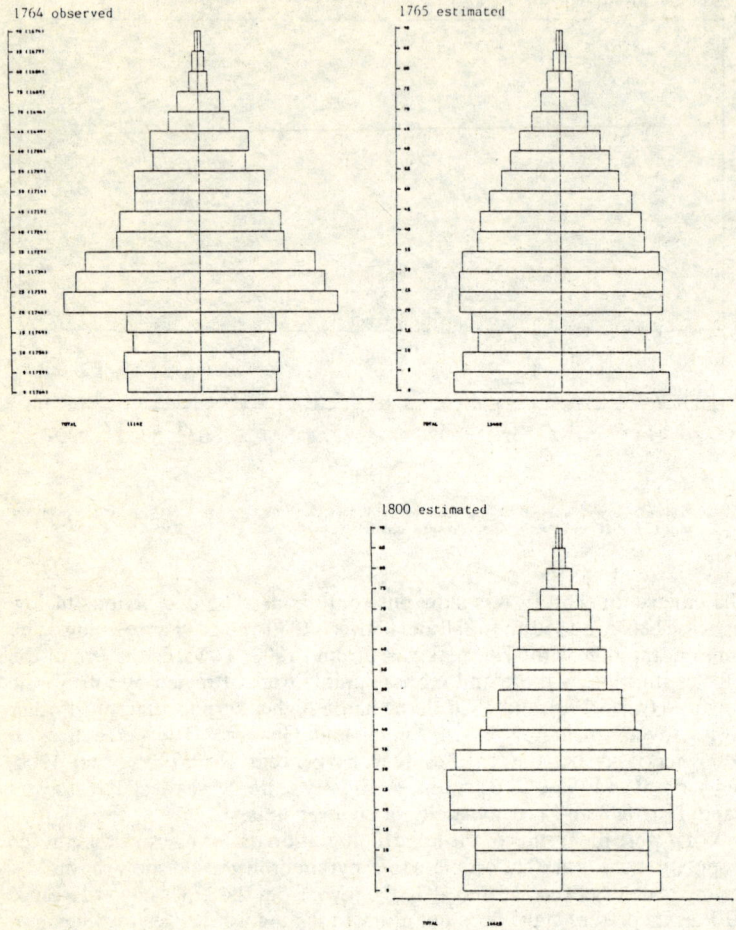

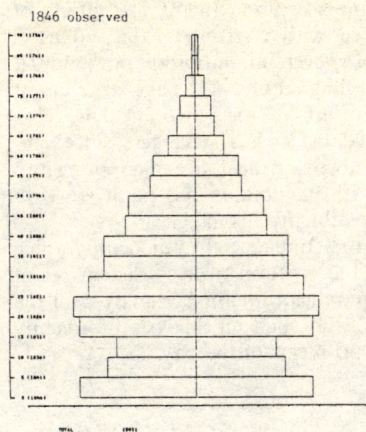

1846 observed

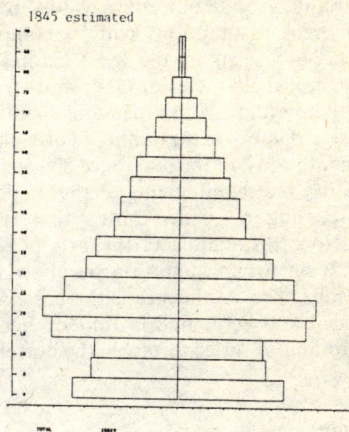

1845 estimated

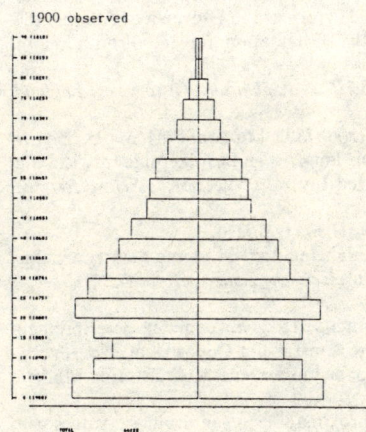

1900 observed

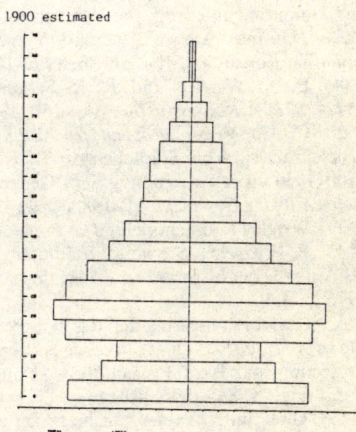

1900 estimated

carefully about our input values to improve upon them. The effects of different assumptions can be compared with registered values. This is especially useful for the age structures. However, it is important not to forget the model character of GIP; short-term fluctuations in the age structure of migrants and deaths are not taken into account. Using a theoretical model to test and improve the quality of historical data also has its dangers, since sight might be lost of the difference between improving the data and adapting it to match the requirements of the model. In our opinion this point is worth discussing in a wider context than is possible in this paper.

Notwithstanding, GIP can improve the confidence in our demographic data on urban migration by allowing the creation of a consistent set of results. This confidence is the basic requirement for further analysis of the social and economic history of Berne, and such an analysis is urgently required in order to tackle the current problems of the city.

Notes

I would like to thank at least four groups of people for their help and support: the Cambridge Group for the History of Population and Social Structure, Christian Pfister and Hannes Schüle from the Department of History at the University of Berne, the Swiss National Science Foundation and the Foundation for the Promotion of Scientific Research at the University of Berne.

1. E. A. Wrigley and R. S. Schofield, *The Population History of England 1541–1871, A Reconstruction*, London, 1981.
2. Cf. J. de Vries, *European Urbanisation 1500–1800*, London, 1984, p. 199, and my article 'Luzern: Vom Städtchen zur Stadt, Die langfristige Bevölkerungsentwicklung 1700–1930 unter Anwendung der "Generalized Inverse Projection"', *Schweizerische Zeitschrift für Geschichte*, 1, 1988, pp. 1–29.
3. Wrigley and Schofield, *The Population History*, p. 220.
4. B. Fritzsche, 'Schweizer Städte im 19. Jahrhundert, Moderne Stadtgeschichte als Aufgabe der historischen Forschung', *Schweizerische Zeitschrift für Geschichte*, 3, 1976, p. 439.
5. It is worth stressing that it is in no way intended to give a complete description of the procedure. For this the reader is urged to consult Jim Oeppen's article 'Inverse Projection and Back Projection: Variants of a more General Constraint Model', Cambridge, 1985, unpublished.
6. These initial values can be rough approximations; even arbitrary values can suffice to start the process. The approximation of the mortality levels is based on J. C. McCann, 'A Technique for Estimating Life Expectancy with Crude Vital Rates', *Demography*, 2, 1976, pp. 259–72.
7. The smoothing of the migration rates over the first t — k periods, where t is the total number of time periods and k the number of age groups in the final census, leads in these intervals to an overestimation of changes in mortality levels as a control of the system, see Oeppen, 'Inverse Projection', p. 14; the system allows the smoothing over cohort or period migration rates. This paper is based on the cohort migration system, since its results match the nineteenth century census observations much better, see in detail, op. cit., pp. 21–2.
8. Statistisches Amt der Stadt Bern, 'Die wichtigsten Ergebnisse der Volkszählung vom 1. Dez. 1920 in der Stadt Bern', *Halbjahresbericht über die Bevölkerungsbewegung und die wirtschaftlichen Verhältnisse der Stadt Bern*, appendix 22, 1, 1921.
9. C. Pfister, 'Menschen im Kanton Bern, Wandlungen in der Bevölkerungsentwicklung und -verteilung seit dem späten Ancien Régime', *Der*

Mensch in der Landschaft, Jahrbuch der geographischen Gesellschaft von Bern, 55, 1983–85, pp. 478–86; H. Stüssi, 'Die Altersangaben bei Volkszählungen', *Zeitschrift für schweizerische Statistik*, 4, 1873, pp. 270–27; W. Bickel, *Bevölkerungsgeschichte und Bevölkerungspolitik der Schweiz seit dem Ausgang des Mittelalters*, Zurich, 1947, pp. 296–7.

10. H. R. Burri, *Die Bevölkerung Luzerns im 18. und frhen 19. Jahrhundert*, Lucerne, 1975, p. 34; Pfister, *Menschen im Kanton Bern*, p. 485.

11. Op. cit., p. 479, W. Sommer, *Beiträge zur Bevölkerungssterblichkeit, Historisch-vergleichende Studie aufgrund der Volkszählungsergebnisse in der Stadt Bern aus dem Jahre 1764*, Berne, 1944, pp. 2–20.

12. I am especially grateful to C. Pfister and his collaborators, who collected the data from the archives.

13. E. Reust, *Die Säuglings- und Kindersterblichkeit in der Stadt Bern in der zweiten Hälfte des 18. Jahrhunderts (1750–1780)*, unpublished master degree thesis, Berne, 1980, p. 16; In catholic Lucerne the average interval between birth and baptism was zero or one day and between death and burial one or two days, see Burri, *Die Bevölkerung*, p. 28;

14. C. Pfister, 'Grauzonen des Lebens, Die aggregative Bevölkerungsgeschichte des Kantons Bern vor dem Problem der totgeborenen und ungetauft verstorbenen Kinder', in *Schweizerische Gesellschaft für Familienforschung*, Jahrbuch 1986, p. 31.

15. See Pfister, 'Grauzonen', p. 28; Between 1866 and 1876 the clerical registers were formally kept as civil registers. Every birth and death had to be written down. Only in 1876 civil registration began, see op. cit., p. 25.

16. Op. cit., pp. 32–3.

17. Op. cit., pp. 90.

18. Op. cit., pp. 29–31 and Burri, *Die Bevölkerung*, p. 140.

19. Pfister, 'Grauzonen', pp. 20–2.

20. Op. cit., pp. 23–5.

21. Op. cit., p. 25.

22. Bernisches statistisches Bureau, 'Statistik der öffentlichen Krankenpflege im Kanton Bern mit Bezugnahme auf die Krankenversicherung', *Mitteilungen des bernischen statistischen Bureaus*, 1. Lieferung, Bern, 1892; in 1924/25 about 32 per cent of the children of the city of Berne were born in a hospital, see Statistisches Amt der Stadt Bern, 'Die Spitalgeburten in der Stadt Bern', *Vierteljahresbericht des Statistischen Amt der Stadt Bern*, 1, 1951, pp. 41–5.

23. A. Vogt, 'Ueber den Unterschied zwischen faktischer und Wohnbevölkerung, sein Einfluss auf die Mortalität der Stadt Bern, mit Berücksichtigung der städtischen Spitalverhältnisse', *Zeitschrift für schweizerische Statistik*, 1, 1875, p. 329.

24. W. Schüpbach, Die Bevölkerung der Stadt Luzern, Demographie, Wohnverhältnisse und medizinische Versorgung, Lucerne, 1983, p. 213.

25. In 1902 a new hospital was built in Lucerne and then the proportion grew rapidly to about 25 per cent in 1914. Nearly a third of them were resident in Lucerne, see op. cit., p. 213.

26. See Swiss Life-Tables 1876 — 1932, published by Eidgenössisches Statistisches Amt 'Schweizerische Volkssterbetafeln 1876 — 1932', *Beiträge zur schweizerischen Statistik*, 4, 1935; in addition tables based on data of the city of Berne were tested, but the results were not promising, see Sommer, *Beiträge*, p. 49 (data from 1764) and W. Grütter-Mojon, 'Konstruktion einer Ueberlebensordnung für die Stadt Bern', *Zeitschrift für schweizerische Statistik*, 3, 1924, p. 308 (based on the death 1919–1922 and the census 1920).

27. See Wrigley and Schofield, *The Population History*, p. 201, table 7·3.

28. See H. S. Shryock and J. S. Siegel et al., *The Methods and Materials of Demography*, New York, 1976, pp. 357–62; although the model is based on a cohort migration schedule, in practical application a period migration schedule is used due to

the lack of more appropriate historical evidence.

29.   Regular listing on the level of districts started in 1841, see Pfister, 'Grauzonen', p. 30.

30.   This material has been analysed by Statistisches Amt der Stadt Zürich in 'Die Bevölkerungsbewegung in der Stadt Zürich 1899 — 1903, Mit besonderer Berücksichtigung der Wanderungen und zwei graphischen Darstellungen', *Statistik der Stadt Zürich*, 4, 1907, and in 'Der Zuzug in die Stadt Zürich nach der kilometrischen Entfernung der Zuzugsgebiete', *Statistik der Stadt Zürich*, 10, 1908. See also H. Wolfensberger, *Die Zuwanderung in die Stadt Zürich seit 1893*, Zurich, 1952. In addition Swedish data was used to distinguish quinquennial cohorts, *Emigrationsutredningen*, Bilaga V, Bygdestatistik (Stockholm 1908 — 1913).

31.   Statistisches Amt der Stadt Bern, 'Zuzug und Wegzug in Bern 1930 bis 1933 mit Rückblicken auf frühere Jahre', *Beiträge zur Statistik der Stadt Bern*, 17, 1934, p. 11.

32.   For example Wrigley and Schofield, *The Population History*, p. 201 n. 18; R. Braun, *Das ausgehende Ancien Régime in der Schweiz, Aufriss einer Sozial- und Wirtschaftsgeschichte des 18. Jahrhunderts*, Göttingen, 1984, p. 154; J. H. Jackson, 'Wanderungen in Duisburg während der Industrialisierung 1850 — 1910', W. H. Schröder, ed., *Moderne Stadtgeschichte*, Stuttgart, 1979, p. 217–37.

33.   Wolfensberger, *Die Zuwanderung*, p. 73;

34.   See op. cit., p. 73; see also R. Heberle and F. Meyer, *Die Grossstädte im Strom der Binnenwanderung*, Leipzig, 1937, p. 26.

35.   J.-P. Bardet, 'Skizze einer städtischen Bevölkerungsbilanz: Der Fall Rouen', N. Bulst et al., eds., *Bevölkerung, Wirtschaft und Gesellschaft, Stadt-Land-Beziehung in Deutschland und Frankreich 14. bis 19. Jahrhundert*, Trier, 1983, p. 61.

36.   C. Pfister, 'Bevölkerung, Wirtschaft und Ernährung in den Berg- und Talgebieten des Kantons Bern 1760 — 1860', in: Allgemeine Geschichtsforschende Gesellschaft der Schweiz, 'Wirtschaft und Gesellschaft in Berggebieten', *Itinera*, 5/6, 1986, p. 361.

37.   Wolfensberger, *Die Zuwanderung*, p. 50; translation by the author.

38.   Statistisches Amt der Stadt Bern, 'Berns Bevölkerung seit der letzten Volkszählung', *Vierteljahresbericht des statistischen Amtes der Stadt Bern*, 3, 1929, p. 160.

39.   For a comparison of the occupational structure of Berne, Zurich and Basel, see op. cit., pp. 149–51.

40.   In the census of 1764 already a clear majority of women was stated in Berne (60 per cent). The reason was that women were preferred as servants and that man in the age of 18 to 30 often were in foreign military duties, see Sommer, Beiträge, p. 31. The following figures underline that the majority of women was slightly reduced until 1920: 1818: 56 per cent women, 1850: 53 per cent, 1880: 54 per cent, 1920: 54 per cent, see Statistisches Amt der Stadt Bern, *Berns Bevölkerung*, p. 159.

The History of Medieval and Early Modern Migration: Computer-Supported Methods and Results

The study of migration in the Middle Ages has come of age.[1] When the authors first discussed a project on medieval and early modern migration and geographical mobility in Austria, about five years ago,[2] we did not foresee that our research would become part of an international arena.[3]

Migration must be seen as a mass-phenomenon. A quantitative approach is thus necessary. For the period we are dealing with, roughly the time between 1300 and 1600, sources covering this mass-phenomenon directly, are, at least for Austria and Germany, rare. We can use a small number of serial sources (university-registers for the migration of students; burgher enrollment-registers as evidence for the immigration to towns; artisan registers). More often though, we depend on lots of scattered evidences mentioned in account-books, last wills, land-registers, travel-descriptions, miracle-registers or even in pictures.[4] No type of source can be excluded. Thus we are dependent on a large number of 'individual cases'. One individual case, i.e. one act of migration, is in our view merely the fact of a 'change of residence' of a person, in the broadest possible sense. Our research, therefore, mainly is based on the comparison of many individual cases of very different character: the migration of individuals and groups, permanent and temporary; migration connected with a change of the social level of the migrant or not; 'forced' and 'voluntary' migration, and so on.

Our interest in migration is not simply concerned with the 'usually relevant' questions of population history and demography. Such 'traditional' migration-studies, particularly done in Western Europe, have been very much connected with concepts of historical demography.[5] They have aimed at making population accounts available in order to describe the basic processes of population history. Having become a rather routine sort of research, with its social historical possibilities exhausted, those demographical questions and methods of analysis do not seem very useful for migration history understood as an integral part of social history. Moreover, these methods can only be applied to medieval sources to a very limited extent.

The approach and questions of sociological migration-studies are certainly much more wide-ranging. Nevertheless, there is no sociological research concept directly relevant to our project. Moreover, sociology has not yet developed a general and/or generally accepted theory able to explain the phenomenon of migration.[6]

Our social historical approach had to be very wide and extensive. It had to recognise the following:

1. Migration is not influenced by one single factor only;
2. The number of factors is not easily determined;
3. The most relevant factors can nonetheless be isolated and determined, and their different influences in certain social spheres may be analysed and described.

To analyse the individual cases they had to be categorised in some way: ranks, classes or social groups. Using a concept of social groups, we are dealing with students, artisans, journeymen, apprentices, burghers, miners, women, peasants, people joining religious communities, etc. Moreover, other levels are studied which exceed this concept of social groups, such as pilgrimages or the mobility of 'criminals'.

A recurrent problem has been the standardisation of the differing contents and structures of the sources. Solutions of this problem were offered by CLIO, the data base management system developed by Manfred Thaller in Göttingen.[7] CLIO makes it possible to record the source-information very precisely and to create for every bundle of cases computer-generated codebooks relevant to the specific subject. One instance ('case') of migration, the lowest level of information, is recorded in a standardised nucleus (see diagram) containing type of migration, source, date, motive of migration (A\$); migrating person: sex, first name, surname, occupation, social rank, other functions (P\$); point of departure of the act of migration (HO\$); destination of the act of migration (ZO\$).[8] Around this unalterably necessary and standardised nuclei other categories are added, in their structure and content dependent on the different sources. In this way, serial sources can be treated as well as travel-descriptions, pilgrimage-records or pictures. The quantitative and statistical analysis is mainly done by using SPSS, CLIO offering the possibilities to create different kinds of thesauri and codebooks and to convert CLIO-datafiles into SPSS-datafiles.

Using some examples, we would like to show to what extent a concept of migration in the Middle Ages and Early Modern period could be developed through evaluation of different patterns of 'change of residence'. We focus here on three relevant issues:

1. Migration driven by market-phenomena;
2. Migration driven by the development or maintenance of social networks;
3. Migration driven by certain concepts of communication.

Needless to say, multiple causation is a common event.

Figure 1

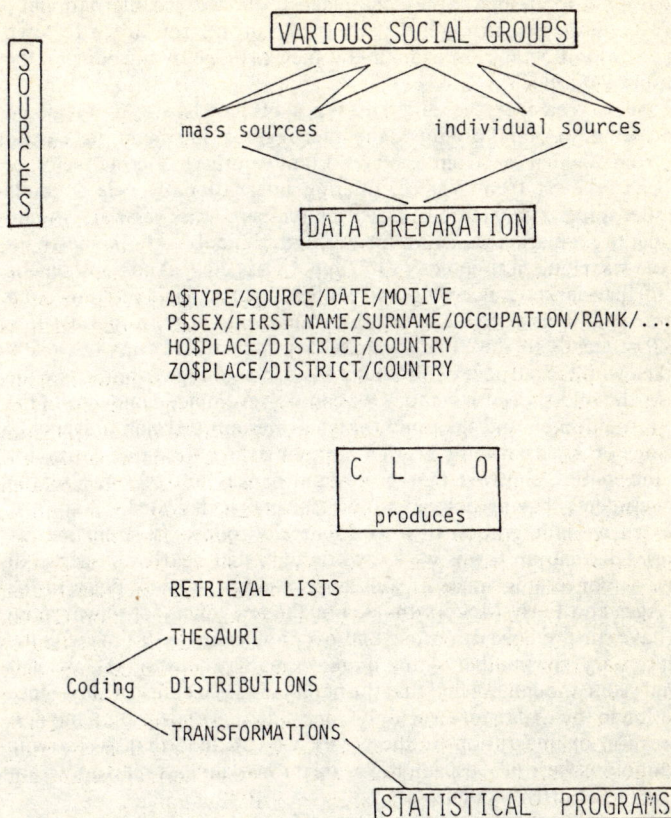

```
A$TYPE/SOURCE/DATE/MOTIVE
P$SEX/FIRST NAME/SURNAME/OCCUPATION/RANK/...
HO$PLACE/DISTRICT/COUNTRY
ZO$PLACE/DISTRICT/COUNTRY
```

Market Phenomena

Market-phenomena play an important role in initiating migration. 'Market' does not only mean the influence of the economic system, but — in the broadest sense — all fields controlling and maintaining a social system.[9] Therefore, we cannot concentrate solely on the pure economic market, which itself shows very different subpatterns of migration. For a number of Austrian communities we could prove the clear difference between certain groups of artisans with regard to their attitude to and patterns of migration: on the one hand the migrant baker or butcher, satisfying basic needs, coming from nearby places to communities where his work is required; on the other hand the specialists originating from specific, often far-away places (e.g. the Italian masons regularly found, particularly in the sixteenth century, in building campaigns of Austrian monasteries, towns or castles);[10] or, again, the specialists with rare skills not necessarily associated with geographic origin such as the clock-makers, who worked internationally in the 1370s, travelling through the whole of Europe from town to town helping communities develop or maintain their prestige by introducing the innovation of the clock.[11]

We have to consider the different types of merchants: the regional merchant selling regional products, the inter-regional merchant, in Austria mainly from Vienna or from the important southern German city of Nuremberg or even from Venice, offering internationally prized goods (Italian silk, spices, rice, almonds, figs or Nuremberg brass vessels).[12] Again we can identify a market structure for vagrant criminals — fairs, merchant routes, the travelling households of the upper class etc.[13] And consider the change of the market concerning universities,[14] particularly in connection with new foundations or, in the sixteenth century, with the religious question, or with first trends to the "Bildungsreise" — educational trips not really undertaken with the purpose of obtaining an academic degree, but to 'see the world'. In the mid-sixteenth century we can, for example, demonstrate the eminent attraction of, and the trend to, the protestant German universities for the sons of Austrian burghers. To a minor degree the same is true for Italian universities, showing that protestantism was not the only reason Austrian students, having only a catholic university, migrated.

The extensive immigration to towns generally follows different market principles. Of Austrian towns we know, though, that nearly no change of their size — concerning space as well as population — took place in the Middle Ages and Early Modern times. For the few towns for which serial sources have survived, we can prove that over longer spans of time (e.g. the fifteenth century) the number of immigrants remained constant. Looking at individual years, though, we find that the numbers varied considerably. Since immigration to towns did not mean only a one-sided act of migration but also the expression of integration by the towns, we conclude that the varying immigration numbers of Austrian towns might be seen as a reaction to ad-hoc needs of the urban systems.[15]

A good example of the interdependance of emigration and immigration could be found for the Reformation and post-Reformation period in Lower Austria. Protestant burghers, particularly the upper class, were forced to leave recatholicised towns at the end of the sixteenth century creating a social vacuum; this in turn forced the authorities to open the communities to others, Catholics, mainly artisans and members of a lower class.[16]

Social Networks

Not all immigration to towns can be explained in terms of market forces. Emigrations and immigrations of social elites often must be seen as following other principles. For Austrian towns we could prove that the local elites were not very stable. In particular, the high mortality rate reduced their number quickly. The vacuum often was not 'refilled' with social 'newcomers' of the own community but with members of the elites of other communities. An important role in this process was played by specific 'marriage-patterns' of the elites — not only in towns, but certainly also in the aristocracy — causing a fusion of the elites in different communities.[17]

Certain groups dominating a monastic community (relatives, persons originating from one place or region, persons of same or equal social rank, persons speaking the same language) obviously had their impact on the entering of novices into that community.[18] On language-boundaries, from Bohemia and Moravia in the North to Slovenia or Croatia in the South, we have not only found quarrels between members of the different language-communities in one monastery but also a pronounced tendency to support one's own group by getting in new members. Monasteries having strong connections to faraway areas, which certainly is in many aspects true for the Cistercians and their system of mother- and daughter-abbey, also sometimes showed the domination of monks originating from there and attempts at maintaining that situation. In the Carinthian monastery of Viktring a very strong group of monks from the Rhineland in the fourteenth and fifteenth centuries dominated the community which, from the viewpoint of members of the monastery originating from nearby, gave rise to quarrels. Their long period of domination clearly shows how the trend to maintain the status quo could create a migration-influencing network.

A similar situation existed in many Austrian monasteries of the Reformation and post-Reformation period. Recruits to the near empty monasteries of the middle and the second half of the sixteenth century were drawn from still strongly catholic Bavaria. Until well into the seventeenth century, when Catholics had regained all positions in Austria and monks from nearby again joined the communities, Bavarians still quite regularly held the lead in those monasteries, obviously by persuading people from their homeland to join the faraway community. Without doubt, however, principles of the market and of communication also played a role in this case.

Communication

Migration as communication again can be seen in many different forms and aspects, often strongly connected with maintaining social networks and market strategies.. Obtaining knowledge and gathering information, taking advantage of such information, or collective knowledge as a factor in technical and social innovation — these are some dimensions of communication as a concept of migration.

Examples are:
— trade-connections sustained during the whole of the period we are dealing with.[19]
— relations of one monastery to other monastic communities, of the same order and/or situated nearby or connected by a mother-daughter connection. Research dealing with the wandering of Cistercian monks from one monastery to others, mainly out of different situations of crises (Hussites; economical shortages; oppression by aristocrats; etc.), showed the very strong connections between those communities, and that communication was the relevant factor for the destinations of the monks.[20]

— the large group of messengers of institutions gathering and distributing information of very different kind, starting from the regular exchange of news between towns, monasteries, towns and court etc. To give a rather isolated example, we might mention the messenger of the small market-town of Obervellach in Carinthia, sent north over the Alps in 1525 to gather information on the peasants' uprisings in Salzburg.[21]
— the transfer of books.[22]
— students joining universities groupwise.[23]
— groups or, sometimes, masses of pilgrims wandering to the holy places, obviously motivating each other, making it possible to create a form of migration more effective, more secure, less tiresome, perhaps cheaper, etc.[24]

Conclusion

In this brief paper we have tried to explain and illustrate three social forces bearing on medieval and early modern migration. Certainly, natural conditions or specific incidents also must be mentioned as being important. Think of the geographical position of places, of traffic- and merchant-routes, of the climate, of 'general' danger or security, of specific incidents causing crises, may they be war, fire, thunderstorms, hunger, etc. Those crises are certainly to be distinguished from the sociological theory of migration as the general result of anomic tensions.[25]

Behind these results, there lies much research, involving a large number of diverse sources, archival and printed.[26] We would like to emphasise again that the very open structure and category-system offered and made possible by CLIO and developed for our project — minimal but strict standardisation of the nuclei; 'standardised openness'[27] for every data type surrounding the nuclei and added to them — has yielded information which demands a new understanding of medieval and early modern migration: contrasting, overlapping, adding to each other, chronologically and regionally changing, individual and general.

Compared to the work of historians using modern source-material our research has disadvantages and advantages. One of the main disadvantages has been that, because of the source-situation, certain results which are a matter of course for everybody dealing with the industrialised period will never be available for us. On the other hand, this shortcoming just might have been a major advantage. We have been forced to free ourselves of the sometimes tight boundaries of the historical-demographical paradigm, and to start again to reflect about the problem of migration as a whole, its theories, its concepts and the possible methods of research for medieval and early modern sources.

Notes

1. See, e.g., B. Geremek, 'Les migrations des compagnons au bas Moyen Age', *Studia historiae oeconomicae*, 5, Poznań, 1970, pp. 61–79; various contributions in *Strutture familiari, epidemie, migrazioni nell'Italia medievale*, ed. R. Comba, G. Piccinni, G. Pinto, (Nuove Ricerche di Storia, 2), Napoli, 1984; Cl. Billot, 'Le migrant en France à la fin du Moyen Age', *Medieval Lives and the Historian. Studies in Medieval Prosopography*, eds. N. Bulst and J.-Ph. Genet, Kalamazoo, 1986, pp. 235–42; various contributions in *Migration in der Feudalgesellschaft*, ed. G. Jaritz, A. Müller, (Studien zur Historischen Sozialwissenschaft, 8), Frankfurt/Main, New York 1988. See also note 3.

2. The project has been funded by the 'Fonds zur Förderung der wissenschaftlichen Forschung in Österreich'. Concerning the project, see G. Jaritz, A. Müller, 'Historia Vaga. Ein computergestütztes Projekt zur Migrationsgeschichte des 15. und 16. Jahrhunderts', *Datenbanken und Datenverwaltungssysteme als Werkzeuge historischer Forschung*, ed. M. Thaller, (Historisch-Sozialwissenschaftliche Forschungen, 20), St. Katharinen, 1986, pp. 93–123; I. Matschinegg, 'Von der Einzelquelle zum Modellfall. Überlegungen zu Datenselektion und Datenstandardisierung', *Datennetze für die historischen Wissenschaften — Data Networks for the Historical Disciplines?*, ed. F. Hausmann et al., Graz, 1987, pp. 159–65.

3. For recent trends in German-speaking countries, see the contributions in *Unterwegssein im Mittelalter*, ed. P. Moraw, (Zeitschrift für historische Forschung, Beiheft 1), Berlin, 1985; G. Jaritz, A. Müller, 'Historia vaga', cit.; N. Ohler, *Reisen im Mittelalter*, Munich, 1986; various contributions in *Migration in der Feudalgesellschaft*, cit.

4. G. Jaritz, A. Müller, 'Historia Vaga', cit., pp. 111–23.

5. See for example J. C. Russell, 'Die Bevölkerung Europas 500–1500', *Europäische Wirtschaftsgeschichte*, vol. 1, eds. C. M. Cipolla, K. Borchardt, Stuttgart, New York, 1983, pp. 38–42; R. Mols, 'Bevölkerung Europas 1500–1700', *Europäische Wirtschaftsgeschichte*, cit., vol. 2, pp. 32–37; Y. Tugault, *La mesure de la mobilité. Cinq études sur les migrations internes*, Paris, 1973, pp. 51–66.

6. See the overview given by H.-J. Hoffmann-Nowotny, 'Paradigmen und Paradigmenwechsel in der sozialwissenschaftlichen Wanderungsforschung. Versuch einer Skizze einer neuen Migrationstherorie', *Migration in der Feudalgesellschaft*, cit.

7. This program-package developed for historians has been documented in several unpublished papers. See, in general, M. Thaller, 'CLIO — Ein datenbankorientiertes System für die Historischen Wissenschaften: Fortschreibungsbericht', *Historical Social Research*, 41, 1987, pp. 88–91.

8. See G. Jaritz, A. Müller, 'Historia vaga', cit., pp. 113–16.

9. See A. Müller, 'Räumliche Rekrutierung und soziale Reproduktion. Beispiele aus dem Städtebürgertum im spätmittelalterlichen und frühneuzeitlichen Österreich', *Migration in der Feudalgesellschaft*, cit.; Y. Barel, *La ville médiévale, système social, système urbain*, Grenoble, 1975, passim.

10. See P. Teibenbacher, 'Die Handwerksbeziehungen des Stiftes Kremsmünster im 16. Jahrhundert, vornehmlich in der Zeit von 1570 bis 1600', *Historisches Jahrbuch der Stadt Linz 1985*, 1986, pp. 437–42.

11. G. Dohrn-van Rossum, 'Migration technischer Experten im Spätmittelalter. Das Beispiel der Uhrmacher', *Migration in der Feudalgesellschaft*, cit., pp.291–314.

12. See for example R. Perger, 'Simon Pötel und seine Handelsgesellschaft', *Jahrbuch des Vereins für Geschichte der Stadt Wien*, 40, 1984, pp. 26 seq.; Ch. Promitzer, *Beispiele spätmittelalterlicher 'Objektmigration' aus Göttweiger Rechnungsbüchern*, unpublished Ms., Graz, 1986.

13. See for example G. Jaritz, 'Probleme um ein Diebsgeständnis des 15. Jahrhunderts', *21. Jahresbericht des Musealvereins Wels 1977/78*, 1978, pp. 77–86; H. Mandl-Neumann, 'Aspekte des Rechtsalltags im spätmittelalterlichen Krems', *Bericht über den sechzehnten Österreichischen Historikertag in Krems/Donau*, (Veröffentlichungen des Verbandes Österreichischer Geschichtsvereine, 25 Vienna, 1985, pp. 314–17; B. Rath, 'Prostitution und spätmittelalterliche Gesellschaft im österreichisch-süddeutschen Raum', *Frau und spätmittelalterlicher Alltag* (Veröffentlichungen des Instituts für mittelalterliche Realienkunde Österreichs, 9 = Sb. Ak. Wien, phil.-hist. Klasse, 473), Vienna, 1986, p. 566.

14. See G. Jaritz, 'Kleinstadt und Universitätsstudium. Untersuchungen am Beispiel Krems an der Donau (Von den Anfängen bis in das 17. Jahrhundert)', *Mitteilungen des Kremser Stadtarchivs 17/18*, 1978, pp. 105–67; 19, 1979, pp. 1–26; 23/24/25, 1986, pp. 153–78. Cf., generally, R. Ch. Schwinges, *Universitätsbesucher im 14. und 15.Jahrhundert. Studien zur Sozialgeschichte des Alten Reiches*, (Veröffentlichungen des Instituts für Europäische Geschichte Mainz, Abteilung Universalgeschichte, 123 = Beiträge zur Sozial- und Verfassungsgeschichte des Alten Reiches, 6), Stuttgart, 1986; idem, 'Migration und Austausch: Studentenwanderungen im Deutschen Reich des späten Mittelalters', *Migration in der Feudalgesellschaft*, cit., pp. 141–55.

15. A. Müller, 'Räumliche Rekrutierung', cit.

16. See, e.g., F. Schönfellner, *Krems zwischen Reformation und Gegenreformation*, (Forschungen zur Landeskunde von Niederösterreich, 24), Vienna, 1985, passim.

17. See for example A. Müller, *Die Bürger von Linz. Soziale Strukturierung und Prosopographie bis zur Mitte des 16. Jahrhunderts*, Diss., Graz, 1987.

18. G. Jaritz, 'Monastische Kommunität und Migration', *Migration in der Feudalgesellschaft*, cit.

19. See the old, but still valuable work of Th. Mayer, *Der auswärtige Handel des Herzogtums Österreich im Mittelalter*, Innsbruck, 1909.

20. G. Jaritz, 'Cistercian Migrations in the Late Middle Ages', *Goad and Nail* (Studies in Medieval Cistercian History, X), Kalamazoo, 1985, pp. 191–200 and pp. 293–99.

21. I. Matschinegg, *Städtisches Botenwesen im Spätmittelalter*, unpublished Ms., Graz, 1986.

22. See, e.g., *Regensburger Buchmalerei. Von frühkarolingischer Zeit bis zum Ausgang des Mittelalters*, (Bayerische Staatsbibliothek, Ausstellungskataloge, 39), Munich, 1987.

23. R. Ch. Schwinges, 'Studentische Kleingruppen im späten Mittelalter', *Politik, Gesellschaft, Geschichtsschreibung. Giessener Festgabe für František Graus*, ed. H. Ludat, R. Ch. Schwinges, (Beihefte zum Archiv für Kulturgeschichte, 18), Cologne, 1982, pp. 319–61.

24. L. Schmugge, 'Kollektive und individuelle Motivstrukturen im mittelalterlichen Pilgerwesen', *Migration in der Feudalgesellschaft*, cit., pp. 263–89.

25. H. J. Hoffmann-Nowotny, *Migration. Ein Beitrag zu einer soziologischen Erklärung*, Stuttgart, 1970, pp. 97–140.

26. Cf. M. Thaller, 'Warum brauchen die Geschichtswissenschaften fachspezifische datentechnische Lösungen? Das Beispiel kontextsensitiver Datenbanken', *Computer in den Geisteswissenschaften*, ed. M. Thaller, A. Müller, (Studien zur Historischen Sozialwissenschaft, 7), Frankfurt/Main, New York, 1988 (in press).

27. See G. Jaritz, 'Offenheit zur Öffnung? Das "Kreuz" mit der Standardisierung', *Datennetze*, cit., p. 133. Concerning the general discussion on standardisation, see **various contributions in** *Datenbanken*, cit., in *Computer in den Geisteswissenschaften*, cit., **and in** *Datennetze*, cit.

VII.

Economy and Society

Social Segregation in Eighteenth-Century Leiden

Problems of Measurement

This essay deals with the problem of social segregation in pre-industrial towns, a major theme in urban history and urban geography. In urban geography the organisation of the urban space is one of the central topics. Are workplaces and residential areas scattered in a random way or is there a pattern to be seen and, if so, why did such a pattern take the form it did? A lot of research has been done on the industrial cities in the United States and Great Britain. The American sociological Chicago-school has become famous for introducing models describing the regularities of the arrangement of the urban space. One of the better known and much discussed models is the one named after the sociologist Burgess. The starting-point of Burgess's model is that urban land use tends to display a zonal organisation concentrically arrayed around the city centre.[1] A major disadvantage of the model is that it reflects the situation typical of big American industrial cities of the 1920s. Therefore the model lacks universality. Gideon Sjoberg has made this very clear. He demonstrated that the pre-industrial city displays different structural features.[2] While in Burgess's model the nucleus of the city is the Central Business District — with few people actually living there —, according to Sjoberg it is the place where the privileged classes gather because they need the closest possible association with the governmental and religious buildings which physically and symbolically represent political power. The two other characteristics of the pre-industrial city, mentioned by Sjoberg, are: spatial differences according to ethnic, occupational and family ties, and secondly the low incidence of functional differentiation of land use patterns. This last point refers to the combination of workspace and living space in a pre-industrial town. One of the basic questions discussing segregation or spatial specialisation or differentiation is the one concerning the unit of analysis or scale. What kind of areas do we distinguish and how do we draw the lines? A danger is that we might be drawing lines that do not adequately represent social borderlines.

A useful synthesis of the methods used in the measurement of homogeneity or segregation has been offered by D. W. G. Timms.[3] He brings forward that it is now well accepted that in the analysis of residential differentiation socio-economic status, differences in family composition, ethnicity and mobility play an important role. For the English industrial city of the nineteenth century Richard Dennis has collected rich empirical data and combined these with the methodology of Timms. Dennis concluded that for the nineteenth century surprisingly little evidence of segregation or increase of segregation has been uncovered. In 1871, even in Leeds, most districts accommodated mixed populations. The question that concerns us here is the same, but referring to eighteenth-century Leiden.

With Delft, Gouda and Harlem, Leiden belongs to the so called 'inland-cities', a category of towns contrasting with the two harbour cities Amsterdam and Rotterdam. The economic basis for the inland cities was distinctive. In Delft distilleries, in Gouda pipemaking, in Harlem linen bleaching and in Leiden clothmaking and the production of other textiles were the main activities. The harbour cities, in contrast, had a diversified economic basis — harbour functions, shipbuilding and industries related to trade such as sugar refineries. The inland towns were much more specialised on one branch of industry. The capital for raw materials and the distribution of the finished products were mainly in the hands of merchants of the harbour cities. When during the eighteenth century the Dutch faced a growth in English competition, Dutch trade was flexible enough to cope with it. The bigger merchants changed their activities and moved into banking. But many of the smaller industrial entrepreneurs in the inland towns did not survive. So Leiden witnessed its greatest number of inhabitants during the last quarter of the seventeenth century, the Golden Age in Dutch history, and a decline during the eighteenth century. Economic success and a great number of inhabitants were synonymous in a period when poor relief was only given on a charitable basis and long periods of unemployment could only be solved by emigration or death. For the Dutch towns we only possess censuses for the years 1622 and 1795. We have to rely on estimates for the intermediate periods. In 1622 we find in Leiden around 45,000 inhabitants and in 1795 around 31,000, a reliable estimate mentions 70,000 for 1675 and on the basis of a tax list of 1749, to be considered as a census, we are able to calculate 37,000 inhabitants for the mid-eighteenth century. So there was a great increase between 1622 and 1675, when a decline started that lasted till the first decades of the nineteenth century.

The increase of the population during the seventeenth century forced the city authorities to enlarge the urban space. We already find an extension in 1611 at the north western and northern side of Leiden. There were two others, one in 1644 at the northern-eastern boundary and the last one in 1659 at the eastern side. The city at that time had reached the spatial boundaries which sufficed for its population till the end of the nineteenth century. The extension of Leiden certainly was the result of planning and planning was necessary because of the administration of the polders and the regulations in respect of the always present threat of flooding. So a spatial arrangement did not develop as the result of an impersonal competition but because of an intently discussed plan.[5] Although urban planning was mainly related to the improvement of the physical environment in general, it also had more distinct consequences for certain people, although only indirectly. These people were the planners themselves, their political supporters, and the upper middle class citizens in general.[6]

The Sources

Before we discuss the question of social segregation and its measurement, we first have to consider the available sources. For the mid-eighteenth century we have a complete tax record containing almost 10,000 households. This list was drawn up when the tax system was revised after the general unrest in 1748. Previously the taxes had been farmed, but misuse was revealed in 1748 when the 'tax-farmers' houses were looted. New tax lists were drawn up with the valuation based on family size and the number of servants living in the house. These family particulars were entered on the tax register by the overseers of the 28 town quarters. In addition the occupation of the head of the household was recorded. Other tax statements provide information concerning householders and property value. These two sources provide the means to analyse house ownership and house values in relation to occupation, size of family and districts of the town. During the first phase of the research project only the number indicating the town quarter and the number within the quarter were coded and added to the data concerning each household for identification purposes.[7] A more detailed address was not coded at that stage. Because of that, the analysis could be carried on only for the town district as a whole. For reasons of comparison and to bring down the great number of districts, the 28 urban quarters were combined into 8 larger units. Here we meet the problem of real thresholds. The 28 town districts had their own administration with social and financial functions. Also a feeling of solidarity and communal activities have been recorded. So the boundaries of these quarters or 'bonnen' as they were called in Leiden, were real social and in some respect financial boundaries. So far about the sources being coded and manipulated, this was ten years ago using punched cards. During a later phase of the project the names of streets, canals, alleys or courtyards were added, to be able to differentiate within the quarters.

Some preliminary results of the later analysis are presented in the three tables. They contain data of the rateable value in respect of the whole town, the eight aggregated quarters and the 28 original quarters or 'bonnen' (see map). We introduce a more detailed analysis for the aggregated quarter 8 composed of the original quarters of 25, 26 and 28. This quarter is to be found at the eastern outskirts of the town. Here we find a concentration of textile workers, together with an absence of professional people and of retail trade. For this district the census lists mentioned the highest percentage of households receiving poor relief. So many characteristics of the Sjoberg model — concentration of an occupational group, the poor living at the outskirts are to be found.

We use five socio-economic variables. Of the variables introduced by Timms — socio-economic status, family composition, ethnicty and mobility-we can only use the first one. We have for our analysis data for the rateable value, ownership of the house, the occupation, the share of households receiving poor relief and the numbers of servants per household.

Figure 1   *Central Leiden*

Figure 2   *Leiden 1749*

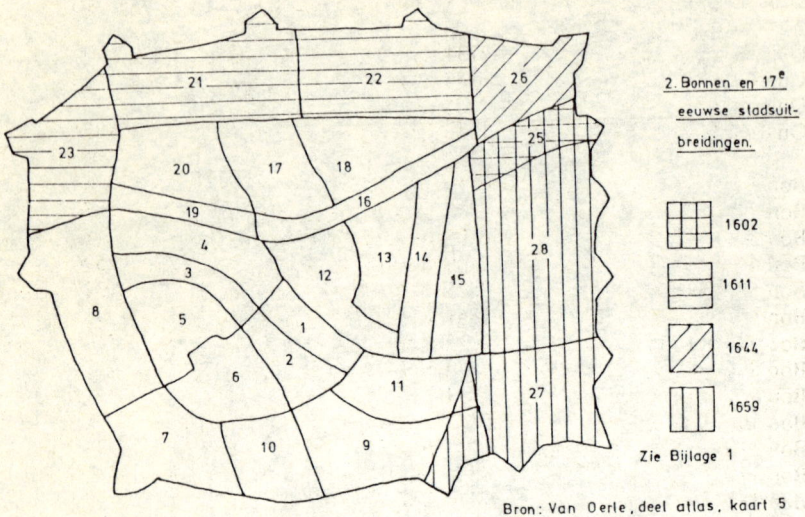

2. Bonnen en 17^e
eeuwse stadsuit-
breidingen.

1602

1611

1644

1659

Zie Bijlage 1

Bron: Van Oerle, deel atlas, kaart 5

Rateable Value

As we have seen Leiden was divided into eight quarters, each subdivided into neighbourhoods (Dutch: *bonnen*). To these two units of analysis we added a third one, the streets with over 75 households. As has been observed, in social area analysis we try to get a meaningful spacial division, i.e. one dividing the area in units with a high degree of social homogeneity. Our hypothesis is that, as large measuring-unit averages tend to blur internal differences, a smaller unit of analysis should lead to more homogeneous and therefore meaningful distinctions. In other words: analysis of the Leiden data at street-level should give more homogeneous results than at 'bon' — or quarter-level.

As a test for the whole of Leiden we use rateable value, being a more trustworthy indicator of household wealth than the amount of tax paid. An adequate measurement of homogeneity is achieved by making use of Theil-coefficients, the value of which varies form 0 (in case of absolute equality) to 1 (in case of absolute inequality). The results can be found in table 1.

Table 1   *The coefficient of rateable value on quarter-, subquarter-, and*
                   street-level.

Unit	Theilcoeff	Unit	Theilcoeff
Quarter 1	.2734	Quarter 5	.2166
Quarter 2	.1956	Quarter 6	.1668
Quarter 3	.1651	Quarter 7	.2461
Quarter 4	.1482	Quarter 8	.1871
Bon 1	.0319	Bon 15	.3035
Bon 2	.1365	Bon 16	.0650
Bon 3	.1505	Bon 17	.2012
Bon 4	.1286	Bon 18	.2596
Bon 5	.0825	Bon 19	.1327
Bon 6	.1861	Bon 20	.1915
Bon 7	.2025	Bon 21	.2486
Bon 8	.2869	Bon 22	.2095
Bon 9	.1793	Bon 23	.1592
Bon 10	.2277	Bon 25	.2983
Bon 11	.1792	Bon 26	.3376
Bon 12	.0834	Bon 27	.3074
Bon 13	.1478	Bon 28	.1501
Bon 14	.2876		
Rijn	.0461	Uiterstegracht	.2943
Breestraat	.0828	Marendorp	.1119
Nieuwe Rijn	.1128	Herengracht	.3554
Langeburg	.0724	Oude Vest	.1416
Steenschuur	.0861	Marend Achtergr	.3575
Rapenburg	.1191	Jan Vossensteeg	.1870
Doelengracht	.1363	Clarensteeg	.3453
Middelweg	.2303	L.Hooglandsekerkst	.1914
Cellebroersgracht	.1415	Vrouwenkamp	.1223
Binnenvestgracht	.1691	Oude Singel	.1459
St.Jacobsgracht	.2270	Langegracht	.1774
Haverstraat	.0105	Kleistraat	.0654
Gortestraat	.0711	Zuidsingel	.3364
Raamsteeg	.1888	Ververstraat	.3894
Koepoortsgracht	.1486	Westhavenstraat	.4853
Hogewoerd	.1088	Looierstraat	.1876
Levendaal	.1756	Langstraat	.3335
Gansoord	.0775	Oranjegracht	.1709
Hooigracht	.1833	Waardgracht	.0185
Oude Rijn	.0861	Singelstraat	.0613
Middelstegracht	.3302	Vestestraat	.1403
Groenesteeg	.0976		

At first sight our hypothesis is confirmed. Average Theil- coefficients 8 on quarter-, bon- and street-level decrease from .1988, through .1916 to .1746. The medians are .1914, .1793 and .1486 respectively. The smaller the unit of analysis, the higher the difference between average and median, which is an indication of more variance between Theil-coefficients on street-level than on both other levels. In fact the lowest and the highest Theil-coefficients (.0105 and .4858) occur at street-level. So a lower measuring level does not necessarily concord with a lower Theil-coefficient for every street, even though on the average it does.

We have to be aware of an important difference between the measuring levels. A high Theil-coefficient on quarter level does not necessarily imply that houses with relatively high and low rateable values are near to each other, while one on street level does, because it applies to a smaller area. In the latter case it may prove to be impossible to find a sensible and homogeneous unit.

Quarter Eight

To find out more about (the lack of) social homogeneity at the three levels, we shall take a more detailed look at Leiden's quarter eight. Quarter eight is convenient in this respect, in that most of the streets in it do not extend beyond its boundaries, nor indeed those of the bon division. The comparison between the three levels of analysis is therefore relatively pure. Also we find in this quarter some of the streets with either very low Theil-coefficients (Waardgracht .0185 and Singelstraat .0613) or very high ones (Westhavenstraat .5852 and Herengracht .3454).

A general impression of the division of wealth within quarter eight can be gained from table 2. At the different levels it gives the percentages of families receiving social aid, of those owning the house they live in and those having one or more servants. The results on bon level already reveals a marked contrast within the quarter. Bon 25 and bon 26 show largely the same pattern, but both 28 has a much lower percentage of families receiving social aid, while relatively more of them own their house and have servants. The contrasts increase very much at street level. The social aid percentage varies from 1·8 to 48·7, the ones concerning house ownership and servants from 43·2 to 2·6 and from 42·3 to 0 respectively. From table 2 it appears that Herengracht is by far the most wealthy part of the quarter. This is confirmed by the median rateable value for this canal, which, being 8·35 guilders, is the highest within quarter 8. The streets with the highest percentage of people receiving social aid are those having the lowest rateable value medians (Singelstraat, Looierstraat and Westhavenstraat; 1·35 guilders)

We can analyse the data of table 2 in different ways: comparing the three levels of analysis could be the first and the second one is comparing the three variables. We can also combine the two approaches. At the level of the whole quarter we find a share of poor families of 22·2 percent, of heads of households owning their house of 15·1 and of families with servants of 7·1 percent. The Herengracht and Oranjegracht score very low in respect of the share of poor families, 1·8 and 3·9 percent respectively. They also lead in respect of the percentages of ownership of the houses; 43·2 and 23·5 percent owned their house respectively. The Oranjegracht is apparently the area of small artisans (weavers) with no indoor servants. There only 3·3 percent of the households contained servants, much less than the average of the quarter (7·1%). The Groenesteeg has more houseowners and more households with servants than the Oranjesteeg, but more people with poor relief. The Herengracht is the most consistent in respect of share of the poor, ownership of the house and the presence of servants, but it had a very high Theilcoefficient suggesting a great lack of homogeneity in respect of rateable value, i.e. wealth.

All these differences within the area would have been blurred when analysing at quarter level only. Table 2 however does not provide us with an explanation for the difference in social homogeneity. Only an exploration of the social differences within the streets can do so.

Table 2   *Percentage of families receiving social aid, owning their house and having one servant or more respectively, at quarter-, subquarter- and street-level.*

Unit	percentage social aid	N	percentage own house	percentage w. servants
Quarter 8	22·2	1480	15·1	7·1
Bon 25	30·3	211	9·5	3·3
Bon 26	30·0	350	12·3	3·7
Bon 28	17·3	919	17·4	7·6
Groenesteeg	10·6	113	27·4	10·6
Vesterstraat	24·6	134	4·5	·0
Herengracht	1·8	111	43·2	42·3
Zuidsingel	25·3	102	7·8	2·0
Ververstraat	32·2	118	9·3	1·7
Westhavenstraat	40·2	82	8·5	·0
Looierstraat	48·1	77	2·6	1·3
Langstraat	21·5	93	5·4	1·1
Oranjegracht	3·9	153	23·5	3·3
Waardgracht	12·3	162	9·3	·0
Singelstraat	48·7	78	6·4	·0

Participation Within Textile Production

Table 3 provides us with an insight into the employment structure of the textile industry by specialised branches: the preparation (combers, wool cleaners), spinners, weavers, workers in the finishing phase, shearcroppers, textile merchants and others. On the basis of the share of some special branches within the textile trade we are able to differentiate within the smallest unit of analysis: the street. It enables us to explain the differences in homogeneity. We can also compare the percentage of the whole quarter with those of the 'bonnen' and the streets. When we take the streets also used in the above mentioned analysis we will find a concentration of persons involved in the textile trade on the Herengracht. While within the whole quarter eight only 2·8 percent of the household heads are working in the textile commerce, almost a quarter of the families living on the Herengracht are involved in this sort of activities. The workers at the lower end of the social scale, the spinners and weavers, are not living at the Herengracht. They are concentrated in the Ververstraat, Singelstraat, Looierstraat and Westhavenstraat. The Oranjegracht shows a concentration of weavers, like the Waardgracht. The concentration of weavers is clear at the Waardgracht and Oranjegracht: of the whole quarter around 25 percent of the household heads were weaver while the families there were for about 55 and 50 percent engaged in weaving.

Table 3   *Percentage of families with head employed in textiles per quarter, subquarter and street*

Unit	1	2	3	4	5	6	7*
Quarter 8	5·1	17·0	25·5	1·5	2·8	2·9	.1
Bon 25	3·3	19·9	10·9	.9	1·4	1·4	.0
Bon 26	2·6	24·6	17·4	1·1	1·1	2·6	.0
Bon 28	6·5	13·5	31·9	1·7	3·7	3·2	.2
Groenesteeg	8·0	4·0	12·0	2·0	14·0	.0	.0
Vestestraat	2·4	23·8	31·0	4·8	4·8	.0	2·4
Herengracht	5·6	.9	13·9	.9	.9	23·1	.9
Zuidsingel	3·9	22·5	11·8	2·0	2·9	1·0	.0
Ververstraat	1·7	34·7	7·6	1·7	.0	.0	.0
Westhavenstraat	3·7	24·4	26·8	.0	1·2	.0	.0
Looierstraat	9·1	27·3	10·4	6·5	.0	.0	.0
Langstraat	8·6	17·2	36·6	2·2	4·3	.0	.0
Oranjegracht	4·6	11·1	49·7	.7	4·7	2·0	.0
Waardgracht	6·8	9·9	55·6	1·2	5·6	.0	.0
Singelstraat	9·0	28·2	14·1	1·3	.0	.0	.0

*1 = preparation; 2 = spinners; 3 = weavers; 4 = finishing; 5 = shearcroppers; 6 = commerce; 7 = others.

In three out of four cases the data concerning occupation provide us an explanation for the extremes in the index of homogeneity per street. For the Westhavenstraat however they do not. It is not too difficult to explain this. While the rateable value is a useful indicator for wealth, it is by no means perfect. There is one other important factor influencing the homogeneity of rateable values per street, and that is town planning. The subdivision of quarter eight reflects its building history. Bon 26 is the oldest part, developing as a suburb at the end of the sixteenth century when Leiden's population was growing explosively, with very little planning and not hampered by building regulations. Bon 25 was constructed from 1644 onward. It was meant to fill up the dead angle between bon 26 and a northern town extension of 1611. Bon 28, part 7 of the last extension of Leiden for the two centuries to come, was very rigidly planned, in 1658/59. Almost every street in this area had uniform houses on uniform plots, the size of which differed per street.[9] It is inevitable that this influenced the variance of the rateable values. In fact the streets in bon 25 and bon 26 all have Theil-coefficients over .3. This does not mean that the degree of homogeneity was determined by town planning only. The Theil-coefficient for the Langstraat (.3335) shows that even in a uniform street rateable values could vary quite a bit. And the combination of a high and low Theilcoefficients (Westhavenstraat and Singelstraat) clarifies that wealth on the whole did influence rateable value very much. Nevertheless the irregularity of houses and plots in the Westhavenstraat may have caused the larger variation of rateable values, rather than that the differences in wealth have.

Conclusion

Our conclusion must be that the analysis at a lower level reveals contrasts within the town quarter that without it would have remained in the dark. Huge differences existed within the quarter in the relative amounts of people receiving social aid, owning their house and having servants. Generally speaking analysis at the street level results in a higher degree of homogeneity in rateable values. Although there seems to be some concordance of homogeneity of rateable values and the share of some occupations of the heads of households on street level, it does not offer in all cases an explanation for the occurrence of high or low Theil-coefficients rateable values.

Notes

1. See Harold Carter, *The Study of Urban Geography*, 1976, 2, pp. 173 ff.
2. Carter, op. cit., p. 177. Gideon Sjoberg, *The Pre-industrial City, Past and Present*, 1965.
3. D. W. G. Timms, *The Urban Mosaic. Towards a Theory of Residential Differentiation*, Cambridge U.P., 1971, especially pp. 85–122.
4. Richard Dennis, *English Industrial Cities of the Nineteenth Century. A Social Geography*, Cambridge U.P., 1984, pp. 200–49.

5.   E. Taverne, *In 't land van belofte, ideaal en werkelijkheid van de stadsuitleg in de Republiek 1580–1680*, Maarssen, 1978.

6.   D. W. G. Timms, *The Urban Mosaic*, cit., p. 121.

7.   H. A. Diederiks, D. J. Noordam and H. D. Tjalsma (eds.), *Armoede en Sociale Spanning, sociaal-historische studies over Leiden in de achttiende eeuw*, Hollandse Studien, 17, Hilversum, 1985, pp. 1–15.

8.   See: J. M. M. de Meere. *De economische ontwikkeling en levensstandaard in Nederland gedurende de eerste helft van de negentiende eeuw*, The Hague, 1982, pp. 136–37, note 86; computation of the Theil-coefficients has been as follows: for every geographical unit the ratal value were divided into categories (from f. 0·00 to f. 0·99; f. 1·00 to f. 2·99; f. 3·00 to 4·99; . . . ; f. 23·00 to f. 24·99; f. 25·00 and more). For each category Y 1n NY is computed, with Y being the share of the category in the sum of ratal values of the unit and N being the share of the total number of observations within the unit. Per unit the results are added, giving the Theil-coefficient, which varies from 0 to 1 nN. This implies that the number of observations per unit influences the value of the coefficient, which makes comparison between the measuring levels difficult. This problem is solved by dividing the coefficient through its own maximum (in N). As a consequence the value of the Theil-coefficient ranges from 0 to 1.

9.   H. A. van Oerle, *Leiden binnen en buiten de stadsvesten*, 2 vols, Leiden, 1975, text volume pp. 301–05 and 361–74.

Urban Wealthholding and the Computer

'The strength of this city', he had said, 'does not lie in its dozen very rich men, but in the hundred or two homely folk who make no parade of wealth. Men like Dickson McCunn, for example, who live all their life in a semi- detached villa and die worth half a million.'

John Buchan, *Huntingtower*, London, 1922, p. 124.

Extremes of wealth have dominated the agenda of many social and economic historians of nineteenth and twentieth-century Britain — the problems of poverty and the prodigious possessions of patricians have mesmerised scholars struck either by guilt or envy. Their investigations have been largely descriptive and static.[1] Few have attempted to investigate the dynamics of poverty or the accumulation of wealth. In the case of the very poor this omission is less blameworthy given the paucity of sources and the presence of penetrating contemporary enquiries into the nature of the domestic economy of the poor. For the wealthy their are no such excuses. Sources exist in abundance which permit detailed enquiry into how fortunes were made and deployed, not only to create and perpetuate business empires, but also to patronise the arts and to support religious and philanthropic endeavour. This paper describes some of the work that is in progress in the Department of Scottish History and the Archives at the University of Glasgow to make good this shortfall of historical enterprise, and to determine methodologies for future research.

Wealthholding by its very nature is complex and the sources, although readily available, are not open to simple interpretation. However they are generally bulky and repetitive, ideal candidates for the application of database techniques. At Glasgow a number of database projects combine to form a profile of the wealthy in late nineteenth century Scotland — from records of land ownership and property ownership through to records of sequestration (bankruptcy) our efforts have concentrated on identifying those whose place in society was determined by wealth rather than by hereditary status.[2] Our current concerns are twofold: with identifying the wealthy from sources describing wealthholding at death, and generating dynamic profiles of individuals' lifetime wealth creation and dissipation. In both of these endeavours we have taken as a starting-point towns and cities as being the context for the generation and destruction of family fortunes. We have also determined that the family, inextricably intertwined with — and for all practical purposes indistinguishable for all nineteenth century men of affairs from — the family firm, was the focus of this process:

as a man lives and gives hostage to fortune, he finds that his money is not his to deal with as he likes. He mortgages his life to his family, the little circle he calls 'his own' — finds its growing claims the most urgent.[3]

Database work at Glasgow is based on the manual construction of datafiles from either original manuscripts, contemporary printed materials or occasionally microfilm copies. We employ the powerful DISHData data-entry package which allows data to be entered into any number of database management systems. For analysis we have used SUPERFILE by Southdata and Microfax GRAPH running under MS WINDOWS.

The printed Calendar of Confirmations for Scotland offers opportunities to identify the wealthy in communities and examine patterns of wealth distribution between both occupations and geographical locations. The Calendar is not without its drawbacks.[4] The Calendar, printed annually from 1876, contains entries for all individuals (men and women) who died leaving personal estate in Scotland, generally in excess of £5. Each entry includes the name and address of the deceased, the deceased's occupation (when provided by his executors), the date and place of death, the names of executors, the place of confirmation, and the total value of personal estate left. When studying individuals these figures must be treated with caution as we have demonstrated elsewhere; but in aggregate they provide unique signposts to the structure and distribution of wealthholding, particularly in towns where estates at death were less likely to be undervalued due to the possession of massive amounts of heritable property.[5]

To demonstrate their utility a small pilot database was developed from the confirmations of all those individuals dying in 1901 whose estates were confirmed at Glasgow Sheriff Court and which were recorded in the Calendar between 1901 and 1906. A total 1,555 cases were identified; 1,464 of these involved deaths within the City's registration districts out of a total of 8,172 adult deaths recorded in the City for 1901. This suggests that well over 80 per cent of the City's population either left less than five pounds at death, or contrived (with the help of friends and relatives) to circumvent the law relating to confirmation and the transfer of wealth at death.[6] The wealth-leavers left a total of £3,645,571, giving a mean value for each estate of £3,156, compared to a median of £309; the distribution of wealthholding was skewed heavily in favour of estates of less than £500. 704 estates fell into this category (with a mean value of £184) compared with 141 in the range £500-£999, 250 in the range £1,000-£10,000, and 60 in excess of £10,000. Only three estates were confirmed at a value in excess of £200,000; those of the ironfounder Robert Gow (£207,593), the iron and tube manufacturer Andrew Stewart (£218,657), and the ironmaster Sir William Laird (£313,648).[7]

Personal data (name, address, occupation, personal estate) relating to confirmees was extracted from the Calendar and supplemented where possible with information on age and occupation from newspaper death notices (around two-thirds of the cases were traced in the death notices of either the Glasgow Herald or the North British Daily Express; of these a half — one third of the total number of cases — had an age at death recorded).[8] Occupations, entered as given in the Calendar, were also classified according to the classification scheme employed by the Registrar General in 1881. The following crude breakdown of wealth by occupational group was obtained:

Table 1   *Wealthholding by Occupation Group*

	cases	% total	total estates	% total	mean estate
Professional	76	(6·6)	274291	(7·5)	3609·1
Domestic	14	(1·2)	4179	(0·1)	298·5
Commercial	169	(14·6)	620805	(17·0)	3673·4
Agricultural	8	(0·7)	13311	(0·4)	1663·8
Industrial	403	(34·9)	2003296	(55·0)	4970·9
Unoccupied	400	(34·6)	567767	(15·6)	1419·4
Not classified	85	(7·4)	161921	(4·4)	1904·9
Totals	1155	(100)	3645570	(100)	

Occupations relating to industry and manufacture clearly dominated the process of wealth generation in Glasgow in 1901 — around 35 per cent of the cases were employed in this group, leaving 55 per cent of the total wealth left in the city. The average estate for those in this group stood at £4,970, although we should remember that the size of this figure was skewed by the presence of the three largest estates in this group, accounting for nearly 40 per cent of all the wealth left by those employed in industrial occupations. Professionals and those involved in commerce shared a mean figure for estates in the region of £3,600. These group included seven lawyers who left an average of £5,570, 15 ministers who left an average of £2,675, six accountants leaving an average of £17,370, nine 'merchants' leaving an average of £6,704, and 25 clerks leaving an average of £423. The group classified as unoccupied, 34 per cent of the total, comprised largely widows, leaving on average around £1,420. The group leaving the smallest estates (on average £298) were those involved in domestic service, with occupations ranging from a doorkeeper who left £53, to the head waiter at the Station Hotel, who left £690. The table reflects the traditional view that Glasgow's economy was dominated by manufacture — although the large range of wealth held by those in this group might lead one to reappraise the importance of the 'small' businessman in the city, so often ignored in favour of the large and perhaps untypical representatives of big firms whose records have survived.[9]

The registration district in which each death occurred, identified by checking the confirmees' address with the street index in the *Glasgow Post Office Directory*, were added to the records in order to observe the extent to which wealthholding reflected social segregation in the city, and to allow some correlation between wealth, locality and morbidity. Wealth was concentrated in three areas of the city — in the two registration districts covering the west end, Kelvin and Partick, and in Kinning Park on the south of the city which included parts of the suburb of Pollokshields. The two west end districts accounted for just under 60 per cent of the total wealth left in the city in 1901, with mean estates of £6,099 and £7,963 respectively. Conversely those areas with low numbers of confirmed estates and the smallest concentrations of wealth, such as the east end districts of Bridgeton and Calton, were among those with the highest number of adult deaths in the city in 1901.

Table 2   *Distribution of Wealth in Glasgow by District*

	estates	% total	value	% total	mean value
Anderston	35	3·0	28842	0·80	824·07
Blackfriars	34	2·9	22901	0·63	673·56
Blythswood	47	4·1	198637	5·45	4226·33
Bridgeton	27	2·3	9209	0·25	341·06
Camlachie	29	2·5	12819	0·35	442·05
Calton	28	2·4	27604	0·76	985·84
Cathcart	52	4·5	101469	2·78	1951·32
Dennistoun	82	7·1	60078	1·64	732·65
Eastwood	7	0·6	6829	0·19	975·51
Gorbals	57	4·9	77526	2·13	1360·1
Govan	49	4·2	18078	0·50	368·94
Hutchesontown	40	3·5	20076	0·55	501·9
Kelvin	150	13·0	914949	25·10	6099·66
Kinning Park	62	5·4	404179	11·08	6519·02
Maryhill	43	3·7	73010	2·00	1697·91
Milton	28	2·4	12212	0·33	436·14
Partick	158	13·8	1258166	34·51	7963·07
Plantation	27	2·3	38776	1·06	1436·16
St Rollox	43	3·7	15446	0·42	359·22
Tradeston	66	5·7	119510	3·27	1810·75
Other	91	7·9	225254	6·18	2475·31

The interesting results of this pilot exercise have encouraged us to embark on a more ambitious project to enter all confirmations in Scotland for the year 1881, supplemented by data extracted from death certificates held in General Register House in Edinburgh that will allow the correlation of wealthholding with age. This undertaking is complete, and work has begun on all the confirmations for 1901.

The total wealthholding at death, particularly for the very rich, naturally leads to enquiry into the ways in which fortunes were assembled. Before the widespread adoption of limited liability after the introduction of death duties in 1894, the financial records for firms often contained detailed transactions of the partners, including expenditure and income unrelated to the business. On the debit side can be found charitable expenditure, *inter vivos* gifts to family members and senior staff, investments in other enterprises, real estate and buildings, loans to individuals, and household expenditure. On the credit side, apart from the share in the profits of the firm, can be found other dividends, rents, capital realised by the sale of investments, real estates and buildings, income from the sale of personal goods like horses and garden produce, and legacies. Such exhaustive entries can be complemented by more summary accounts in balance sheets and profit and loss accounts and sometimes by an abridged ledger series. For example, in the case of the shipbuilder William Todd Lithgow each annual balance sheet includes a summary statement of the partners' transactions during the year.[10] Financial records from firms can sometimes be supplemented by private personal accounts books, such as investment ledgers and estate rentals. Since partnerships created financial records to suit their own and the partners' needs, the value of their content for our purpose cannot be assessed without detailed examination and an understanding of the context in which the business and its members operated.[11] The business record collection in Glasgow University Archives contains several series of such records for West of Scotland manufacturing and commercial enterprises. Amongst these are the extensive financial records of the firm of William Denny & Brothers of Dumbarton, shipbuilders on the lower Clyde.[12] The firm's general ledger series contains detailed transactions of the individual partners from the foundation in 1846 until it adopted limited liability in 1917. For much of this period the dominant partner was Peter Denny. His private accounts have been converted into a simple database structure by treating each entry (debits and credits) as single records. A typical initial entry looks like this:

Date	1879 03 31
Amount	−5·13
Description	Repairs Genoa chair
Reference	938
Code	1601

In all 3,777 records were created. Our ambition was to mirror the ledger in the database — no attempt was made to corrupt the integrity of the clerk's work, no matter how idiosyncratic, or occasionally incorrect it may have appeared. When all the data had been entered in this fashion it was manipulated by sorting, string searching and matching routines to bring together records that had similar descriptive entries (whether debits or credits). It was then possible to approach the problem of classifying the entries by type. The typology that was used emerged naturally from the data; no attempt was made to impose a predetermined structure derived from presupposed models of behaviour in order to simplify analytical problems. For example, all the entries that related to shipping investments were classified in one group with sub-codes for individual ventures. Similarly all entries relating to dividends from shipping investments were allocated to a common group. Not all transactions could confidently be allocated to specific types, principally because the descriptions in the ledger entries were not sufficient. This was particularly the case for a large number of trivial transactions which probably related to household expenditures and the sale of garden produce.

When all the entries had been classified they were aggregated by type and over time to reveal the dynamics of Peter Denny's wealth creation and dissipation. A detailed account of the results of this analysis will shortly be published elsewhere, in which some general conclusions will be made in relation to investment patterns and the life-cycle of the middle-classes.

Although trends in economic activity are discernible in his income over his lifetime, this offers only a partial explanation for the level of income or peaks in expenditure. The first peak in expenditure in 1868 (Figure 1) can be explained by a large *inter vivos* gift to his son William Denny III, when he was admitted to the partnership. Subsequent peaks relate to major investments particularly in shipping ventures (Figure 2) that might bring custom to the yard, for an example an investment of £25,000 in the Glasgow firm P. Henderson & Co. and £6,000 in Albion Shipping Co. in 1874, and the investment of £25,000 in the Irrawaddy Flotilla Steam Navigation Co. between 1868 and 1876. The largest single outgoing took place on the day of Denny's death when £82,000 was written off against his estate in the disastrous La Platenese Flotilla Co. Ltd., in which he and the firm had become heavily involved in 1882. As might be expected his largest single source of income was derived from the profits and interest on capital in the family firm (Figure 3); but perhaps surprisingly a sizeable proportion of it was derived from other sources in small sums, director's fees, dividends from investments, interest on personal loans to business associates and friends, rents from property and profits from sales of garden produce and other goods. By far the greatest proportion of this other income was derived from shipping investments (Figure 4) illustrating that market values of individual shares in inventories are not always a reliable guide to relative success or failure.[13] Finally this analysis of income and expenditure reveals Peter Denny's deep involvement in his local property market — a type of investment known to have been popular amongst the Victorian middle classes but often difficult for historians to unravel (Figure 5). Like many of his contemporaries in the Clyde Peter Denny spent heavily on his home, a large mansion (called Helenslee after his wife), which cost him some £9,845 between 1866 and 1868. The rest of his investments in property was made up of the construction of a model town for his workforce at Dennistoun in 1862–63, extended in 1866–68, and in the 1860s and 1880s several villas for his sons, relatives and senior employees. This house-holding was neither conspicuous consumption nor philanthropic; Helenslee was expected to yield income through the sale of hay, manure, vegetables and other produce from the kitchen garden, and workers and relatives were expected to pay rents not simply to cover repair charges and rates, but also to contribute a profit. Finally, the land itself could act as vital security for short-term loans in a crisis.

This brief description of some of the findings from our investigation into Peter Denny's financial transactions suggests something of the complexity of the affairs of the Victorian businessman. Although these are based firmly in the context of the family firm, it is clear that, for the most enterprising, other investments either related or unrelated to the core activity could make substantial inroads into expenditure hopefully balanced by equally large contributions to income, and the family fortune.

Taken with other less detailed case studies we have completed, the analysis of Peter Denny's lifetime transactions suggest that this approach offers a route towards an explanation of business and investment behaviour in the nineteenth century, not only in Scotland, where our initial investigations have been conducted, but elsewhere in the United Kingdom and on the

Figure 1(a)   *Peter Denny: all Income and Expenditure, 1845–70*

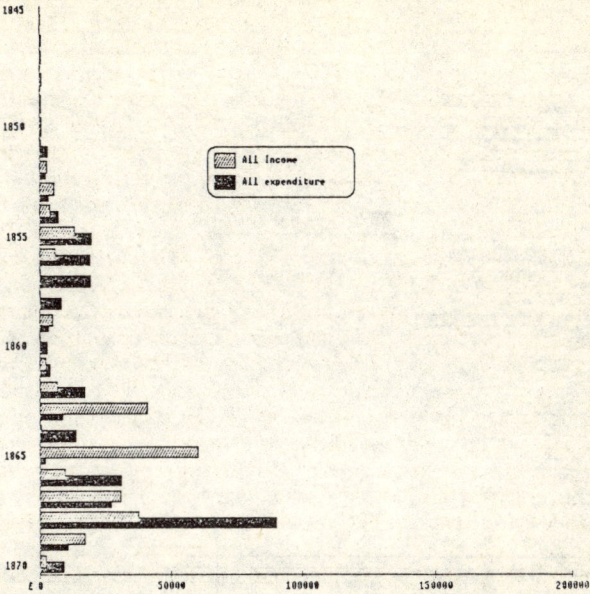

Figure 1(b)   *Peter Denny: all Income and Expenditure, 1870–95*

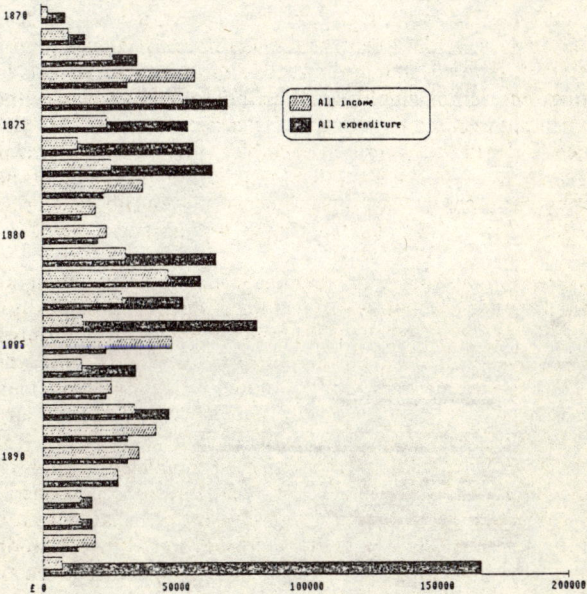

Figure 2   *Peter Denny: Investments in Shipping, 1870–95*

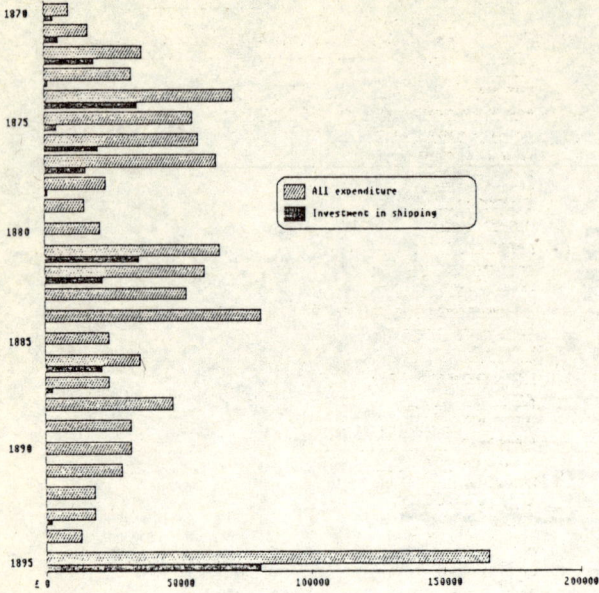

Figure 3(a)   *Peter Denny: Sources of Income, 1847–70*

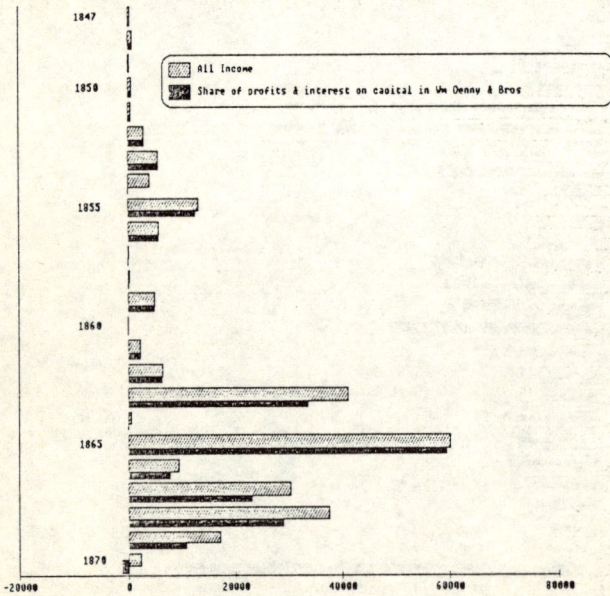

Figure 3(b)   *Peter Denny: Sources of Income, 1870–95*

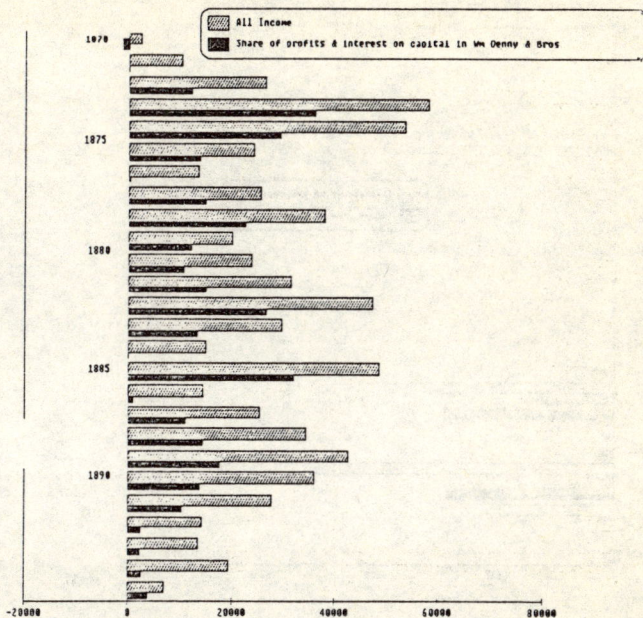

Figure 4   *Peter Denny: Income from Shipping Investments, 1870–95*

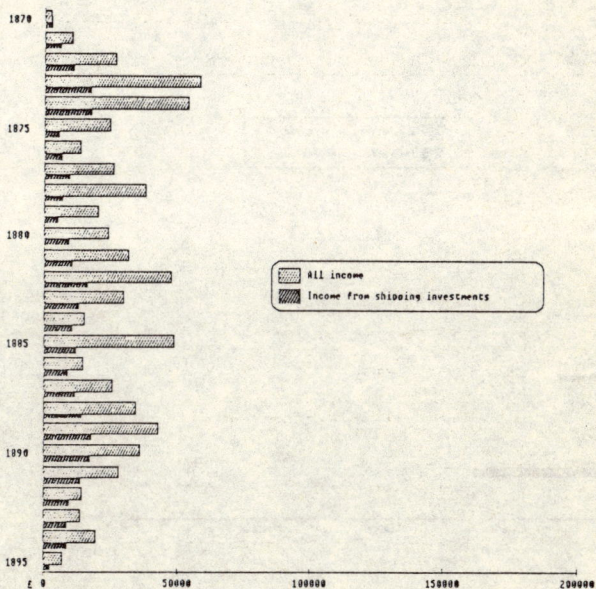

Figure 5(a)   *Peter Denny: Expenditure on and Income from Property,*
                     1845–70

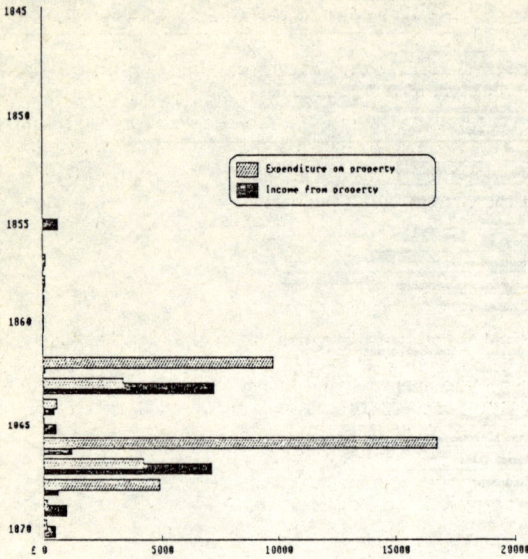

Figure 5(b)   *Peter Denny: Expenditure on and Income from Property,*
                     1870–96

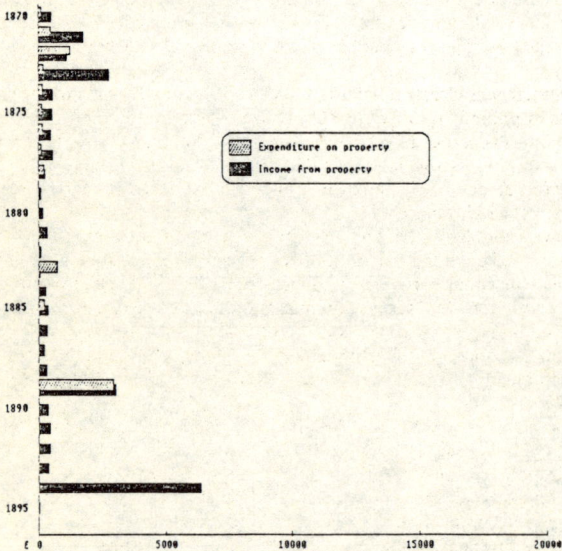

continent. This level of scrutiny is not confined to the very wealthy; it extends, where sources allow, to the influential but frequently overlooked men of enterprise whose individual fortunes were modest by comparison, but who collectively accounted for much of the process of wealth generation and economic growth in the Victorian age. More than this; it promises to unlock the private world of the Victorian family, showing how wealth was used for business, pleasure and philanthropic endeavour, and, as importantly, how it was passed on to succeeding generations. Combined with the insights into the distributions of wealth derived from confirmations, this information will advance our understanding of the dynamics of Victorian urban society considerably from the current static position.

Notes

1. For example W. D. Rubinstein, 'British Millionaires 1809–1949', *Bulletin of the Institute of Historical Research*, 47, 1974, pp. 202–23; idem, Men of Property: the Very Wealthy in Britain Since the Industrial Revolution, 1981, passim; Rachel Britton, 'Wealthy Scots, 1876–1913', *Bulletin of the Institute of Historical Research*, 58, 1985, pp. 787–94. See also James H. Treble, *Urban Poverty in Britain 1830–1914*, 1983, pbk., who suggests that 'the nature of the data effectively preclude any meaningful exercise in comparative quantification' (p. 161).
2. These databases include the Scottish Sequestrations database and the Valuation Rolls database, details of which may be obtained from the authors.
3. William Smart, *Second Thoughts of an Economist*, 1916, pp. 19–20.
4. We have explored some of these in 'Listing the Wealthy in Scotland', *Bulletin of the Institute of Historical Research*, 59, 1986, pp. 189–95. We are grateful for the comments of our colleague, Professor R. H. Campbell, who urges even greater caution in using totals given at confirmation on the basis of a preliminary examination of Inland Revenue files relating to death duties. The total figure finally arrived at by the Revenue for an estate, he suggests, could vary considerably from the figure first given in the Calendar.
5. Although there was clearly much heritable property to be owned in towns and cities, the results of preliminary analysis of valuation roll data for Glasgow in 1861, 1881 and 1911 confirms earlier published findings for 1900 that the average unit of property-ownership in Glasgow, and probably in other Scottish urban centres, was small; see N. J. Morgan and M. J. Daunton, 'Landlords in Glasgow: a Study of 1900', *Business History*, 25, 1983, pp. 264–86.
6. 'The man was very light and it was easy to carry him in the little black box and place him in his home below the red earth of Kinlochleven. The question as to what should be done with his money arose later. I suggested that it should be used for buying a little cross for Sandy's grave. "If the dead man wants a cross he can have one", said Moleskin Joe. And because of what he said and because it was more to our liking, we put the money up as a stake on the gaming table.' For this semi-fictional account of how confirmation might be avoided, see Patrick MacGill, *Children of the Dead End*, 1983 edn., p. 241.
7. This massive concentration of estates in the £0–1,000 category is confirmed by our preliminary analysis of data for the whole of Scotland for 1881.
8. This crude method of proceeding was adopted due to lack of funds to pay travel to, and the fees imposed for access to registers in, HM Registrar General's House in Edinburgh. A generous grant from the Wolfson foundation has subsequently allowed us to overcome this problem in our research on 1881 confirmations.

9.   Similar views are expressed in Richard Rodger, 'Capital, Labour and the Structure of Mid-Victorian Scottish Industry', *Journal of Urban History*, 14, 1988, pp. 178–213.

10.   M. S. Moss, 'William Todd Lithgow: Founder of a Fortune', *Scottish Historical Review*, 62, 1983, pp. 47–72.

11.   M. S. Moss, 'Forgotten Ledgers, Law, and the Business Historian: Gleanings from the Adam Smith Business Records Collection', *Archives*, 16, 1984, pp. 354–75.

12.   University of Glasgow Archives, UGD 3/2/1–12; for Peter Denny's biography see A. Slaven & S. G. Checkland, *The Dictionary of Business Biography*, 1986, vol. 1; and Paul L. Robertson, 'Shipping and Shipbuilding; the Case of William Denny and Brothers', *Business History*, 16, 1974, pp. 36–47.

13.   'These investments proved to be unprofitable in the sense that the market value of the shares, in 1895 at least, was almost invariably much less than they had cost' (ibid, p. 41).

Population and Settlements in Central Greece: Computer Analysis of Ottoman Registers of the Fifteenth and Sixteenth Centuries

1. Introduction

There is little agreement in the literature on the demographic consequences of the Turkish occupation of Greece. In particular little is known about the regional and local effects of Turkish domination, because of the relative scarcity of concrete information on the conditions in many of the peripheral areas. Many studies are especially influenced by the harsh oppression and consequent struggle for freedom in the late years of the domination. For this reason it is often assumed in the literature that the Ottoman conquest of the Balkans had a tremendously destructive effect. According to these views, the local population in the conquered lands was either exterminated or enslaved, or withdrew to inaccessible mountain areas, while the fertile plains and coastal areas became populated by the Turks.[1]

A closer examination of the sources, especially the study of detailed Ottoman registers and censuses in various Turkish archives, which have become available only quite recently, suggests that these notions are too crude and that they do not hold for the whole period of Ottoman rule and for the whole territory of the Empire, though they may have some validity in some periods and selected regions.[2]

The aid of computers proved to be indispensable in the analysis of the registers. In the first place, the computer was used to order the data and to link and identify the settlements mentioned in the sources. Next, various analyses were carried out in order to describe the developments of the settlement structure and population in a quantitative way.

The wealth and quality of data on the socio-economic and demographic conditions at the local and regional levels that the Ottoman registers offer is unsurpassed until the twentieth century, when modern census material becomes available. The detail of the material is overwhelming, especially when compared to the almost complete lack of information on the Byzantine or Latin periods. The study of this data has only just begun and is likely to overthrow a number of seemingly well-established views on Greece under Ottoman rule. Despite considerable difficulties of interpretation, it is now possible to form a notion of the living conditions of the population of Turkish Greece since the second half of the fifteenth century.

This research was carried out within the compass of a longitudinal project on the occupational history of eastern Aetolia from antiquity up to the present.[3] The research area, roughly defined by the present-day eparchy (province) of Doris in Central Greece, consisted of two Ottoman administrative areas in the fifteenth and sixteenth centuries: the districts of Lidoriki and Vitrinitsa (Figure 1). The developments in the Turkish period in this region have never been studied in detail before. This contribution will be limited to the changes in the settlement structure and population growth in the early phases of the Ottoman domination, based on the computer analysis of registers from the fifteenth and sixteenth centuries.

Figure 1   *The eparchy of Doris in Central Greece*

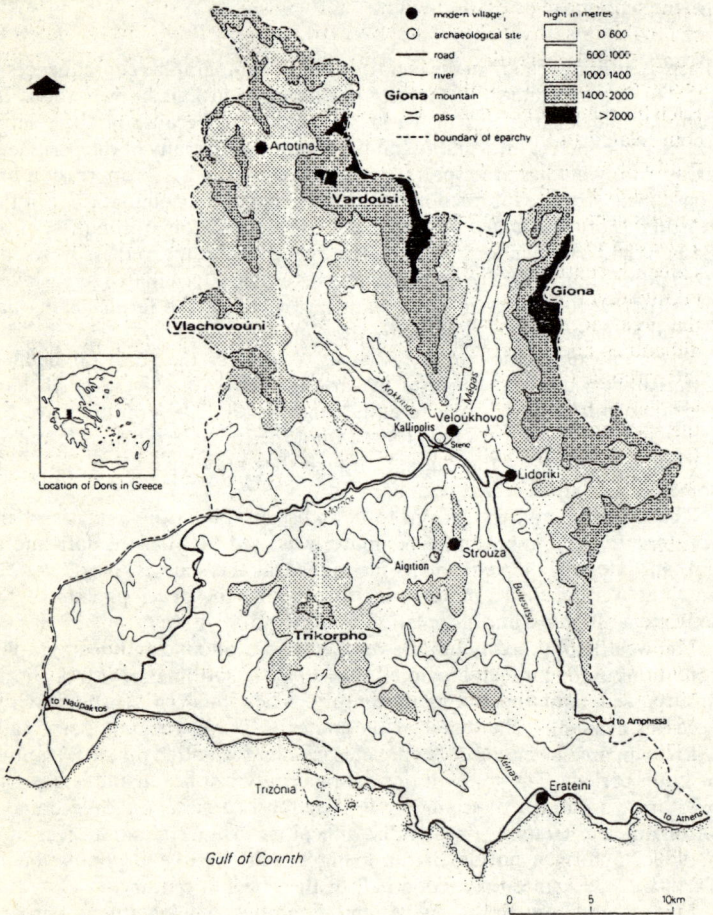

2. The Ottoman administrative system in the fifteenth and sixteenth century

Large parts of Greece and the rest of the Balkans have been under Turkish domination for over four hundred years since the fifteenth century. A solid and strictly hierarchical organisation of the state, with a strong central authority and based on a thorough bureaucratic system, formed the backbone of the Empire.[4] The Ottoman authorities started to register the population for the purpose of taxation and control as early as the late fourteenth century.

The Ottomans kept two types of census and tax registers. One of these was a detailed register (*mufassal defter*), the other one was a synoptic register (*icmal defter*), which was made on the basis of the *mufassal*. The information in the synoptic register was limited to the name of each village and its number of inhabitants, divided into households, bachelors (boys in the age group from *c.*13–14 years till *c.*22–25 years old), and widows. The comprehensive registers contained additional information on the taxation of many products. Each household or *hearth* paid a fixed tax sum (*ispence*) in *akçe* (a small silver coin related to the gold ducat). There were also taxes levied on goods and production, paid in kind or cash.[5]

Documents of the *nahiyes* of Olendirek or Olunduruk (Lidoriki) and Vitrinitsa have been preserved at the *Başbakanlik Arşivi* in Istanbul and at the *Tapu ve Kadastro Genel Müdürlüg* in Ankara for five years in the fifteenth and sixteenth centuries: 1466, 1506, 1521, 1540 and 1570 (Table 1). Without taking anything away from the enormous administrative achievement and the great accuracy displayed by the Ottoman bureaucrats, a number of difficulties and imperfections must be reckoned with when analysing and interpreting the data. In the first place the translation of the sources is associated with a number of paleographic difficulties,[6] especially regarding the spelling of place names. These are Ottoman transliterations of mostly Greek, Albanian, and Slavonic toponyms in the Siyakat handwriting. Secondly, the registers are not always entirely preserved, because some pages

Table 1   *The Ottoman sources on the districts of Lidoriki and Vitrinitsa*

District of Lidoriki
1466/7:   Maliyeden Mudevver 66, fol. nr. 149–51 (Istanbul).
1506:   Tapu Defter 36, fol. nr. 73–82, 97–109, 1255–59 (Istanbul).
1520/1:   Tapu Defter 105, fol. nr. 435–38, 586–96, 615–23 (Istanbul).
1540:   Tapu Defter 445, fol. nr. 14–18, 162–87 (Istanbul).
1570:   Kuyudu Kadime (K.u.K.) 50, fol. nr. 31–51 (Ankara).

District of Vitrinitsa
1466:   Maliyeden Mudevver 66, fol. nr. ? (Istanbul).
1506:   Tapu Defter 35, fol. nr. 735–44 (Istanbul).
1521:   Tapu Defter 367, fol. nr. 94 (Istanbul).
1540:   Tapu Defter 431, fol. nr. 1070–84 (Istanbul).
1570:   Kuyudu Kadime (K.u.K.) 183, fol. nr. 188–203 (Ankara).

have been lost or damaged. In the third place a few internal inconsistencies turned up after the data were computerised. The sum of the number of families on the village level, for instance, is sometimes not in accordance with the aggregate number for the district as a whole as it is mentioned in the sources. These discrepancies are however very small. Fourthly, it is difficult to associate the fifteenth and sixteenth century toponyms with known villages or locations. Many Greek place names have changed in the course of time. All kinds of foreign sounding names have been Hellenised since the 1920s, but many other changes of names and variations in spelling of toponyms can be observed. The fifth and final problem is to estimate total population numbers on the basis of the numbers of families, bachelors and widows. The average household size in this period and area is not known. In several studies a number of five persons per family is used, but there are also advocates of fewer or more members per household.[7] The earliest information on household size in these parts of Greece on the village level dates from after the Turkish period. Around 1850 the average family size was about 5·5 persons. Later, in the early twentieth century this number was reduced to around 4·5 persons. In this research, we prefer not to convert the number of families into numbers of inhabitants, in order to keep the data as pure as possible. For a few general indications of total population numbers we will use the number of five persons per household for the sake of simplicity.

3. Data processing and identification of settlements

The data from the registers was entered into the computer in a transliterated form, using a database program (dBASE). In the original sources, the information is already ordered by village. The database structure could therefore be straightforward in the form of one rectangular table, each village forming one record. Originally, for each year a separate file was created, but these were later combined into a single file.

Because of spelling variations and place name changes, computerised toponymical research was carried out in order to systemise these changes and in order to link the settlements in the Ottoman registers both mutually and with later known villages and sites of former villages. A toponymical database was created containing all place-names mentioned on modern topographical maps (scale 1:50,000) of the study area. The database was enlarged by the names of villages and former villages from a variety of sources: Greek censuses since the independence, old maps, travel literature, local publications and village interviews. In this way, a file containing over a thousand toponyms was compiled. Of each toponym, the type (hodonyms, choronyms, hydronyms, and oronyms), the location (quadrant on the 1:50,000 map), and occurring spelling variations were recorded.

The identification of the settlements was not completely automatic, but the computer offered suggestions for the linkage on the basis of the toponymical information. By carrying out several different sorting routines, we were able to identify the majority of the Ottoman toponyms within reasonable margins of certainty. For another group of settlements suggestions for possible identifications were made, and a small group remained unidentified. After the linkage was completed, the datafile was transferred to a larger computer system for further statistical analysis.

4. The districts of Vitrinitsa and Lidoriki

4·1. *Vitrinitsa*

The district of Vitrinitsa, in the south of present-day eparchy of Doris formed a separate *nahiye* within the *kaza* of Salona, which in its turn formed part of the *sandjak* of Egriboz (Negroponte or Khalkis). The district was a grand-fief (*ziamet*) with a special status. The register of 1466 stipulates that the district of Vitrinitsa counted one village (the capital of the same name as the district, nowadays Tolofon) and 15 *katuns* of *Arnavudan* (pl. of *Arnavud* = Albanian). It is noteworthy that after 1466 the status of the *katuns* appears to be upgraded to that of regular villages or *karye*. Only in some isolated cases the terms 'Albanian' and '*katun*' remained in use. This may be an indication for a stabilisation of the settlement pattern. Thirteen villages can be followed from 1466 until 1570. Two villages were deserted after 1466. One village was newly founded between 1466 and 1506. Two places were deserted throughout the whole period under consideration, but they were later refounded. Their desertion during the early Ottoman period was probably related to their location on the coast, which was repeatedly plundered by pirates.

We have been able to identify and locate nine of the villages in the Vitrinitsa district mentioned in the censuses on the basis of the toponymical research (Table 2). After plotting these settlements on maps the approximate boundaries of the district could be assessed. Between five and seven villages could not be traced. It is interesting to note that also about six villages are found after the Turkish period, for which we have no fifteenth and sixteenth century pendants, disregarding the recently developed coastal locations. It is probable that several of the unidentified villages correspond with these modern successors or that they were located elsewhere within the modern village territories.

4·2. *Lidoriki*

The *nahiye* of Lidoriki constituted part of the *sandjak* Trikala since 1393, which is confirmed in 1466. After the conquest of Navpaktos by Bayezid II in 1499, the new *sandjak* Navpaktos was created between 1521 and 1540. Lidoriki became a district of the new *sandjak*, where it remained till at least 1570. The district was divided into two *ziamets* and one *timar* (feudal fief holding) in 1466. It consisted of the town of Lidoriki, three villages and 21 *katuns*, together inhabited by 626 households. One *katun* was uninhabited in 1466 and four others were newly founded. The second *ziamet*, 'the accessories of Lidoriki', consisted of one village and 11 *katuns*, of which two were newly founded, with 327 households. The timar consisted of six *katuns*, inhabited by 253 households. As in Vitrinitsa, most of the settlements in Lidoriki had the status of *katun* in 1466. After that year all settlements were upgraded to villages. Several names of settlements are Albanian, although it is not mentioned that all *katuns* were inhabited by Albanians. In 1506, it is explicitly stated that six villages were Albanian. In later years only two villages are called Albanian.

Mention should also be made of another special status that some villages possessed: the privileged position of *derbend*. This status of 'pass guardian' was granted to villages protecting vital routes. The *derbend* status included a considerable reduction of taxes and, in the case of Lidoriki, the dispensation of the *devshirme* (recruitment of Christian janissaries for service in the army and duties in the palace). Of a total of 57 different village names in the district (not including double names for one village), we came across 33 in all five registers. Seven villages were mentioned in four of the registers. Of the 16 remaining villages that were found three times or less, 13 were only mentioned once. It is possible that a few settlements could not be correctly linked because of the paleographic problems.

It must be noted, that most of the infrequently registered villages were very small. It is self-evident that hamlets with only a handful of families are problematic. They may be satellites of larger settlements, that are counted separately only in certain years, a phenomenon which remains after Greek independence. They are also more likely to originate or disappear according to relatively small demographic and economic fluctuations. It is possible, then, that villages which are one or more times missing in the registers were uninhabited at the time of the enumeration, but we must also reckon with the possibility that they either belonged to another administrative district or that there are imperfections in the registers.

Despite these changes, the total number of inhabited settlements in Lidoriki remained fairly stable throughout the whole period from 1466 till 1570, i.e. around 41. Only between 1540 and 1570 can an increase in the number of villages can be observed, but most of the settlements mentioned for the first time in 1570 were very small. At the same time there was probably an expansion of the area in northerly and westerly directions, respecting the location of some of the identified new settlements.

Depending on the year of registration, we have been able to identify and locate between 29 and 32 settlements in Lidoriki (about three quarters of the total number of settlements) in each year of registration (Table 2). Between six and eleven settlements remain unidentified, and a doubtful identification is suggested for between three and six settlements in each census year. Combining the Lidoriki and the Vitrinitsa data, two thirds of all settlements were identified, about one quarter is unidentified, and the identification of the remaining fraction is uncertain. The identified settlements were plotted on maps in order to study their spatial distribution and to assess the approximate boundaries of the district (Figure 2). Inspecting the distribution, it is striking that no villages are identified in the area around Steno, a strategic node in the network of communication north-west of Lidoriki. The castle of Lidoriki almost certainly crowned the ancient ruins of the *kastro* of Veloukhovo above Steno, but it is unknown whether the defenses were still in use by the Ottomans.

In the post-Ottoman period about six villages were situated around Steno. Most of the names of these villages are of Slavonic origin, which might

Table 2   *Identified and unidentified villages*

Villages	1466	1506	1521	1540	1570	ca. 1780
Identified	30	29	29	29	32	35
Unidentified	7	9	10	6	11	5
Problematic	4	4	3	5	6	3
Lidoriki	41	42	42	40	49	43
Identified	8	9	9	9	9	20
Unidentified	7	5	5	5	5	3
Vitrinitsa	15	14	14	14	14	23
Identified	38	38	38	38	41	55
Unidentified	14	14	15	11	16	8
Problematic	4	4	3	5	6	3
Total	56	56	56	54	63	66

Figure 2   *Geographical distribution of settlements, districts of Lidoriki and Vitrinitsa, 1466–1570*

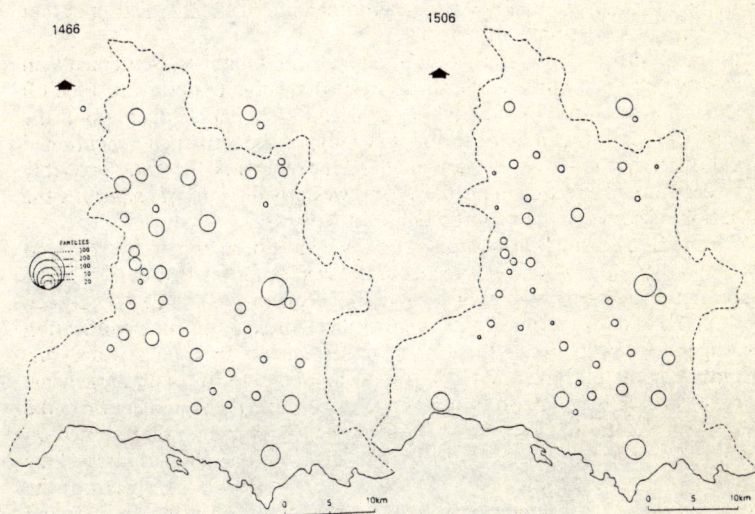

1521

1540

1570

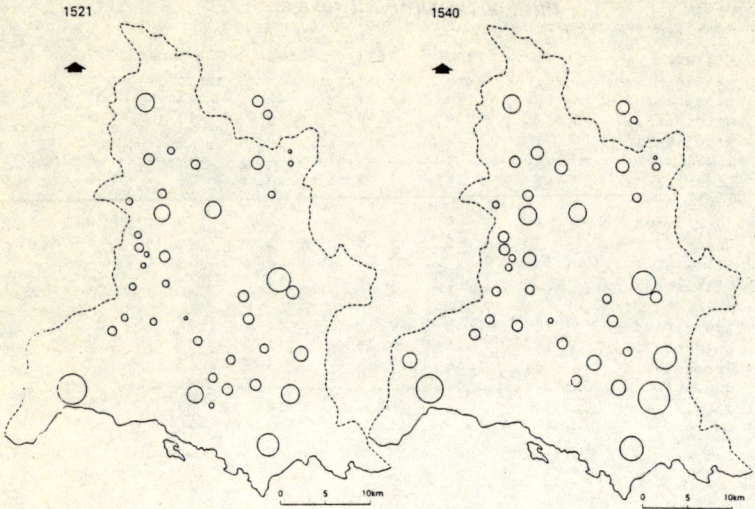

Settlement numbers refer to list
of (identified) settlements

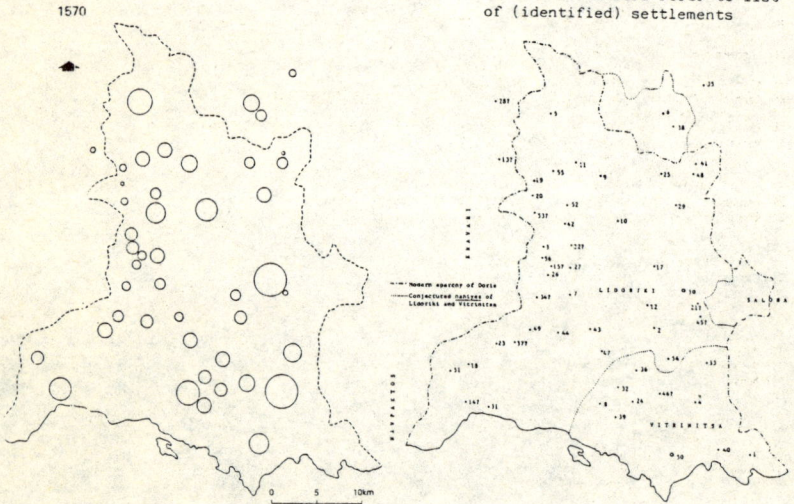

IDENTIFIED SETTLEMENTS (referring to Fig. 2)   31

NR	MODERN TOPONYM	OTTOMAN TOPONYM	LOCATION
1	Agioi Pandes	Vidavi (deserted)	ITE C8
2	Aigition	Usturuza (-utse?)	AMY K1
		Ustr(o)uza	
3	Al(e)pokhorion	Elpohor	LID B11
		Alpohor(i)	
4	Amygdalea	Plessa	AMY N5
5	Artotina	Artotina	LID C3
6	Athanasios Diakos	Megali Musonitsa	LID K3
	(Ep. Parnassis)	(Musinitsa)	
		(Musikice)	
7	Avoriti	Yorgi Avoridi	LID E14
		(Turk) Agorin	
8	Dafnokhorion	Marazye	AMY F5
		Taruna	
9	Dafnos	Vost(in)its(a)	LID F7
10	Diakopion	Granitsa	LID H10
		Agranits	
11	Dikhorion	Gostarditse	LID H10
		Gostanits	
		Gostarince	
		Kostaric (-its)	
12	Dorikon	Sindi Viko	LID J15
		Surediko	
		Somadiko	
		Sevedik	
13?	Elatovrysi?	Palyo Voyic	KLE N6
	(Ep. Navpaktia)		
14?	Evpalion?	Megali Lambino	NAV K5
		Lambina (Megali)	
15	Itia	Itiye	LID A14?
		Atya	
16?	Kakouri?	Kakuri	(near Lidoriki?)
17	Kallion	(mills of Lidoriki)	LID K12
18	Karya (Ano, Kato)	Kokos(a)la(vo)	NAV L3
		Karya	
19	Keraseai	Sur(u)tsi	LID A7
		Surlisti	
20	Kerasia	(Nihor) Kerasa	KLE O9
		Nicor	
21?	Kharmenorema?	Harmena	(near Karoutai?)
		Platano	
22?	Klimaki?	Kalimaki	LID E12
23	Koimiseos Theotokou	Varnakova	NAV M2
	Varnakovis (Mon.)		
24	Kokovista	Kokoviste	AMY G4?
25	Koniakos	Konyako (-ka)	LID K7
		Kopako	
		Kamoano	
		Kanbako	
26	Koupakion	(Ko-) Kupaki	LIO B13
27	Krokyleion	Palyo Kat(o)una	LIO O12
		Paliokatuna	
28?	Kydonea?	Zanliste	KLE M3
	(Ep. Navpaktia)	Megali Toma	
29	Levkadition	Levkadit(i)	LIO L9
30	Lidorikion	Olunduruk	LID M14
		Evlenderek	
		Olendirek	
31	Magoula	Agios Ioannis (Mon.)	NAV M6
32	Makrini (-si)	Makrizi	AMY H4
33	Malandrino	Malandrino	AMY O3
34?	Maravelli?	Maravik (-vali)	LID C14?
		Karaul	
		Ava Paraskevi	
35	Mavrolithari	Mavro Lisari (1570-)	LID N2
	(Ep. Parnassis)		
36	Milea	Milea	AMY I3
37?	Moundounia?	Hondoni	NAV O2?
		Mondon(i)	
		Brades	
		Mundut	
38	Mousounitsa, Kato	Makri (-o) (Mikri)	LID L4
	(Ep. Parnassis)	Musonitsa	
		(Musokice)	
39	Palaio Velenikos	Velaniko (1506-)	AMY H6
40	Panormos	Kisseli (deserted)	AMY O8
41	Pelesi (Palaio)	Peles(ovo)	LID N6
		(Ku-) Kokla	
		Plesve (-vsa)	
		Ayo Dimitri?	
42	Pendagioi	Pendapes (-ayos)	LID D10
		Petiryos	
		Pendepos (-poyi)	
43	Perithiotissa	Peri Litotiye?	AMY F1
		Perlitotisa?	
		Perlototisa?	
44	Potidania	Palyo Kursaz	AMY O1
		Palio (Ka-) (Ku-)	
		Kosari	
45?	Skaloula?	Uskurla (1506-)	LID N15
46?	Sotaina?	Eustatia	AMY K5
		Ousoutia	
		Evsanika	
		Esvetina	
47	Stilia	Istiliye	AMY G2
		Istilic	
48	Sykea	Siki	LID N7
		Sik(e)a	
		Senka	
49	Teikhion	Liko(c)hor(i)	AMY A1
50	Tolofon	Vitrinitsa	AMI L8
51	Trikorfon	Vlacho Kat(o)una	NAV J4
		Ayo Laho Katuna	
52	Tristenon	Dristena	LIO D9
		Tirstena	
		Dirstana	
53?	Vlakhovouni?	Olahovuni	LID A9
		Vlacno Vuni	
		Vlachovuni	
54	Vraila	B(i)raila	AMY L3
		Perapila?	
55	Ypsilon Khorion	Noc(i)miro	LID C7
		Noc (Is-) Esmiro	
		Nuc Ismiro	
56	Zorianos	Leka Usqura	LID B12
		Leka (As-) Uskura	
		Skouros	
		Zorpano	

UNIDENTIFIED SETTLEMENTS

NR	MODERN TOPONYM	OTTOMAN TOPONYM	LOCATION
57	?	Askorpo Lisari	?
58	? (deserted)	Kalami (-1506)	(near Milea)
59	?	Kokovakilo (-ito)	?
60	?	Lanbino	?
		Lambano	
61	?	Likotoni	?
62	?	Mavronik	?
63	?	Mirsi (-as) (-is)	?
64	?	Nikola Gramatiko	?
		(incl. Sirako)	
65	? (deserted)	Ogurus (-1466)	?
66	?	(Van-) Panaki	?
		Pataki	
67	?	Pirgoro	?
		Progon(i)	
68	?	Pirikoti	?
69	? (deserted)	Pyrvus (-1506)	?
		Sirvus	
70	?	Rinsi	?
		Ainsi	
71	?	Stanitsa (1521-)	?
		(I)stanic	
		Ispalince	
72	?	Tovinzi (1521-)	?
73	?	Xiro Pigadi (1506-)	?
74	?	Yani Marivat (-iuta	?
		-iota; -buta)	
		Duskonor	
75	?	Zenebis	?

prudent. It is characteristic for the 1506 register that parts of villages are counted with other districts. Nevertheless, the demographic decline may also be related to the campaign of Bayezid II against Lepanto (Navpaktos) in 1499, because the Turkish army marched through our research area to Lepanto.

After 1506 the demographic situation began to recover, especially in the Lidoriki district, where the total number of families was back at the level of 1466 in 1521. In many villages, annual growth rates of over two percent were quite normal. Also in Vitrinitsa the population grew, though not as fast as in Lidoriki. In the next twenty years until 1540 the situation was just the reverse and Vitrinitsa grew faster than Lidoriki. In Vitrinitsa the number of families doubled, whereas the growth of the Lidoriki district was less than ten percent over the whole period from 1520 till 1540. In the last thirty years of the period under study, the roles are once again reversed. Between 1540 and 1570 Lidoriki grew apace (40 per cent), while the growth of Vitrinitsa stagnated.

As mentioned before, not only the numbers of families, but also numbers of bachelors and widows are recorded. The development of the number of widows does not show a specific pattern, but the bachelors are interesting (Table 4). In most years about one bachelor (per five households) is found in both Lidoriki and Vitrinitsa. This proportion can be regarded as the average or normal situation, which was also found elsewhere in the Ottoman Empire. In 1506 and 1521, however, the number of bachelors in Lidoriki was greatly reduced to only three or four percent. The decline was less dramatic in Vitrinitsa, where the rate in 1506 amounted to about ten percent. Later the situation returned to normal in both districts.

The extremely low proportion of unmarried men was most probably related to the *devshirme*, the recruitment of janissaries for the army. Passing through Lidoriki and Vitrinitsa on his campaign against Navpaktos in 1499, Bayezid must have recruited many janissaries. In the Lidoriki district, there were only a few villages where any boy was left in 1506. The town itself must have been privileged already, because the situation was quite normal there. In six other villages there were between one and three boys. All other villages were completely deprived of bachelors. The situation in the district was only slightly better in 1521, although there were still twenty villages without any boys, and no village (excluding the capital) counted more than five bachelors. It is noteworthy that the *devshirme* had a rather uniform effect on all villages. In Vitrinitsa the *devshirme* also pressed comparably hard on all villages, although the situation was not as bad as in Lidoriki. Everywhere at least some boys were present. Two important conclusions can be drawn about the *devshirme*. In the first place, it is undeniable that the profoundness of the child tribute must have temporarily had some severe drawbacks on the

Table 4   *Number of bachelors per family*

District	1466	1506	1521	1540	1570
Lidoriki	19	3	4	22	21
Vitrinitsa	24	10	22	ND	21
Total	20	6	10	ND	21

indicate that the area was inhabited before the arrival of the Turks. It is unlikely that this region was only uninhabited in the early Ottoman period. As a number of settlements of that time was not identified, it is probable that at least some of them correspond with locations in the Steno area.

5. Development of population and settlement structure 1466–1570

5·1. *Population growth and decline*

Apart from some fluctuations in the Lidoriki district, the total number of settlements in the area was fairly stable. Between 1466 and 1540, the total number of settlements in both districts was around 55. In 1570 the number of settlements increased to 63, due to a number of new settlements in Lidoriki (Table 3). The development of the total population, however, was not as smooth as the settlement numbers suggest. In the Lidoriki district, the population diminished by one third between 1466 and 1506. In the same period, the number of families in the Vitrinitsa district remained virtually stable. The interpretation of this initial decline or stagnation has to be

Table 3   *Number of villages, number of families and village size (in families per village)*

Villages	1466	1506	1521	1540	1570	ca. 1780
Lidoriki	41	42	42	40	49	43
Vitrinitsa	15	14	14	14	14	23
Total	56	56	56	54	63	66

Families	1466	1506	1521	1540	1570	ca. 1780
Lidoriki	1206	805	1263	1378	1928	1141
Vitrinitsa	447	486	590	1206	1174	535
Total	1653	1291	1853	2584	3102	1676

Vill. size	1466	1506	1521	1540	1570	ca. 1780
Lidoriki	29	19	30	34	39	27
Vitrinitsa	30	35	42	86	84	23
Total	30	23	33	48	49	25

Notes: In 1506 parts of at least five villages in the district of Lidoriki are counted with other districts. The number of famlilies actually living in the villages was therefore at least 110 higher than mentioned in the Table.

Data on five of the fourteen villages in the Vitrinitsa district are missing in 1540 (pages lost). The number of families in these villages was estimated to be 400, which is 1·5 times the number mentioned in the source. In all further tables the data are corrected for the missing values.

In Granitsa, a village in the Lidoriki district, the number of families is incomplete in 1540, also due to missing pages. Because of its size in other years, the number of families was estimated to be 50 higher than the 14 mentioned in the source (corrected). The data from ca. 1780 are based on Pouqueville (1820, 1826) and are included to facilitate comparisons.

development of the region. It is nonetheless remarkable that despite the forced recruitment of productive young men, who would otherwise have formed new households, a population growth could be realised in the Lidoriki district. Secondly, the registers point out that the *devshirme* took place only once in this district over a time period of at least seventy years, which is in contrast to suggestions of a regular 'blood tax' every few years.[8] Thus, the often heard hypothesis that the *devshirme* had a long-term devastating effect on the Greek demographic and economic development is not supported by the evidence for this district and period.

The Muslim population was inconsiderable in these districts. There were only a few Muslim households in the study area, most of which lived in the town of Lidoriki.

To sum up, the population development in Lidoriki is characterised by a period of decline from 1466 till 1506, which is followed by a growth, though with varying pace, until 1570. In the Vitrinitsa district the population growth over more than a century, between 1466 and 1570, is concentrated in the twenty-year period between 1520 and 1540. Before 1520 and after 1540 the number of families remains almost stable. Adding the two districts together the general trend is one of initial population decline followed by a substantial population growth. The minimum number of inhabitants recorded was six to seven thousand people in 1506, the maximum was about 15 to 16 thousand people in 1570. It can be inferred that the early phase of the Ottoman domination in these parts of Greece brought about some severe demographic setbacks, but that the situation improved enormously in the sixteenth century. The more than redoubling of the population in a period of barely 65 years can be seen as a remarkable fact, especially in the light of the thesis posed by Braudel and others that a population growth of 100 per cent in a pre-industrial society within one century is already a great achievement.[9]

5·2. *Settlement structure*

On the basis of the numbers of settlements and families the average village size was calculated (Table 3). This amounted to about 30 families in both districts in 1466, but in later years the situation diverged. In Lidoriki the mean village size dropped to 20 families due to the general population decline. Later it recovered and reached a maximum of about 40 families in 1570. In Vitrinitsa the mean village size initially increased. Later, because of the rapid population growth between 1521 and 1540, it rose to about 85 families per village.

The size distribution of settlements is reflected in Figure 3. In 1466 more than half of the villages in Vitrinitsa and Lidoriki counted 20 families or less (i.e. about 100 inhabitants). The initial demographic stagnation or decline is reflected in 1506 by a marked increase of the group hamlets with ten families or less and a decline of the number of villages with more than 20 families (now comprising only one third of all settlements). The demographic recovery of 1521 is reflected by an increasing settlement size, especially in the group with between 21 and 30 families. In 1540 and 1570 the process of settlement growth is illustrated by a steady increase of the number of larger settlements at the cost of the smaller hamlets.

Figure 3 *Size distribution of settlements, districts of Lidoriki and Vitrinitsa, 1466–1570*

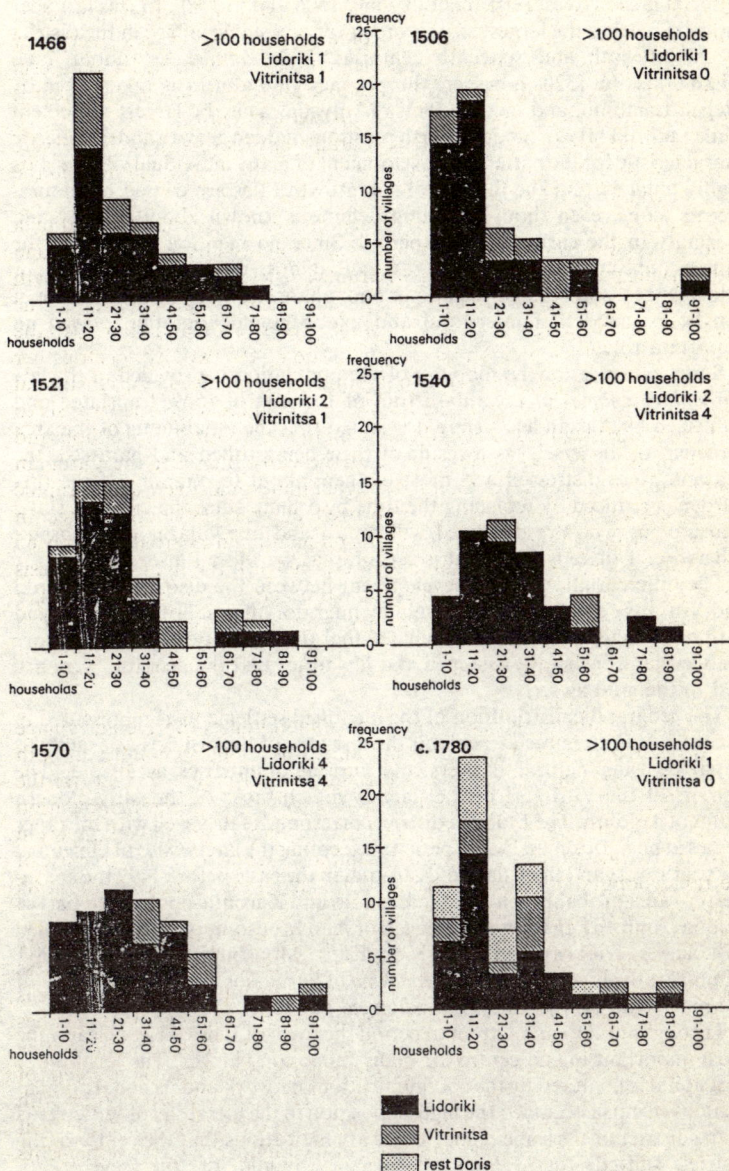

At the other end of the scale, the number of large settlements with over a 100 families increases. The growth of these settlements is far from steady. There are also shifts in the ranking of settlements according to their size. Lidoriki is the largest settlement in 1466, 1506 and in 1570. In this last year Lidoriki reaches the largest size recorded for any single village in the district in the fifteenth and sixteenth centuries: 262 families, i.e. about 1300 inhabitants. In 1520, however, the primacy of Lidoriki is taken over by Megali Lambino, and in 1540 Plessa (Amygdalea) is the largest settlement while Lidoriki takes a modest fourth position. Sudden growth and decline are characteristic for the pattern of development of many individual villages. It is highly unlikely that the fluctuations in growth rates are caused by natural factors alone, even though nothing definite is known about natality and mortality in the early Ottoman period. Since no mention is made in the sources about disasters such as contagious diseases, hostilities or catastrophes, and because the booms and falls are strongly local in nature, it can be assumed that inter-local and inter-regional migration played an important role.

Some evidence for the mobility of the population is provided in the law book (*kanunname*) of the sub-district of Lidoriki in 1569, translated and published by Alexander.[10] Here it is stated that the inhabitants of the area threaten to 'disperse': 'as a result of their being tithed and harassed, the peasants were distressed and most of them about to migrate'. If the tax-burden is reduced by replacing the tithe by a lump sum, the villagers state: 'those of us who are dispersed will return and our villages will prosper; otherwise, if there is tithing, it is certain that we will all disperse'.

The differentiation in the development between the districts of Lidoriki and Vitrinitsa can be explained only by migratory flows, both mutually and with other regions. It can be concluded that the population was much more mobile than is generally assumed and illustrates that the peasants were not tied to the land as serfs.

The geographic distribution of the identified settlements is represented in Figure 2. It is attempted to delimit the territory of the districts as exactly as possible, using natural barriers and current boundaries as an aid. The borders of the Vitrinitsa district largely match those of the early-modern *dimos* of Tolofon. The Lidoriki district corresponds fairly well with the other demes in post-Ottoman Doris, perhaps excepting the later *dimos* of Oineon in the south-west and the village of Karoutai in the east. Before 1499 the south-western area probably belonged to Lepanto and Karoutai constituted part of Salona (Amfissa). In the north, Megali or Ano Mousounitsa (presently called Athanasios Diakos) and Mikri or Kato Mousounitsa are nowadays administratively reckoned to the *eparkhia* of Parnassos, but in the first half of the nineteenth century they still belonged to Doris.

Throughout the early Ottoman period the town of Lidoriki was clearly the most important inland centre for many mountain villages. The location of the capital is favoured by the communications network and its nodal point at Steno. Vitrinitsa occupied the highest position in the hierarchy of settlements in the district of the same name. There are indications that the centre of the district shifted to Malandrino in the middle of the seventeenth century.[11] Malandrino may have had primarily a military function to protect the Belesitsa valley and to control the road from connecting the valley with the sea.

6. Conclusion

For the first time it has been possible to assess the continued existence of a large number of settlements in the districts of Lidoriki and Vitrinitsa in Central Greece in the fifteenth and sixteenth centuries. About three quarters of the settlements mentioned in Turkish sources could be identified and located. It is not yet possible to explain what has occurred to the remaining quarter. Part of these may have disappeared or shifted to other sites, as particularly happened towards the end of the Turkish domination under the harsh oppression of Ali Pasha of Ioannina. Several villages were moreover destroyed during the War of Independence. Some other villages may have changed their names but otherwise remained where they were. At least, the total number of settlements in both districts was of the same order as the number of settlements in the nineteenth and early twentieth centuries. In the early phases of the Ottoman domination, the districts of Lidoriki and Vitrinitsa witnessed a considerable demographic growth. After an initial stagnation at the end of the fifteenth century and the repercussions of the recruitment of janissaries, the population grew rapidly, at least until the last quarter of the sixteenth century. The computer proved to be indispensable for this research. In the first place, the linkage and identification of the settlements would have been much less complete without the computer. Secondly, the mere quantity of the data in the Ottoman defters simply necessitates the use of computers to organise the information. Further statistical analysis is facilitated after a data-base is constructed. The wealth of the material is by no means yet exhausted. Further quantitative research by the application of multivariate statistical techniques will offer more insight in the socio- economic and demographic development of these districts.

Notes

1.   L. S. Stavrianos, *The Balkans since 1453*, London, 1950; A. E. Vacalopoulos, La retraite des populations Grecques vers des régions éloignées et montagneuses pendant la domination Turque', *Balkan Studies*, 4, 1963, pp. 265–76; B. G. Spiridonakis, *Essays on the Historical Geography of the Greek World in the Balkans during the Turkokratia*, Thessaloniki, 1977.

2.   D. N. Karydis and M. Kiel, 'Sandzaki tou Evripou: 15os 16os ai'. (Sandjak of Egriboz: 15th–16th century), *Tetramina*, 28/29, 1985, pp. 1859–1903.

3.   The Strouza Region Project and the Aetolian Studies Project by the Dutch Archaeological School at Athens; L. S. Bommelje, & P. K. Doorn (eds.), *Strouza Region Project: an historical topographical fieldwork*, (three interim reports) Utrecht, 1981–84; L. S. Bommelje, P. K. Doorn et al., *Aetolia and the Aetolians: towards the interdisciplinary study of a Greek region*. Utrecht, Studia Aetolica I, 1987.

4.   N. Beldiceanu, *Le monde Ottoman des Balkans (1402–1566)*, London, Variorum Reprints CS 35, 1976; I. G. Giannopoulos, *I dioikitiki organoseis tis Stereas*

Ellados kata tin Tourkokratian (1393–1821) (the administrative organisation of Central Greece during the Turkokratia), Athens, 1971; G. Finlay, *History of Greece under Ottoman and Venetian domination*, Edinburgh & London, 1906; W. Miller, *The Latins in the Levant: a History of Frankish Greece (1204–1566)*, New York, 1908; H. Inalçik, *The Ottoman Empire: the Classical Age 1300–1600*, London, 1973; idem, *The Ottoman Empire: Conquest, Organization and Economy*, London, Variorum Reprints CS 117, 1978; idem, *Studies in Ottoman Social and Economic History*, London, Variorum Reprints CS 214, 1975.

5. O. L. Barkan, 'Les grands recensements de la population et du territoire de l'empire Ottoman, et les registres impériaux de statistiques I/II'. *Revue de la Faculté des Sciences Economiques de l'Université d'Istanbul*, 2, 1940/41, pp. 21–34 and 168–70; J. C. Alexander, *Toward a History of Post-Byzantine Greece: the Ottoman Kanunnames for the Greek Lands*, c.1500–c.1600, Athens, 1985.

6. L. Fekete, Die *Siyakat-Schrift in der Türkischen Finanzverwaltung*, Budapest, 2 vols, 1955.

7. For example N. Beldiceanu and P. S. Nasturel, 'La Thessalie entre 1454/55 et 1506', *Byzantion*, 53, 1983, pp. 104–56, who suggest a figure of between 4·3 and 6.

8. e.g. A. E. Vacalopoulos, *The Greek Nation, 1453–1669: the Cultural and Economic Background of Modern Greek Society*, New Brunswick, N. J., 1976; D. A. Zakythinos, *The Making of Modern Greece: from Byzantium to Independence*, Oxford, 1976, pp. 23–33; Spiridonakis, *Essays on the Historical Geography . . .* , cit., pp. 131–35.

9. F. Braudel, *La Méditerranée et le monde méditerranéen à l'époque de Philippe II*, vol. I, Paris, 1962.

10. *Toward a History of Post-Byzantine Greece . . .* , cit., p. 298.

11. Giannopoulos, *I dioikitiki . . .* , cit., pp. 107–08.

Masters and Apprentices in Genoese Society, 1450–1535

1. Introduction

During the past years, a group of scholars of the University of Genoa have been engaged in a computer-based data recording of apprenticeship contracts drawn up in Genoa between 1450 and about 1540, i.e. during the eighty years prior to Andrea Doria's constitutional reform and those immediately following it. The people usually mentioned in the apprenticeship contracts are:

1. the person who entrusts the apprentice to the master craftsman;
2. the master;
3. the *famulo* or apprentice;
4. the witnesses, guarantors, procurators, etc.

An average of 4·7 people per contract have been recorded. Besides having a first name and a surname, each of them can also be identified by his father's name, his residence and his craft. We have called them nominal records. Information about paternity has led to the compiling of the relative nominal records. The surname is often composed of several parts, one of which can be a place name derived from the place of origin of the subject. The age of each apprentice is also usually given. Quite frequently, the persons mentioned in the contract are related either by kinship or neighbourhood, and this is nearly always explicitly stated.

The apprenticeship contracts, with their fixed formal structure and detailed information are particularly suitable for computer analysis, and provide ideal material for a prosopographic mass research aiming at the reconstruction of Genoese handicraft activity and following its development over a period of several generations.

2. Nominal record linkage and the construction of individual dossiers

In computer research, the best results are obtained by working on an amount of data large enough to trigger off a mechanism of increasing output. This is particularly true in the field of prosopographical research. In fact, the greater the number of documents, the greater the probability of finding the same persons at different stages of their career. Thanks to this mechanism, the data can be easily and usefully integrated later on with different kids of sources.

The records of the most commonly recurring individuals forms the basis of this research, taking into account the wide range of its sources, the large number of recurring names and the many variations in the spelling of surnames. Instead of separately comparing the data of each nominal record in our files, we have chosen, for obvious economic reasons, the method of preliminarily grouping together the nominal records that seemingly refer to the same person (candidate records). Therefore we have written a programme which automatically assigns to each nominal record a ten-character identifier consisting of three groups of characters. The first group of characters comprises the first two consonants of the first part of the surname.[1] The second group consists of the first four letters of the name. The third group is composed of either:

1. the first four letters of the father's name; or
2. the first four letters of the second part of the surname, if the father's name is not given and the surname consists of more than one element; or
3. the first four letters of the name of the craft, if the father's name is missing and the surname consists of one element only. Craft is not always a reliable criterion for identification, but, given the nature of our records and the considered period, we found it useful to use it as such.

Each of the three above-mentioned cases led to the compiling of a different list, and an automatic sorting of each list has been carried out according to identifier, surname and date, and subsequently the nominal records with the same identifier have been grouped together. By comparing the three lists, it has been possible to compile the individual dossiers (Figure 1). An initial experiment was carried out on about 7,000 contracts (out of the 8400 recorded to date) with the main purpose of verifying the validity and time-saving quality of the identifier method and this produced satisfactory results. The most dangerous mistake, i.e. the grouping of personal records referring to different people under the same indicator, only recurred in a limited number of cases: less than 20 per cent in the first list, less than 8 per cent in the second, and less than 5 per cent in the third.

At the moment, owing to the availability of more up-to-date hardware support at the Computer Centre of the University of Genoa, advanced experiments are being carried out with a new method of identification capable of operating with one identifier only (thus producing only one list), and of taking into account any eventual incompatibility in grouping the nominal records in dossier form. This procedure, carried out on line during data input, gives an immediate indication of the eventual linkage with an already existing record. This should greatly reduce the likelihood of mistaken or doubtful identification, while at the same time increasing the efficiency of the identifier. It is possible that a certain number of nominal records may be excluded from the process of automatic identification, i.e. from being grouped in individual dossiers. This may be due to the different forms in which the same surname appears in the documents, or to reading and transcription errors which may occur at the time of the disclosure of the data, or else during their input into the computer, notwithstanding the necessary checks for each operation. However, one of the most important aims of this

Figure 1

```
1           2      3 4       5                        6          7    8     9
----------  -----  - -----   ---------------------    --------   ---  ----  --

FSBAR DOM   44582  A BAR     FASTAZIO                 DOM        CLL  1469
FSBAR DOM   47385  T BAR     FASTAZIO DE LEVANTO      DOM        CLL  1476
FSBAR DOM   57034  G BAR     FASTAZIUS                DOM        CLL  1480
FSBAR DOM   55493  A BAR     FASTAZIO                 +DOM       CLL  1483

FSBAR LEVA  45374  G BAR     DE FASTAZIO DE LEVANTO              CLL  1470
FSBAR LEVA  58993  A BAR     FASTAZIO DE LEVANTO                 CLL  1472
FSBAR LEVA  55042  A BAR     FASTAZIO DE LEVANTO                 CLL  1475
FSBAR LEVA  47303  A BAR     FASTAZIO DE LEVANTO                 CLL  1476

FSBAR CLL   44913  A BAR     FASTAZIO                            CLL  1470
FSBAR CLL   89544  D BAR     FASTAGIUS                           CLL  1476

----------------------------

1  Identifier
2  Record number
3  Rôle: A=Accettante (master), D=Dante (who entrusts the apprentice),
       G=Garante (guarantor), T=Testimone (witness)
4  Name
5  Surname
6  Father's name
7  Craft: CLL = callegarius (shoemaker)
8  Date
9  Age
```

The example shows a dossier relating to a person who has been mentioned in all three lists, i.e. *Bartolomeus Fastazius* or *Fastagius* or *de Fastazio*. The first and second group of letters composing the key of all three lists is always FSBAR, regardless of how the first part of the surname appears. The additional data which enables the person to be identified within each list is, respectively, the father's name (DOM, i.e. *Dominicus*), the second part of the surname (DE LEVANTO) and the craft (CLL, i.e. *callegarius*, shoemaker). The linking and thus the reunification of these three findings have been made possible by the redundancy of information with which every nominal record appears in each list.

initial experiment has been the identification of spelling variations and, above all, of reading and transcription errors in a list of about 5,000 surnames.

Having eliminated the errors from the list by the identification method already described, there still remains a somewhat remote possibility that, due to the exchange of the first two consonants, certain surnames, which are in fact identical, appear not to be so and recur far away from one another (Figure 2). In order to pinpoint these cases we have adopted a procedure of automatic identification which, by analogy with a similar procedure in statistics, we have called 'mutual correlation' of surnames.[2]

3. The database

A considerable part of our preliminary operations was mainly concerned with the planning of the database which was to process the information contained in the apprenticeship contracts. In particular, for the purpose of our prosopographic research, it seemed necessary for us to organise the database around the structure of the individual dossier. The latter was to gather all the non-redundant information concerning one individual: name

Figure 2   *Nominal Record Linkage*

```
1              2    3 4        5                          6        7  8    9
----------     ---- - -------- ------------------------   ------   --- ---- --

BSBAR PELE   620:23 F BAR      BESATIA DE RAPALLO         PELEGRI  XPS 1473 15

BZBAR PELE   78183 F BAR       BEZATIA DE RAPALLO         PELEGRI  XPS 1471 13


--------------------

1 Identifier
2 Record number
3 Rôle: F=Famulus (apprentice)
4 Name
5 Surname
6 Father's name
7 Craft: XPS = Textor pannorum sete (silk weaver)
8 Date
9 Age
```

The name–surname first element–father's name identifier fails (Z character exchanged with S). The name–surname second element–father's name identifier will succeed.

and surname (and their frequent variations), father's name, age, craft or crafts, roles played in the different contracts, and dates.

3·1 *The first database.*
The database available in the Computer Centre of Genoa University soon proved to be inadequate for our requirements. It had a rather limited hierarchical structure, which hindered the processing of our historical data. It was therefore decided to devise a nine inverted-list system, with each list corresponding to a primary direct access key to the data (name, surname, father's name, etc.). Access could also be provided by multiple keys obtained by different combinations of the nine primary keys (Figure 3). The programme was written in FORTRAN, interfaced to allow direct access to the various files of the database with ISAM (Index Sequential Access Method) procedures.

3·2 *Drawbacks of the first database and construction of the new one*
Our first database, while allowing a wide range of direct access method to the data, was somehow restricted by its hierarchical structure. Different unforeseen demands required the construction of specific query programmes which were, in fact, rather complex, as it was necessary to know exactly where and how to retrieve the data by using the languages available (COBOL, PL/I, FORTRAN, etc.). Besides, the foreseen extension of our documentary basis by using different sources apart from the apprenticeship contracts, implied a modification of the structure of the database and, consequently, a modification of its processing. Taking into account that not all the modifications could be foreseen, as some of them depended on the intermediate results of the research, it was obviously convenient to build a more flexible instrument, capable of adapting itself to documents of different origin and structure, and to the new and not always foreseeable requirements of the research.

Figure 3   *Diagram of Access to the Database*

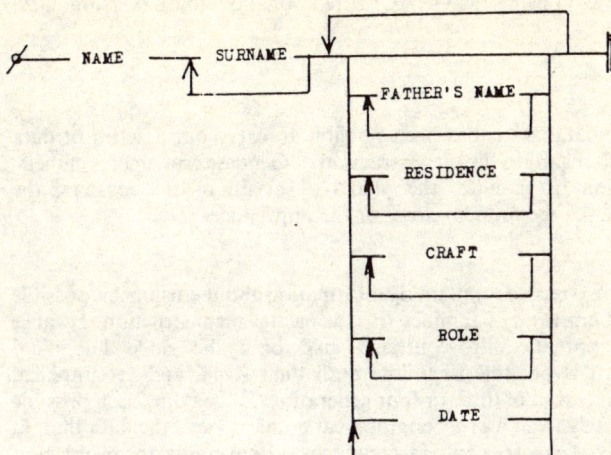

The diagram of access by name–surname is shown. Other accesses (not shown) are: name–father's name, surname–father's name, surname, residence, record number, contract number, dossier number.

3·3 *The relational database and the logical reconstruction of the document*

The relational database model meets these requirements fairly well. Generally, it offers some advantages which satisfy many of the necessities of the historian's research work, namely:

1. The possibility of easily re-defining the structure of the database.
2. The independence of the data from their applications. This means that it is possible to write applications independently from where the data was originally found or from the access method which one wishes to follow in order to retrieve it.
3. The possibility of reconstructing the logical structure of the document. This is a particularly important point. Together with an analysis of the information contained in the document, a historian needs the document itself or at least an accurate transcription of it. By using the traditional databases, it was not easy to obtain a true reconstruction of the document without a cumbersome duplication of data. On the contrary, by using the relational databases (without having to write ad hoc programmes) it becomes easy to obtain the virtual representation of a whole document, even if the data of which it consists belongs to different structures.[3]

At this stage of our research, we are in the process of converting the old database into a new one with a relational structure. As soon as this operation is over and the necessary reference manual is ready, the new database installed in the computer of Genoa University, which is connected to the EARNET network, will be made available to scholars. We are also working on a program which runs on personal computer (IBM AT or compatible with expanded memory) using the ORACLE relational database (version 5·0).

4. Some results

With our first database it has been possible to carry out a series of data processing with regard to the reconstruction of Genoese craftsmen's careers, the composition of families, the places of origin of the masters, the distribution of the recruitment areas of the apprentices, etc.

4·1 Families.

From the nominal records containing information about kinship it is possible to reconstruct craftsmen's families (it is a partial reconstruction, because usually the apprenticeship contracts give only the male line) and consequently, it is possible to follow both their social and geographical mobility over a period of three or four generations. It has thus been possible to examine closely from a prosopographical point of view, the data that, in statistical analysis, emerges only as a tendency. For example, the problem of the propensity among kinsmen to carry on a craft can be studied from a statistical point of view as a tendency of reciprocal relationship between the various crafts (some of them being more 'open', others being more 'closed', some having a higher or lower level of economic activity, greater or less social status, etc.). Figure 4 shows the propensity among kinsmen (usually fathers and sons) to carry on the craft. The propensity of sons to carry on the craft of their fathers (observed frequencies) reaches values twice as great as those one should reach if there was not any preference (expected frequencies). Conversely, for different fathers and sons crafts' observed frequencies are less than the expected ones.

Figure 4   *Father's and Son's Crafts*

Observed and (in brackets) expected frequencies.

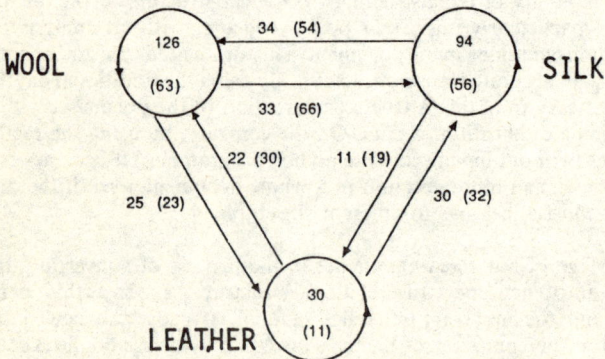

In the prosopographic analysis, this can also be linked to the different family strategies, aiming at consolidating or extending their own positions. Figure 5 shows four generations of the De Florentia or Florentinus family (two variants of the family name). Filipus, silk weaver, is the son of Blasi, whose craft we do not know, and he is the father of Baptista, who is also a silk weaver. After two generations, with Iacopus, silk merchant, the family gets a real social promotion.

Figure 5   *Apprenticeship Contracts. Family and Crafts*

DE FLORENTIA

FLORENTINUS

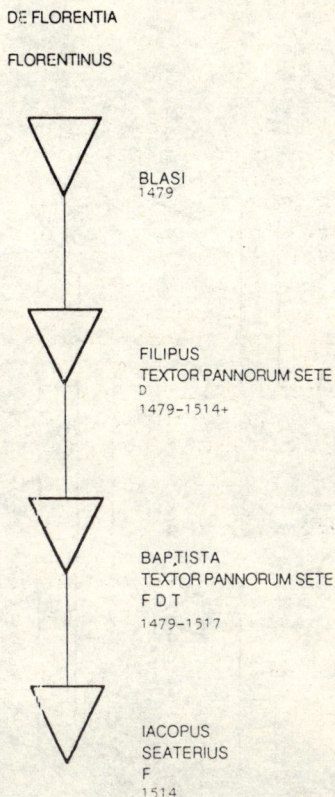

BLASI
1479

FILIPUS
TEXTOR PANNORUM SETE
D
1479–1514+

BAPTISTA
TEXTOR PANNORUM SETE
F D T
1479–1517

IACOPUS
SEATERIUS
F
1514

4·2 Comparisons with other sources

Our research has now reached the point of comparing the data obtained from the apprenticeship contracts with those taken from different types of documentary sources: craft rolls, assembly reports, fiscal registers, dowries, wills, etc. From the earliest exploratory comparisons with other documents, a considerable probability of nominal links with the apprenticeship contracts has emerged. By extending our research to other sources, it will be possible to integrate with the female line the families which have been constructed by means of the apprenticeship contracts. Figure 6 shows an example of linking apprenticeship contracts with dowries and wills.

Figure 6   *Linking Apprenticeship Contracts with Dowries and Wills*

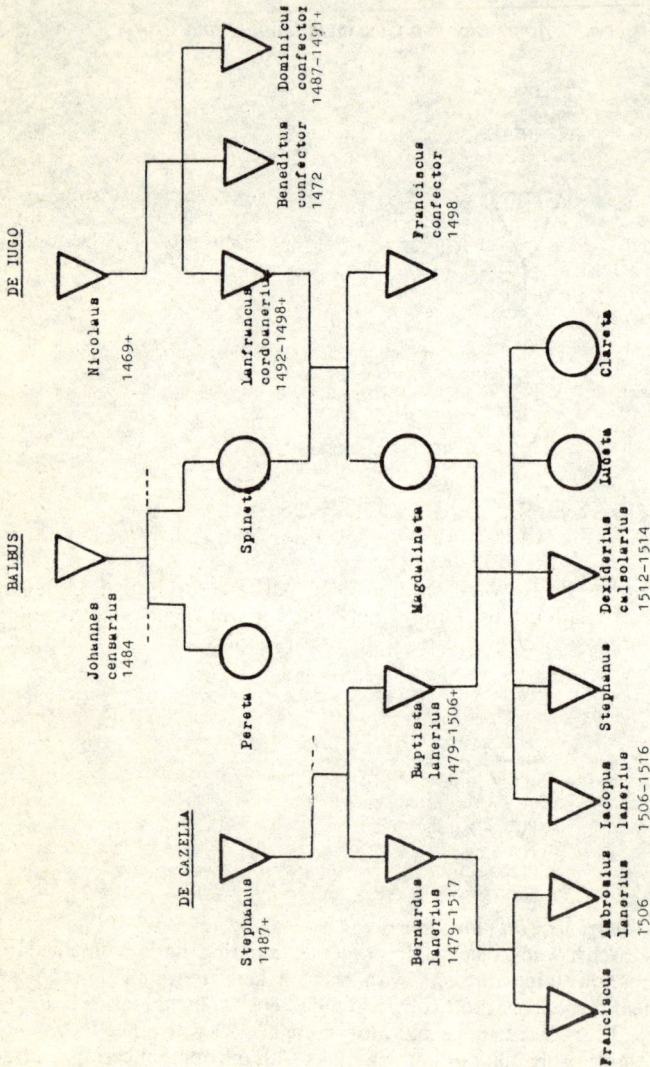

The example shows:

I) From apprenticeship contracts.

a)   The members of the family De Cazella are almost all *lanerius*. One of them, Desiderio, is *calsolarius* (shoemaker). He uses for his job both wool and leather.

b)   The members of the family De Iugo are *confector* and *cordoanerius* (leather manufacturer).

c)   Johannes Balbus is *censarius* (cattle-broker).

II) From wills.

a)   Johannes Balbus' will (1493). He leaves his property to Pereta (his illegitimate daughter). If Pereta died without sons, he would leave his property to his grand-daughter, Magdalineta.

b)   Baptista De Cazella's will. He designates his brother, Bernardo, as his testamentary executor. He leaves an amount of money for the dowries of his daughters, Luceta and Clareta. The rest of his property is left, in consequence of the minorities of Stephanus, Iacopo and Dexiderio, in usufruct to his wife, Magdalineta.

III) From dowries.

a)   Lanfranco De Iugo married Spineta, Johannes Balbus' daughter.

b)   Baptista de Cazella married Magdalineta, Lanfranco De Iugo's daughter

Examples like these will enable us to study the Genoese craftsmen families as work groups, their social and geographical mobility on a wider scale and over a longer period, also in relation to the policy of marriage alliances carried out at the time. In other words, from professional careers and their close-knit network of relationships (family, work, etc.) it will be possible to obtain numerous prosopographic data of historical significance .

Notes

1.   If surnames consist of more than one element, the elements are permuted cyclically . Thus, each element of the surname contributes to build, one at a time, the first group of two letters of the identifier.
2.   The algorithm that measures the 'mutual correlation' of surnames is similar to the one known as Guth's algorithm (See Guth G., Surname spellings and computerized record linkage, *Historical Methods*, 1976).
3.   Of course one should reserve the possibility of direct access to a 'real representation' at any time, by keeping copies of all the documents.

Bibliography

Maestri e garzoni nella società genovese fra XV e XVI secolo. (*Quaderni* published by the Centro di studio sulla storia della tecnica del C.N.R.). Vol. I (*Quaderni* n. 3, 1979): O. Itzcovich, 'Trattamento automatico dell'informazione archivistica: prime elaborazioni delle acordaciones famuli'; C. Ghiara, 'I contratti di apprendistato: esplorazione e selezione del fondo notarile'; G. Casarino, 'Notai e "accartazioni". Elementi per una critica della fonte'; L. Gatti, 'Mestieri e carriere artigiane. Problemi e prospettive di ricerca'. Vol. II (*Quaderni* no. 4, 1980): L. Gatti, 'Un catalogo di mestieri'. Vol. III (*Quaderni* no. 5, 1980): O. Itzcovich, 'Metodi e programmi per l'elaborazione elettronica'. Vol. IV (*Quaderni* no. 9., 1982): G. Casarino, 'I giovani e l'apprendistato. Iniziazione e addestramento'. Vol. V (*Quaderni* no. 13, 1986): L. Gatti, 'Artigiani delle pelli e dei cuoi'.

G. Casarino, 'Una ricerca prosopografica sugli artigiani genovesi', *Quaderni storici*, no. 41, 1979.

G. Casarino, 'Mondo del lavoro e immigrazione a Genova tra XV e XVI secolo', *Strutture famigliari, epidemie e migrazioni nell'Italia medievale*, Siena, 1983.

G. Casarino, 'Note sul mondo artigiano genovese tra XV e XVI secolo', *Atti del convegno di studi sui ceti dirigenti nelle istituzioni della Repubblica di Genova*, Genova, 1985.

L. Gatti, 'Mestieri e organizzazione corporativa a Genova fra XV e XVI secolo', *Studi e Notizie*, no. 5, 1979.

C. Ghiara, 'Mestieri e organizzazione del lavoro a Genova nella seconda metà del Quattrocento', *Studi e Notizie, Centro di studio sulla storia della tecnica del C.N.R.*, no. 1, 1977.

C. Ghiara, 'Filatori e filatoi a Genova tra XV e XVIII secolo', *Quaderni storici*, no. 52, Bologna, 1983.

C. Ghiara, *Famiglie e carriere artigiane a Genova tra XV e XVI secolo. Il caso dei filatori di seta* (in press).

VIII.

Political Studies

Electoral Behaviour in England, 1700–1872

Definition

Psephology is the scientific measurement of electoral behaviour. The word derives from the Greek 'Psephos' meaning 'pebble' and recalls the Greek custom of voting by dropping tiny pebbles into boxes. The word 'psephology' is very much a vogue word of the 1970s and 1980s. It was first coined in 1964 during the American presidential campaign of that year by Michael Demarest, an American writer for Time magazine. It acquired currency in academic circles in and after 1970, and the publication of *The Real Majority*, a sophisticated analysis of the American electorate by M. Scammon and B. J. Wattenberg.

Historiography

Until the 1960s research into the behaviour of the British electorate in the eighteenth and nineteenth centuries was fragmentary and anecdotal. Even at its best, in the work of writers like Namier and Hanham, it lacked a sophisticated statistical dimension. Consequently, the interpretation of electoral behaviour usually involved the deployment of fairly simplistic notions concerning what Dr Nossiter has described in a slightly different context as 'the politics of opinion', 'the politics of influence' and, more sordidly, 'the politics of the market'. This last, the idea that something generic called 'corruption' accounted for an obligingly wide variety of forms of electoral activity, has been perhaps the most popular and most enduring concept used to explain electoral behaviour.

In the 1960s, nevertheless, the modern, empirical study of British electoral behaviour in the eighteenth and nineteenth centuries arose out of the discovery of Poll Books and some understanding of the possibilities of their exploitation. A number of scholars seem independently to have discovered these most basic of all sources for the statistical analysis of electoral behaviour in the period of their publication, from 1696 to 1872, when the Secret Ballot replaced public, and thus recordable forms of balloting. Although Professor Vincent's *Poll Books: how Victorians Voted* is often taken to be the trigger of the 'Poll Book Revolution', it was rather a collective than an individual undertaking.[1] Already when Vincent published in 1968 Professor Moore had begun his own characteristic analysis of the structure of electoral politics in the age of the 1832 Reform Act.[2] As Professor Phillips has remarked, Moore's controversial theories concerning 'bloc voting' and 'deference communities' could only be tested by seeking out still more Poll Books.[3] About the same time, Professor Rudé was making startlingly different use of county Poll Books, together with an impressive range of other local sources, to investigate the Middlesex electorate in the age of Wilkes. For the time, Rudé was able to provide a remarkably detailed profile of the occupational and geographical foundations of Wilkite support and he depicted an electorate which was, as Rudé put it, 'perfectly well aware of the issues at stake'.[4] For the seventeenth century. meanwhile, Professor Plumb was already making his own discovery of the Poll Books. In his *Growth of Political Stability*, published in 1967, he had already drawn attention to the numerical increase in the size of the electorate in the later seventeenth century and had begun to work out some of its implications.[5]

By the end of the 1960s the empirical and statistical investigations of the behaviour of the electorate was developing rapidly and excitingly. It was at this point exactly that the first computer aided research programmes began to make their mark. The scholars already mentioned did not, so far as I am aware, take advantage of the computer facilities which were in the 1960s beginning to become available. Bill Speck, together with successive associates, Alex Gray and Bob Hopkinson, used the computing facilities of the University of Newcastle-upon-Tyne to investigate the electoral behaviour of county voters in the reign of Anne. In 'The Computer Analysis of Poll Books: an Initial Report', published in the *Bulletin of the Institute of Historical Research* in 1970, Speck and Gray examined the behaviour of the Hampshire electorate at the elections of 1705 and 1710.[6] In 'A Further Report', published five years later, Speck, Gray and Hopkinson went much further. They not only described the behaviour of five county electorates at fourteen contested elections but felt able to advance a 'participatory' model of electoral behaviour, over and against the 'deference' model which had until then prevailed, at least implicitly.[7] By this time, the use of the computer had extended beyond the Reform Act of 1832. In 1971 Michael Drake published a most interesting small study of the voters of Ashford in Kent in the 1850s and 60s.[8] Although his work concerned only some 2–3 per cent of the electors of Kent East, Drake managed to raise some interesting questions concerning voter turnout, voter residence and voter partisanship. If his analysis of the occupations of voters left much to be desired his study was remarkable for his longitudinal analysis of the electors. Hitherto, studies of electoral behaviour after 1832 had restricted themselves to a static, cross-sectional analysis. Drake wished to see how the same electors would vote at successive elections. Many of these themes were developed, though with improved methodological sophistication by Jeremy Mitchell and James Cornford in their unfairly neglected study of the electorate of Cambridge between 1832 and 1868.[9] Their study was remarkable for the use of census schedules, rate books, denominational records and other sources to supplement the Poll Books. Moreover, like Drake they employed longitudinal analysis to effect a perceptive investigation of the realities of electoral behaviour over time.

By far the most ambitious analysis of electoral politics after 1832 was Tom Nossiter's *Influence, Opinion and Political Idioms in Reformed England.*

Although it was sub-titled 'Case Studies from the North East' Nossiter included data from other regions, too. His work, published in 1975, is a telling commentary upon the increasingly sophisticated technical and conceptual methodologies which were becoming available to historians in the years after the publication of Vincent's *Poll Books* in 1968. Nossiter investigated the social and economic structure of the electorate, related the distribution of the voters' two votes to a variety of variables, not least geographical variables, and, in a novel and pioneering manner, endeavoured to relate party preference to the age at which voters reached political maturity. There was a lot to admire in Nossiter's work, not only his book but in the related articles which he published.[11] Not least there was its statistical sophistication, but parts of it were not for those of a nervous disposition and the technical virtuosity which it displayed in some chapters may have weakened its impact. Nor was it always clear which parts of the work had been aided by computer methodologies and which not.[12] Nevertheless, as a general analysis of the electoral behaviour of the 1832 electorate it still stands without peer. Nossiter's counterpart for the unreformed electorate has unquestionably been Professor John Phillips of the University of California. Professor Phillips completed his Ph.D. Dissertation in the University of Iowa in 1976, a study which formed the basis of his noteworthy book: *Electoral Behaviour in Unreformed England, 1761–1802*, published by Princeton University Press in 1982. Phillips' marvellous book is a prodigiously detailed examination of every voter who voted — all 15,000 of them — at eight general elections between 1761 and 1802 in the four constituencies of Norwich, Maidstone, Lewes and Northampton. The genuine merit of Phillips' research lies in his combination of cross-sectional and longitudinal analyses of electoral behaviour in his chosen boroughs together with the theoretical and methodological rigour with which he proceeds. Future psephological work in modern British history must be judged alongside the standards exemplified in the work of Professor Phillips. Nevertheless, it would be mistaken to believe that Phillips has said the last word about electoral behaviour even within the periods which he has studied, nor has he ever claimed that he has. Reviewers noticed that the dates that Professor Phillips had chosen for his study, 1761 to 1802, lacked particular significance and it remained to be seen whether the patterns of electoral behaviour which Phillips had delineated in that period derived naturally from those of earlier decades or, indeed, whether they held good after it. In particular, what some have judged to be the most exciting of Phillips' discoveries — the increasing partisanship which the electorate displayed towards the end of the eighteenth century — could not without considerable further enquiry be projected into the early nineteenth century. Many writers wondered, too, whether his four constituencies were quite as typical as they might have been. Were not those constituencies which experienced an impressive run of contested elections perhaps a little unusual and atypical of the normal run of constituencies?

So far, so good, but I am not at all certain that the above account of the development of psephological studies of Britain in the eighteenth and nineteenth centuries does full and effective justice to all the individuals involved. I am very conscious, for example, that for the early eighteenth century I have said nothing about the very positive contributions to psephological understanding made by Geoffrey Holmes,[13] Aubrey Newman[14] and Karl von Steinen.[15] The work of John Phillips on the later eighteenth century directly inspired the computer work of Professor Bradley[16] and must have been known to Dr Knox in his work on the North east.[17] Three other unpublished doctoral dissertations contain manually worked psephological analyses of different geographical areas for the later eighteenth century onwards: Moses for Nottinghamshire, Childs for Sussex and Stoker for the Northern counties.[18] Slightly later in period of coverage, Jaggard's published work on early nineteenth century Cornish electoral behaviour has made a very valuable contribution to our understanding of the pre-reform electorate[19] while Speight's dissertation on Colchester should be consulted by any student who is interested in the working of the unreformed electoral system.[20] Strangely, the period after 1832 has perhaps not attracted the attention of scholars in quite the numbers that may have been expected, following the pioneering work of Vincent, Nossiter and others. Nevertheless, there have been a number of studies, Fisher's, Fraser's and Wright's, among others,[21] but the only ambitious computer project known to me is that of the industrious Professor Phillips, who has already published one important article on the impact of the 1832 Reform Act.[22]

Two things, I think need to be said about this accumulation of research. First, even though the quality of much of the research is unquestionable it is, inevitably, fragmented, localised and even, perhaps, confusing. How, for example, does the electorate of Professor Speck square with that of Professor Phillips, and his with that of Dr Nossiter? However excellent the individual research programmes were, there can be no doubt that different scholars were doing different things. Speck, for example was studying the county electorate, Phillips the borough electorate, and so on. Secondly, with the possible exceptions of Professor Phillips and Dr Nossiter, none of the scholars dealt with above tried to produce a synthesis of electoral behaviour at any given period, still less for the totality of the Poll Book period, from 1700 to 1872. Professor Moore, it is true, did try to give his theories of deference some general application but I do not think I am being discourteous to Professor Moore if I observe that almost all writers have refused to accept the model which he offered.

Issues and Evidence

What seemed to me to be needed was an attempt to bring together the psephological work, manual as well as computer driven, which had been accumulating since the early 1960s, no less than a quarter of a century now. Further, the existing work needed to be supplemented with fresh research, designed to test hypotheses, fill gaps, extend the area of existing data to different types of constituency, of different size and with differing social and economic patterns, with different franchises, in different geographical areas and at different periods. On the basis of this research, it might be possible to establish not merely a provisional synthesis of electoral behaviour but a viable working model into which my own thoughts and research might fit and from which my future work might take some sense of direction.

Over the last few years, I have been working on the published literature on electoral behaviour and steadily reading through all the major (and many of the minor) unpublished collections of manuscripts and other sources which arose out of the election contests. (Candidates' and agents' papers, canvassing records and the like). In particular, however, I wished to observe a manageable number of constituencies and voters at closer quarters. Therefore I began collecting and processing data from fifty seven contested elections in twenty two constituencies at different general elections from the mid-eighteenth century to the Reform Act of 1832. I put Poll Book information for over 22,000 voters who voted in 22 contested elections in six constituencies onto a database written to a S.I.R. format. (The constituencies and the date of the elections are: Chester, 1812, 1818, 1826; Cirencester, 1768, 1790, 1802; Colchester, 1790, 1796, 1806, 1807, 1812, 1818, 1820; St. Albans, 1820, 1821, 1830, 1831; Shrewsbury, 1806, 1807, 1814, 1819, 1826, 1830, 1831; Southampton, 1774, 1790, 1794, 1806, 1812, 1818, 1820, 1831). This now exists on a PRIME 9955, located at the University of Manchester Regional Computer Centre, where I was fortunate enough to receive indispensable and technically proficient advice and guidance. (For obvious reasons to do with time and the sheer scale of the task in front of me I fairly early abandoned the idea of incorporating the post-1832 electorate in all this. It seemed to me that if we could establish a fairly sound working model of the political behaviour of the unreformed electorate then the character of the reformed electorate would eventually fall more graphically into place). This is what I have endeavoured to do. What follows, then, is a progress report on a selected few of the major issues which I have attempted to confront.[23]

I think I might by saying that in general I found the unreformed electorate much more interesting and compelling than I had been led to expect. For one thing, I found it to be considerably larger than I had imagined. Few writers had done more than repeat nineteenth century estimates of the size of the electorate and it soon became clear to me that these were much too low. They were much too low because they did not allow for turnout. That is to say, what was being counted was not the numbers of voters who could have voted but the (much smaller) number of voters who actually did vote. Although it is difficult to estimate exactly how many people had the right to vote in the unreformed electoral system it is not impossible. As I have argued elsewhere, then,[24] we must review upwards out estimates of the size of the electorate. It must have included over 310,000 electors in 1715 (not the 250,000 usually quoted), rising slowly to over 350,000 by the later eighteenth century, then more rapidly to over 450,000 on the eve of the 1832 Reform Act. The increase in 1832, then, up to 650,000 from 450,000, while impressive, was nothing like the reported doubling in the size of the electorate which books on the subject have for a century and a half repeated, reinforcing a legend which prevailed for so long. One of the essential characteristics of the unreformed electorate, then, especially in the last fifty or sixty years of its existence, was its tendency fairly steadily to increase in size.

With respect to the unreformed electorate, Professor Cannon has observed that between 1754 and 1832 'there was a sharp decline in the proportion of people who had even a formal share in the political life of the nation'.[25] Such a view receives no support from electoral analysis. As far as we can tell, turnout was steadily increasing from the miserably low figures achieved in the early eighteenth century to the much higher figures (around 80 per cent) which were common in the early nineteenth century. (They continue to increase slightly after 1832, sometimes attaining quite spectacular levels of participation over 90 per cent). There are at least three types of explanation for this:

1. Improvements in communications.
2. More effective techniques of voter mobilisation.
3. Higher levels of communal involvement and participation.

Whatever the precise mix of these in particular situations, there can be no doubt that a further defining characteristic of the unreformed electorate was a tendency over time to steadily enhanced participation.

It is, of course, entirely natural to talk of 'the electorate' in this manner but we should remember that it was not a static and unchanging entity: its personnel was not fixed but varied from election to election. We should remember, too, that contested elections were not the norm: only about one quarter of constituencies were contested at general elections before 1832. 'New' voters might appear through the acquisition of the franchise, through coming of age, through the purchase of property or, not least, by choosing to exercise the franchise which they already possessed. 'Old' voters, similarly, might disappear through death, through the loss of the franchisal qualification or, of course, through a decision not to exercise the franchise which they had exercised on the previous occasion. What is not so obvious is the sheer extent of electoral turnover. Usually, somewhere between 25 per cent and 33 per cent (not infrequently more) of the electorate would be 'new', at those contested elections held at regular general election intervals of approximately six years. The average *annual* figure for turnover normally varies between 4–6 per cent (Detailed analysis of my Shrewsbury voters, to whom I had applied a system of nominal record linkage, revealed that when elections were separated by a fairly lengthy period of five or six years the annual turnover figure was around 4 per cent. When the period was shorter, e.g. 1806 to 1807, the figure rose to around 10 per cent per annum). When contested elections were separated by longer periods, then an even higher proportion of the electorate would be 'new': usually around one half if one contested election was missed out. Turnover on this scale emerged from Holmes' work on the reign of Anne, from Phillips' and Stoker's work on the later eighteenth century and it emerges from my own in all the constituencies I have studied. There is no doubt whatsoever that the electoral pool — those who had at any one time actually voted as opposed to the number of people who *did* vote at a general election — must have been very large. Professor Holmes estimated that in the reign of Anne it must have been around two and a half times the size of the electorate.[26] On a Triennial convention that may well have been the case. In the early nineteenth century, on a Septennial convention, the figure is naturally a little lower. A longitudinal analysis of all voters at Shrewsbury at eight elections between 1806 and 1831 suggested that the electoral pool was roughly double the size of the electorate. My guess is that after 1832, with a formally defined (i.e. registered) electorate, and higher turnouts, the ratio of the size of the electoral pool to the size of the electorate probably falls quite markedly.

There emerges from all this, then, the picture of an electoral system in which many voters cannot have voted very often. The irregularity of contested elections together with the operation of electoral turnover constitute some of the most basic characteristics of electoral behaviour in the unreformed period. At Liverpool in the later eighteenth century I have calculated that about one third only ever voted once, about two thirds voted at least twice and only half at least three times.[28] It was a shifting, swirling and slightly raw electorate in which experienced voters were perhaps at something of a premium. When elections were separated by five or six years the number of experienced voters could shrink to 60 per cent, and even 50 per cent. It was a mobile electorate in which rather few participated with any *great* regularity but in which rather many participated with *some* regularity.

Who were these voters and what did they do? Most Poll Books, of course, provide occupational descriptions usually furnished by the voter himself at the taking of the Poll. How reliable are these for purposes of analysis? Obviously, statistical data, whether put through a computer or not is only as reliable as the units of information themselves. There are at least two reasons for thinking them to be, on the whole, reasonably reliable. Firstly, in all but the few largest constituencies, before 1832 at least, the background of individual voters would be known, or could be known, and their credentials checked and exaggeration of the wilder sort eliminated. Secondly, it is possible, if exhausting, to check the individual voter's self ascribed occupation in other sources, Directories, Rate books and the like, as well as with the same voter's descriptions at earlier and later election. The results of such an analysis are interesting. Up to one third of the voters do give a different description or are given a different description BUT the differences are usually amount only to a terminological inconsistency. E.g. a joiner becomes a carpenter, a hairdresser a barber, a bricklayer a bricksetter, and inevitably smiths become more or less anything, gunsmith, whitesmith, blacksmith and so on. The point is that these inconsistencies — for that is what they are — do not destroy the integrity of the data.

Since each fair-sized Poll Book includes around one hundred occupational descriptions some scheme of categorising occupations is required. Although, as Professor Katz has memorably remarked: to impose categories upon the sensitive and bewildering data of occupations 'bristles with ambushes'[29] psephologists have been remarkably unanimous in selecting their categories. Most schemes of classification at least separate out:

1. Gentlemen/Professional/Respectables.
2. Merchants and Manufacturers.
3. Retailers.
4. Craftsmen with some skill.
5. Unskilled craftsmen/labourers.
6. Agriculture.

This is not a perfect scheme and one or two fairly obvious defects should be admitted. There is overlap between 3 and 4, the retailers and the craftsmen. Nossiter's dictum is useful enough — that the craftsmen make a product and the retailers sell it — but it does not solve the problems attached to people like Bakers, who both make and sell.[30] They can only be solved with the benefit of contemporary writers on occupational descriptions and through consistency of practice. Another problem is that occupational terms are too insensitive. Professor Neale drew attention to this problem l almost twenty years ago now when he argued that the work 'shoemaker' could mean either a large employer of other shoemakers or, indeed, one of the large number of shoemakers employed by a few large shoemakers.[31] Two ways out of this nasty little quandary might be to remark that it relates to a relatively small number of such occupations. I believe that Professor Neale only noticed a handful. Most occupations seem to be unaffected. Furthermore, Neale raised this very interesting issue in the context of an urban situation after 1832. It has perhaps less relevance to the market towns of eighteenth century England.

What, then do detailed statistics for successive elections in the same constituencies tell us about the structure of the unreformed electorate?

Table 1   *Occupational Structure of the Electorate in Six Constituencies (1768–1831)*

Constituency	Year	1	2	3	4	5	6	Constituency Type
Chester	1812	11·2	4·5	26·2	53·1	3·4	1·6	Large Freeman
Chester	1818	9·4	4·7	24·7	56·0	3·6	1·6	Large Freeman
Chester	1826	7·9	4·2	26·4	55·2	4·7	1·6	Large Freeman
St.Albans	1820	12·8	3·7	19·3	29·2	32·8	2·2	Medium Freeman
St.Albans	1821	17·2	3·5	21·4	28·1	27·4	2·4	Medium Freeman
St.Albans	1830	15·7	3·7	25·9	29·6	22·9	2·2	Medium Freeman
St.Albans	1831	14·2	3·7	23·3	29·7	26·5	2·6	Medium Freeman
Southampton	1774	31·6	2·2	19·7	30·5	13·9	2·1	Medium Freeman
Southampton	1790	31·5	5·7	25·2	25·2	10·9	1·5	Medium Freeman
Southampton	1794	30·4	6·3	24·9	26·3	10·8	1·3	Medium Freeman
Southampton	1806	31·4	10·0	22·4	24·1	10·5	1·6	Medium Freeman
Southampton	1812	28·8	8·6	23·8	24·6	12·2	2·0	Medium Freeman
Southampton	1818	28·0	8·2	25·6	24·1	12·6	1·5	Medium Freeman
Southampton	1820	25·1	8·1	24·3	24·1	14·8	3·6	Medium Freeman
Southampton	1831	19·3	7·6	25·1	30·6	14·2	3·2	Medium Freeman
Cirencester	1768	3·0	8·6	17·0	47·4	22·8	1·2	Householder
Cirencester	1790	5·4	5·2	21·7	39·0	26·7	2·0	Householder
Cirencester	1802	9·0	5·9	19·7	33·3	31·9	0·2	Householder

Shrewsbury	1806	16·4	4·0	25·8	43·4	7·5	2·9	Small Freeman
Shrewsbury	1807	14·6	5·5	27·2	43·4	8·3	1·0	Small Freeman
Shrewsbury	1812	9·2	3·1	22·2	53·7	11·0	0·8	Small Freeman
Shrewsbury	1814	11·5	3·7	22·4	50·2	11·0	1·2	Small Freeman
Shrewsbury	1819	12·4	6·4	24·4	45·9	10·0	0·9	Small Freeman
Shrewsbury	1826	11·2	4·0	25·6	50·5	7·8	0·9	Small Freeman
Shrewsbury	1830	11·0	6·2	24·2	49·0	9·0	0·6	Small Freeman
Shrewsbury	1831	9·6	6·9	26·1	50·5	5·9	1·0	Small Freeman
Colchester	1790	8·6	4·0	14·0	46·4	20·6	6·4	Large Freeman
Colchester	1806	8·7	5·1	12·9	36·6	28·0	8·7	Large Freeman
Colchester	1807	8·8	4·3	12·4	34·4	31·2	8·9	Large Freeman
Colchester	1812	9·6	5·7	13·5	34·8	25·7	10·7	Large Freeman
Colchester	1818	9·9	2·6	15·1	42·8	25·4	4·2	Large Freeman
Colchester	1820	12·1	5·5	14·9	35·1	26·4	6·0	Large Freeman

Table 1 gives the results of a very detailed computer survey of the occupational structure of the unreformed electorate based on an examination of six constituencies at slightly different periods. Attention is drawn to the following:

1. The first Category — that's the Gentlemen, Professionals etc. — shows a certain consistency. (That's quite something for Poll Book analysis where local variations are so pronounced.) In four of the six constituencies under review, in Chester, Colchester, St. Albans and Shrewsbury, it ranged around the 10–15 per cent band. In Cirencester it is much less because Cirencester is a Householder borough in which all resident householders have the vote. As this is over 50 per cent of the adult male population, then the significance of this upper class group becomes diluted. The opposite is true at Southampton, a medium-sized Freeman borough, in which the naval presence is strong and the existence of a large number of respectable families swells the presence of this group.

2. The percentage of merchants and manufacturers among the electorate is fairly small and fairly steady, around 5 per cent of the total perhaps. Notice that it is higher at Southampton, as one might expect, but even there it is still usually under 10 per cent.

3. It is Categories Three and Four which numerically dominate the electorate. The Craftsmen (Four) are more numerous than the Retailers (Three) by a ratio of about three to one at Colchester and by two to one at Chester, Cirencester and Shrewsbury. At St. Albans and Southampton they are roughly equal.

4. The number of electors in the fifth Category would depend upon a number of considerations. The Householder franchise at Cirencester was undoubtedly responsible for the large number there while at Colchester it was the structure and number of unskilled marine occupations. At St. Albans, I

must confess, I do not know really what explains the high figure apart from the consistent inclination of those who compiled the Poll Books to assign every fourth elector to a Category simply and repeatedly know as 'Labourers'.

5. The number of voters in the sixth Category (Agricultural) was necessarily tiny in borough seats but something of the persistently agricultural nature of Colchester can be seen in the figure for that constituency.

6. One general point; while each constituency has its own distinctive occupational structure of the electorate, it must be said that on the whole that structure does not change much. Southampton and Shrewsbury are very different seats, as even a quick glance at Table One demonstrates, but the point is that they *stay* different. Look too, at how little Chester and St. Albans change, although admittedly the chronological periods involved are not lengthy ones.

To act as some sort of check upon these findings, I have over the years found it useful to look at some other constituencies to see if the (admittedly rather broad and variable) pattern which is emerging could be regarded as typical. I have summarised these findings in Table 2. Here, in some cases, I have simply taken a series of structural snapshots, looking at a particular constituency just once in order to sample its electoral composition. In others, notably Liverpool and Minehead, I have looked at several Poll Books. In general, I would suggest that there are no significant surprises. The variations which occur offend neither common sense not an appropriate knowledge of local history and local economies. For very different reasons, ecclesiastical rather than maritime, Canterbury looks a little like Southampton. Liverpool has an enormous craftsman-dominated electorate, a little like that of Nottingham, though not, of course, dominated by a single industry like the textile industry, Minehead is a slightly strange example of a ruralised borough in which local farmers voted while rural Lincolnshire is a most interesting example of a very rural county in which less than one half of the electorate were actually farmers.

Table 2   *Occupational Structure of the Electorate in Constituencies of different franchise types*

	1	2	3	4	5	6
Large Freeman						
Lincoln 1826	7	2	14	38	27	12
Liverpool 1780	4	4	18	67	6	1
Liverpool 1784	7	8	16	63	5	1
Liverpool 1790	7	8	12	66	6	1
Liverpool 1802	7	8	13	67	4	1
Liverpool 1818	9	7	9	69	5	1
Oxford 1820	13	2	26	44	12	3
Nottingham	-8	615	65	4		2
Medium Freeman						
Newcastle-u-Lyme 1790	6	1	13	62	16	2
Small Freeman						
Boston 1826	6	2	18	57	16	1
Grantham 1820	12	1	15	48	23	1
Grimsby 1826	1	-	17	30	51	1
Wigan 1830	21	10	20	40	7	2
Scot and Lot/Householder						
Abingdon 1802	16	17	29	38	-	-
Minehead 1768	13	8	9	21	12	37
Minehead 1796	19	3	7	20	12	39
Minehead 1802	18	2	9	20	13	38
Preston 1818	6	5	12	22	53	2
Preston 1820	6	3	9	30	50	2
County						
Lincolnshire 1818	14	1	8	14	14	49
Lincolnshire 1823	16	1	9	15	14	45

I do not wish to go further into the structure of the electorate. I would only observe that very similar conclusions emerge from the work of Professor Phillips, Dr Stoker and others who have, on a more restricted basis, analysed the social and occupational structure of the unreformed electorate. Professor Phillips' boroughs *were*, after all, quite representative enough. There are, of course, other ways of measuring and estimating the social of the electorate in addition to the adoption and categorisation of occupational descriptions. Wealth and income, value, style and place of residence and numbers of servants all provide alternative possible guides to the structure of the electorate. Nevertheless, occupational descriptions are the most easily available of any of these and, indeed, those most likely to offer comparative possibilities. For the moment, then we must use these descriptions as the starting point of our enquiries.

One other suggestion needs to be made. In many of the places that were enfranchised before 1832 it is possible that the structure of the electorate was not too bad a representation of the social structure as a whole. At least, the structure of the electorate did register some of the most stark social and economic realities: the presence of a large, rurally dominated, civilian élite, the existence of a numerous and influential professional sector, the sub-division of crafts and the existence of a numerous retailing sector. The unreformed electorate reached quite far down the social scale, much more so than did the electorate *after* 1832 when the number of labourers in the electorate was drastically diminished.

Nevertheless, how did these electors actually distribute their votes? Most constituencies were two-member constituencies and therefore voters had two votes. The extent of partisan voting has been a natural concern of psephologists although the explanation for it has been something of a mystery. Professor Speck and his associates established that in the (largely county) elections that they studied for the reign of Anne around 90 per cent of voters delivered a party ticket.[32] A very similar phenomenon has been established for the post-1832 electorate by Dr Nossiter. At most General Elections, partisan voting is exhibited by well over 80 per cent of voting electors: in 1841 the figure rises to over 90 per cent, in 1865 it is over 87 per cent and at the first election after the 1867 Reform Act that figure of over 87 per cent is maintained. The only exceptions to this pattern occur at the General Election of 1832, in the immediate aftermath of the Reform Act, and at the General Election of 1847, immediately after the confusion to party alignments effected by the Repeal of the Corn Laws. Even on these occasions, however, the figure for partisan voting was 74 per cent and 73 per cent respectively.[33] Now, this phenomenon of partisan voting may in the early eighteenth century be related to 'the Rage of Party' and after 1832 to the effective party organisations presided over by Bonham and Parkes. How do voters vote in the intervening period of the unreformed electorate, a period in which party alignments were by no means as well established aa those which occur immediately earlier and later?

I would not like to claim too much but it is not at all apparent that the unreformed electorate exhibits significantly weaker patterns of partisan voting at all. Certainly, it is possible to find many examples of partisan voting after 1715 which match figures of 90 per cent and over which may be seen in Anne's reign. (This is, of course, in four-cornered contests). Even when party divisions at Westminster were relaxing in the middle years of the century partisan voting figures in excess of 90 per cent are still to be found. Where it is possible to measure the extent of partisan voting in the same constituency over time partisan voting does decline a little but it does not decline very much: say from 85–90 per cent down to 75–80 per cent by the mid-century but thereafter reviving once again.[34] Even after the middle of the century, where a local confrontation was represented by two candidates against two opponents a high figure for partisan voting, usually in excess of 90 per cent, can usually be established. Even in three-cornered contests, when levels of partisan voting were significantly lower, partisan figures in excess of 50 per cent can usually be found, depending, of course, upon the nature of the election itself and the traditions of the constituency. (We do not have comparable figures for partisan voting in three cornered contests in the reign of Anne so we do not know whether there was any decline after 1715 on present evidence). It is not my purpose here to account for this phenomenon of partisan voting without parliamentary parties. No doubt some mixture of locally directed partisanship, of awareness of past party conflicts together with what may best be euphemistically termed competitive organisational activity collectively account for it. But it is there.

Partisan voting, nevertheless, is clearly less forthcoming in three-cornered contests and this for very good reasons. By definition, a three-cornered contest demanded single votes of voters wishing to support the party or side which had only one candidate. (In some three-cornered contests, indeed, there are three different candidates, each standing singly). Yet voters were under enormous pressure to use both their votes. To use one only might involve them in a fairly sizable financial loss. To use one only might require an act of political sophistication and sacrifice of which some would not be capable. If a voter split his two votes, giving one to each, then everyone would be happy and no one offended. No wonder then that split voting was much higher in three cornered than in four cornered contests. Interestingly, in four cornered contests split voting, i.e. voting across the parties, was more or less unknown. (Often less than 1 per cent of voters split their votes between the parties). But in three-cornered contests it was inevitably much higher. Figures of 30 per cent are not uncommon.

Does not partisan voting increase during the unreformed period and split voting decrease? One of Professor Phillips' most interesting findings was that partisan voting tended to increase in his four constituencies. I cannot thoroughly endorse that conclusion. I have found some constituencies where over a lengthy period some types of partisan voting do increase. At Southampton, for example, between 1774 and 1831 and at St. Albans in the early nineteenth century. At Cirencester and at Shrewsbury, however, over 20–30 year periods in the late eighteenth and early nineteenth centuries it was on the decline. Everything seems to depend on the nature of the contest — disrupted patterns seem particularly common in this type of enquiry — and on the background of the constituency. What the psephological historian ought to do in this situation, it seems to me, is not to wrangle fruitlessly over whether the unreformed electorate exhibited increasing, steady or declining patterns of partisan voting — evidence can be marshalled to support all three of these propositions — but to establish the conditions in which partisan voting could appear, might increase or could decline.

One way of approaching the question of partisan voting more closely is to raise the question of the extent to which the same electors were able to sustain the same pattern of partisan voting over time? To adopt slightly technical jargon: so far I have been adopting a cross sectional analysis, looking at the behaviour of the electorates of constituencies in general when dealing with partisan voting. I want to look at the electorate longitudinally. Now, this is an exhausting business, only possible with the aid of a computer. In some places, a fairly high level of consistency can be observed. Around three quarters of the electorate can be seen to have voted for the same party at successive elections, according to Professor Bradley — at Bristol between 1781 and 1784, or at Newcastle-upon-Tyne between 1774 and 1777 and between 1777 and 1780.[35] These figures, I am sure, are exceptional. Professor Phillips produced figures for Norwich ranging from 45 per cent to 65 per cent for 1761–1802, but Maidstone and Lewes were much less impressive — from 30 to 50 per cent — and Northampton failed even to exceed 40 per cent.[36] My own investigations into the behaviour of the Shrewsbury electorate of the early nineteenth century more than confirmed these lower figures. Less than a quarter of the Shrewsbury electors normally sustained their initial party preference. There are a number of reasons for this. Party differences were much less thoroughly developed in Shrewsbury than they were in Bristol, Newcastle and Norwich. Traditions of family loyalty and the cry of electoral independence seem to have counted for more in Shrewsbury politics than the party conflict of Whig and Tory. Three-cornered contests, moreover, were far more common than four-cornered contests in Shrewsbury and it is not always easy to see exactly how electors *could* have voted with consistent partisanship even if they had wanted to, given the confusions and ambiguities of the politics of the borough. Consequently, the figures for partisanship at Shrewsbury are particularly low, certainly lower than those achieved by Professor Phillips. I am led, therefore, to envisage an electorate in the unreformed period which exhibits high levels of partisan voting in some places where the right conditions existed for it but in others relatively few of the electors would be capable of sustaining their partisanship.

Does this mean that large numbers of the electors were floating voters? I do not believe that it does. If floating voters are to be defined as voters who, having voted for one side at one election, vote entirely in the opposite manner at the next, then there are signs that from a slightly higher figure in the mid-eighteenth century the figure for floating voters sinks to around 10 per cent by the early nineteenth century. That is not only my figure but that computed by Professor Phillips and others.[37] Voters who fail to vote consistently with their previous party affiliation do not float to vote in clear contradistinction to it. Some partly lapse: e.g. by giving one, not two, votes to the same party. Others partly renege: giving one vote against or splitting. The number of permutations of vote distribution at successive elections is a large one. What we can say is that consistent party support is by far the most common pattern of voting, and floating voting one of those manifestations of relatively intermittent, and in some places, unenthusiastic and short lived patterns of party support which characterised the electoral behaviour of voters before 1832.

This is in no sense apologetically stated. I do not believe that early eighteenth century voters behave very differently over time. The floating vote seems, if anything, higher in the early compared to the late eighteenth century and the figure for consistent partisan support no greater, depending, of course, upon the type of constituencies under review.[38] There are, however, clear indications that more distinctive signs of consistent party support can be seen in the behaviour of the post-1832 electorate. Percentages from Ashford and Leeds reach the high 70s for consistent party support,[39] for Cambridge the 80s,[40] while Professor Phillips' most recent published work shows that after 1832 there occurred a very real increase in levels of sustained partisan voting.[41] At the same time, there is accumulating evidence that floating voting was becoming markedly less common, often falling to very low figures, often just a few percent.

Future Research

Of course, we should not get our heads so far inside our databases that we begin to take our figures too seriously. After all, partisan voting does not occur in a vacuum; it arises from the context of the election itself, from the opinions and personalities of the candidates, perhaps the political activities of sitting Members, and so on. In other words, it is possible for us to become so enticed by our Poll Books that we pay inadequate attention to other forms of evidence. Now, it is, I think, inevitable, and even advisable, that psephological research before 1872 begins with Poll Books but it should not end there. Let me suggest a number of alternative categories of data which are available, sometimes in copious quantities, which have been rather neglected by psephologists and which can yield important data about residence, occupation, status and wealth. First, there are official and semi-official sources such as Quarter Sessions books, Court Leet books, Freemen's Rolls, admissions records and even registers of apprentices. Secondly, there are taxation records such as Church Rate books, Land tax assessments, churchwarden's assessments, assessment for highway repairs and the rest. Thirdly, there are Militia records such as Cash account books and ledgers, lists of militia men and details concerning them, subscription accounts and so on. Fourthly, there are sources which tell us something about religious affiliation — not very much, it may be added, since it is notoriously difficult to glean data on religious observance — but sources like Parish Registers, Nonconformist Church registers, Methodist Registers of Baptisms, Congregational lists etc. do help.

It is possible, therefore, through the utilisation of sources such as these — and there are others which I have not mentioned such as Directories — to enhance psephological research which runs the danger of depending too exclusively upon Poll Books. It is through the exploitation of these sources, exhausting as it will be to relate them to the data given in the Poll Books, to erect alternative models of the structure of the electorate, to name just one possibility. Nevertheless, the time and energies required will be enormous and the times are not favourable to the prospect of unlimited personal initiatives.

What types of solution to this problem might be envisaged? There is urgent need for co-ordination or, at very least, some centralisation of information about the psephological research that is taking place. There is such a fragmented degree of local and personal effort going on, unplanned, unco-ordinated and, to some degree, even unknown. Thankfully the regular meetings of this Conference, together with the facilities afforded to us in *Social History*, may take us some of the way. Furthermore, local record offices have mountains of material which can be exploited for our purposes and, within the realms of what is practical and possible, they perform noble services. What I should like to see is some greater co-operation between interested psephologists and archivists, designed to promote psephological research in some systematic rather than purely competitive and localised basis. This would involve a register of research in progress, some institutional contact — perhaps under the auspices of this Conference in the first instance — and some coordination of research and computer methodologies. This would, of course, promote co-ordination and comparabilities, prevent needless duplication and assist and encourage researchers in the field.

Conclusion

In conclusion, then, and in the light of the realities which I have just described, I should like to make a number of suggestions based upon my own experience and upon my own knowledge of the requirements of psephological research. a) Psephological research should proceed via the establishment of databases, each relating to a particular constituency or group of constituencies and, so far as possible, uniformly, or, at least, comparatively formatted. Electors ought where possible to be identified via systems of nominal record linkage, proceeding upon common ground rules. It would be unfortunate if the pioneering work of Professor Phillips in this regard were to be followed by a multiplicity of systems. b) Provision ought to be made for the accumulation, at some time or other, of further information derived from the sources additional to Poll Books which I described earlier. c) There ought to be some central agency for information concerning psephological data, and, indeed, common ground rules for accessing that data. Large databases are very expensive, of time and money, to establish and they can only be cost effective if they are accessible generally. There is a lot of activity at the moment — at the Universities of Manchester, Leeds and Hull and at the Open University, with its Barnstaple data-base — activity which needs to be further co-ordinated and made more generally known. More, much more, progress could be made if the further expertise of archivists, librarians and others were drawn in to psephological research and, indeed, if the expertise of the Cambridge Group were more intensively cultivated. d) In formatting these databases, historians should take the major decisions, so far as this is practicable. I am old-fashioned enough to think that for some time, at least, fairly traditional questions and issues should force us into using computer technology, not the other way round. I have discovered myself that slightly greater familiarity with the computer leads one to be more sensitive to the sorts of possibilities, sometimes quite unexpected, with which the computer confronts us. Certain patterns of voting behaviour only become evident with the use of the computer, unlikely alliances between unlikely sets of candidates, unexpected disposals of second votes and the like.

By now, the pioneering work has been done and the methodologies tested. The limitations in what we now do are more evident than they were ten years ago and we are certainly less utopian about the usefulness of high tech. Computer technologies do not answer all out questions. Indeed, it is we who have to ask them, formulate them and reformulate them. The computer is at its most indispensable in establishing correlations between data already input and categorised, especially in relating the distribution of votes to particular variables and clusters of variables. Similarly, in keeping track of voters, in noting how often they voted and how consistently, they are absolutely invaluable. In locating mobile voters who change their residence, and possibly their occupation, and in enabling us to speak with some confidence about the stability of the electorate they can perform tasks that earlier generations of historians scarcely envisaged. In relating voting behaviour to community environments during a period of industrialisation, urbanisation and modernisation the computer enables us to open up enticing practical and theoretical issues, especially those of an interdisciplinary character, which promise to reinvigorate the study of electoral history and promote it to a new, and possible more important, place within historical studies in general.

Notes

1. J. Vincent, *Poll Books: How Victorians Voted*, Cambridge U. P., 1968.
2. Although *The Politics of Deference* was not published until 1976 (Hassocks, Sussex) D. C. Moore's run of influential articles had begun in 1961 with 'The Other Face of Reform' *Victorian Studies*, 5, 1961, pp. 7–34.
3. See Phillips' Introduction to *A Handlist of British Parliamentary Poll Books* (ed. J. Sims), 1984, pp. vi-vii.
4. G. Rudé, *Wilkes and Liberty*, Cambridge U. P., 1962, p. 78; 'The Middlesex Electors of 1768–69', *English Historical Review*, 75, 1960, pp. 601–17.
5. J. Plumb, *The Growth of Political Stability in England, 1675–1725* (MacMillan, 1967), especially pp. 34–47. His pioneering article 'The Growth of the Electorate in England from 1600–1715', *Past and Present*, 45 1969, pp. 90–116, further developed these themes.
6. W. A. Speck and W. A. Gray, 'The Computer Analysis of Poll Books an Initial Report', *Bulletin of the Institute of Historical Research*, 43, 1970, pp. 105–12. Speck published independently in 1969 *Tory and Whig: The Struggle in the Constituencies, 1701–15*, Macmillan, 1969.
7. W. A. Speck, W. A. Gray and R. Hopkinson, 'The Computer Analysis of Poll Books: a Further Report', *Bulletin of the Institute of Historical Research*, 48, 1975, pp. 64–90. See also, 'Londoners at the Polls under Anne and George 1st', *Guildhall Studies in London History*, 1, 1975, pp. 251–62.
8. M. Drake, 'The Mid-Victorian Vote', *Journal of Interdisciplinary History*, 1, 1971, pp. 473–90.
9. J. G. Mitchell and J. Cornford, 'The Political Demography of Cambridge, 1832–68', *Albion*, 9, 1977, pp. 242–72. See also Mitchell's dissertation, 'Electoral Change and the Party System in England, 1832–68', Unpublished Ph. D. Dissertation, University of Yale, 1976.
10. T. J. Nossiter, *Influence, Opinion and Political Idioms in Reformed England*, Hassocks, Sussex, 1975. The book arose out of Dr Nossiter's unpublished D. Phil. Dissertation 'Elections and Political; Behaviour in County Durham and Westmorland, 1832–74', University of Oxford, 1968.
11. T. J. Nossiter, 'Voting Behaviour, 1832–72', *Political Studies*, 18, 1970, pp. 380–88; 'Aspects of Electoral Behaviour in English Constituencies', *Mass Politics*, E.

Allardt and S. Rokkan (eds.), New York, 1970.

12. Idem, 'Voting Behaviour', p. 385 and no. 3.

13. For the most recent summary of Holmes' opinions see *The Electorate and the National Will in the First Age of Party*, Kendal, 1976.

14. A. Newman, 'Elections in Kent and its Parliamentary Representation, 1715–54', Unpublished D. Phil. Dissertation, University of Oxford, 1957.

15. K. Von den Steinen, 'The Fabric of an Interest: the First Duke of Dorset and Kentish and Sussex Politics, 1705–65', unpublished Ph. D. Dissertation, University of California, Los Angeles, 1969.

16. James E. Bradley, 'Whigs and Nonconformists: Presbyterians, Congregationalists and Papists in English Politics, 1715–90', unpublished Ph. D. Dissertation, University of Southern California, 1978; 'Whigs and Nonconformists', *Eighteenth Century Studies*, 9, 1975, pp. 1–27; 'Religion and Reform at the Polls: Nonconformity in Cambridge Politics, 1774–84', *Journal of British Studies*, 23 (2), 1984, pp. 55–78. Professor Bradley's Forthcoming *Religion and Revolution* is the first comprehensive analysis of the nonconformist vote.

17. T. R. Knox, 'Popular Politics and Provincial Radicalism: Newcastle-upon-Tyne, 1769–85', *Albion*, 11, 1979, pp. 220–39; 'Wilkism and the Newcastle Election of 1774', *Durham University Journal*, 72, 1979–80, pp. 23–37.

18. J. H. Moses, 'Elections and Electioneering in Nottinghamshire Constituencies, 1702–1832', unpublished Ph. D. Dissertation University of Nottingham, 1965; A. R. Childs, 'Politics and Elections in Suffolk Boroughs during the late eighteenth century and early nineteenth century', unpublished M. Phil. Dissertation, University of Reading, 1973; D. Stoker, 'Elections and Voting Behaviour: A Study of Election in Northumberland and Durham, Cumberland and Westmorland, 1760–1832', unpublished Ph. D. Dissertation, University of Manchester, 1980.

19. E. Jaggard, 'The Parliamentary Reform Movement in Cornwall, 1805–26', *Parliamentary History Yearbook*, 11, 1983; 'Cornwall Politics, 1826–32; Another Face of Reform', *Journal of British Studies*, 22 1983, pp. 80–97.

20. M. E. Speight 'Politics in the Borough of Colchester, 1812–47', unpublished Ph. D. Dissertation, University of London, 1969.

21. J. R. Fisher, 'Issues and Influence: Two By-elections in South Nottinghamshire in the Mid-Nineteenth Century', *Historical Journal*, 24, 1981, pp. 155–65; 'The Limits of Deference: Agricultural Communities in a Mid-Nineteenth century Election Campaign', *Journal of British Studies*, 20, 1981, pp. 90–105; D. Fraser, *Urban Politics in Victorian England*, Leicester, 1976; 'The Fruits of Reform: Leeds Politics in the 1830s'; *Northern History*, 7, 1972; D. G. Wright, 'A Radical Borough: Parliamentary Politics in Bradford, 1832–1841'; ibid., 4, 1969.

22. John A. Phillips, 'The Many Faces of Reform: the Reform Bill and the Electorate'; *Parliamentary History Yearbook*, 1, 1982, pp. 115–35.

23. For some published details see my paper 'The Unreformed Electorate of Hanoverian England; the mid-eighteenth century to the Reform Act of 1832', *Social History* 2 (1), 1986, pp. 33–52.

24. Ibid, pp. 36–7.

25. J. Cannon, *Parliamentary Reform*, Cambridge, 1972, p. 42.

26. J. Phillips, op. cit., p. 98; G. Holmes, *The Electorate and the National Will*, 21–4; D. Stoker, 'Elections and Voting Behaviour', p. 205.

27. G. Holmes, op. cit., p. 24.

28. Professor Phillips puts the figure for the third time slightly lower, ranging from 27 per cent to 40 per cent, at Norwich, 30 per cent to 42 per cent at Maidstone, from 19 per cent to 30 per cent at Northampton and from 22 per cent to 34 per cent at Lewes (loc. cit. pp. 99).

29. M. B. Katz, 'Occupational Classification in History', *Journal of Interdisciplinary History*, 3 (1), 1972, p. 63.

30. T. J. Nossiter, op. cit., p. 145.

31. R. S. Neale, 'Class and Class Consciousness in Early Nineteenth Century England', *Victorian Studies*, 12, 1986.

32. See notes 6 and 7 above.

33. T. J. Nossiter, 'Aspects of Electoral Behaviour in English Constituencies, 1832–68', *Mass Politics: Studies in Political Sociology*, E. Allardt and S. Rokkan, (eds.), 1970, pp. 164–65.

34. 93 per cent at Hereford in 1741, 98 per cent at Shrewsbury in 1747 and 97 per cent at Bristol in 1754.

35. I am grateful to Professor Bradley for allowing me to see a pre-publication typescript of his forthcoming *Religion and Revolution*.

36. J. G. Phillips, op. cit., pp. 232–38.

37. Ibid pp. 232–37; D. Stoker, op. cit., p. 206; R. W. Davis, *Political Change and Continuity*, Newton Abbot, 1972, pp. 49.

38. W. A. Speck, W. A. Gray and R. Hopkinson, 'A Further Report', cit., pp. 23–25.

39. M. Drake, 'The Mid-Victorian Voter', loc. cit; idem, *Introduction to Historical Prephology*, 1974, pp. 91–93.

40. J. Cornford and J. Mitchell, 'The Political Demography of Cambridge, 1832–68', loc. cit.

41. J. G. Phillips, 'The Many Faces of Reform: the Reform Bill and the Electorate', *Parliamentary History*, 1, 1982, pp. 131–32.

Social Structure and Political Behaviour in Westminster, 1784–1788[1]

We are familiar today with the idea of political differences as an expression of social conflict. Though caution now qualifies Pulzer's assertion that "class is the basis of British politics; all else is embellishment and detail",[2] we remain aware of political manifestations of social differences. This paper is part of a larger research project to examine the social context of political behaviour in urban England in the late eighteenth and early nineteenth centuries. Some contemporaries were aware of the possibility of social conflict in Parliamentary elections, as the defeated candidate in the Leicester by-election of 1800 declared, the "contest [was] between the rich and the poor, the oppressors and the oppressed".[3]

This study is based on the poll books for the Westminster elections between 1774 and 1820. The constituency had a wide franchise, of adult male rate paying householders, and it was the largest electorate regularly to go to the polls in the period. Data exist for 7,500 voters at the election of 1774, and for over 10,000 voters in the election of 1818. In the election of 1784 over 12,000 electors voted: given a total of 18,000 inhabited houses in Westminster recorded in the census of 1801, this suggests that at least two thirds of the households provided a voter. Westminster was one of the large open constituencies to which others in the country looked for evidence of popular political behaviour.[4]

The examination of this large constituency over eleven contested elections has led to the creation of a database of about 55,000 voting acts and nearly 25,000 parish rate records. The analysis of the data is still at a preliminary stage and what follows is an overview of this rich source of data, followed by a more detailed examination of the relationship between the social structure and political behaviour at two fiercely contested elections in the 1780s.

Westminster was not dominated by any single industry, interest, landlord or employer. Its economic structure was dominated throughout the period by artisan trades and handicrafts and a large service sector. The occupational descriptions given by the voters to the poll clerks have been allocated to nine broad economic sectors, following the classification adopted by Booth and amended by Armstrong for the analysis of nineteenth-century census data.[5] The occupational structure remained broadly constant throughout the period: a third of the voters in 1774 worked in the distributive trades, and a third in manufacturing. By 1818 these proportions were virtually unchanged. Similarly, in 1774 13 per cent of the voters so described themselves to allow them to be placed in a category of rentiers, and the same proportion did so in 1818. The building trades account for 9 per cent of the voters in 1774, and 8 per cent in 1818. In 1774 these four broad economic sectors accounted for 90 per cent of the voters; by 1818 their proportion was 86 per cent.[6]

The overall impression given by an analysis of the geographical distribution of occupations is of the occupational heterogeneity of Westminster during the period. Rich and poor, rentiers and professionals, artisans and dealers, all lived in close propinquity in the grand thoroughfares or in the mean streets and mews behind. There were variations in detail between the old urban centre in the east of the constituency and newer developments in the more fashionable west. Dealers and manufacturers were most strongly represented in the eastern parishes in 1774, and least strongly in the western parishes of St George and St Margaret. But it was in those western parishes that the rentiers and those in the professions and public service were most strongly represented. This broad outline of occupational distribution between the parishes holds good for the election of 1818. The different sectors accounted for roughly the same proportion of the total of voters throughout the period, and their geographical distribution remained broadly similar.[7]

In 1774 both the Administration and their opponents put up slates of two candidates in the election, in which 91·5 per cent of the voters polled for one or the other straight ticket. There was a very high degree of partisan behaviour among the electorate. The opponents of the Administration did very badly among the public servants and professionals, and especially among the rentiers, only 12·9 per cent of whom voted for the straight anti-Administration ticket. But the opposition did rather better than their average of 30 per cent of all voting acts among the builders, the dealers, the domestic and personal servants, and among the manufacturers. In what was essentially a two-way fight, the Administration candidates outperformed their opponents in all economic sectors. But they did exceptionally well among the rentiers, receiving straight votes from over 80 per cent of them, and among the professionals and public servants, receiving straight votes from over 70 per cent.

The remainder of this paper is a more detailed study of voters in the fiercely contested elections of 1784 and 1788.[8] In 1784 the poll continued for forty days between Lord Hood and Sir Cecil Wray in the Administration interest, and their opponent Charles James Fox. The by-election of 1788 was contested between Hood and Fox's colleague Lord John Townshend. Voting in 1784 was dominated by partisan behaviour: 88·7 per cent of the voters either plumped for Fox or polled the straight Hood-Wray ticket. In the by-election of 1788 voting was necessarily partisan as only one of the seats was vacant.

In the 1784 election, 42·6 per cent of all voters plumped for Fox: 41·4 per cent of the dealers did so, and 41 per cent of the manufacturers. The straight Hood-Wray ticket was the choice of 41·6 per cent of the voters, and again we find no great divergence from this figure among either dealers or manufacturers. But Fox received plumpers from over half of those in the agriculture sector, over half of those in the building sector, over half of those in the sector of domestic and personal services, and over half of those in the transport sector. The relative strength of the Administration vote lay with the rentiers, over half of whom polled the straight Administration ticket, and with the sector of professional and public services. But in neither of these sectors were the Administration candidates as dominant as in 1774.

In 1788 Townshend, the opposition candidate, received the votes of 52 per cent of those for whom data have survived; and 52·3 per cent of the dealers voted for him. Townshend's supporters sought to rally the shopkeepers behind their candidate, on the grounds that Hood supported Pitt, whose Shop Tax fell heavily upon the prosperous commercial parishes of Westminster.[9] The attempt failed. There was no shopkeeper vote in late eighteenth century Westminster: shopkeepers were subjected to the influence, among others, of a multitude of customers of differing political persuasions. A wider difference may be seen in the voting of manufacturers, 56·4 per cent of whom voted for Townshend and 43·6 per cent for Hood. Over 60 per cent of both the rentiers and those in the sector of professionals and public servants voted for Hood in 1788. But the building workers, the domestic and personal service sector, and the sector of transport workers continued to favour the Opposition as they had done four years earlier.

The social context of voting behaviour in the combined western parishes of St Margaret and St John may now be examined in more detail with reference to the parish rate books.[10] These books record the names and addresses of rate payers, together with an annual value or rack rent of the property on which the rate was levied. Computerised files have been created of the names and addresses of rate payers, together with the rack rent values of their property. These have been linked with the poll books for the parishes on the basis of matching strings for surnames, Christian names and addresses. Since payment of rates was a necessary condition of voting, a high level of linkage might be expected. In the event rate book values could be found for the properties of only half of the voters in St Margaret and St John in 1784 and 1788. It is on these combined files of rate paying voters in 1784 and 1788 that the following analysis is made.

Evidence survives of the voting behaviour of 2,337 electors in St Margaret and St John in 1784, but rate book data can only be found for 1,249 of these, or 53 per cent of them. The subset is not exactly representative of the larger group: whereas 44·9 per cent of St Margaret's voters polled for Hood and Wray, 52 per cent of those for whom we have rate book data did so. And the plumpers for Fox were correspondingly under-represented among the rate paying voters. 44·2 per cent of St Margaret's voters plumped for Fox, but among those for whom rate book evidence has survived only 36·9 per cent did so.

The file of 1,249 rate paying voters in 1784 has been divided into quintiles to reveal the distribution of votes. The plump for Fox was the choice of 48·1 per cent of those in the lowest quintile, with property assessed at £7 or less. Fox's partisan support held up well through the middle quintiles, but dropped off to 28·7 per cent of those in the highest quintile. Conversely, only in the lowest quintile did Hood and Wray receive straight votes from less than half the rate paying voters. In that quintile of those with property assessed at £7 or less they received straight votes from 39·1 per cent of the rate paying voters. In the middle three quintiles they received votes from roughly the same proportion as their average of all rate paying voters. But in the top quintile, of those with property assessed at £24 and above, 65 per cent polled for them. The cells for the other four types of non-partisan votes contain only a small number of rate paying voters and display no such clear pattern.

In 1788, 2,061 voters are recorded as having polled in St Margaret and St John. Rate book data exist for 1,090 voters, or 52·9 per cent of the total. Hood received votes from 54·1 per cent of St Margaret's voters, but of 63·9 per cent of those for whom we have rate data. So in both 1784 and 1788 the sub-set of rate paying voters exaggerates the support given in St Margaret and St John to Administration candidates. As in 1784, the division of the file into quintiles reveals a progressive increase in support for the Administration candidate with the inferred wealth of the voter, and a corresponding decline for his opponent. The results in 1788 show less of a plateau in the middle quintiles than is apparent in 1784, with a steady decline in support for Townshend from 48·3 per cent of those in the lowest quintile to 22·7 per cent in the highest.

We have no direct knowledge of the wealth of eighteenth century voters. The evidence given here suggests that one way forward for psephological studies of the eighteenth century may lie in the combination of occupational data and information on the values of property occupied by the electors.

Notes

1. This paper is based on research in progress for a London University Ph.D. thesis 'Social Structure and Political Allegiance in Westminster, 1774–1820'. I am grateful for advice and assistance to my supervisor, Dr P. J. Corfield, and to Dr C. Harvey and the Computer Centre of Royal Holloway and Bedford New College. The research was supported by the E.S.R.C., the Central Research Fund of the University of London, and Royal Holloway and Bedford New College.

2. P. Pulzer, *Political Representation in Britain*, 1966, p. 98.

3. *A Copy of the Poll . . . in the Borough of Leicester . . . 1800* (1801).

4. L. B. Namier and J. Brooke (eds), *The House of Commons, 1760–1790*, 1964, I, pp. 336–37.

5. C. Booth, 'Occupations of the people of the United Kingdom, 1801–1881', *Journal of the Statistical Society*, xlix, 1886, pp. 314–444. A. Armstrong, 'The use of information about occupation', *Nineteenth Century Society*, ed. E. Wrigley, 1972, pp. 191–310. The sectors are of agriculture, domestic and personal services, building, dealing, industrial service, manufacturing, professional and public services, rentiers, and transport. The sector of rentiers, absent from Booth's occupational classification and Armstrong's revision, has been included to accomodate those many voters who described themselves by such statuses as 'gentleman', 'esquire', 'knight', 'baronet', or with some title of nobility.

6. *A Correct Copy of the Poll . . . for the City and Liberty of Westminster (1774)*. *The Poll Book . . . for the City and Liberty of Westminster* (1818).

7. Further details of the spatial distribution of occupations and voting will be contained in my thesis.

8. Greater London Record Office, WR/PP/1784 and WR/PP/1788.

9. *The Times*, 31 July 1788.

10. Westminster Archive Office E/504–06 (1784) and E/523–25 (1788). I am grateful to Miss M. Swarbrick for the loan of microfilms of these documents. Full statistics will be available in my thesis.

Sex, Age and the Labour Vote in the 1920s

The problem

British historians have always been fascinated by the struggle for the franchise, and the campaigns for female suffrage in the twentieth century have received their full share of attention.[1] But few historians have taken a serious interest in the political consequences of female enfranchisement. How many new female voters were there? Did they alter the political balance? Was it more than chance that their entry into politics coincided with the downfall of the Liberal Party and the rise of Labour, and a long period of Conservative domination? Did anybody care?

In fact contemporary politicians did care very much. The decision to extend the franchise to some women in 1918 was taken deliberately. Its purpose was to find a way around a potential parliamentary deadlock between the two wings of the ruling Lloyd George coalition. When the reform of the franchise was forced into discussion by Conservatives as a price for the prolongation of the wartime parliament, they intended to secure the vote for servicemen, expecting that this would consolidate their domination of post-war politics. With the subject open, Liberals, Labour members and some suffragists on the Conservative benches insisted on female enfranchisement to meet a long-standing grievance. They were opposed by the more anti-democratic Conservatives, who also opposed adult suffrage for men. In due course a compromise was struck in which women over 30 got the vote if they were married to local government electors (that is to say householders) or if they would have been eligible in their own right for the local government franchise before 1918 if they had been men. For the suffragists this represented all they could get. For the others the 30-year rule was an arbitrary device to ensure that the number of female electors did not exceed the number of male electors; and for some of the more clear-sighted Conservatives the female vote was a potential secret weapon against the domination of a post-war mass electorate by trade union activists.[2]

Female enfranchisement had a larger numerical effect on the franchise in 1918 than the granting of the suffrage to hitherto unenfranchised adult males (in fact there were rather more than twice as many female voters as new male voters on the 1918 register, and more female voters in 1918 than there had been male voters in 1915). The electorate in Great Britain in 1915, the last register taken under the old legislation (excluding university electors) was 7,608,840, all men. The first register under the new legislation was taken in a hurry in 1918, and included 10,926,461 men and 7,775,211 women (41·5 per cent female). These figures certainly underestimated the numbers of those eligible to vote, both male and female: and the male figure included a number of serving soldiers between 18 and 21. The Autumn 1921 figures, published in the Census volumes, were probably more representative of the true weight of the female vote under the new franchise. Women on that register comprised 42·5 per cent of the electorate.[2]

The next major electoral reform was the equalisation of the franchise between men and women in the Act of 1928. This granted the suffrage to all women over the age of 21, and was calculated at the time to add 5·25 million to the electorate, of whom 1·8 million would be women over 30 who had not previously qualified, 16 thousand would be men now entitled to a second vote because of their wives' occupation of business premises, and the rest (3·5 million) would be women between the ages of 21 and 30. The Act appears to have been passed in a genuine fit of absence of mind by William Joynson-Hicks, one of the most reactionary Home Secretaries of this century, and it was accompanied by a strident newspaper campaign against the 'flapper vote'. In defence of his measure, Joynson-Hicks urged that the large majority of women newly enfranchised would either be married women or gainfully employed: only about 400,000 would be unoccupied women between the ages of 21 and 30, flappers properly so called. He was warned of all sorts of dire consequences if women were made a majority in the electorate, including national bankruptcy and the dissolution of the empire, but the government persevered.[3] The result of a wider and much simplified qualification for female enfranchisement was that the proportion of enfranchised women in the appropriate age group went up from 79·5 per cent (of women over 30) in 1921 to 98·5 per cent (of women over 21) in 1931, while male enfranchisement rates went up from 94·5 per cent to 99·5 per cent between the censuses. Women in 1931 constituted 53·8 per cent of the electorate.

The consequences of reform?

The first election held on the new franchise was in 1929 and the Conservatives lost heavily, through a combination of Labour revival and a large, albeit temporary increase in the Liberal vote. The relationship between the new electorate and the election result has remained a mystery. The consensus among historians and political scientists is that within all classes and all regions in Britain women tend to a greater extent than men to favour the Conservative party over all other parties, though the best predictor of the political allegiance of a wife is the political allegiance of her husband and the best guide to a wife's social class is her husband's occupation.[4] The most direct evidence for this comes from sample opinion surveys taken almost entirely after 1945, when the two-party system was at its strongest. For the inter-war period, in a three-party system, there is evidence of a rather different kind. A study of constituency voting patterns after 1918 suggested that in the immediate post-war elections the size of the female proportion of the electorate was an important determinant of the size of the anti-Labour vote in a constituency.[5] This relationship held good over two elections and over a number of different regression models of Labour voting, and was the most robust of all explanatory variables examined in a study of the relationship between the class, gender, socio-economic composition and religiosity of the electorate, the party-political characteristics of the candidates, and voting outcomes in England. The conclusion of that study was, emphatically, that the female electorate in 1918 and 1922 was a considerable advantage to the Conservative party and a handicap to Labour.

Further investigation of the same material has not fundamentally altered this conclusion, but the study of a longer period has revealed new perspectives and perhaps a new interpretation of the evidence. Like any study of twentieth-century British electoral behaviour, these fresh conclusions only emerge after a battle with methodological problems. With no poll books after 1872 and no relevant sample surveys before the Second World War, the behaviour of individuals has to be estimated from the behaviour of aggregates. Constituencies are the smallest unit for which parliamentary votes are recorded, and no socio-economic data beyond the barest demographic information is available for constituencies. The behaviour of female voters, for example, has to be inferred from the varying behaviour of constituencies with varying proportions of female voters.

This leaves us with two classic statistical problems. The first is the problem of aggregate *versus* individual level analysis. It is notoriously unsafe to infer individual level behaviour from information about aggregates such as polling districts, let alone anything so big as a parliamentary constituency. Jews in New York and Irishmen in Lancashire provide the examples best liked by the statistical textbooks. Every American schoolboy knows that until the 1970s Jews voted Democrat; most English historians would agree that between 1885 and 1918 most Irish immigrants voted Liberal or Labour, usually the former. Nevertheless the New York city wards with high proportions of Jewish voters tend strongly to be Republican, while high proportions of Irish immigrants in Lancashire constituencies are associated with Conservative voting. The reasons for this are similar, though not identical, in the two cases. Besides being Democrat, Jewish New Yorkers are socially mobile and tend to move to the wealthier suburbs, where most of their Gentile neighbours, who outnumber them, are Republican. They are a deviant minority in their residential districts. The Irish were also generally a minority, with the added difficulty that their presence in significant numbers tended to excite the politics of Protestant bigotry, which inspired much 'popular Toryism' in Lancashire. Significantly, the Scotland division of Liverpool, which alone among British constituencies actually had an Irish Catholic majority, reliably returned an Irish Nationalist M.P. until 1929. In both these cases inference from the aggregate figures would suggest conclusions about the Irish and Jewish vote which are precisely opposite to the true state of affairs.[6]

The risk of this error being made is fortunately smaller with the female vote in Britain between the wars. Though women were a minority in the pre-1928 electorate, they were a very large minority which could not be 'swamped' by male voters as Jewish and Irish voters were swamped. Moreover it was very difficult to know whether a constituency was more or less influenced by female voters, and thus very unlikely that the politics of reaction could persuade the male majority to vote against the female minority: in any case there was no suggestion that either party was 'the woman's party', to be voted against by men. The problem of aggregate level inference is therefore not so severe as might first appear, though it cannot be dismissed entirely.

The second classic problem is more difficult to argue away. The high correlation between female electorates and Conservative voting may be explained not by a causal link between the two, but by an unspecified third factor, correlated with both variables and causing them both. It is not hard to see what sort of variable that might be in inter-war Britain. Women were not distributed evenly or even randomly across the country. In rural areas and heavy industrial areas the normal excess of females over males in the population, especially the economically active age-bands, was very much reduced and in some cases even reversed, because there were few employment opportunities for women. Mining, farming, and heavy industrial constituencies were likely to have smaller female electorates because of their economic structure, though this was partially offset by higher rates of female enfranchisement in those areas before 1928 because younger women (between 21 and 30) were more likely to leave. There is no easy way to exclude the possibility that it was their economic structure, rather than their small female electorates, which were responsible for their lesser sympathy for the Conservative party.

To these statistical problems must be added a third problem which dogs the explanation of post-1918 female electoral behaviour. The female electorate for ten years was, by the deliberate wish of parliament, both older and more concentrated in the propertied or at any rate settled classes than the male electorate. Young women, poor women, and even a large number of female domestic servants without access to a ratepayer franchise, were prevented from voting. This quality of maturity, stability and 'independence' had been part of the attraction of the female electorate for Conservative woman-suffragists. Might Lord Selborne not have been right, that 'women will prove to be the most stable and conservative element in the constitution'?[7] Were the women electors pro-Conservative and anti-Labour simply because they were drawn from an older population?

Finally, there are tiresome problems in the data. The 1921 and 1931 census volumes contained registration data drawn from the autumn registers of the previous year, and included limited data on the population within each parliamentary constituency. In 1918 the register was published to illustrate the effects of the 1918 Representation of the People Act, and the 1919 Autumn register was also published. The 1920 registers were not published, but those for 1921 to 1939 were. In 1928 the Registrar-General was asked to estimate the impact of the new legislation on the size and sex-ratio of the electorate. His office published a tabulation which included the 1927 register results, together with an estimate of the number of women who would be enfranchised which was apparently based on otherwise unpublished estimates of the age-structures of populations within constituencies: it correlated well with the 1928 register. Thus there are a number of cross-sectional breakdowns of the structure of the electorate over the period, no two of which give the same data beyond the minimum, a report of the number of men and women in the electorate for each constituency. Both census reports give the number of men and women in the population on census night, but only the 1921 census gives the number of men and women of franchise age. The 1931 census and the published registers show separately the number of residential qualifications and business (occupation of business premises) qualifications.

Worse than this, no published tabulation, indeed no data obtainable by any means, makes it possible to discover the economic and social characteristics of constituencies, since all the census reports and tables except for registration material are tabulated by administrative units rather than electoral areas. The raw data is gone for ever. The enumerators' books for the 1931 Census were destroyed by enemy action in the 1939–45 war and the punched-cards on which all the data was recorded (potentially the largest machine-readable dataset which has ever existed for Britain before 1951) was pulped by order of the Registrar-General's department after the 1931 Census volumes were published.[8] Consequently, all full scale studies of electoral behaviour in the early twentieth century have used the method of constant unit analysis pioneered by William Miller.[9] Constituencies are grouped into larger units for which full census data is obtainable, and which maintained their boundaries effectively unchanged for a long period. In practice this means that large boroughs, divided into a number of parliamentary divisions, serve as constant units between the wars, as do the administrative counties whose boundaries were undisturbed by successive local government legislation. In counties with substantial urban settlement, the 'county remainder' becomes a constant unit alongside the boroughs. This aggregation brings disadvantages. Constant units were not genuine political units, and some arbitrary assumptions have to be made when (as is typical in the 1920s) not all seats in a unit are contested by all the major parties. Using constituencies as the units of analysis, while attributing to them the socio-economic data of the constant unit of which they are a part, may be misleading if the constant unit is not socially or economically homogenous. It also brings severe technical drawbacks in a regression analysis, which is the most powerful analytical tool available for this data. In brief, such a use of 'split-level' data tends to depress correlations between voting behaviour and socio-economic characteristics. Nevertheless, split-level data is used in the analysis which follows because some important data (not used, for example, in Miller's own study) is available at constituency level and would be lost in a constant unit analysis.

The study

By using constant unit data for socio-economic variables and constituency data for demographic and political data it is possible to test a number of regression models which relate female enfranchisement to the vote for major parties. The core hypotheses to test are threefold:

1. That the correlation between female enfranchisement and Conservative voting is a genuine sex-difference between male and female voters.
2. That it is a function of the different age structure of the female and male electorates.
3. That it is an artifact of the distribution of women over the constituencies, reflecting merely the smaller female population in mining and heavy industrial districts whose partisanship is determined by their economic characteristics.

The critical data which make it possible to differentiate between these hypotheses are contained in the Registrar General's 1928 paper and the 1931 Census, from which one can calculate the change in the level of female enfranchisement brought about by the equalisation of the franchise in 1928. Other things being equal, that change score should be related to shifts in partisan voting in one of three ways. Taking the Labour vote as the dependent variable, these would be:

1. If anti-Labour voting is strictly the result of a sex difference, higher change scores (more women) should be associated with shifts away from Labour (Hypothesis 1).
2. If anti-Labour voting is associated with the age-structure of the pre-1928 female electorate, higher change scores (younger women) should be associated with shifts towards Labour (Hypothesis 2).
3. If anti-Labour voting is merely an artifact of the economic structure of constituencies, change scores should be uncorrelated with shifts in Labour voting (Hypothesis 3).

Regression models can therefore be used which relate changes in voting between the 1924 and 1929 general elections, and changes in female enfranchisement in 1928. The general form is that for each constituency:

Partisan   =   National Swing + Local Factors + Female Vote + Error
Shift

In a standard regression equation, the partisan shift will be the dependent variable, the National Swing will be taken up in the Constant term, and the local factors will be a set of variables which include socio-economic data and also the variations in the structure of the contest between the two election years. In a three-party system partisan proportions will be markedly different in two-way and three-way contests. The error term will have to accommodate a great deal of life's rich pattern, including local political issues and the personality of the candidates, but that is a cross that all quantitative electoral studies must bear. Following Miller's conclusions and the results of previous work, it seemed important to include at least religious variables and class and occupational variables, which would be expected to affect not only the absolute level of partisan allegiance but also the varying response of different constituencies to the political situation in 1929.

The results

The 1929 election was an inglorious defeat for the Conservatives but it left the opposition parties in some doubt about their achievements. The Conservatives found that 'Safety First' was no better than Protection as an elction slogan; they returned to the position they had been left in by the 1923 election, with 260 seats, a net loss of 152. Labour made a net gain of 136, from 151 to 287, and the Liberals a net gain of 19, from 40 to 59.

In terms of votes, the pattern of gains and losses is rather complex. The

Tories' heaviest losses were in middle class urban constituencies and in mining communities, while they held their own much better in working class and rural constituencies. (See Table 1) In contrast, Labour's greatest improvements were in mining constituencies and working class urban constituencies, with less distinguished performances in rural areas and in urban middle-class constituencies. The explanation of this odd mismatch is the peculiar effect of Liberal intervention: the party put up 173 more candidates than they had done in 1924, and concentrated them in middle

Table 1   *Conservative Losses and Labour Gains, 1929*

Shifts in Conservative share of the vote (per cent)

	Middle Class	Mixed Class	Working Class	Urban/ Rural	Rural	Mining
London	-11	-13	-2	n/a	n/a	n/a
South East	-14	-13	-1	-17	-3	n/a
East Anglia	-9	-8	n/a	-10	-11	n/a
Central England	-11	-12	-5	-13	-9	n/a
Wessex	-21	-20	n/a	-12	-11	n/a
Bristol	-12	-2	0	-14	-9	-15
Devon & Cornwall	-5	-5	-6	3	-7	n/a
West Midlands	-13	-14	-9	-9	-7	n/a
East Midlands	n/a	-10	2	-11	-12	-8
Lancastria	-18	-9	-7	-8	-6	-4
Yorkshire	-18	-12	-6	-7	-6	-5
North of England	n/a	-6	-10	-11	-15	-5

Shifts in Labour share of the vote (per cent)

	Middle Class	Mixed Class	Working Class	Urban/ Rural	Rural	Mining
London	-1	3	3	n/a	n/a	n/a
South East	2	1	5	-1	0	n/a
East Anglia	3	0	n/a	6	2	n/a
Central England	1	-3	2	7	6	n/a
Wessex	-11	1	n/a	2	3	n/a
Bristol	9	6	8	3	5	4
Devon & Cornwall	4	3	0	10	8	n/a
West Midlands	16	2	5	7	-2	n/a
East Midlands	n/a	6	6	8	6	7
Lancastria	11	4	5	12	0	2
Yorkshire	10	9	5	-1	0	9
North of England	n/a	4	1	4	-6	1

class areas. Moreover, where they had put up candidates in both elections, they tended to gain (at the expense of Conservatives) in middle class areas and lose (to Labour) in working class and mining districts: they were also relatively strong in agricultural areas.

It is possible to devise fairly good descriptive models of variations in the Labour and Conservative votes in 1929. These are illustrated in Figure 1.

Figure 1   *The Election of 1929 in England: Explaining the Labour Vote*

A. EXPLAINING THE LABOUR VOTE

452 English Constituencies

Dependent Variable: Labour proportion of total votes cast

Independent Variables:	*Coeff.*	*Signif.*
Female % of Electorate	-2.767	<.0001
Agricultural % of workforce*	-0.525	<.0001
Two-way contest (Y/N)	0.127	<.0001
Working Class Constituency (Y/N)	0.086	<.0001
Mining Constituency (Y/N)	0.104	<.0001
Anglican Ministers per head*	-36.983	<.05
(Constant)	1.856	

Adjusted R Squared   .6745   F = 156.78 <.0001
S.E.   .0957

Figure 2   *The Election of 1929 in England: Explaining the Conservative Vote*

411 English Constituencies

Dependent Variable: Conservative proportion of total votes cast

Independent Variables:	*Coeff.*	*Signif.*
Female % of Electorate	1.573	<.0001
Anglican Ministers per head*	59.571	<.0001
Middle Class Constituency (Y/N)	0.042	<.005
Miners/Quarrymen as prop. of workforce*	-0.151	<.001
Two Party Contest (Y/N)	0.121	<.001
T.U. Officials as prop. of workforce*	-203.617	<.001
Female Servants per head*	0.764	<.005
(Constant)	-0.458	

Adjusted R Squared   .4350   F = 46.101 <.0001
S.E.   .0765

* Constant unit level data; all other data at constituency level

Figure 3   *Explaining (or Rather, not Explaining) Changes in the Labour Vote, 1924 to 1929*

400 English constituencies

Dependent Variable: Change in Labour Vote (Prop. in 1929 – Prop. in 1924)

Independent Variables:	*Coeff.*	*Signif.*
"Non-operatives" in workforce*	-0.389	<.0001
Agricultural prop. of workforce*	-0.151	<.0001
Persons per Room*	-0.096	<.001
Change in Female prop. of electorate	-1.601	<.12
Adjusted R Squared	.1087	F = 17.215 <.0001
S.E.	.0528	

* Constant unit level data; other data at constituency level

This is rather a dog bites man story. Labour turns out to be the party of the urban working class and the miners, the Conservatives, ostensibly, a middle class party much beloved by vicars and housemaids, or at any rate by the sort of constituencies in which vicars and housemaids tended to gather. But the overwhelming importance of the female electorate in this descriptive model is as striking as it was for 1918. The big question has by no means gone away.

Yet the prediction of change scores, the nub of this whole investigation, suggests that this apparently very strong relationship between female voters and anti-Labour voting is an artifact of the socio-economic composition of constituencies. No predictive model fits the relationship well: the example in Figure 2 is one of the best, explaining just over 10 per cent of the variance, though rather better predictions can be obtained by breaking the country into regions or splitting the population in other ways, as in Figure 3. This is not surprising in itself: change scores are inherently difficult to predict, since they involve the behaviour of smallish minorities of the population. Even so, within this weak model, the role of change in the female proportion of the electorate is not strong enough to allow Hypothesis 3, the null hypothesis (of 'no relationship' between change in female enfranchisement and change in Labour voting), to be rejected. On this evidence, we must regard Hypothesis 3 as the best description of the relationship. What is important, then, is not the change in enfranchisement, but the socio-economic characteristics which were present before and after the franchise revision.[10]

Furthermore, the pattern of new enfranchisement in 1928 (Table 2) suggests that not only were the female proportion of the electorate before 1928 and the female proportion afterwards both related strongly to class differentials, but also that the extra enfranchisement was itself skewed towards middle class constituencies and away from mining constituencies. Differences between constituencies were made larger, not smaller, by the 1928 Act. Not only was the proportion of women in mining populations smaller than that in middle class constituencies, but also a far higher

Table 2   *Females as Proportion of the Electorate*

1928 Register (per cent)

	Middle Class	Mixed Class	Working Class	Urban/ Rural	Rural	Mining
London	46.56	45.29	43.47	n/a	n/a	n/a
South East	46.51	45.19	43.39	44.87	44.82	n/a
East Anglia	46.55	45.14	n/a	43.26	42.58	n/a
Central England	45.36	43.39	43.86	43.35	43.35	n/a
Wessex	50.29	44.38	n/a	44.40	43.32	n/a
Bristol	47.96	44.17	43.42	41.33	44.54	41.06
Devon & Cornwall	49.71	45.70	44.02	47.93	44.79	n/a
West Midlands	44.86	42.38	41.98	41.69	42.59	n/a
East Midlands	n/a	44.50	44.10	42.50	42.07	39.73
Lancastria	45.79	42.51	43.57	44.59	41.94	39.13
Yorkshire	43.18	43.29	43.93	43.87	41.89	38.51
North of England	n/a	41.65	42.22	41.40	43.24	39.44

1931 Census (per cent)

	Middle Class	Mixed Class	Working Class	Urban/ Rural	Rural	Mining
London	57.52	54.33	52.00	n/a	n/a	n/a
South East	55.83	53.29	52.41	53.97	54.01	n/a
East Anglia	56.33	54.41	n/a	51.52	51.21	n/a
Central England	54.96	53.86	53.02	51.75	52.23	n/a
Wessex	62.14	52.25	n/a	53.26	52.25	n/a
Bristol	57.70	53.43	53.10	50.44	53.56	51.67
Devon & Cornwall	57.80	53.61	50.87	55.86	53.54	n/a
West Midlands	54.81	52.47	52.62	51.67	52.55	n/a
East Midlands	n/a	53.98	53.35	52.15	51.22	49.88
Lancastria	55.86	53.47	53.51	54.89	53.47	51.49
Yorkshire	53.88	53.50	54.00	54.00	52.21	48.95
North of England	n/a	51.55	51.67	50.92	53.65	49.41

proportion of women were enfranchised in the middle class areas. About 70 per cent of all females in London middle-class constituencies were enfranchised by 1931: only about 60 per cent of all females in the Yorkshire and Durham coalfields. Women in their twenties were especially likely to migrate, for example to London. Here lies the most probable explanation of the relationship between female electorates and the Labour vote.

Conclusions

This has rather larger implications for the analysis of twentieth-century voting behaviour than merely the answer to a conundrum in 1920s politics. It would appear from this study that the proportion of women in a constituency's electorate is not merely a demographic variable, as first appears, but a rather subtle and interesting social indicator. It is more like an index number than a simple variable, combining (and thus of course confounding) class and type of economic activity. If anything it might be a better index of 'class' than most of the other measures derived from the census. If gender is not a straightforward indicator, despite its repeated appearance in models predicting voting behaviour, can we be sure of the other standby, religion? One of the main achievements of Miller's study was to restore religious differences as determinants of voting behaviour after 1918. In this instance we can perhaps be a little more confident. Anglicanism clearly has an independent effect, in the statistical sense, from female electorates and other social measures. On the other hand, the strong relationship between the distribution of clergymen (of all denominations) among constituencies and other social variables such as the number of female servants suggests a causal model which is at any rate not entirely confessional. Certain constituencies attracted clergymen. These constituencies tended to vote Tory. But this, at most, suggests that clergymen, not Anglicans at large, were the Tory voters.

Investigating the psephological history of the twentieth century is, on the whole, more difficult than investigating that of the nineteenth century. We are confronted not with fragmentary sources, but with what Winston Churchill described as 'a great fog of information'. Cutting through that fog to reveal a version of reality will always be a problematic historical exercise. To call it political science would be outrageously ambitious.

Notes

1. David Morgan, *Suffragists And Liberals: The Politics of Woman Suffrage in England*, Oxford: Blackwell, 1975; Brian Harrison, *Separate Spheres. The Opposition to Women's Suffrage in Britain*, London: 1978; Brian Harrison, 'Women's Suffrage at Westminster 1866–1928', in Michael Bentley and John Stevenson, eds, *High and Low Politics in Modern Britain* Oxford: Clarendon Press, 1983, pp. 80–122.

2. For the 1918 Act see Martin Pugh, *Electoral Reform in War and Peace*, London: Routledge & Kegan Paul, 1978; D. Rolfe 'Origins of Mr Speaker's Conference during the First World War', *History*, 64, 1979; D. Close, 'The Collapse of Resistance to Democracy: Conservatives, Adult Suffrage and Second Chamber Reform 1911–28', *Historical Journal*, 20, 1977.

3. H. C. Dods, vol. 215, 1359–1482.

4. e.g. David Butler and Donald Stokes, *Political Change in Britain*, New York: St Martin's Press, 1971, p. 100, which (in a footnote!) observes casually that the greater Conservatism of women is partly explained by their greater religious observance; for the recent discussion of social class see e.g. R. Erikson, 'Social Class of Men, Women and Families', *Sociology*, 18, 1984, pp. 500–14, answering J.H. Goldthorpe, 'Women and Class Analysis: in Defence of the Conventional View' *ibid.*, 17, 1983.

5.   John Turner, 'The Labour Vote and the Franchise after 1918: an Investigation of the English Evidence.', in Peter Denley and Deian Hopkin, *History and Computing*, Manchester: Manchester University Press, 1987, pp. 136–43.

6.   For the Irish and anti-Irish vote in the North West, see Henry Pelling, *Social Geography of British Elections*, London: Macmillan, 1967, pp. 239–87.

7.   Selborne to Salisbury, 12 September 1916, quoted in George Boyce, ed., *The Crisis of British Unionism*, London: Historians' Press, 1987, p. 200.

8.   For this information I am grateful to Dr E. Higgs of the Public Record Office.

9.   W. L. Miller, *Electoral Dynamics*, London: Macmillan, 1977.

10.   Jorgen Rasmussen, 'Women in Labour: the Flapper Vote and Party System Transformation in Britain', *Electoral Studies*, 1984, pp. 47–63, reaches the same overall conclusion about the relationship between a constituency's behaviour and the proportion of women in the electorate, but prefers the view that women *per se* behaved differently.

IX.

Regional Data Banks

The Stockholm Historical Database at Work

Introduction

"Reported dead in New Zealand, the 15th of March 1960". This short note is to be found in one of more than 26,000 ledgers that forms the Roteman Archives. The Archive was the result of a special population register for the city of Stockholm between 1878 and 1926. Made by one of the Archive officials long after the abandonment of the Roteman System, this entry is an indication of the benefits of a bureaucratic society for historians among others. It creates records for the future and a future for historians. Even though the Roteman System only accounts for people living in the city of Stockholm over a period of 50 years, in the ledgers there can be found groups of people with connections with almost every country in the world, either by origin or through migration.

The Roteman System

The rate of increase in the population of Stockholm before 1850 was rather slow. After that, however, the increase accelerated and the population really began to expand. On top of that, the population turnover was so high that the parish priests could not cope with the problem of keeping accurate Parish Registers of the people. At a time when city authorities really needed a good account of demographic changes to plan for housing, water supplies, schooling, and medical care for its inhabitants, it was these shortcomings that made necessary a new way of keeping track of the population — the Roteman System.

In order to do this, especially with very high population turnover rates, the records had to be longitudinal rather than cross-sectional. This also meant that the most appropriate reading unit was the single unit of real estate. In this new system, many of the parishes were too large in terms of population to be a secondary administrative level, hence a new division in wards was designed (rotar). Each rote was headed by an official called the Roteman. But apart from just being a population registrar, the Roteman had to serve the boards of education, poor relief, etc., with information. You had to get a certificate from the Roteman, for instance, in order to claim relief. In this capacity, the Roteman became a sort of agent of social control.

The division into wards (rotar) was based on an estimate of the number of poor people in the area and on average included 10,000 citizens. Figure 1 below shows the rote boundaries, the population in 1880 as well as the population on a property level for rote 1. With a population of 160,000 at the

Figure 1   *The Roteman System 1880*

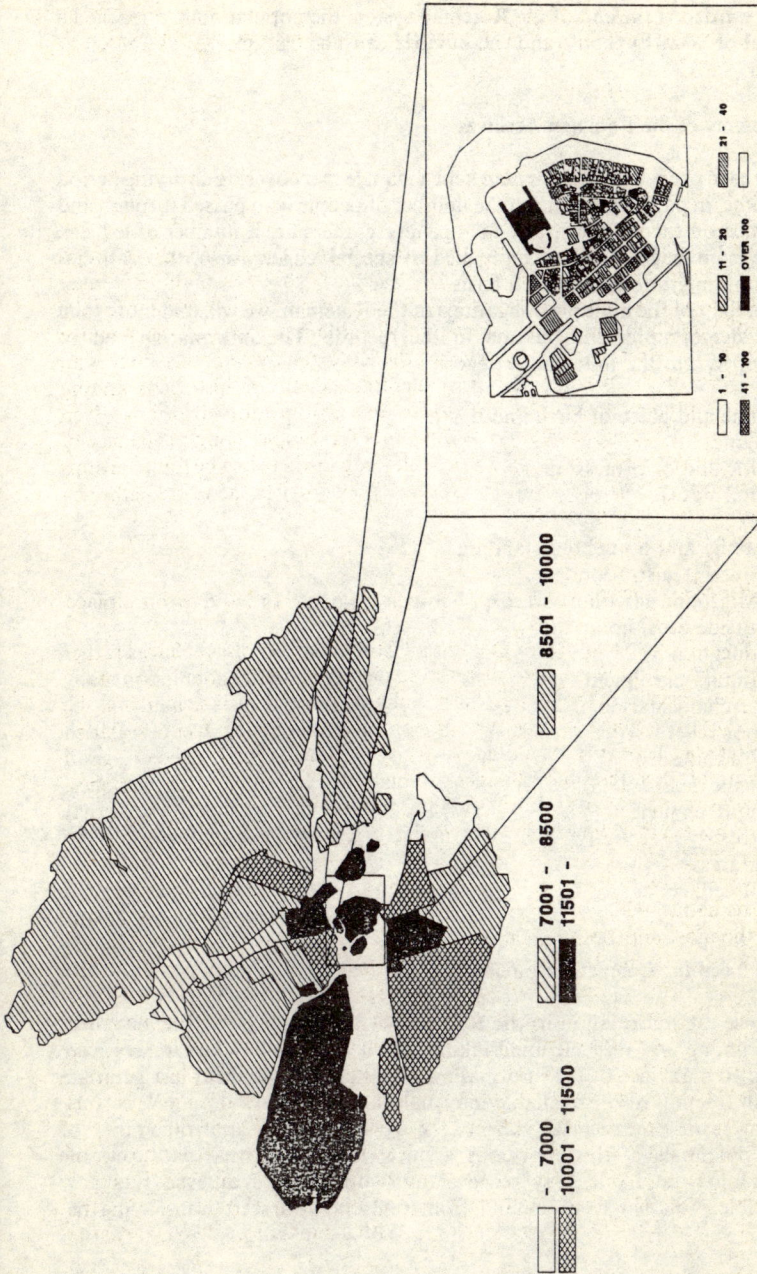

start of the Roteman system, the city was divided into 16 rotar. The rapid increase in population called for successive divisions and rearangements of the wards. At the end of the Roteman system the population had reached a total of 360,000 people and the number of rotar was 36.

Contents of the Roteman Archives

For each property, the Roteman kept a main ledger covering a varying period of time, in part dependent on the number of people who passed through and resided on the property. For each property, there are a number of ledgers. The main ledgers were accompanied by special ledgers for birth, death, in- and outmigration on a ward basis.

In light of the multiple obligations of the Roteman, we will find more than just demographic information in the records. The information can be grouped into the following categories:

* Time and place of birth and death
* Name
* Title and/or profession
* Civil status
* Sex
* Family and household standing
* Church registration
* Migration (within wards, between wards, to and from places outside Stockholm
* Education
* Military enrolment
* Merchant marine
* Poor relief
* Workhouse
* Medical care
* Imprisonment
* Property
* Address
* Miscellaneous

The Need for Computer Systems

To use the information in the Roteman Archive manually is a very time-consuming and difficult undertaking. Until recently few researchers have tried to make use of the information and they spent months just getting a small fraction of the available information.

It was these pioneers who opened the eyes of social historians and others to the potentials of this enormous archive; to the fact that with new the technology at hand, easy retrieval and sophisticated analysis was now feasible. This led to a demand from reseachers to start transferring the contents of the ledgers kept by the Roteman to a more appropriate media. This was one of the reasons for the establishment of the Stockholm Historical Databas (SHD). The transference of this large archive is still the primary task for SHD. The total volume of the paper database is not known. Estimates vary between 7 and 9 million entries. Of this, 1·2 millions are computerised already. But apart from the Roteman ledgers, SHD adds information from other sources as well. Some of the additional data are registered to enhance the use of the information in the Roteman Archives. For example coordinates for mapping administrative and property boundaries. The coordinates also serve as keys to linking data within the system. Other records that are presently processed by SHD are registers on causes of death, crimanal records and the 1900 census for Stockholm. The cross-sectional census data will enable us to compare with the longitudinal data of the Roteman system and thus be of use in a qualitative evaluation of the Roteman Archives.

Concepts and System Design

Starting this long term undertaking called for a number of considerations for system design and concepts. The long "production" phase means that the system design should not be based on the hardware and software constraints of today. To get around this problem we used the internal structure of the source to create software and hardware independent logical relationsships within the database. The primary key in the system is the source address made up of two variables:

* the ledger number
* page and row in the ledger.

This gives each entry a unique identifier. In the transference process we also attach a unique identifier to the household attachment of each entry. Thus we can reconstruct family and household composition over time. The accuracy of the information on date of birth together with sex and county of birth makes it our primary fields for the linkage of the total number of entries for one individual. We use these features in the source for a number of variables which by themselves or in combination may serve as keys for various kinds of record linkage within the system. Some of these are:

Variable	Used for	Based on
ID	Linking records for an individual	Date of birth, sex and county of birth
HEFTE SIDR1	Source address and primary key for linking	Ledger number and page and line number
HEFTE SIDR2	Household linking	Ledger number and page and line number for head of household

HEFTE	Family linking	Ledger number, page and line
SIDR2		number, family standing and
FAMST		relation to head of household
RELAT		

HEFTE	Key to property and geographic location and map data sets	Ledger number

With this limited number of key variables we have the means for restructuring the database in a number of different ways. The primary divisions that may be made are as follows:

Demographic data:

* Individual base
* Family base
* Household base

Administrative and Spatial data:

* Property

Apart from the key variables presented above, we have added special code variables to simplify and speed up the retrieval process. The recorded information is computerised as it stands in the source, that is as text. The code variables enables us to restructure the information in the Roteman Archives in still more problem approriate fashions. With these concepts, we have all the information needed for various linkage operations inherent in the database and are thus not software-dependent. However, because of the large volume of data to be handled, we do need powerful software for data processing as well as hardware with good storage capacities. In these respects, we have been very fortunate in having the following hardware and software facilities at our disposal in our own office.

Hardware: IBM4341 II (8Mb CPU)

Total disc space 5·6 Gbyte of which SHD can use 1·5 Gbyte for "permanent" direct access data storage.

Terminals — both alphanumeric and graphics with hardcopy and plotters.

PCs with digitisers and COAX-connections to the mainframe for up- and downloading of data.

Software: On the mainframe SAS under MVS/TSO/ISPF we have the following SAS (Statistical Analysis System) modules:

* Base SAS
* SAS/FSP
* SAS/GRAPH
* SAS/AF
* SAS/ETS

On the PCs we have a number different software packages available.

With this hardware and software set up, in combination with the data at hand, we have created a good research environment, that we hope can serve as a base for a History Laboratory. The basic tools are there. However, we are still lacking simple to use and yet powerful user interfaces. For that development we need feedback from different kind of user experiences in dealing with the information in the database.

SHD at work

When the registration of the Roteman Archives started, historians at universities were considered to be the primary potential user group. This view has since changed and today we find users from a number of different disciplines and at different levels in the educational system. We regard this as an advantage in order to develop a user-friendly environment at SHD, especially since SHD is a division of the City Archives in Stockholm, and as such does not have any obligations to undertake research based on the computerised information.

Working in close cooperation with users has also enabled us to become participants in various development projects, where we get the chance to test new software and hardware as well as creating software shells for easy utilisation of SHD data. Our cooperation with researchers so far has been predominantly of an *ad hoc* nature. To give some examples of these joint efforts and illustrate what kind of research undertakings that can be made using SHDs material we will refer to ongoing works by a sociologist, two historians and a human geographer.

"Household structure in Stockholm 1880–1925" is part of a larger project "Household structure in Sweden 1860–1930: Continuity and Change" by Mona Martensson, Department of Sociology, University of Stockholm. Her primary interest in the data from the Roteman Archives is in information on household standing, which can be used to generate datasets on the composition of households. It is the kind of information that is very lean in the aggregated statistical summaries of the Population censuses, which is the major national source. To meet her needs and enable comparisions between Stockholm and the rest of the country, we generated cross-sectional datasets for rotar of different socio-economic compositions.

One of the things Ms. Martensson looks at as part of her study is standing in the household with regard to age and sex. By a combinatory classification based on variables describing family standing and relation to head of household we can create the very categories she needs for her work. For analysis we have generated a sequence of graphs for different years, areas and sex. Figure 2 illustrates one type of graphic design used for her interpretations.

Figure 2   *Household Standing in Rote 1*

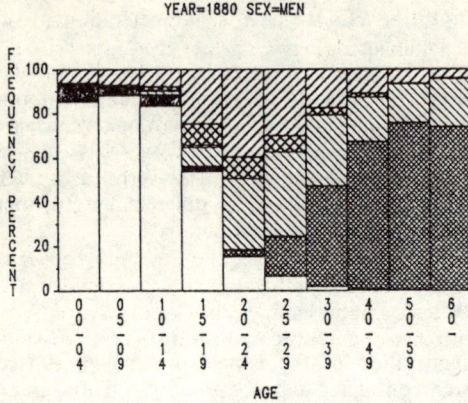

YEAR=1880 SEX=MEN

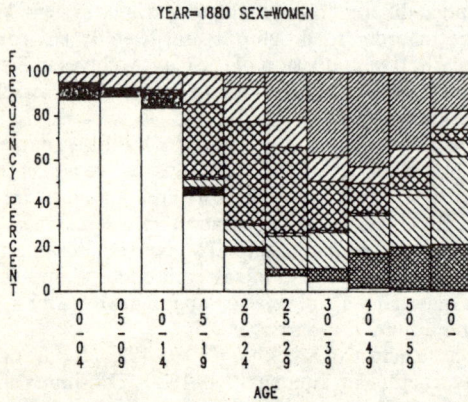

YEAR=1880 SEX=WOMEN

☐ OWN CHILDREN	■ OTHER CHILDREN
▦ HEAD.O.HOUSEHOLD	▨ SING.PERS.HOUSEH
▧ RELATIVES	▨ EMPLOYES
▨ LODGERS	▨ WIFES

"Rural to Urban migrants in turn of the century Stockholm" is the project of Roger Miller, Department of Human Geography, University of Stockholm and University of Minnesota. His work involves two studies. They both explore the potential for combining information from the two major demographic databases in Sweden, SHD and DDB (Demographic Database in Umeå-Haparanda). The first study is focused on a qualitative evaluation of a small population of urban migrants from one rural parish. Since both databases provide longitudinal information on individuals Roger Miller has been able to create detailed biographies describing the migrants social mobility and professional careers. Living conditions in Stockholm were extremely poor for most migrants. Because of a severe shortage of housing the practice of taking lodgers was common. Households were large, with many unrelated individuals living together in cramped circumstances. Under these conditions geographic mobility was extremely high, resulting in a number of entries for each individual. The qualitative evaluation of these records gives only limited evidence of upward social mobility in the rigidly hierarchial social structure of turn-of-the-century Stockholm. Most social mobility occured within the framework of specific trades, and was associated with normal life-path progression through the apprenticeship, journeyman, and master stages of craft organisation.

A second part of the study involves the interaction between Stockholm and the region of Sundsvall, a rapidly developing sawmill industry. In this study the focus is on demographic characteristics and chages over time, illustrated in Figure 3 with the age and sex composition of migrants at different periods in time.

Figure 3   *Age-Sex of Medelpad Migrants*

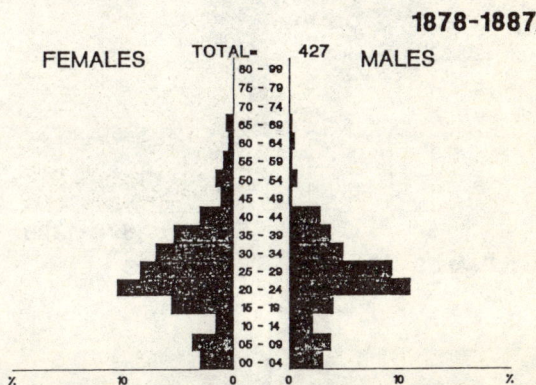

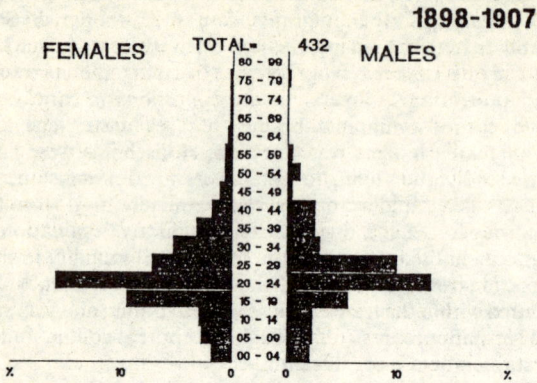

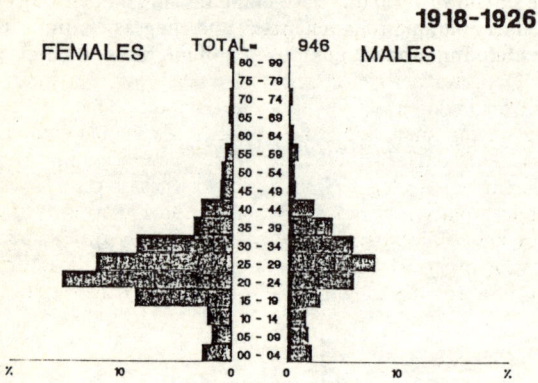

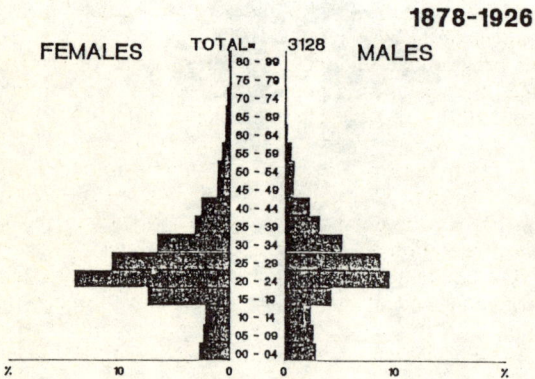

"Foster-children and foster-homes" is the project of Lisa Oberg, Department of History, University of Stockholm. The study is focused on the conditions for foster-children in the households where they were staying. One part of the study was based on a cohort in which biographies were compiled for persons who had been categorised as foster-children at least once before the age of 15. It also involved retrival of all the household members. The approriate selections were made by using the key variables listed above in a three step retrieval process. First identification of "identity". In step two researching the files for all entries the "foster-children" and retaining information on "head of household", which was used to retrieve all household members. With the longitudinal cohort data it was possible to calculate to what extent the foster-children became legalised. Another question, for which the cohort data set was useful, was to what extent the foster-home families used foster-children as a substantial source for income. Another part of the study is based on cross-sectional data for different years for households with foster-children. The size and composition of the households were calculated. The findings give no indication of a foster-child industry, which was one of the things Lisa Oberg wanted to investigate.

"Single Female Emigrants to the USA, 1880–1920" is the project of Joy Lintelman, Department of History, University of Minnesota. Joy Lintelman's primary interest is in the social standing, age and geographic origin of the single female emigrants to USA. To enable comparision we provided her with data for married women, married and single men. Questions she raised with regard to her primary interest were: to what extent was Stockholm a place for transit? Was emigration the result of a lack of opportunities in Stockholm and a sort of last hope? Since almost 60 per cent of the population in Stockholm was born outside the city, the information in the roteman files provides a good base for answering the questions posed.

Conclusion

SHD has the means, in terms of hardware, software, and, most important, a well-structured data model, to create and restructure data to meet the needs of a large number of different research problems.

The *ad hoc* programming adopted for the examples presented above is complemented by work for school authorities in Stockholm. We are preparing specially designed menu systems for PC-networks. The undertakings we have at present focus on applications for the upper secondary schools. In this work we download subsets from the mainframe in a form that can be used by the database systems presently at use in the schools. As a part of these development works, we are at the same time engaged in the preparation of the exercises, that accompany the applications software. SHD staff are also engaged in schools, introducing materials and methods and guiding students. In this way we get direct feedback of value in planning future developments, as well forming a bond with the next generation of reseachers who will exploit the riches of SHD.

A Computerised Medieval City Archive: the Project 'Regensburger Bürger- und Häuserbuch'

1. Introduction

Regensburg was founded as a military camp by the Roman Emperor Marcus Aurelius in 179 A.D. In the fifth century it became the residence of the Dukes of Bavaria and from the ninth century the Carolingians used it as an occasional residence. As a trading and cultural centre, Regensburg was proclaimed 'Freie Reichstadt' by a decree of the emperor Friedrich II. in 1245. From 1663 until 1806, when the 'Altes Reich' came to an end, Regensburg was the seat of the 'Immerwährender Reichstag', an assembly of German princes, counts, knights and independent towns. Today Regensburg has one of the best preserved medieval city centres in Germany with about 1,400 surviving buildings.

In the archives and museums of Regensburg and Munich one can find such a large volume of historical material about Regensburg, that until today nobody has attempted a complete history of this city.

In light of this fact, the idea emerged in 1984 of computerising the city archive, when three historians started a project called 'Regensburger Bürger- und Häuserbuch'. The aim of the project is to build a database covering all available data about the history of the city of Regensburg and make them accessible for scientific analysis.

The title 'Regensburger Bürger- und Häuserbuch', just as a working title, resulting from an old desire of the Regensburg city historians to put together data about 'Bürger' and buildings. The project however will not only construct listings of persons and buildings but make it possible to retrieve the whole biography of individuals and buildings as well as descriptions of art and households.

2. The Sources

The construction of the database is closely related to the original sources. We distinguish three areas important to 'everyday life' in medieval times: people, buildings and objects. In the first stage of the project we will concentrate on the sources of the 'Reichsstadt', leaving the sources of the religious institutions aside for the time being. Below we give a short description of the sources to be analysed in the next few years as well as an overview of current developments in our work.

The 'Neubürgerbücher' (1419–1869) include about 25,000 entries about people who came to Regensburg and received civil rights. These entries are already completely recorded and their analysis has commenced. The 'Heiratsbücher' (1551–1600) is a listing consisting of approximately 5,000 records, dealing with persons who got married in the 'Reichsstadt'. Recording and analysis of this source has been prepared for a course at the University of Regensburg which will begin shortly.

In the 'Totenbücher' (1650–1812) there are about 98,000 entries concerning people who died in Regensburg. Work on these 'Totenbücher' will follow after the recording of the 'Heiratsbücher'.

The major group of medieval sources, the documents (12th—18th century), have been part of our endeavours for two years now. The large number (about 18,000 records) and lack of formal structure of these documents make it necessary to prepare the registration of this information in the form of abstracts (in German 'Regesten'). Preliminary studies of 8,000 wills (13th—18th century) are almost finished. A data structure for and analysis of the 'Urfehdebriefe', documents of the municipal court, which include oaths of persons swearing not to take revenge, is being tested. The recording of the 'Siegelprotokolle', a very central group of sources, which include roughly 80,000 contracts of private law, will begin in 1990. One of three volumes of inscriptions is now going to press, the other two are being prepared. Work on the 'Rechnungsbücher' (14th, 15th, 17th, 18th centuries), books of bills of the Reichsstadt, was started in 1986.

The 'Beisitzprotokolle' (1604–1812), books including citizens of a legal status inferior to ordinary citizens, consist of about 50,000 entries. The registration of this source will be a follow-up project to the analysis of the 'Neuburgerbücher'. An important source for the analysis of buildings is the 'Baualtersplan', which includes the history of every building by its architectural characteristics.

The confluence of all these sources is shown in Figure 1.

3. Construction of the Database

In developing the Regensburg database we start with persons. Data relating to single persons or families will not only include information about their individual biography, they will also offer information about the buildings they owned or lived in, and the objects they dealt with.

The identification of most of the buildings, for example, makes it necessary to know the owners or residents of the neighbouring buildings. If one tried to identify a building by its house number or the name of its owner one might not be very successful. People moving to another building sometimes took their old house numbers with them. That is why one can have the same number for different buildings over the course of years. The name which one reads in a document and which one thinks to be the name of the owner of a building can also be the name of a former owner which meanwhile has become the name of the house itself. Thus, 'Baker's house' can either be the house of Mr Baker or the house of a baker or a house which once belonged to a baker and which is called 'Baker's house' ever since. So it will be useful to

Figure 1   *Basic Sources Confluencing in the Area of Persons, Buildings and Objects*

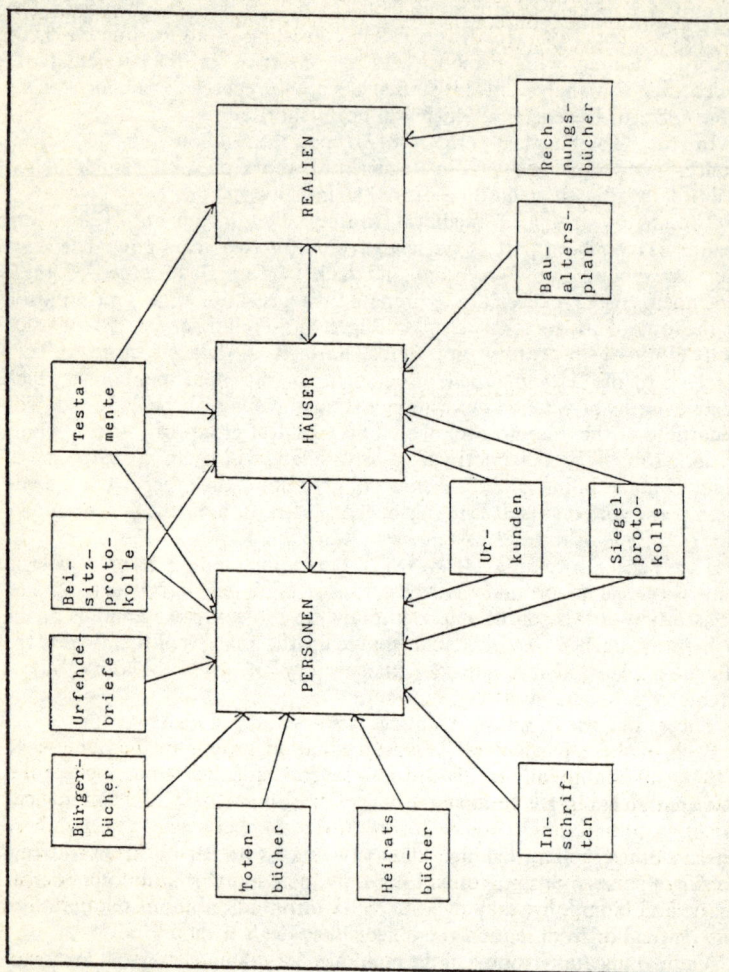

know that by 'Baker's house' we mean the house next to the house of Hanns the shoemaker and across the street from the house of good old Paulus, whose family name has not been recorded. So what we need is a record of 'Hanns the shoemaker' and 'old Paulus' to identify 'Baker's house'. These records will be available in our database after the first stage of the project.

Every person mentioned in the sources will get a record in the database, which is made up of a specific code number and a basic set of particulars for every individual, including name, christian name, sex, date of birth, date of death, birth place, additional references to places, address in Regensburg, burial place, profession, office, status, religious denomination, reference to the person in other sources (naming), partners in marriages, relatives and 'connections' (see Figure 2).

Figure 2   *General Structure of Records (Persons)*

```
code number:number

name:name/date/id_number
christian name:christian_name(s)/id_number
sex:sex

date of birth:date/id_number
date of death:date/id_number

birth place:place/id_number
other places:place/date/id_number
adress in Regensburg:place/date/id_number
burial place:place/date/id_number

profession:profession/date/id_number
office:office/date/id_number
status:status/date/id_number
religious denomination:religious_d./date/id_number

naming:named_as/date/id_number

wife/husband:name/chr_name/code_number/date/id_number
relatives:name_of_the_relationship/name/chr_name/
          code_number/date/id_number

connectiones:named_as/name/chr_name/code_number/
          date/id_number
```

Each of these particulars, called information groups in the context of CLIO, can additionally be divided into several subfields, which include the information as regards content, the date of the source (to give a chronological orientation) and other code or identification numbers. The code numbers refer to other persons, the identification numbers refer to different sources. Each of the information groups, except the code number, can occur several times, accounting, for example, for the information group of relatives, for different children, parents, wives or husbands of a person.

Figure 3 gives an example for a record of an individual person. We have chosen a person who belonged to the patricians, who made up the 60 top families of Regensburg. Admittedly the person of our choice, Gottfried der Prewmeister, was not one of their most prominent representatives. Gottfried's data sheet, like all the other data sheets starts out with a unique personal code number. The will with the identification number TLK67 from 11 November 1406 gives a hint to the full name of our person. His name was 'Gottfried Prewmeister'. The meaning of the name Prewmeister is 'master brewer'. His sex was male. Gottfried was born about the year 1360. This date can be deduced from his first appearance in a document (here called STB1383). The date of the Prewmeister's death is inferable from his will.

Figure 3   *Example of a Record for an Individual Person*

```
code number:p10001

name:Prewmeister/23.11.1406/TLK67
christian name:Gottfried/TLK67
sex:M

date of birth:1360-  /STB1383
date of death:1406/TLK67

birth place:Regensburg/EWR1370
adress in Regensburg:Westnerwacht ander gang vor
                     Prukh/1370/EWR1370
adress in Regensburg:Westnerwacht ander gang vor
                     Prukh/1391/STRL1391
burial place:Niedermünster/1406/TLK67

profession:Brauer/1383/STB1383
profession:Kaufmann/1390/BZR1390
office:Steuerherr/1385/RBR1385
office:Steuerherr/1387/STJ1387;RBR1387
office:Münzherr/1403/MZB1392
office:Baumeister/1399/RBRW1399
status:Bürger/23.11.1406/TLK67
religious denomination:K

naming:Zeuge/1390/Heiratsvertrag

wife/husband:/Kathrein/p10003/1394/LRR1394
relatives:Sohn//Jacob/p10005/1394/LRR1394
relatives:Tochter/Hofmeister/Anna/p13004/1406/TLK67
relatives:Tochter//Barbara/p12050/1406/TLK67
relatives:Schwester/Notscherff/Anna/p10009/1406/TLK67

connectiones:/Reich/Agnes/p1234//UK
connectiones:/Reich/Jörg/p10056//UK
connectiones:/Ingolstetter/Heinrich/p10089/1406/TLK67
```

The birth place of Gottfried was Regensburg. He was probably born in his father's house, which also became his life-long residence. The address of the building can be found in the registers of taxes and inhabitants. The biography of Gottfried ends in 1406. As the place of his burial he chose the tomb of his family in Niedermünster. Gottfried's profession was master brewer. Besides that, he dealt in building materials, which means he was also a businessman, according to the bridge toll registers. Additionally Gottfried held some municipal offices: from 1385 to 1389 he was 'Steuerherr' (master of taxes) and municipal master builder. For about ten years the Prewmeister owned a share of the municipal mint. Gottfried's status was that of a 'burgher', his religious denomination was roman catholic.

Gottfried appears as a witness in a marriage contract. He was married to Kathrein and father of one son and two daughters. One of them, Anna, was married in 1406. That is why she was called Anna Hofmeister at that time. Additionally, the will of Gottfried names a number of further persons, whose 'connections' to him are still unclear. Some of them, like the Ingolstetter, belonged to the patricians of Regensburg. Information about the others will have to be found during the following stages of our work.

The following step in constructing the Regensburg database will be the registration of buildings. Starting out from 1,400 buildings within about 500 years we expect roughly 700,000 data items. The data structure of the records is being worked on at the moment. At any rate we have to start again with a code number for every building, possibly identifying single buildings with the help of the neighbouring buildings or their residents. The field of the code number is followed by the definite location and description. A problem occurring with both of these fields is that size and function, as well as location, may have changed in the course of the centuries due to modifications made by the owner. Owners and residents must be recorded together with the date of the sources in which they are mentioned. An additional information group should contain data about contracts and wills concerning the building. Finally the 'Baualtersplan' will add information about the architectural characteristics of the building (see Figure 4). All these information groups, except the code number, can be repeated just as with the information groups we already have for the database of persons.

The third stage of the project 'Regensburger Bürger- und Häuserbuch' will deal with objects called 'Realien' in German, which means articles of art or objects of 'everyday life'. The data structure of the 'Realien' will include a code number as well, but in this case the code number will at the same time specify a classification of the object. Besides that, the date of appearance and description of the objects are the central criteria for this part of the database. Linguistic variations of object names will be mentioned in a separate data field. Preliminary work in this area of the project will begin in parallel with the registration and analysis of wills.

Figure 4   *Provisional Structure of Records (Buildings)*

```
code number:number

location:adress
neighbour building:position/code_number/id_number

general description:description/date/id_number
size:size/date/id_number
function:function/date/id_number

owner:name/code_number(person)/date/id_number
resident:name/code_number(person)/date/id_number
house name:name/date/id_number

mentioned in:source/date/id_number

Baualtersplan:id_number/date/description
```

4. Organisation of the Project

The project 'Regensburger Bürger- und Häuserbuch' is a common endeavour of the archive of the city of Regensburg, the University of Regensburg, and industry, principally the Siemens Corporation. Registration of data is done by student assistants who transcribe and record data directly from the original sources to the computer. This method of working makes it necessary for us to have a data processor of our own at the archive. At this time we have eight terminals there, and are working together with four historians and about twelve student assistants. We hope however to enlarge our staff as well as machine capacity later this year. In addition we intend in the near future to begin to analyse our data with CLIO/C instead of using our own programs which were designed simply for the first stages of the project.

In addition to the work at the archive we are going to teach six courses at the university. Two of these courses will be supplemented by a subsequent practical training either in an archive, a museum, a library or in industry. The seminars will include an introduction to computing and quantitative methods in history, including EDP, various software packages, especially CLIO/C, and the programming language C. In this way we want to improve the chances of historical science students getting a job after their final examination, whilst training them for the work on our project.

This summer (1988) a special series of publications will be started. For each source there will be a scientific edition, an analysis and a detailed index, which at the same time will be part of a complete index of the city history of Regensburg. The setting of these publications will be done directly form our floppy disks by a local publishing house.

The project 'Regensburger Bürger- und Häuserbuch' has already become a model for other cities in Bavaria. At the moment we are advising colleagues of five archives inside and outside of Regensburg, who wish to initiate similar projects. So, in a few years we hope to be able not only to give an overview over the sources of the 'Reichsstadt' Regensburg and its religious institutions, but also the history of neighbouring cities and the region in general.

Who's Who in the Medieval Southeast of Germany: the Design of the Prosopographical Data Bank at Graz University

In 'some elementary remarks' L. Genicot emphasised the importance of computer applications even in the field of medieval history,[1] although he mentioned only one of the various possibilities in computer-supported historical research. In medieval history especially we need working tools to help extract information from rare and unrefined source material, information which for the most part is already available to the historian who deals with modern or recent history.[2] What follows is neither a discussion about the definition, methods or special problems of prosopography, nor a presentation of results.[3] The aim is to provide a simple introduction into a new research tool, the *Prosopographical Data Bank for the History of the South-East Territories of the Roman Empire until 1250 (PDB)*,[4] and to demonstrate its contents, functions and practical uses. In order to do this, it will be necessary to make clear the creation and prerequisites of the PDB and give an overview of its realisation and organisation.

1. The Prerequisites: Content and Aims

At Graz University the *Forschungsinstitut für Historische Grundwissenschaften* is carrying out two large editing projects with the aid of the computer: the *Urkundenbuch der Steiermark und ihrer Regenten* (Charters of Styria and its Regents) and the *Urkundenbuch des Patriarchats Aquileia* (Charters of the Patriacate Aquileia). To ensure the correctness of dates and authenticity of persons mentioned in the documents according to the *discrimen veri ac falsi*, the computerised processing of person records seemed desirable.[5] This was the hour the PDB was born, but how should the data bank be organised, how should it be related to the projects mentioned above?[6]

Initially, the PDB was intended solely as an aid to ensure an assignment of time and place to the undated documents and *notitiae traditionum*, to ascertain their degree of authenticity. Once the importance for building indices of chartularies was recognised, applications in other fields of historical research — especially in analyses of the medieval society — became possible. This development of the PDB makes clear that it is not a prosopography in the common sense, but a first stage in the collection of materials on persons mentioned in the documents, without regard to a particular class or group. Of course in a second stage the identification of individuals must be the basis for a lot of analysis; in this way PDB sees itself as an approach to a prosopography of the southeast of the Empire. Furthermore it wants to fulfil the same function for other historical reserach, whenever information on persons is needed.

For reasons already mentioned there are prerequisites if such a data bank is to be successfully established, with regard to the process of data entry as well as subsequent analytical procedures. If the PDB is to be available for use to the largest group of researchers possible, records must remain true to the source. There should be neither a reduction in information nor should personal interpretation intrude. The application of predetermined models, terms or categories could lead to a distortion of information. On the other hand, records must be economically organised, due to the mass of data.

The 'history' of the PDB, the requirements of several projects and experience gained by the pilot tests revealed five concrete prerequisites for the successful implementation of projects of of this type:

1. The data bank has to be established according to the principles of source-oriented data processing.[7] If source structure and content information are reflected, this means adopting all inconsistencies shown by the historical sources from orthographical variations to inconsistency in terminology as well as reliable numerical data.

2. It must be guaranteed that information not included at present can be added to the data bank. The possibility of adding to the data bank and the link between differently structured information is indispensable for computer supported editing as well as for the realisation of the concept of machine readable *regesta*.

3. In data analysis different processes of research have to be considered.[8] In addition to the necessary control of validity and plausibility an explorative phase of analysis is needed, focussing on retrieval methods. In this case we have to evaluate inconsistencies in the source,[9] we have to allow for changes and exchange of functions in different conceptual categories. Furthermore we need the support of the technique of record linkage,[10] often applied in the field of the PDB as well as machine-supported coding, in order to 'translate' parts of the PDB into numerical files to be analysed by the well-known statistical packages.

4. Because of the complexity of these transformations every user must be able to reconstruct every procedure step by step. The addition of auxiliary support should guarantee intersubjective comparisons.

5. Finally one administrative demand should be mentioned. The PDB should be able to be run even on PCs as well in special environments. This means that people often will not access the whole data bank one time, but special components for special topics.

2. The Realisation: Software and Design

3·1. κλειω— a DBMS for Historians

The prerequisites mentioned are being realised with the support of a special data bank design and a specially designed software package for historians. The first developments of PDB have been undertaken using the prototype of the CLIO system. This package provides for high-flexible input, supporting a wide range of different data structures as well as modules for evaluating and transforming the data, i.e. data retrieval, preparation for statistical analysis, nominative record linkage, file merging and text processing by means of either a command language or menus.[11] By now, the first release of the new implementation, baptised κλειω and almost machine-independent, is available.[12] Although this first version includes only a part of the aforementioned modules, in the near future all components of the PDB, listed below, will be supported by κλειω. The design of the PDB is very closely related to the development of this package.

3·2. Primary Data Banks

The basis of the PDB are its so-called *Primary Data Banks*. They contain all information to be gained in a first step of modern editing of documents; in a second step the document samples of the diverse archives will be listed. What is contained in these Primary Data Banks?

Figure 1   *Structure of the PDB Primary Data Banks*

```
Document:  Reference/Dating/Place-of-Issue/Tradition
 |
 |------ Person:  Identifikation/(First)Name/Description/Function/
 |                Number-of-Function/Status/Genealog-Relationship
 |
 |------ I(nstitution):  Function/Type/Name/Place
 |
 |------ Dating-Line:  Text
```

In the data model, the single document is also the superordinate information unit, which is described by reference, date and place of issue, and its type of tradition. Within the documents we are most of all interested in people mentioned but also in the institutions that stand in relation to them and for control in the dating line of the document.

Each person can be found with the assistance of an identification code within the all-encompassing data bank as well as in the source from which it was taken. This code is also the passive part of the network expressing genealogical relationships. The names of the people have been left in original spelling, likewise the description of persons in direct semantical link to the person, such as surname, status, rank, profession etc. or predicates, that express several of these simultaneously — this is why no *a priori* assignments can be made. The personal description is completed with information on function in the document, the position in the list of functions, the status (alive, dead, not clear) and the active genealogical relationship.

From every collection of documents, whether they are books or archives, a Primary Data Bank is generated in that way.[13] These data banks can either be analysed for themselves according to different methods or they can be altered by various procedures or expanded for more detailed analysis.

3·3. The Secondary Data Banks

Alterations are achieved through the generation of *Secondary Data Banks*, which can appear completely different depending on particular research needs. performances required.

3·3.1. The Cumulative Index of Entries.   The simplest of all Secondary Data Banks is a mere listing of Primary Data Banks. It represents the sum of the contents of all linked Primary Data Banks with an identical structure. Through this only a data bank expansion is achieved. Like the Primary Data Banks, these are indices of persons names arranged according to the original documents. The very simple procedures to generate a Cumulative Index of Entries are managed in a kind of *Toolbox* or library, which is, as well, a part of PDB.

3·3.2. The Prosopographical Catalogues.   After persons are identified and the single namings assigned to them, every Primary Data Bank will be linked within itself. The identification and linkage is carried out through semi-automatic Record Linkage and — due to the small amount of information offered by the sources — this is the most difficult part of the entire analytical procedure. After the identification and linkage of individuals a new data bank structure must be generated, the result of which can be described in the following way:

Figure 2   *Structure of a Prosopographical Catalogue (PDB Secondary Data Bank)*

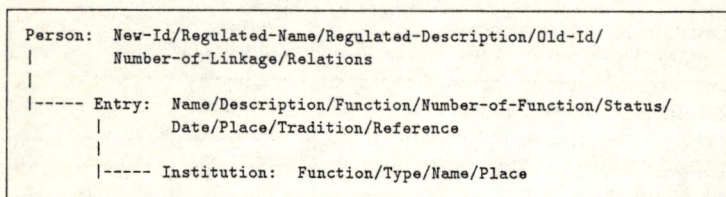

```
Person:   New-Id/Regulated-Name/Regulated-Description/Old-Id/
|         Number-of-Linkage/Relations
|
|----- Entry:   Name/Description/Function/Number-of-Function/Status/
|               Date/Place/Tradition/Reference
|
|----- Institution:   Function/Type/Name/Place
```

The individual who is described with his/her new identification, regulated name, description, as well as identifications mentioned and pertinent relations, becomes now — instead of the document — the superordinate unit. Subordinate are the individual records of their appearance that essentially constitute the primary data bank information, thus avoiding any loss of information in this field. For this reason, institutions that stand in any relation to the individual are integrated into the PDB Secondary Data Bank. In this case the very complicated procedures of identification and generation are managed in the PDB Toolbox, too. Furthermore it is necessary to document these steps as exactly as possible to keep them transparent. In this way, from every single Primary Data Bank, a respective Secondary Data Bank is created through extensive steps of analysis. This Secondary Data Bank consists of the information content of the Primary Data Bank, and the added information from identification of the individuals. That means, it is a meta-source although it was only created from one source group, namely documents.

3·3·3. The Cumulative Prosopographical Catalogue. Through further linkage procedures which are simplified through the regulation of name forms and verification of dates, a cumulative prosopographical catalogue can be established from the *Secondary Data Banks*, which are prosopographical catalogues of the document collections themselves.

3·3·4. Further (non PDB-) Data Banks. Some other data banks, not belonging to the PDB itself, are related at the level of the Secondary Data Banks. As mentioned before, PDB should be useful to the largest possible circle of interested scholars, regardless of their special fields of research and applied methods. The latter is guaranteed by the neutral processing of data. Further information content can be linked with the PDB by the techniques of record linkage, too. One of the applicationss is computer-supported editing. The full text of charters and some other components of an ordinary printed edition are linked with the relevant PDB Primary Data Bank.[14]

4. The Environment: Modularity within a Historical Workstation

The PDB is not a single, unified large scale data bank, it is rather a modular form of data bank organisation. Modularity allows the possibility of changing the data bank through operations limited to single parts, for analytical reasons or because of restrictions of the computer system used. The fundamental building blocs of the system are source-oriented Primary Data Banks, representing a special printed edition or a collection of original documents. Primary Data Banks can be linked with others, including non-PDB data banks, so that they can be used for many different research purposes. The result of every linkage procedure is called a Secondary Data Bank. Special ones are the prosopographical catalogues, which show how individuals should be identified. We emphasise transparency, so that all steps towards identification and execution can be intersubjectively tested and reconstructed with the help of the complementary toolbox and documentation.

In the near future the PDB will be available as a Public Domain Data Bank providing parts of the source as well as knowledge about them within the concept of Historical Workstations.[15] So the PDB will be distributed in modules consisting of individual data banks and the procedures on how to handle them, laid down in the toolbox. In this way we aim to make a contribution to more efficient research in the history of south-east Germany in the Middle Ages.

Notes

1. Léopold Genicot, 'Some Elementary Remarks on the Utility of Computers in Medieval History', *Computer Applications to Medieval Studies*, ed. by Anne Gilmour-Bryson, Kalamazoo, 1984 (Studies in Medieval Culture 17), pp. 45–50.

2. Here is no place to discuss the wide field of computer applications in medieval history. For the different approaches see *Informatique et histoire médiévale*, ed. by Lucie Fossier, André Vauchez and Cinzio Violante, Rome 1977 (Collection de l'Ecole

Française de Rome 31); *Computer Applications to Medieval Studies*, ed. by Anne Gilmour-Bryson, Kalamazoo, 1984 (Studies in Medieval Culture 17).

3. For this purpose see the different papers in the volume *Informatique et prosopographie*, ed. by Hélène Millet, Paris, 1985.

4. The PDB has also been presented at the *International Conference on Data Bases in the Humanities and Social Sciences* in Montgomery/Alabama, July 1987; the proceedings of the conference are in print. — For conceptual considerations and a short documentation see also Ingo H. Kropač and Peter Becker, 'Die Prosopographische Datenbank zur Geschichte der südöstlichen Reichsgebiete bis 1250: Konzepte und Kurzdokumentation', *Medium Aevum Quotidianum Newsletter*, 10, 1987, pp. 30–48.

5. For the concept of computer-supported editing see Reinhard Härtel and Ingo H. Kropač, 'Edition und Auswertung mittelalterlicher Urkunden: Probleme bei Standardisierung und Transfer fortlaufender Texte', *Data Networks for the Historical Disciplines? Problems and Feasibilities in Standardization and Transfer of Machine Readable Data*, ed. by Friedrich Hausmann et al., Graz, 1987, pp. 100–12. Some more papers on this subject are still in print.

6. A short description of the projects and their relations is given in Ingo H. Kropač, 'Computergestützte Projekte am Forschungsinstitut für Historische Grundwissenschaften der Karl-Franzens-Universität Graz', *Fakten — Daten — Zitate*, 6/1, 1986, pp. 9ff.

7. The term *source-oriented data processing* — contrary to *method-oriented data processing* — has been introduced by M. Thaller. For the problems and their solution see Manfred Thaller, 'Ungefähre Exaktheit. Theoretische Grundlagen und praktische Möglichkeiten einer Formulierung historischer Quellen als Produkte 'unscharfer Systeme'', *Neue Ansätze in der Geschichtswissenschaft*, ed. by Herta Nagl-Docekal and Franz Wimmer, Vienna, 1984 (Conceptus-Studien 1), pp. 77–100; Manfred Thaller, 'Vorüberlegungen für einen internationale Workshop über die Schaffung, Verbindung und Nutzung großer interdisziplinärer Quellenbanken in den historischen Wissenschaften, *Datenbanken und Datenverwaltungssysteme als Werkzeuge historischer Forschung*, ed. by Manfred Thaller, St. Katharinen, 1986 (Historisch-Sozialwissenschaftliche Forschungen 20), pp. 9–30.

8. A description of an iterative process is given in Manfred Thaller, 'Zur Formalisierbareit hermeneutischen Verstehens in der Historie', *Mentalitäten und Lebensverhältnisse. Beispiele aus der Sozialgeschichte der Neuzeit. Rudolf Vierhaus zum 60. Geburtstag*, Göttingen, 1982, pp. 439–54.

9. Historical sources can be considered as 'fuzzy sets'; to retrieve them procedures for evaluationg variations in spelling as well as 'fuzzy-set-parameters' must be provided. For solutions of these problems see Thaller, *Exaktheit*, pp. 91–94.

10. For an introduction into the problemes of this technique see *Identifying People in the Past*, ed. E. A. Wrigley, London, 1973; Ian Winchester, *Record Linkage in the Microcomputer Era: A Survey*, Umea, 1985 (Demographic Data Base Newletter 3).

11. A summary of these approaches is given in Manfred Thaller, 'Methods and Techniques of Historical Computing', *History and Computing*, ed. by Peter Denley and Deian Hopkin, Manchester, 1987, pp. 147–56. — For a short but recent overview on the abilities of the prototype see Manfred Thaller, 'Beyond Collecting: The Design and Implementation of CLIO, a DBMS for the Social-Historical Sciences', *The International Conference on Data Bases in the Humanities and Social Sciences 1983*, ed. Robert F. Allen, Osprey, 1985, pp. 328–34.

12. Manfred Thaller, $\kappa\lambda\epsilon\iota\omega$. A Data Base System for Historical Research (version 1·1.1, β-test-version), Göttingen, 1987.

13. For a documentation of the several entries in the Primary Data Banks see Kropač–Becker, PDB, pp. 41–49.

14.   An overview on this application and a description of the singular components is given in Härtel–Kropač, *Edition*, pp. 108–10.

15.   For the requirements of a historical workstation and the role of accessible data bases (libraries of sources as well as background knowledge) see Manfred Thaller, 'The Daily Life in the Middle Ages. Editions of Sources and Data Processing', *Medium Aevum Quotidianum Newsletter 10*, 1987, pp. 22–28.

BERNHIST: a Laboratory for Regional History

Building up a dynamic database for the spatial analysis of population, economy and the environment in the Canton of Berne (Switzerland) 1700–1980

1. An open-ended process

In Central Europe the term 'regional history' refers to a branch of the historical sciences which attempts to investigate the relationship of local groups or larger socio-economic groupings with their natural, social and political environment and which is related to both society and space. Public interest in this dimension of research has increased markedly during the last decade, when a small scale structure and ecological quality emerged as a new basic value of the post-industrial society. Also, economic historians have realised that modernisation must be conceived in a regional context.[1] There is agreement on the growing need for 'approximation to the detail' (Gert Zang) in order to examine, refine and revise the body of current theories. This requires the building up of large standardised databases which may be linked or merged into larger units.[2] However, the recent debate[3] reveals that 'regional historians' in Germany are still engaged in reviewing past research and in assessing the value of traditional theories rather than exploring research strategies for the future and the development complementary theories.

The emphasis put on systems theory and the rapid progress of computer technology suggests that future 'regional histories' will be couched in ecological terms and founded on a broad quantitative basis. The concept of regional history which underlies the present approach is that of society embedded in and dependent on a natural habit which is transformed by human actions and natural impacts. This broad issue extends across three structures of thought — economics, social sciences and natural sciences — that are known to be very divergent because their focus has been directed towards different facets of man's existence:

— the role as a self-oriented optimising agent in the market place and a change creator in the technology arena.

— the role as a social being, who strives to maintain or improve his status in society.

— the role as a biological input-output organism, who contends to survive and reproduce himself.[4]

Institutional economics may offer ways for avoiding some of the pitfalls inherent in an ecological approach which attempts to combine these divergent patterns of thought into a coherent synthesis. From this perspective the 'social system' is made up of a set of elements (or subsystems) which includes natural resources, population, technology, institutions, cognitive and behavioural patterns. These elements are interconnected by feedback mechanisms. The basic goal of society, i.e. the overall effort to keep scarcity away at one level or the other, is not associated with any particular event or invention. Instead is it an expression of a combined societal, economic and technological system's effort over many years which is related to changes in the natural and economic environment.[5] While institutions, cognitive and behavioural patterns are less suited for quantification, one focus of a quantitative analysis might be natural resources and technology (e.g. land-use, production), another the domain of population (reproduction, consumption, wealth, health, social security).

It is, of course, impossible to provide a body of quantitative evidence which might fully document such a complex web of interrelations in time and space. However, a well-founded regional history may attempt to systematically collect all the relevant data which have actually been recorded in the past. In a first step this objective requires tailoring the framework of a database according to the specific territorial structure of the region of analysis and its changes over time. This spatial network should permit the integration of all quantitative evidence for the entire period of analysis, for all levels of administration. In a second step, data referring to specific subsystems — e.g. population, resources — should be analysed within their own context. In a third step the relationship between subsystems is investigated requiring a higher degree of sophistication. Model building is, of course, not an end in itself. It is directed to decompose and weigh key factors and to find the way in which they interact. Often the results point to features which are connected to institutions and behavioural patterns. These patterns have to be studied at the level of small spatial units on the basis of non-quantitative sources. The success of this approach depends on the appropriate choice of testing ground. A database which caters for the definition of communities which are the most representative for a given problem is very helpful in this respect. As new variables will always be included and fresh questions asked the building up of such a database is an open-ended process. At present the main objectives of the analysis may be summarised as follows:

1. Examining the spatial distribution of population, resources and infrastructure of different points of time. This will allow the assessment of the magnitude of regional imbalances in economic development, and the measurement of flows of energy, money and labour along the gradients of poverty.

2. Investigating changes in the distribution between the points of reference and relating them to environmental, economic, demographic, cognitive and behavioural parameters.

3. Attempting to model some of the interactions between man, economy and the environment.

The numerical results will be published together with methodological and statistical comments (Historische Statistik des Kantons Bern); the main lines of interpretation and the maps will be contained in a computer atlas.

2. *Spatial framework and logical structuring of BERNHIST*

The Canton of Bern, for which such a 'dynamic' database is in creation, comprises roughly one seventh of the surface area and population of Switzerland. In what follows the spatial framework and the logical structuring of this database will be discussed.

In the original sources the variables are recorded at four different levels of administration. The canton is hierarchically made up of six regions, 27 districts, 184 parishes and 410 communities of different size. Since 1798 the perimeter of the Canton has been altered several times. For instance, the Jura region was incorporated in 1815, of which the northern part was hired off as an individual canton in 1978. Also the internal structure of some districts and parishes has been modified. However, the territorial perimeters of the basic units, the communities, were only rarely altered. This has allowed holding the territorial structure roughly constant over time by aggregating parishes and districts according to the same scheme (which is that of 1980) for the entire period under investigation. Variables which are only available at the district level, had to be estimated in some cases for the time prior to 1900. Within this framework the concept of 'region' has also been within this flexible way which is bound to natural parameters or those entities, for which Mitterauer (1986) has coined the term 'ecotypes'. At present all the evidence contained in the database may be analysed within 'ecotypes' (according to the importance of grain, wine or dairy production for the period before the coming of the railway) or 'mountain zones' (mainly defined by natural parameters such as altitude, exposition and slopes). For instance it came as a surprise, in this context, that mortality levels before the late nineteenth century were clearly connected to 'mountain zones'.

A systematic search (which included the local archives in the Canton) has up to the present brought to light an unexpected wealth of quantitative evidence. This is related to the fact that as early as the mid-eighteenth century the Bernese administration was well organised and ahead of time in its fervour to set up statistical surveys. The data which, at present, amount to more than a thousand raw variables and several thousand composite variables (e.g. percentages, ratio, per capital figures etc) are processed using SPSSX; all the graphic output (maps, barcharts etc.) is prepared by SASGRAPH for electrostatic and pen plotters on the basis of SPSSX 'export-files' which can be read by SAS.

Where the original data in the sources are set up in form of a time- series (e.g. annual aggregate numbers of baptisms and deaths) they are read into a corresponding SPSSX file-structure ('time-file') in which temporal units are defined as cases. Where the original sources are set up according to spatial structures (e.g. in a census) they are integrated into a 'space-file' in which the cases are spatial units. In the 'time-file' the handling of data is straightforward as long as both the sequence and the number of the variables are not modified. Because the LEAVE and LAG command allows only including the previous case, the file must be rearranged several times in order to compute moving averages. This makes the handling very cumbersome and tedious. On the other hand the DO REPEAT utility allows the creation of large number of new variables using a small list of commands. Because the length of variable names is restricted to 8 bytes, a logical system for naming the thousands of variables had to be created: the first few letters define the content of the variable, a subsequent code of numbers characterises the spatial unit to which it refers (four numbers for parishes, two numbers for districts, one number for regions, zero for the entire canton). An example: MORT0301 stands for mortality in the city of Bern (01) which is itself part of the Bern district (03).

The definition of variables in the 'space-file' is somewhat different: in most cases a prefix of one letter defines the unit (e.g. calories, hectares, currency units), the subsequent three letters marks the content of the variable. They are followed by a code of three numbers which stands for the year of the census and a suffix of one letter which indicates the unit of reference (e.g. per capita, per hectare, percent etc). An example: CGET847P = calories (C) produced in GETreide (= grain) in (1)847 as a percentage (P) of total agricultural output. The date are read in at the spatial level in which they are recorded in the sources and then aggregated into larger units (i.e. parish, district, region) using the AGGREGATE command. With the ADD FILES command the files aggregated at deferent spatial units are then merged into a file which hierarchically includes the variables at all levels.

The transfer of variables from the 'time-file' to the 'space-file' and vice-versa cannot be done using SPSSX. This problem is handled in three steps. First a SPSSX-program writes the needed variables in a fixed sequence into a data file. Then a PL-1 step (which needs an enormous amount of storage) reads this matrix and reverses it. The reversed matrix is then read into the target files. For editing data from the 'time-file' SPSSX programs are written on the basis of a PL-1 algorithm for each of the 230 spatial units. Only the name of the parish in the headline and the spatial codes are different. Editing from the 'space-file' is not as easy since every census has its peculiar combination of variables. Nevertheless the LIST VARIABLES command combined with SET WIDTH and LENGTH are sufficient to issue all the data. However, a next version of SPSSX should allow the inclusion of more than two headlines and include bottom lines as well (such as SAS does).

3. Classification of variables

The data are classified according to the numerical classification of present-day statistical surveys.

1. *Population:* Size; structure (age, sex); households; births, deaths and marriages; citizenship; religion; migration.

2. *Space and environment:* Quality of soil; climate (temperature and precipitation) are quantified on the level of the individual month for the entire period[6]; exposition.

3. *Livelihood:* Occupation; labour-market; wages.

5. *Prices:* Prices for basic commodities (mainly food),

7. *Agriculture and forestry:* Land-use; production (grain, potatoes, fruit, milk

and cheese); livestock, size, scattering and property of holdings; amount and composition of stored food.

8. Energy: Production and consumption (firewood, peat, coal)

9. Buildings: Number and size.

13. Social indicators: Orphans; widows, landed property; number of paupers according to degree of dependance; expenditures for poor-relief.

14. Health: Number of doctors and midwives; number and size of hospitals; nutrition (derived from other parameters).

18. Public finance: Revenues from income and property tax.

Most of the variables have not been measured for the entire period of investigation, except population, where births and deaths are available at the level of the parish and population size, where annual figures have been interpolated from a sequence of 24 censuses.[7] The combination of this data has allowed estimating fertility, mortality and migration.

4. Steps of the analysis

The building-up of the database involves the following four steps:

1. Data collection and control: two students with a portable PCs gather the data in the archives. Then the evidence is transmitted to the main computer. The subsequent control of the data is the most tedious and time-consuming part of the work.

2. Homogenisation of data and disclosure of structures: composite variables such as percentages and per capita values are computed in order to summarise the evidence. At this level, structures emerge within different concepts of 'region' which are statistically tested and mapped.

3. Interpreting changes over time and model building: changes in spatial variables over time are computed and mapped — e.g. increases or decreases in the birth-rate — and submitted to more sophisticated statistical analyses. Models will be built in order to better understand the nature of the processes involved.

4. Counterfactual history: the suitability of the models will be tested using hypothetical data. Also hypothetical questions will be asked such as: how would the economy and the environment of the canton have supported a prolonged population growth of 2 per cent to 3 per cent during the nineteenth century, as is common in Africa or Latin America today?

This procedure may lead to a new kind of regional history which will shed more light upon the interaction of economic forces, the ecological surroundings and mental patterns which, in their interaction, are underlying the feature of uneven growth. Also a broad database may become a useful tool for all those who are engaged in local history. In most cases local historians do not have the time nor the facilities to collect and check quantitative evidence across a broad spectrum of manuscript and printed statistics. If these data are readily available the integration of local findings into a larger context is greatly facilitated.

Notes

This research is supported by the Swiss National Science Foundation.
1. R. Fremdling & R. Tilly (eds.), *Industrialisierung und Raum. Studien zur regionalen Differenzierung im Deutschland des 19. Jahrhunderts*, Stuttgart, 1979.
2. M. Thaller, 'Vorschlag für einen internationalen Workshop über internationale Datenbanken', in M. Thaller (ed.), *Datenbanken und Datenverwaltungssysteme als Werkzeuge historischer Forschung*, St. Katharinen, 1986, pp. 9–30.
3. C. H. Hauptmeyer (ed.), *Landesgeschichte heute*, Göttingen, 1987.
4. U. Svedin, 'Economic and Ecological Theory: Differences and Similarities', in D. O. Hall & N. Myers (eds.), *Economics of Ecosystem Management*, Dordrecht, 1985, pp. 31–40.
5. R. Steppacher, 'Institutionalismus', in J. Jarre (ed.), *Die Zukunft der Oekonomie. Wirtschaftswissenschaftliche Forschungsansätze im Vergleich*, Rehberg-Loccum, 2nd edition, 1985, pp. 30–95.
6. C. Pfister, *Klimageschichte der Schweiz 1525–1860. Das Klima der Schweiz von 1525–1860 und seine Bedeutung in der Geschichte von Bevölkerung und Landwirtschaft*, Bern, 1984.
7. C. Pfister, 'Menschen im Kanton Bern 1764–1980. Wandlungen in der Bevölkerungsentwicklung und -verteilung seit dem späten Ancien Régime', in *Der Mensch in der Landschaft. Festschrift für G. Grosjean*, Bern, 1986, pp. 475–499.

The Computer, Oral History and Regional Studies

An oral history archive has recently been established at the Department of Economic and Social History of Graz University. The archive is responsible for several projects concerning the recent history of Styria in south eastern Austria. One of them is presented in this study. Our primary interest lies in using a living person as an historical source, and thus we are concerned mainly with facts, not in sociological or social-psychological questions like the social dimension of memory. Of course, these areas can never be divided completely, but we think it is important not to lump them together. However, the question of what influences the memory of a person naturally is included in source-criticism.[1] But the primary task of oral history is to research the past and not actual situations as in sociological field-research.[2]

1. The Region

The starting point of the work is an attempt to establish a local history on the basis of oral history. The specific place should represent a micro-region which is defined as an area of distinctive conditions and solutions in the frame of extraterritorial processes: 'The historical reality to be searched out is seen as some in contradictions moving on entirety, as a "concrete totality"'.[3] The region in question might be described as removed from channels of traffic, trade and communications, and as being agriculturally structured. At the other extreme, the region, in the period researched (the years towards the end and just after the Second World War) witnessed the death throes of Nazism and invasion by the Red Army — it was a focus-point for the end of the War in Austria. The period researched was dominated by a break away and a new beginning built on the foundations of what was acquired before or during the war.

2. Sources

The method of data collection is that of the narrative interview within a framework of semi-standardised questions. Thus individual interviews are conducted in the manner of a historical workshop involving inhabitants and members of our institute. Interviews in groups are held to resolve cases of contradiction between the testimony of individuals in personal interviews. The personal interviews naturally contain many individual data, interviews in groups produce more general data, but there are many common basic facts. Also personal sources of inhabitants (books, scripts, photos etc. are collected). Each interview is marked by date, time and type. Thus each individual person and each interviewed group has its own 'act'.

In a second stage general sources are collected: local newspapers or news about that region in other newsletters, official acts, statistics about the population, the economy, etc. Thus a lot of comparable data from different sources can be used to extract external realities and perceptions.[4] The institute evaluates the data, derived from personal interviews or published sources, and the results, along with the collected data, will eventually be handed back to the village community. At the end, the inhabitants should be able to write their history by themselves, on the basis of all collected data, and with the help of our institute. Thus by selecting inhabitants to be interviewed out of various social and functional groups, this work makes a contribution to a more democratic way of dealing with sources and therefore with the basic 'objects' of history, namely subjects and individuals.[5]

3. Data Derived from Individual Interviews

Each interview is recorded in full and typed out. The data, established by individual interviews, are stored and processed with the help of various source-oriented database-systems, text-retrieval and statistical-packages. Each interview forms a document which divides into 'hard' and 'soft' data. The hard data contain personal data of an interviewee and are more or less sharp (date of birth, occupation etc.). These data can be proved with legal documents and other sources. In this way a legal part is created whose data can at all times be used for various descriptive analyses. The soft data of the documents (points of view, experiences, perspectives etc. of the person, a so-called 'interior reality') are written in each document in an extractive way: marked by semi-standardised key-words and listed in an original text-field, containing characteristic expressions or sequences of the original text. Additionally this information is edited in the beginning with the aid of an information field and a reference to the page number within the transcript, so that the link to the original text will be evident. The structure is directed toward the attainment of factual information and to a lesser degree on emotional experience. However, non-verbal expressions are added in standardised symbols according to the state of agitation of the person. The parallel examination of hard and soft data enables the discovery of relations between an 'objective' and a 'subjective' person, and for fresh data to be uncovered. The entire file (these are interviews in structured data format and documents) should serve three purposes:

1. An archival purpose: the data should be easy to search through with the help of simple data- and text-retrieval software, acting quickly on specified contents (such as keywords, persons, places, events, facts, etc.). The occurence of desired contents should be easily obtainable and the respective passage should be made available through reference in the transcript and the recording. For that reason the entries should be unique, thus questions and answers or the mentioning of certain events and their evaluations should

appear in one place; the dataset should be more transparent and more easily 'processable', even without the aid of a background system-file. The data- and text-retrieval procedures can be carried out using BYU (WORDCRUNCHER) or the module CLIO(KLEIO)-IAC). Already, at this stage, simple frequencies of certain persons, events or terms and their textual surroundings are ascertainable.

2. In a second step a system-file of the entire file is established. With the help of this file, univariate analyses can be made, and indexes and registers can be produced. Furthermore CLIO(KLEIO) makes the record linkage possible which helps prove the identity of persons or events in one or several data sets.

3. In a third step, a SPSS file of the 'hard' data is established by using CLIO(KLEIO) routines. The coding is performed by hand. Thus complex social-scientific analyses are facilitated. These three data-files, the transparent dataset in CLIO(KLEIO) format, the CLIO(KLEIO) system- file, and the SPSS system-file, are kept separate and are available for various retrievals and analyses.

4. The Data Structures

The data structure for the 'hard' data include personal data on the interviewee, as well as recollected 'facts' within a time-period.[6]

IP[interviewed person]$data concerning biological and social origin
IPR[interviewed person at the point of remembered time]$data concerning social roles(divided by signs like '/','£' and '%')
IPM[interviewed person at points in the meantime]$ --'--
IPP[interviewed person at the point of interview]$ --'--

The data structure for the 'soft' data follows evident facts along the line of life[7] and embraces three entities: the event, the person and the fact.

ME[mentioned event]$election of the mayor%not remembered£Mr. Y/. . ./time
ME. . .
MP[mentioned person]$name/function/ . . ./time
MP. . .
MF[mentioned fact]$less food%everybody was starving/. . .
MF. . .

With the help of markers '£' and '%' it is possible to include comments or to append original expressions of the interviewed person (the tagged fields may be included or excluded at each step of data processing).

5. Questions and Aims

The analyses refer to four levels:

5·1. The obtainment of, up to the researched time, not yet evident data of a personal, eventful or factual nature and relating to a person in the network of village society and the micro-region.

5·2. The obtention of knowledge about the common ethos of an era.

5·3. The obtention of knowledge about the general and individual horizon of memory.

5·4. The obtention of knowledge about the general and individual horizon of values.

5·1. Individual data are checked against all sources. With the help of record-linkage operations we can identify persons, events and facts mentioned in different interviews. In that way we can idendify social relations (important or remarkable persons, events etc.), channels of communication (who knows what about whom)[8] and, eventually, functional qualities of certain persons or functional relations of the inhabitants with each other. In addressing questions such as who was at a given place at a given time and why, we can learn a lot about the status of persons, events, etc. and their significance in the collective memory.

5·2. The appreciation of an era by its contemporaries might be understood through reference to fields of factual events, which contain general statements, notes and opinions about general conditions, such as the economic situation or personal security.

5·3. By using record linkage the general file should be examined for identical events mentioned, and a frame of events remembered might be established. All this will contribute generalisations about the local consciousness and the consciousness of individuals with different functions, relations, social backgrounds, etc. The question: 'How is an era remembered' naturally throws a light on the present and its appreciation in opposition to the past; notions like 'mastering the past' or 'working up the past' could be dealt with.

5·4. The personal values of individuals and groups might be deduced with the aid of entries in the field of original expressions regarding mentioned persons, events and facts. This should throw a light on matters like community feeling, solidarity and formation of groups among the whole population.

The associative facility of a computer helps to process complex data and to redraw networks; it enables us to cross-check and quantify; it helps us to exhaust our data completely.[9] A structured database, combining 'hard' and 'soft' data, supports direct cross-checks between these areas and can throw light on dependencies, and, the structuring of the database itself is a method of standardising data and making them more comparable. When researching the history of communities and roles of individuals in them, the parallel or crossing paths of individuals in a community is a particular argument for working with sophisticated database management and data analysis systems.

Notes

1. Of course each interview is a social meeting and therefore a theory of interviewing is necessary, cf. A. V. Cicourel, *Methode und Messung in der Soziologie*, Frankfurt/M, 1974, pp. 110–51; cf. W. Fuchs, *Biographische Forschung. Eine Einführung in Praxis und Methoden*, Opladen, 1984, esp. pp. 154–90. Our interviews are based on a questionnaire, containing standardized questions building a framework; see also footnote 2.

2. Cf. A. V. Cicourel, as in footnote 1, pp. 63–109, esp. p. 63; beyond that distinction there are various methods of field-researching by an oral historian, cf. *Oral History: A Guide for Teachers*, eds. Th. Sitton, G. L. Mehaffy and O. L. Davis, Jr. (and others), Austin, 1983, pp. 83–114; we are using various types of field-research in oral history: in individual interviews we are using the method of formal interviewing, in groups we are using informal interview, unobtrusive observation and participant observation, cf. Sitton, et al., cit., pp. 111–14.

3. Cf. H. Haumann, 'Neue Regionalgeschichte: Linke Heimattmelei oder kritische Gesellschaftsanalyse', *Das Argument*, 126, 1981, pp. 239–52, esp. p. 242.

4. On the problems of validity in retrospective interviews and solutions by referring to common parts of data as result of cross checks cf. R. Mann. 'Validitätsprobleme retrospektiver Interviews', *Mündliche Geschichte und Arbeiterbewegung*, eds. G. Boltz and J. Weidenholzer, Vienna, 1984, pp. 355–70, esp. pp. 366ff.; St. Humphries, *The Handbook of Oral History: Recording Life Stories*, London 1984, pp. 47–49; J. Kirk and M. L. Miller, *Reliability and Validity in Qualitative Research*, Beverly Hills, 1986[2].

5. Cf. G. Paul and B. Schoaig, eds., *Die andere Geschichte. Geschichte von unten, Spurensicherung, ökologische Geschichte, Geschichtswersättten* Cologne, 1986; *Geschichte von unten. Fragestellungen, Methoden und Projekte einer Geschichte des Alltags*, ed. H. Ch. Ehalt, Vienna, 1984.

6. To the problem of various times in a life cf. A. Lehmann, *Erzählstruktur und Lebenslauf, Autobiographische Untersuchungen*, New York 1983, pp. 13–39, esp. p. 13; A. Schütz and Th. Luckmann, *Strukturen der Lebenswelt*, Neuwied 1975, p. 67.

7. To a method of describing narrative interviews cf. R. Sieder, 'Geschichten erzählen und Wissenschaft treiben', Ed. G. Botz and J. Weidenholzer, like footnote 1, pp. 203–32, esp. pp. 210–22.

8. Cf. P. Malina, 'Lokalkommunikation und Regionalgeschichte. Zur Annäherung an die Geschichte lokaler Räume und ihrer Kommunikationsstrukturen', in *Zeitgeschichte*, 14, 1986, Heft 2, pp. 69–88.

9. Cf. P. Thompson, 'Das Problem der Repräsentativität am Beispiel eines Familienprojektes', *Lebenserfahrung und kollektives Gedächtnis. Die Praxis der 'Oral History'*, Ed. L. Niethammer, Frankfurt/M, 1980, pp. 273–85, esp. p. 285.

10. On the problems of combining qualitative and quantitative methods cf. C. Hopf-E. Weingarten, *Qualitative Sozialforschung*, Stuttgart, 1984[2], pp. 23–34 and cf. G. Botz, 'Neueste Geschichte zwischen Quantifizierung und 'Mündlicher Geschichte'', *Geschichte als demokratischer Auftrag*, Vienna, 1983, pp. 13–36; cf. also W. Fuchs, as in footnote 1, pp. 158–61; M. B. Miles and M. A. Huberman, *Qualitative Data Analysis. A Sourcebook of New Methods*, Beverly Hills, 1986[4], esp. pp. 215–230; W. Voges, *Methoden der Biographie- und Lebenslaufforschung*, Opladen, 1987. Nevertheless the opinion is dominant, that both methods are combinable, and that both can profit from each other.